Attack on Titan: Lost Girls volume 2 is a work of fiction. Names, characters, places, and incidents are the products of the author's imagination or are used fictitiously. Any resemblance to actual events, locales, or persons, living or dead, is entirely coincidental.

A Kodansha Comics Trade Paperback Original
Attack on Titan: Lost Girls volume 2 copyright © 2016 Hajime Isayama/ Hiroshi Seko/Ryosuke Fuji
English translation copyright © 2016 Hajime Isayama/Hiroshi Seko/Ryosuke Fuji

Published in the United States by Kodansha Comics, an imprint of Kodansha USA Publishing, LLC, New York.

Publication rights for this English edition arranged through Kodansha Ltd, Tokyo.

First published in Japan in 2016 by Kodansha Ltd., Tokyo as *Shingeki no kyojin LOST GIRLS*, volume 2.

ISBN 978-1-63236-418-0

Printed in the United States of America.

www.kodanshacomics.com

9 8 7 6 5 4 3 2 1
Translation: Ko Ransom
Lettering: Steve Wands
Editing: Haruko Hashimoto
Kodansha Comics edition cover design by Phil Balsman

Afterword

The characters in Attack on Titan are all so captivating that I keep finding myself wanting to mess around with them. Over and over during my work, I'd end up doodling and playing with the cast. It was a lot of fun to work on this manga, from start to finish.

While it was brief, this brings Attack on Titan: Lost Girls to an end, thanks to the help of many different people. I'm planning on enjoying the world of Titan as a regular reader from now on. Thank you all.

·Ryosuke Fuji

As Mr. Fuji said, all of the characters in Attack on Titan are so captivating, and I personally think that quality comes from each character's soul. For example, Mikasa's fierce yet pure soul; Annie's introspective and isolated soul; and so on.

As I watched this story becoming remolded into a new shape, and turned into a manga, I started to think that Attack on Titan: Lost Girls may be a story about the souls of these two girls who often keep to themselves.

·Hiroshi Seko

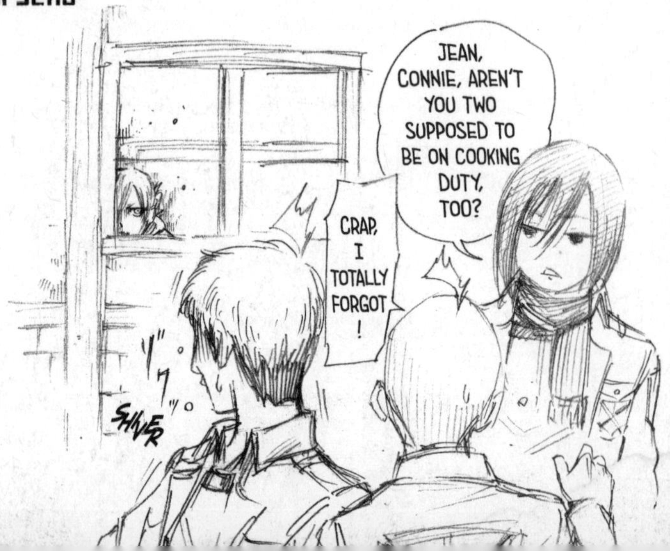
JEAN, CONNIE, AREN'T YOU TWO SUPPOSED TO BE ON COOKING DUTY, TOO?
CRAP, I TOTALLY FORGOT!
SHIVER

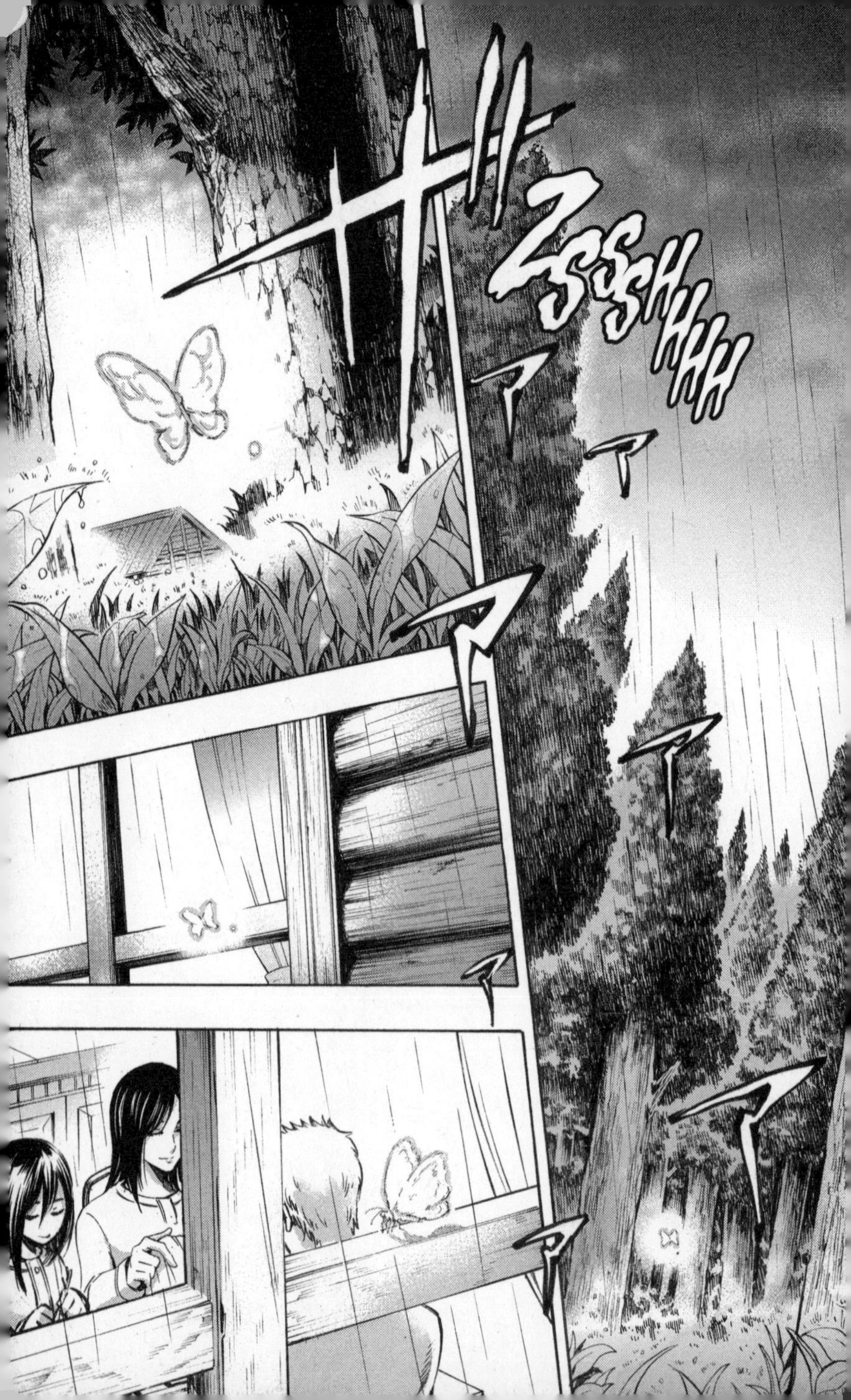
ZSSHHHH

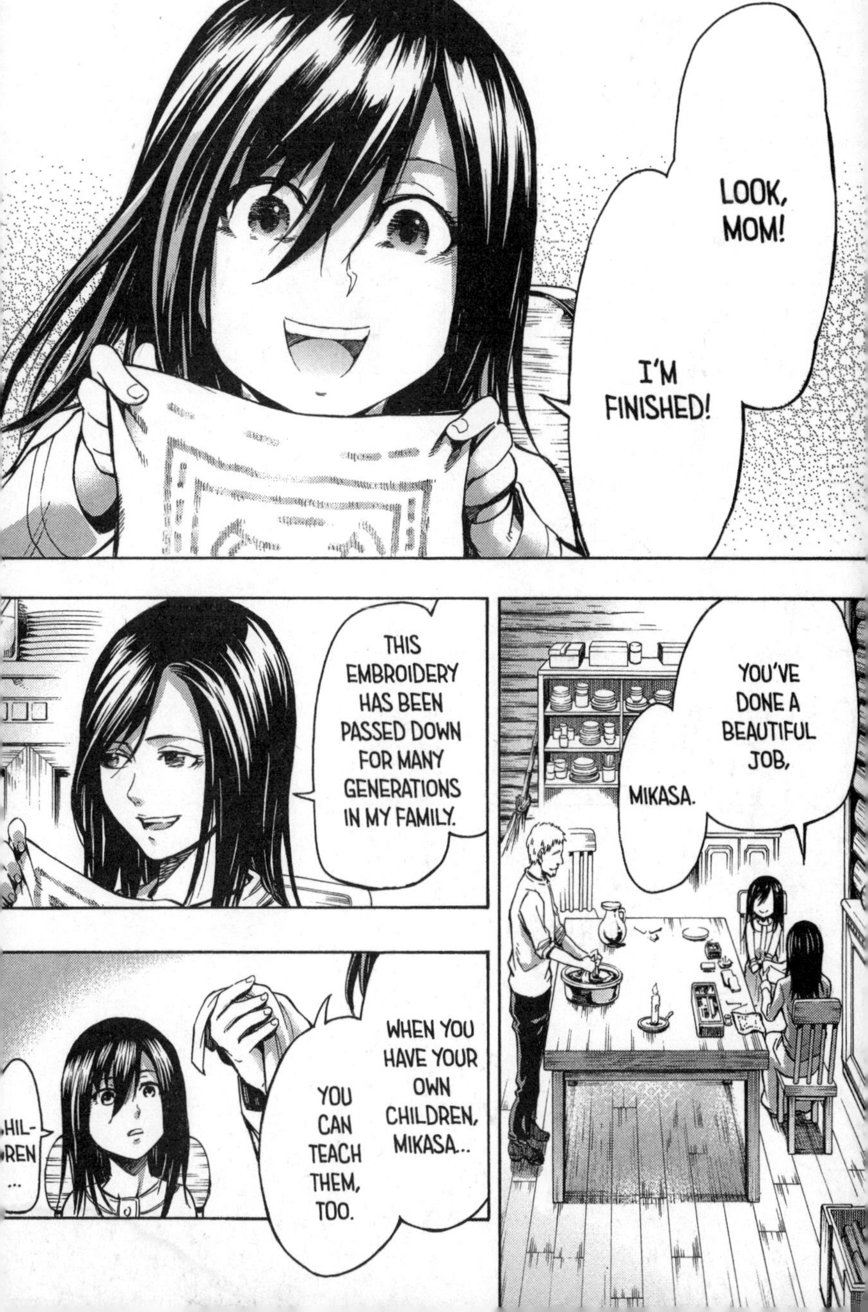
LOOK, MOM!
I'M FINISHED!
YOU'VE DONE A BEAUTIFUL JOB, MIKASA.
THIS EMBROIDERY HAS BEEN PASSED DOWN FOR MANY GENERATIONS IN MY FAMILY.
WHEN YOU HAVE YOUR OWN CHILDREN, MIKASA...
YOU CAN TEACH THEM, TOO.
HIL- REN ...

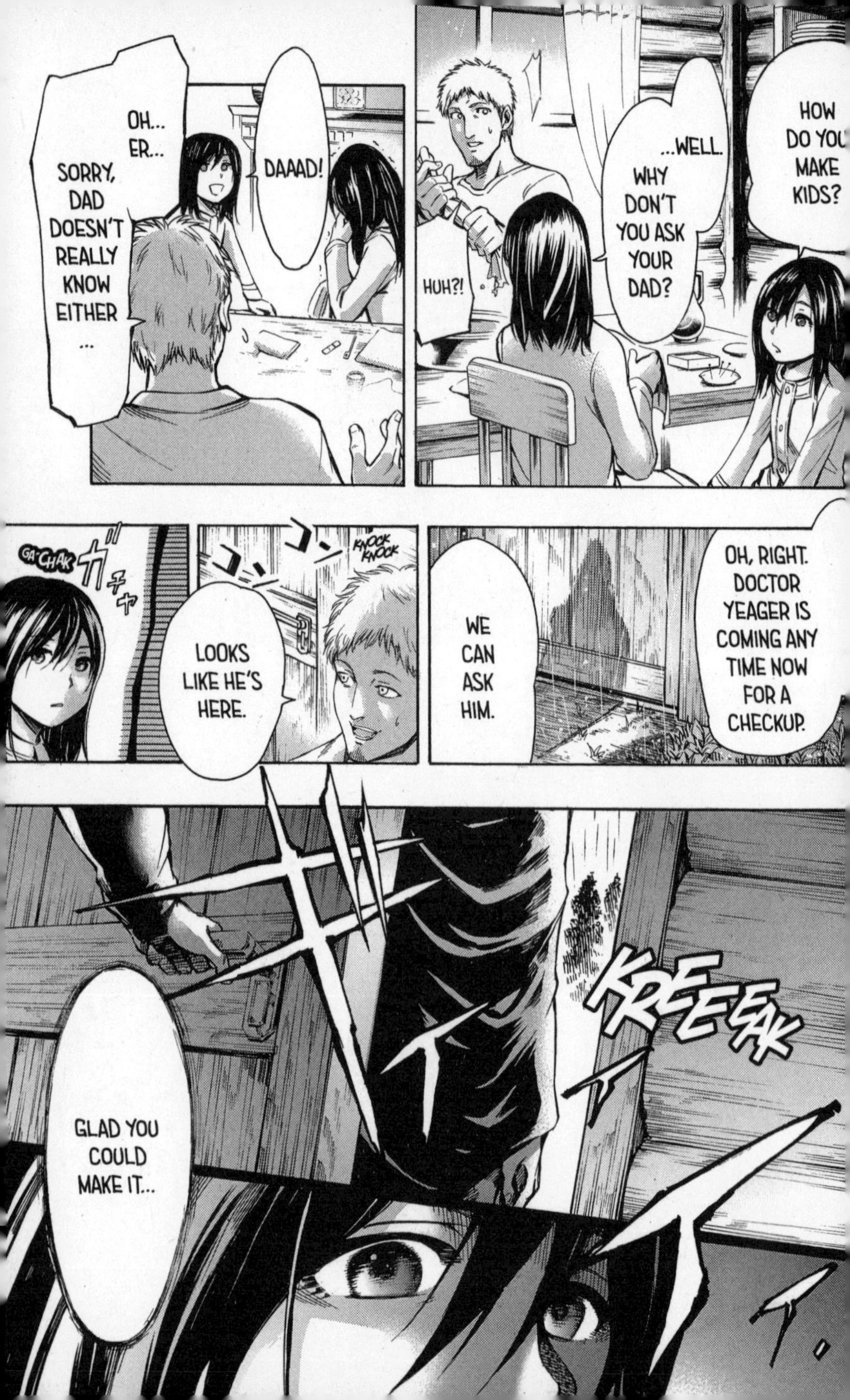
HOW DO YOU MAKE KIDS?
...WELL.
WHY DON'T YOU ASK YOUR DAD?
HUH?!
DAAAD!
OH... ER...
SORRY, DAD DOESN'T REALLY KNOW EITHER ...
OH, RIGHT. DOCTOR YEAGER IS COMING ANY TIME NOW FOR A CHECKUP.
WE CAN ASK HIM.
KNOCK KNOCK
LOOKS LIKE HE'S HERE.
GA-CHAK
KREEEAK
GLAD YOU COULD MAKE IT...

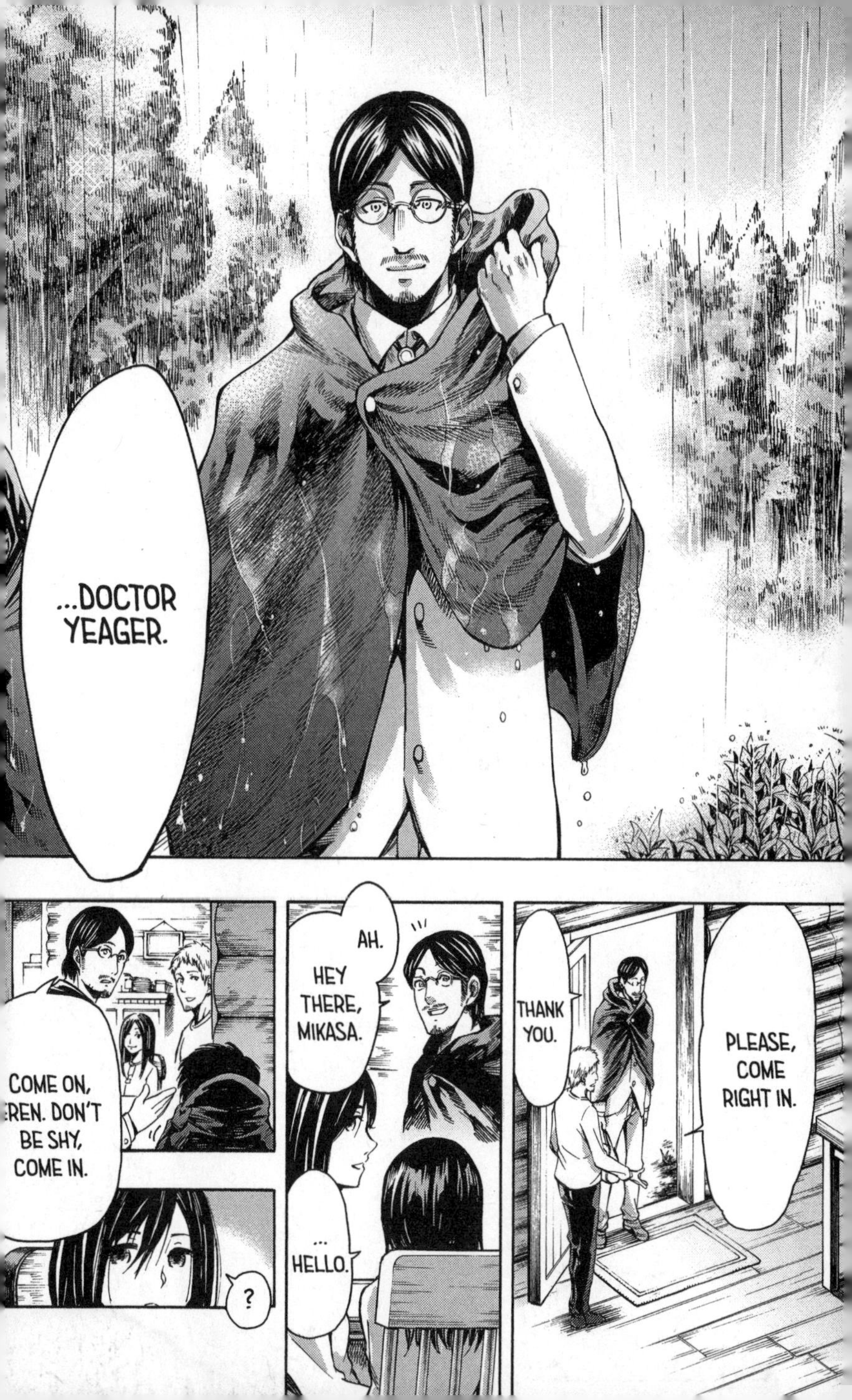

...DOCTOR YEAGER.
PLEASE, COME RIGHT IN.
THANK YOU.
AH.
HEY THERE, MIKASA.
...HELLO.
COME ON, REN. DON'T BE SHY, COME IN.
?

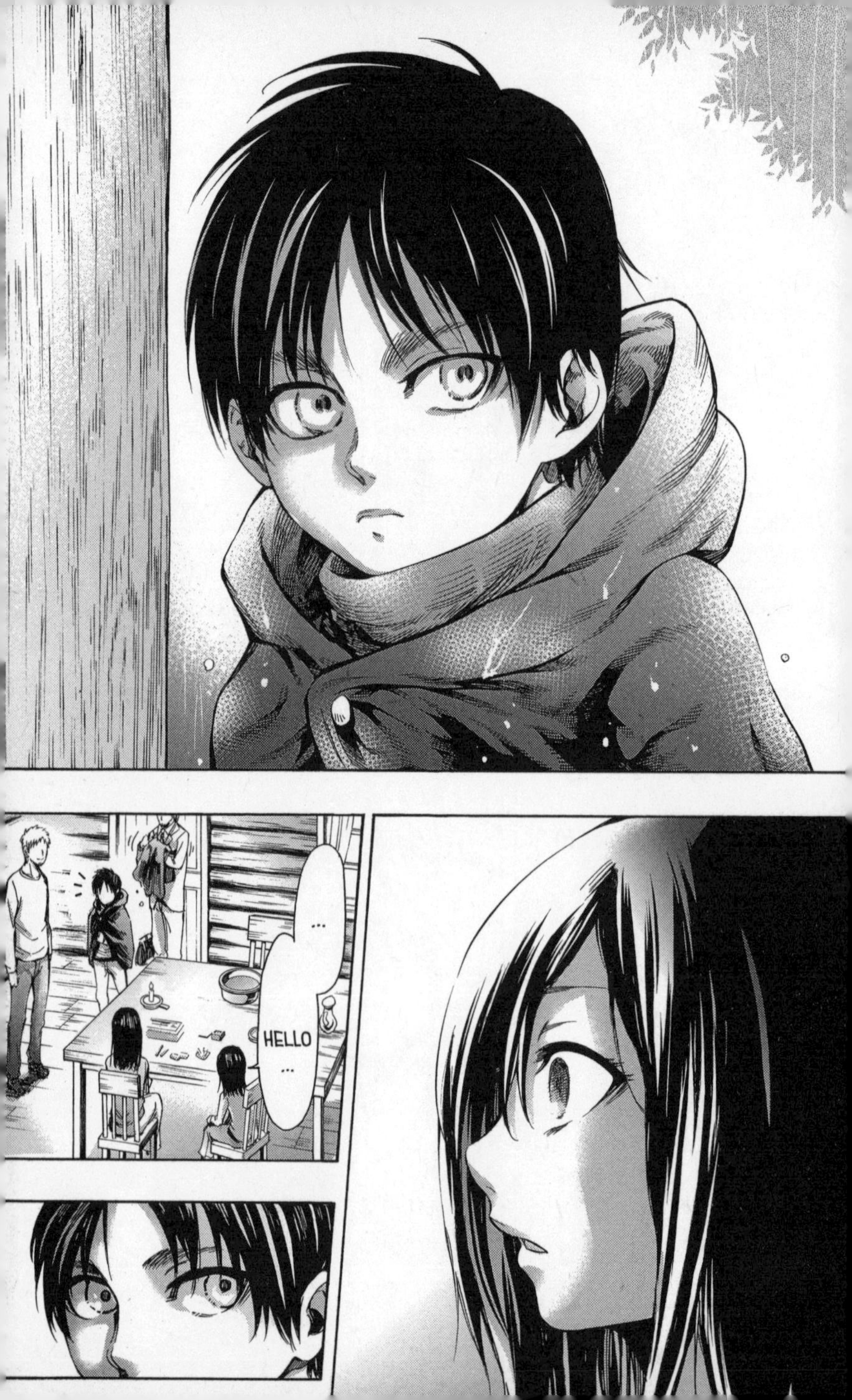
...
HELLO
...

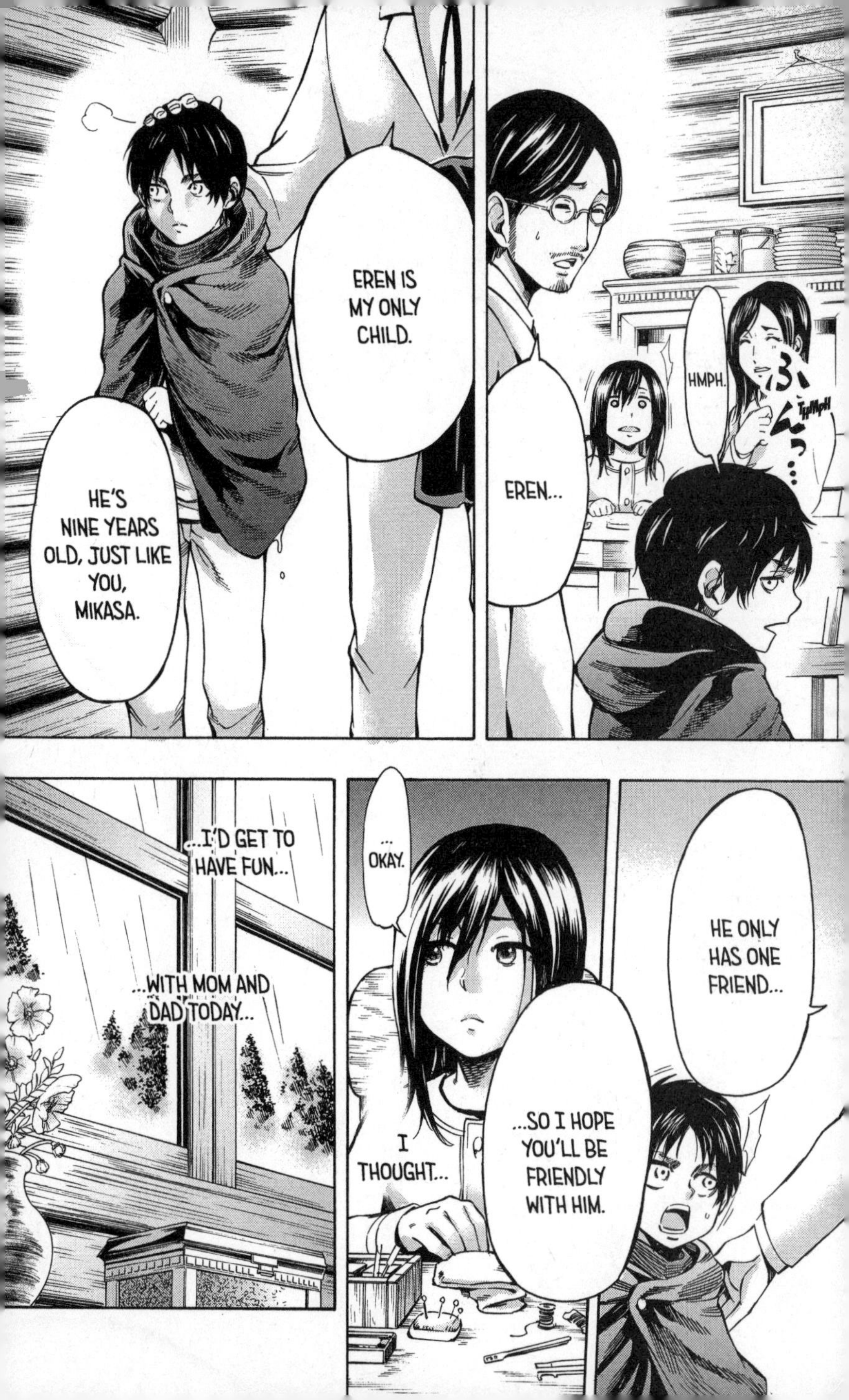
HMPH.
ふんっ…
EREN...
EREN IS MY ONLY CHILD.
HE'S NINE YEARS OLD, JUST LIKE YOU, MIKASA.
HE ONLY HAS ONE FRIEND...
...SO I HOPE YOU'LL BE FRIENDLY WITH HIM.
... OKAY.
I THOUGHT...
...I'D GET TO HAVE FUN...
...WITH MOM AND DAD TODAY...

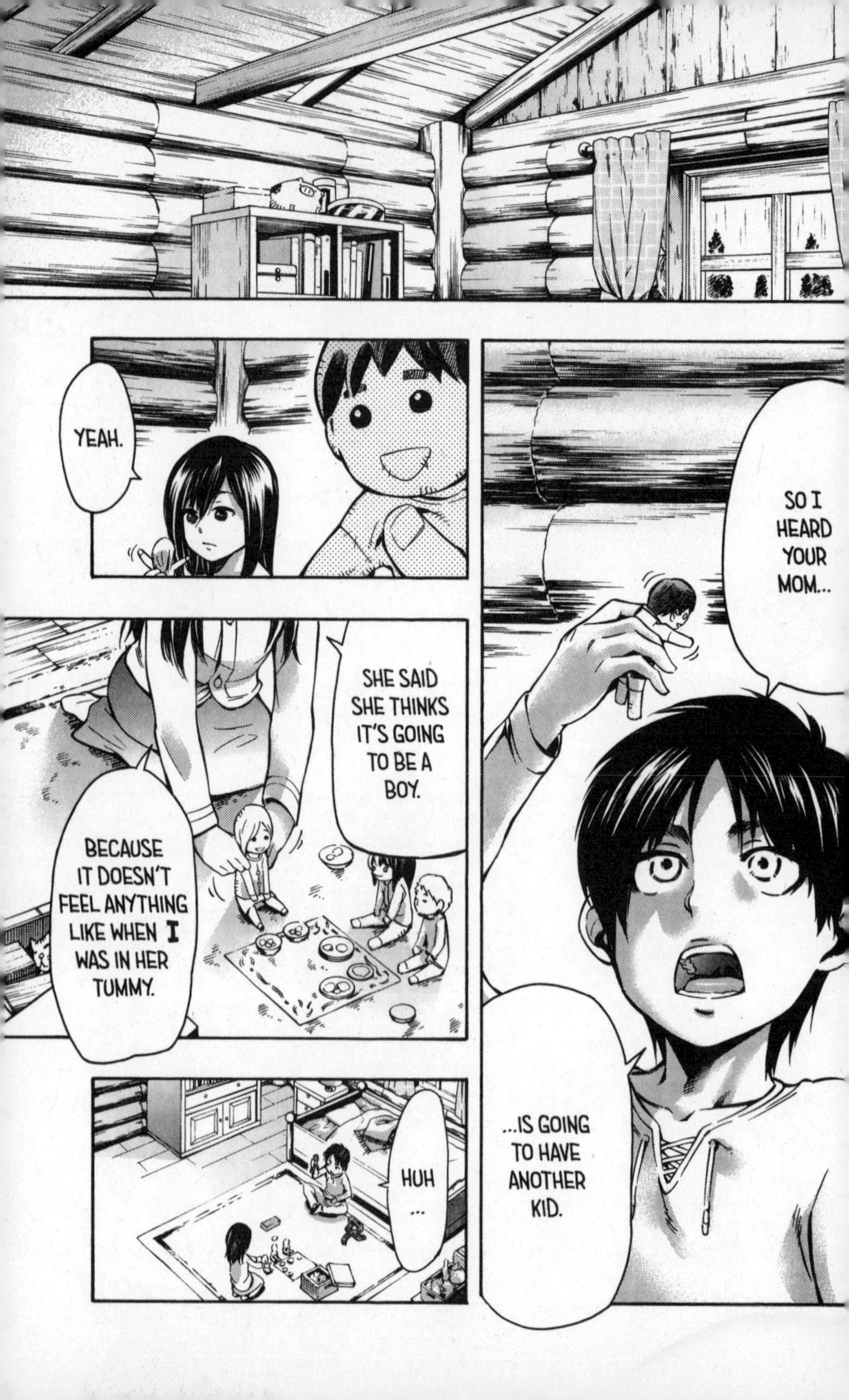
SO I HEARD YOUR MOM...
...IS GOING TO HAVE ANOTHER KID.
YEAH.
SHE SAID SHE THINKS IT'S GOING TO BE A BOY.
BECAUSE IT DOESN'T FEEL ANYTHING LIKE WHEN I WAS IN HER TUMMY.
HUH ...

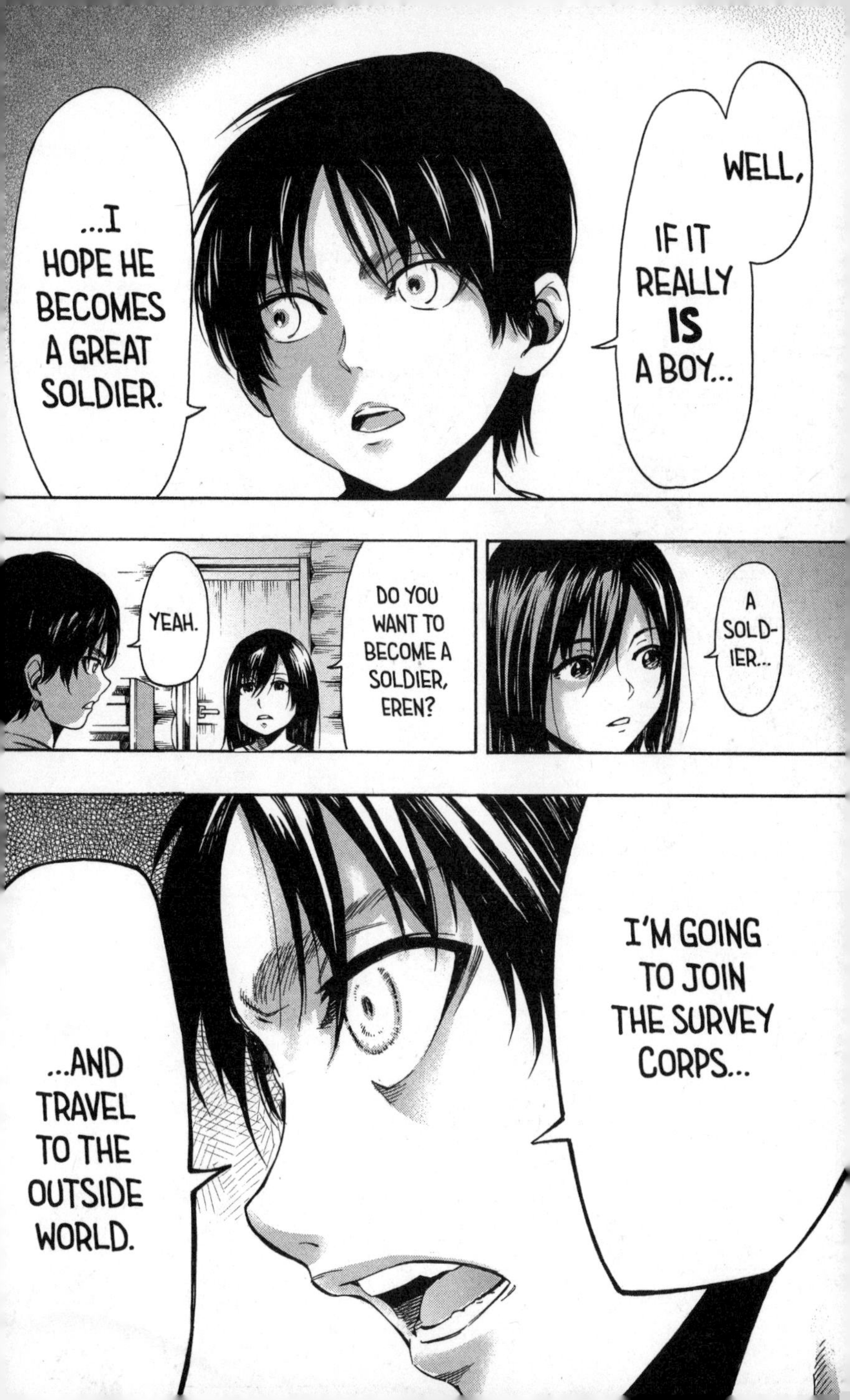
WELL, IF IT REALLY **IS** A BOY...
...I HOPE HE BECOMES A GREAT SOLDIER.
A SOLD-IER...
DO YOU WANT TO BECOME A SOLDIER, EREN?
YEAH.
I'M GOING TO JOIN THE SURVEY CORPS...
...AND TRAVEL TO THE OUTSIDE WORLD.

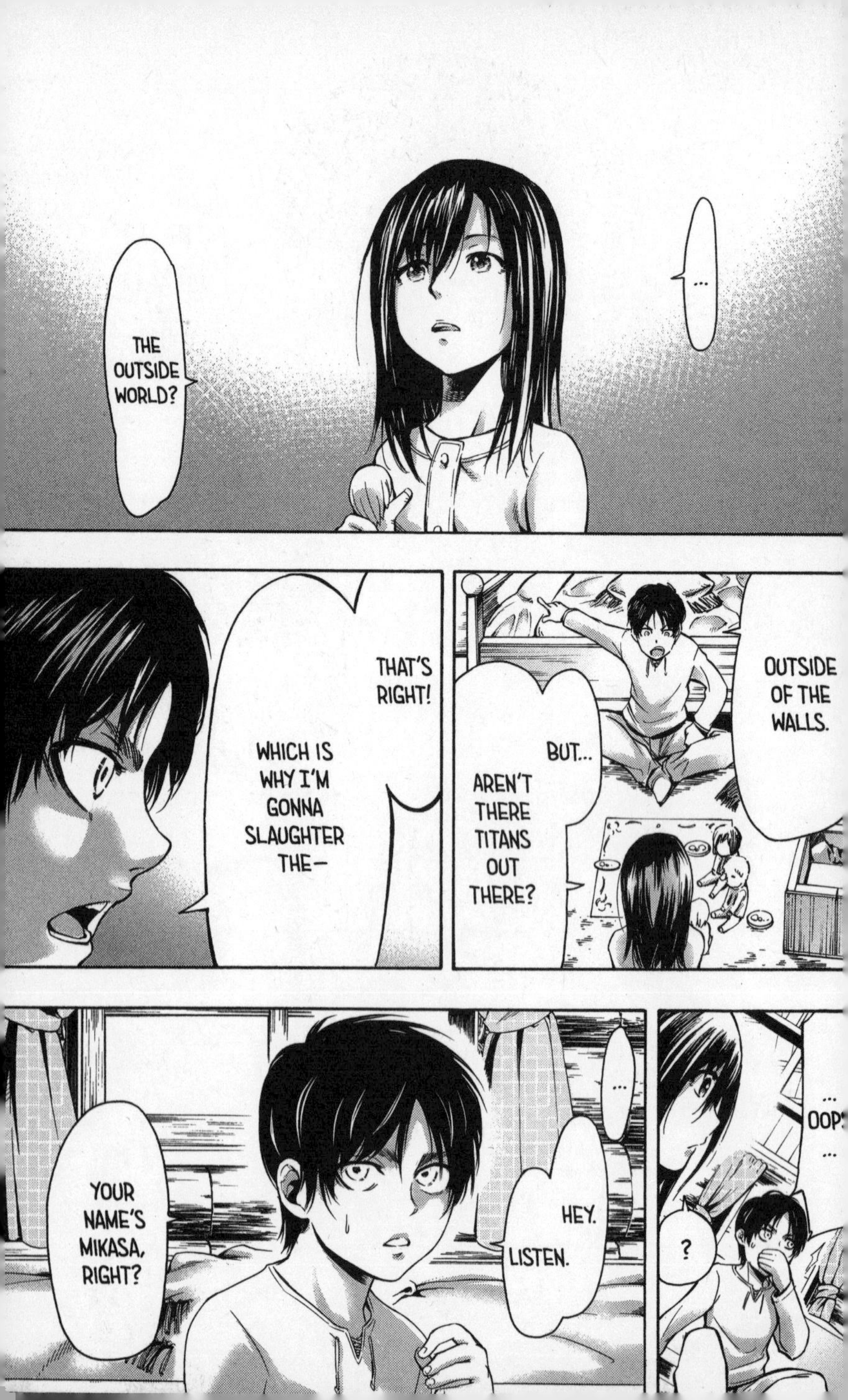
...
THE OUTSIDE WORLD?
OUTSIDE OF THE WALLS.
BUT... AREN'T THERE TITANS OUT THERE?
THAT'S RIGHT! WHICH IS WHY I'M GONNA SLAUGHTER THE—
... OOP ...
?
...
HEY. LISTEN.
YOUR NAME'S MIKASA, RIGHT?

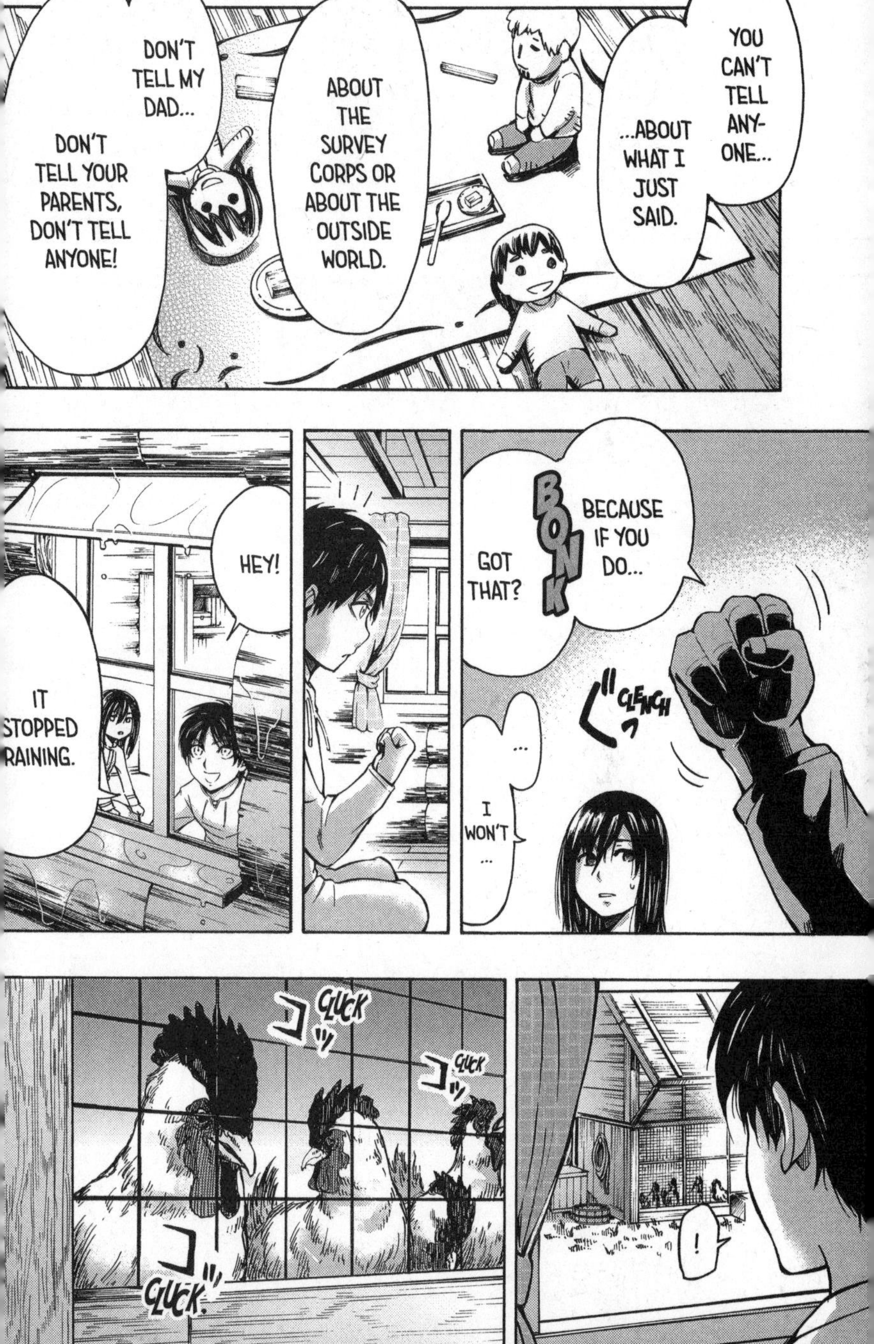
YOU CAN'T TELL ANYONE...
...ABOUT WHAT I JUST SAID.
ABOUT THE SURVEY CORPS OR ABOUT THE OUTSIDE WORLD.
DON'T TELL MY DAD...
DON'T TELL YOUR PARENTS, DON'T TELL ANYONE!
BECAUSE IF YOU DO...
BONK
GOT THAT?
CLENCH
...
I WON'T ...
HEY!
IT STOPPED RAINING.
!
CLUCK
CLUCK
CLUCK

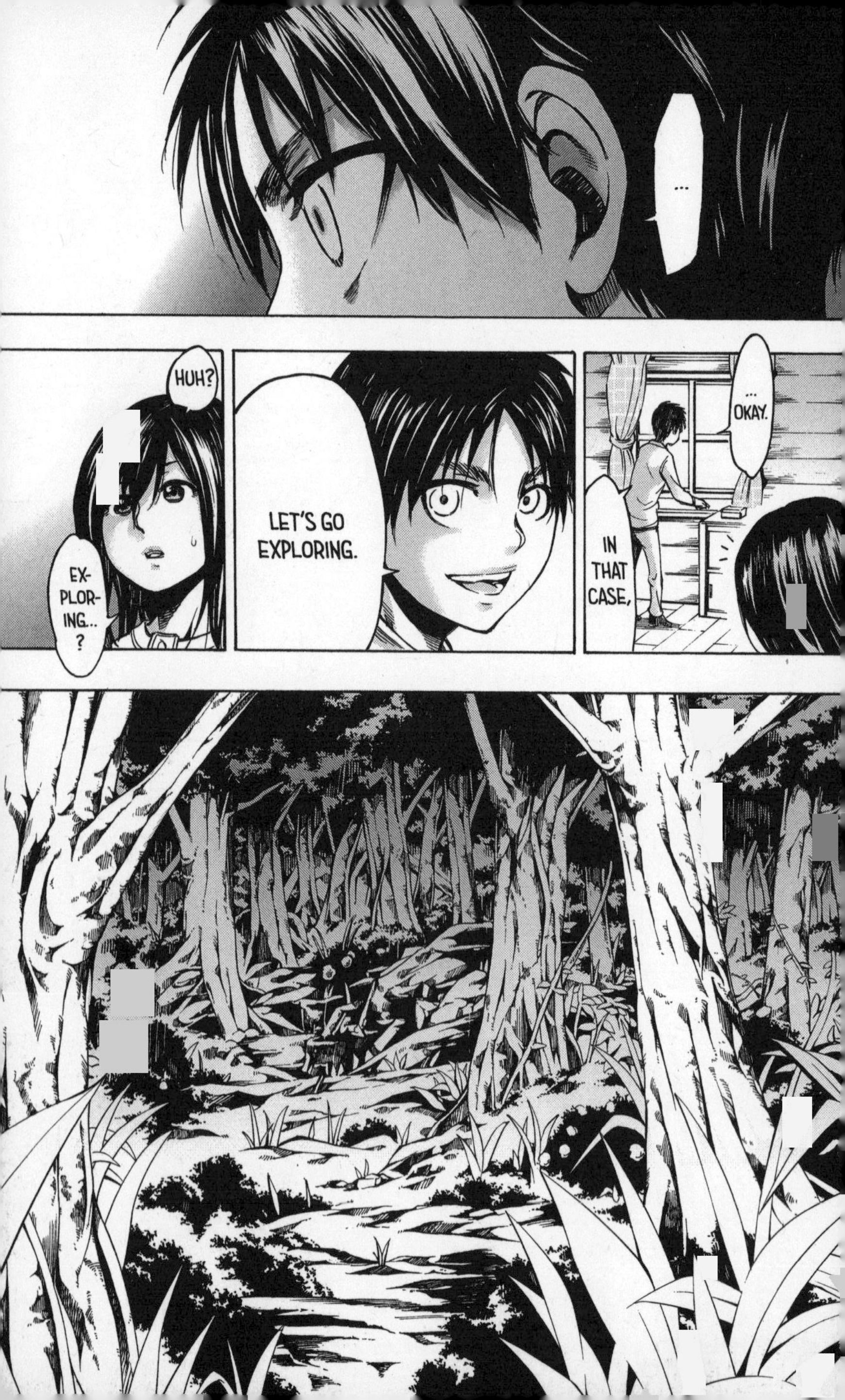
...
... OKAY.
IN THAT CASE,
LET'S GO EXPLORING.
HUH?
EX-PLORING...?

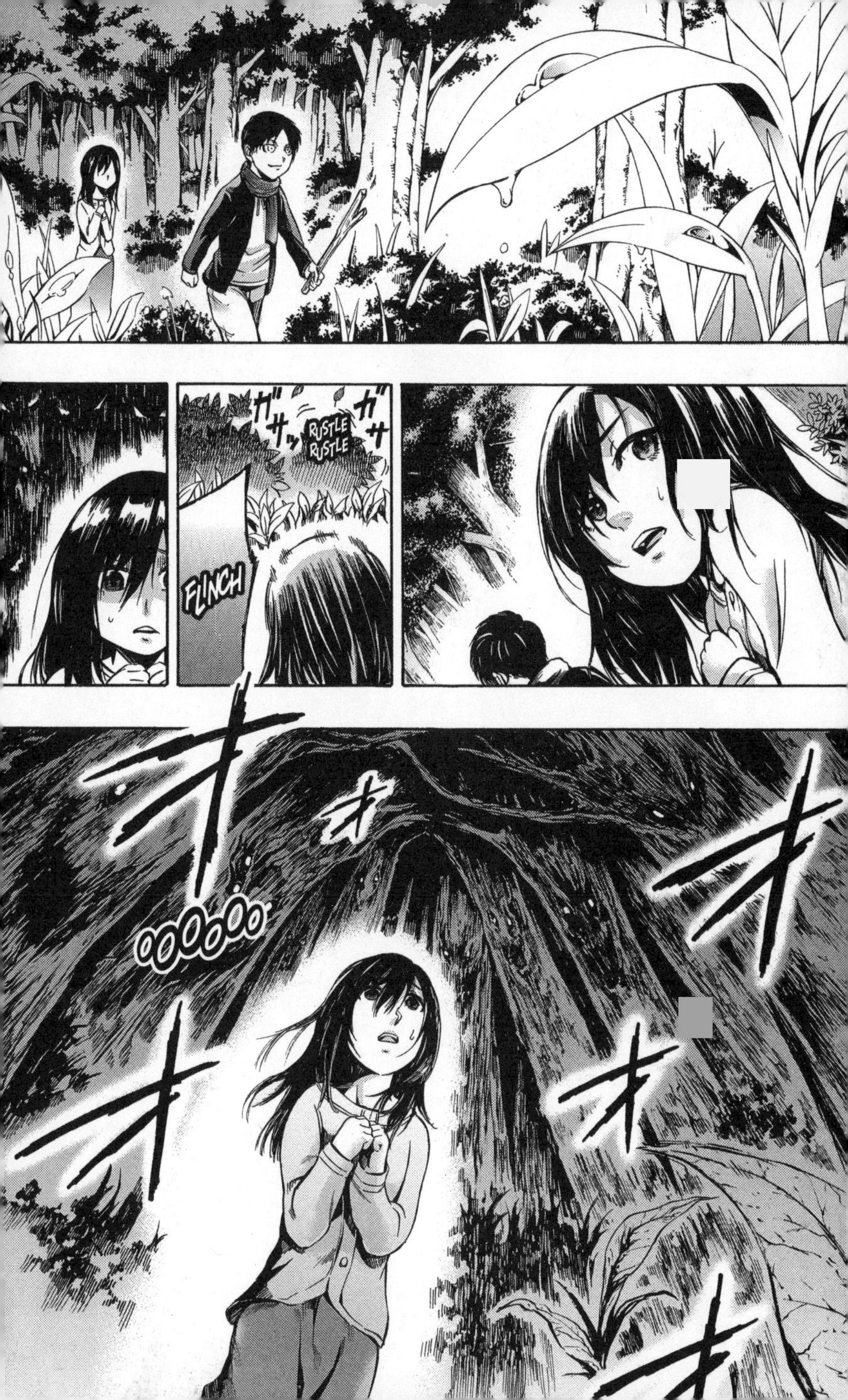
ガサッ
RUSTLE RUSTLE
ガサ
FLINCH
オ
オ
オ
OOOOOO
オ
オ
オ

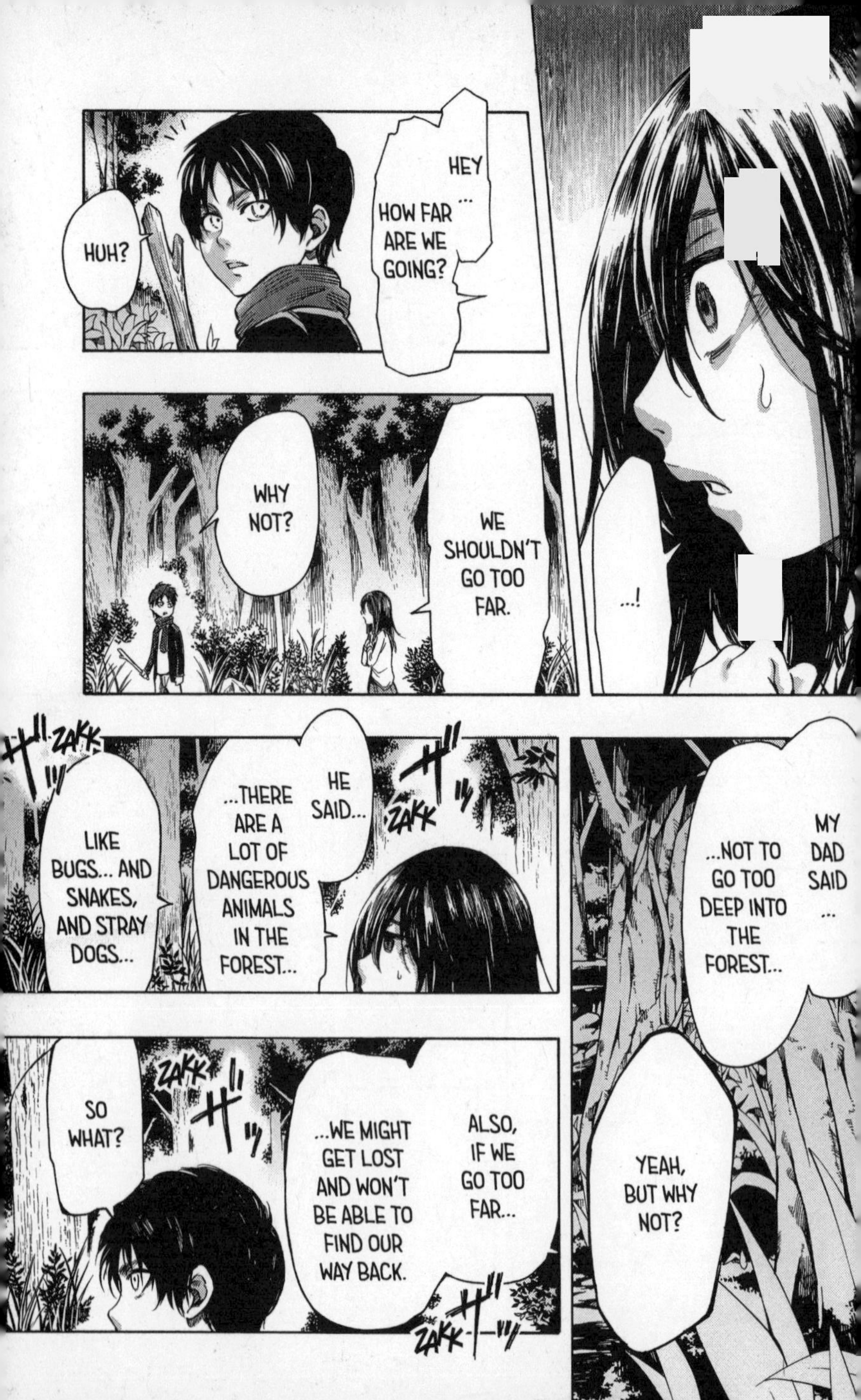
...!
HEY ...
HOW FAR ARE WE GOING?
HUH?
WE SHOULDN'T GO TOO FAR.
WHY NOT?
MY DAD SAID ...
...NOT TO GO TOO DEEP INTO THE FOREST...
YEAH, BUT WHY NOT?
ZAKK
HE SAID...
...THERE ARE A LOT OF DANGEROUS ANIMALS IN THE FOREST...
ZAKK
LIKE BUGS... AND SNAKES, AND STRAY DOGS...
ALSO, IF WE GO TOO FAR...
...WE MIGHT GET LOST AND WON'T BE ABLE TO FIND OUR WAY BACK.
ZAKK
ZAKK
SO WHAT?

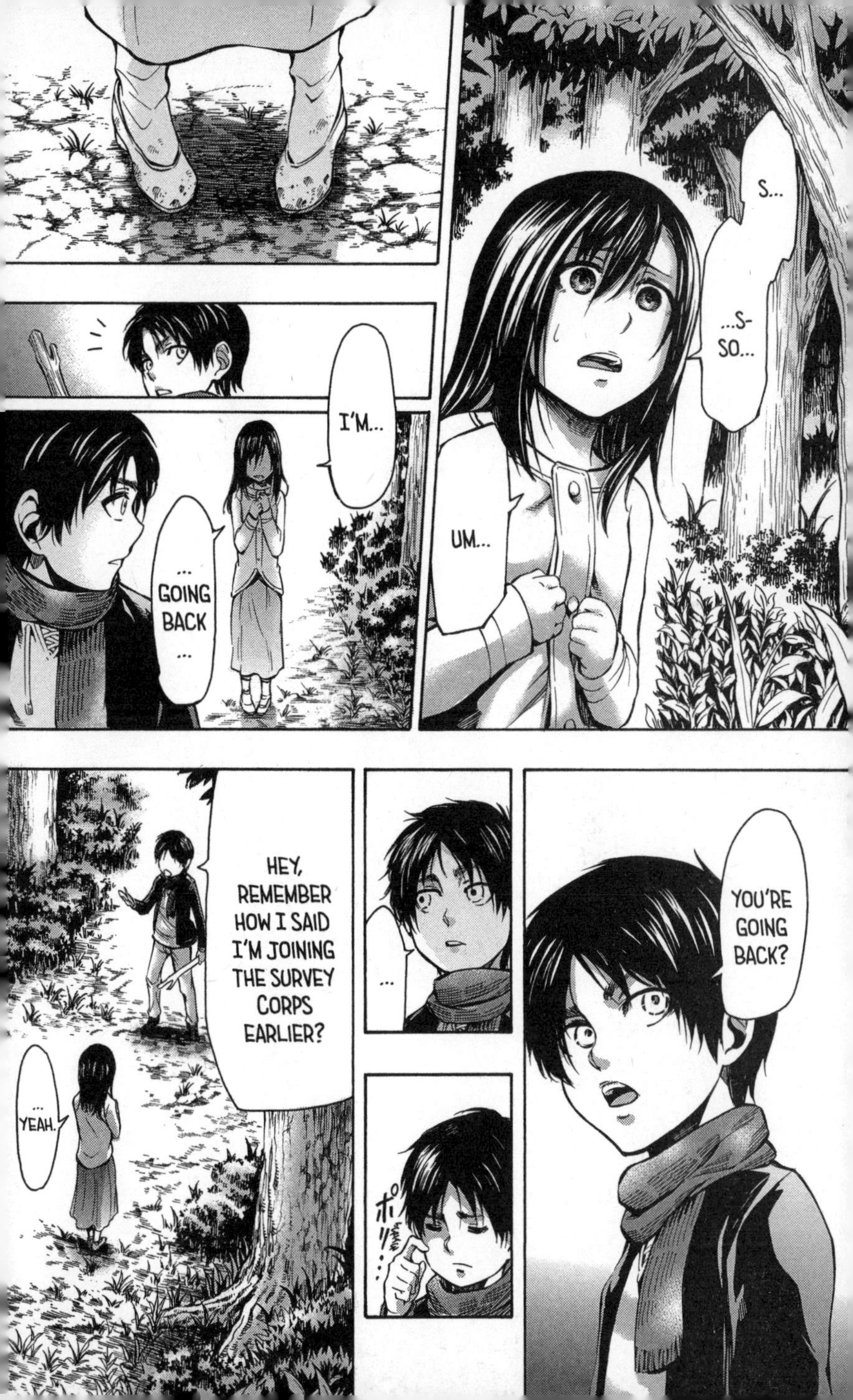
S...
...S- SO...
UM...
I'M...
... GOING BACK ...
YOU'RE GOING BACK?
...
ポリ…
HEY, REMEMBER HOW I SAID I'M JOINING THE SURVEY CORPS EARLIER?
... YEAH.

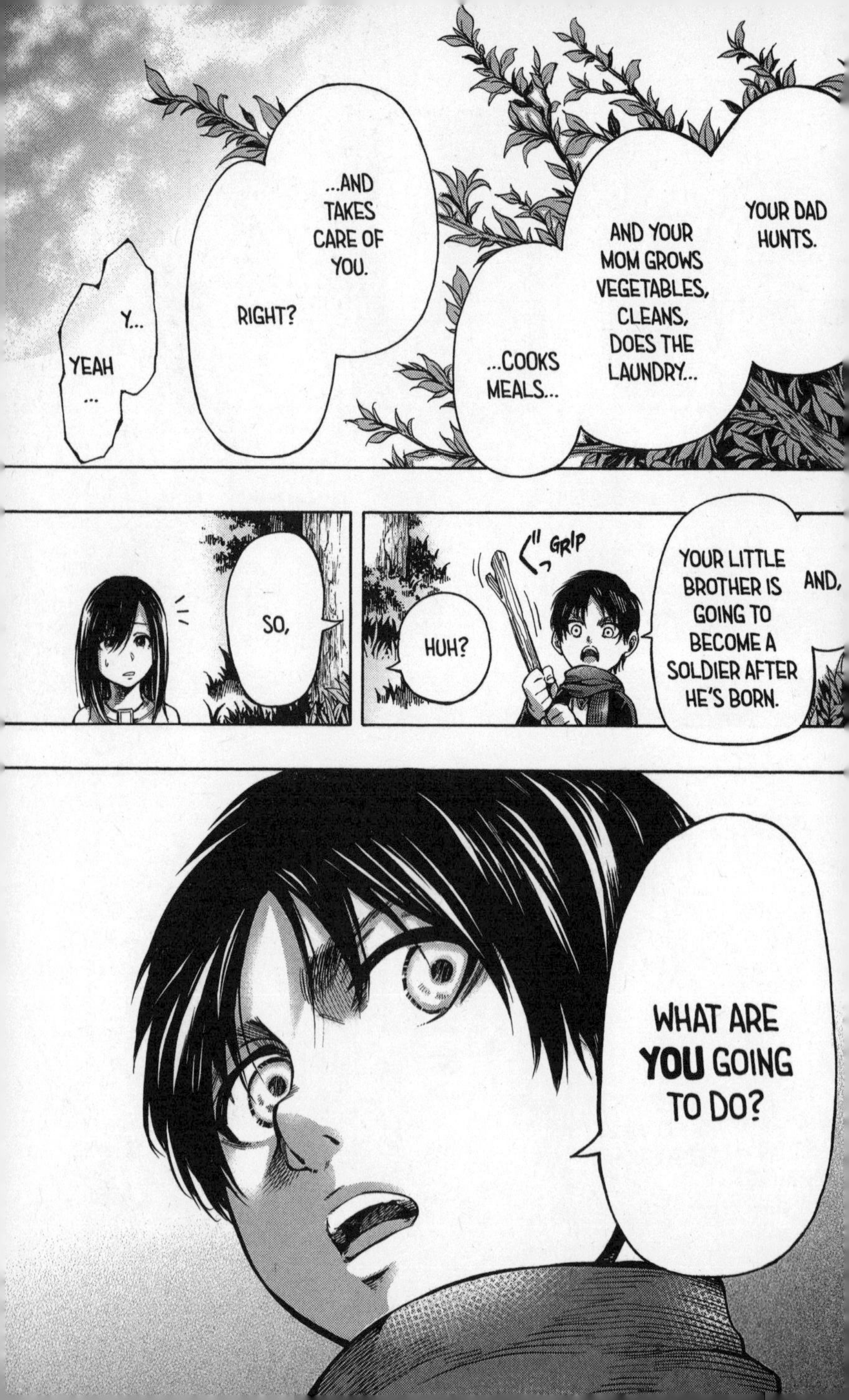
YOUR DAD HUNTS.
AND YOUR MOM GROWS VEGETABLES, CLEANS, DOES THE LAUNDRY...
...COOKS MEALS...
...AND TAKES CARE OF YOU.
RIGHT?
Y... YEAH ...
AND,
YOUR LITTLE BROTHER IS GOING TO BECOME A SOLDIER AFTER HE'S BORN.
GRIP
HUH?
SO,
WHAT ARE **YOU** GOING TO DO?

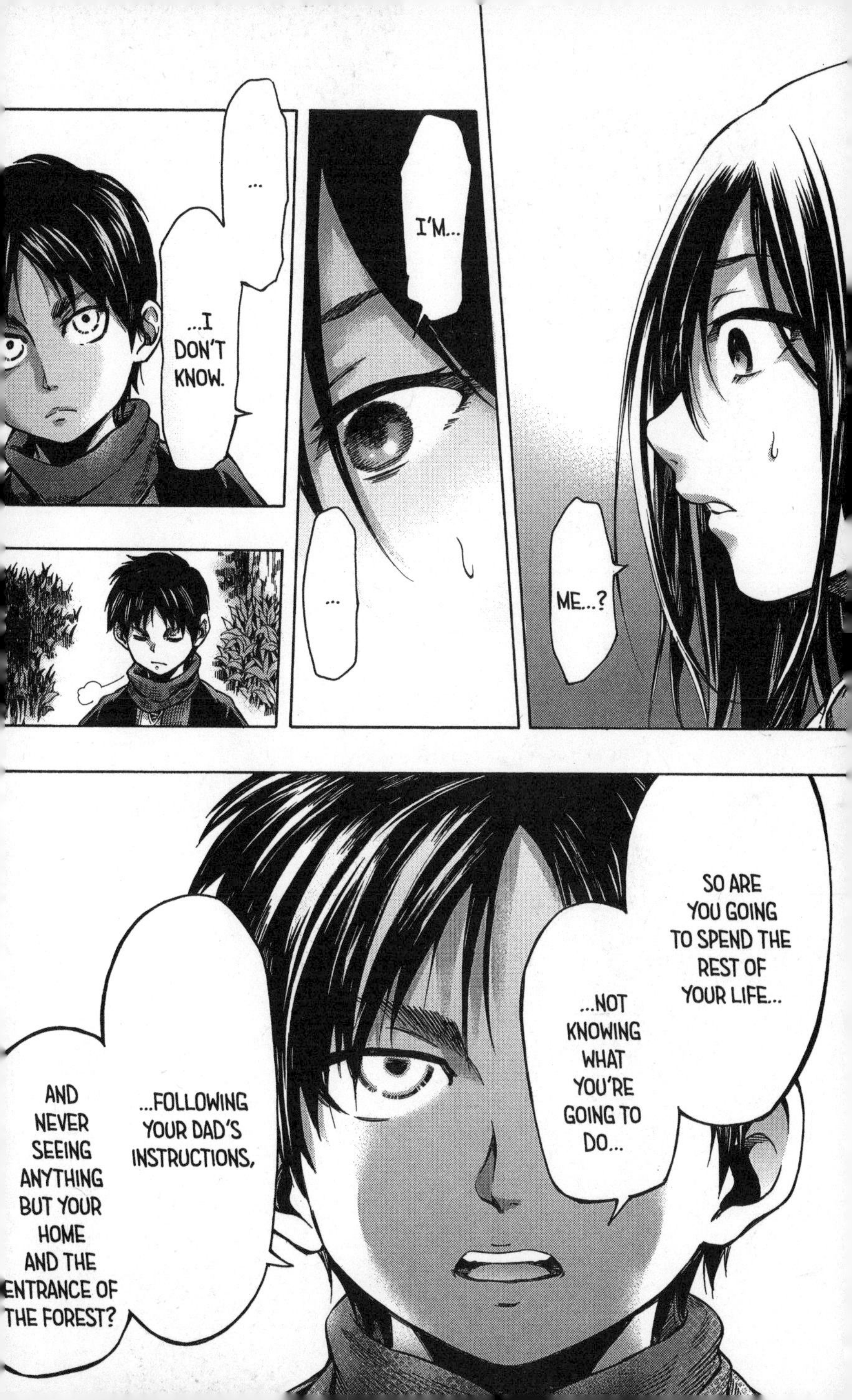

ME...?
I'M...
...
...
...I DON'T KNOW.
SO ARE YOU GOING TO SPEND THE REST OF YOUR LIFE...
...NOT KNOWING WHAT YOU'RE GOING TO DO...
...FOLLOWING YOUR DAD'S INSTRUCTIONS,
AND NEVER SEEING ANYTHING BUT YOUR HOME AND THE ENTRANCE OF THE FOREST?

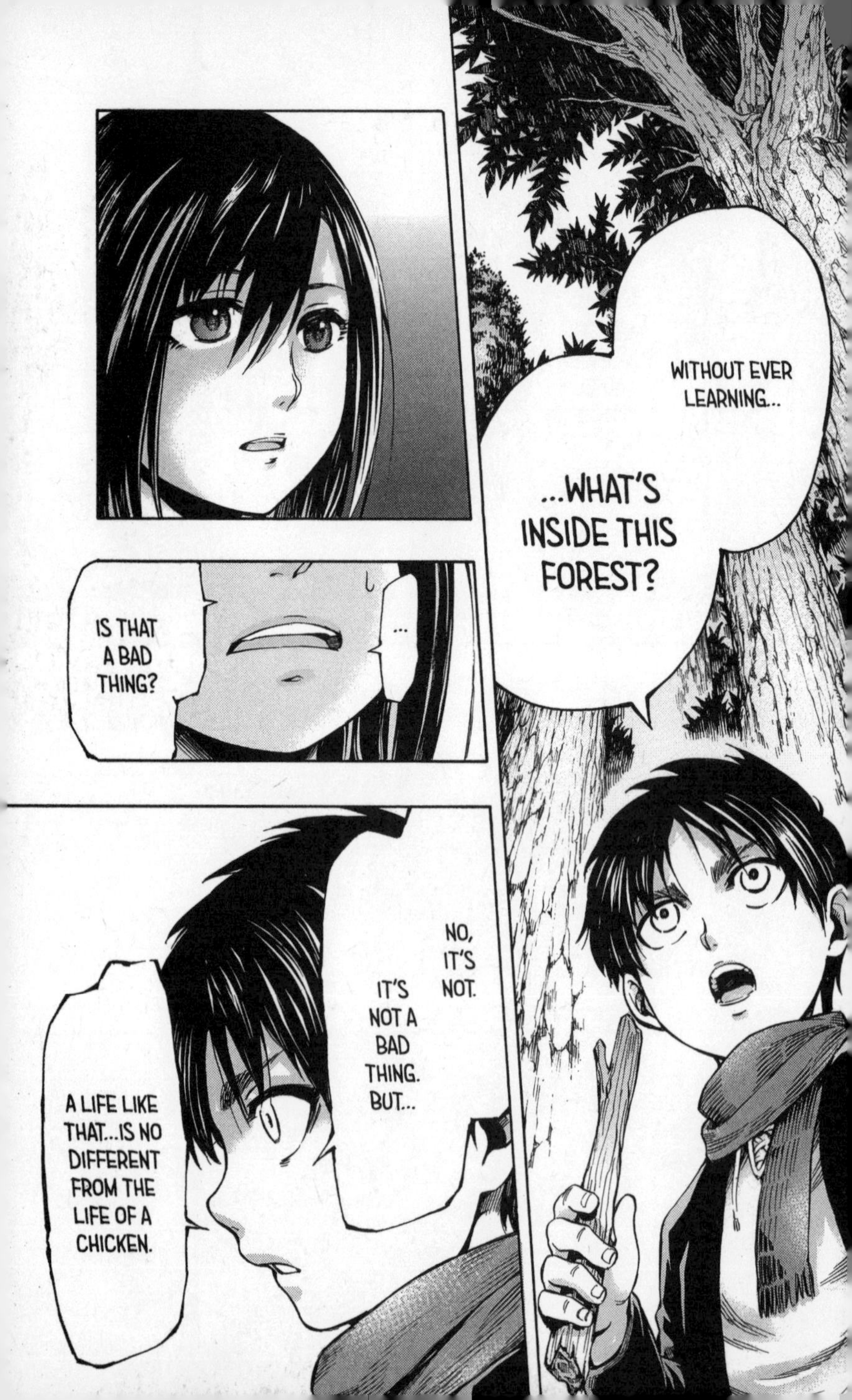
WITHOUT EVER LEARNING...
...WHAT'S INSIDE THIS FOREST?
...
IS THAT A BAD THING?
NO, IT'S NOT.
IT'S NOT A BAD THING. BUT...
A LIFE LIKE THAT...IS NO DIFFERENT FROM THE LIFE OF A CHICKEN.

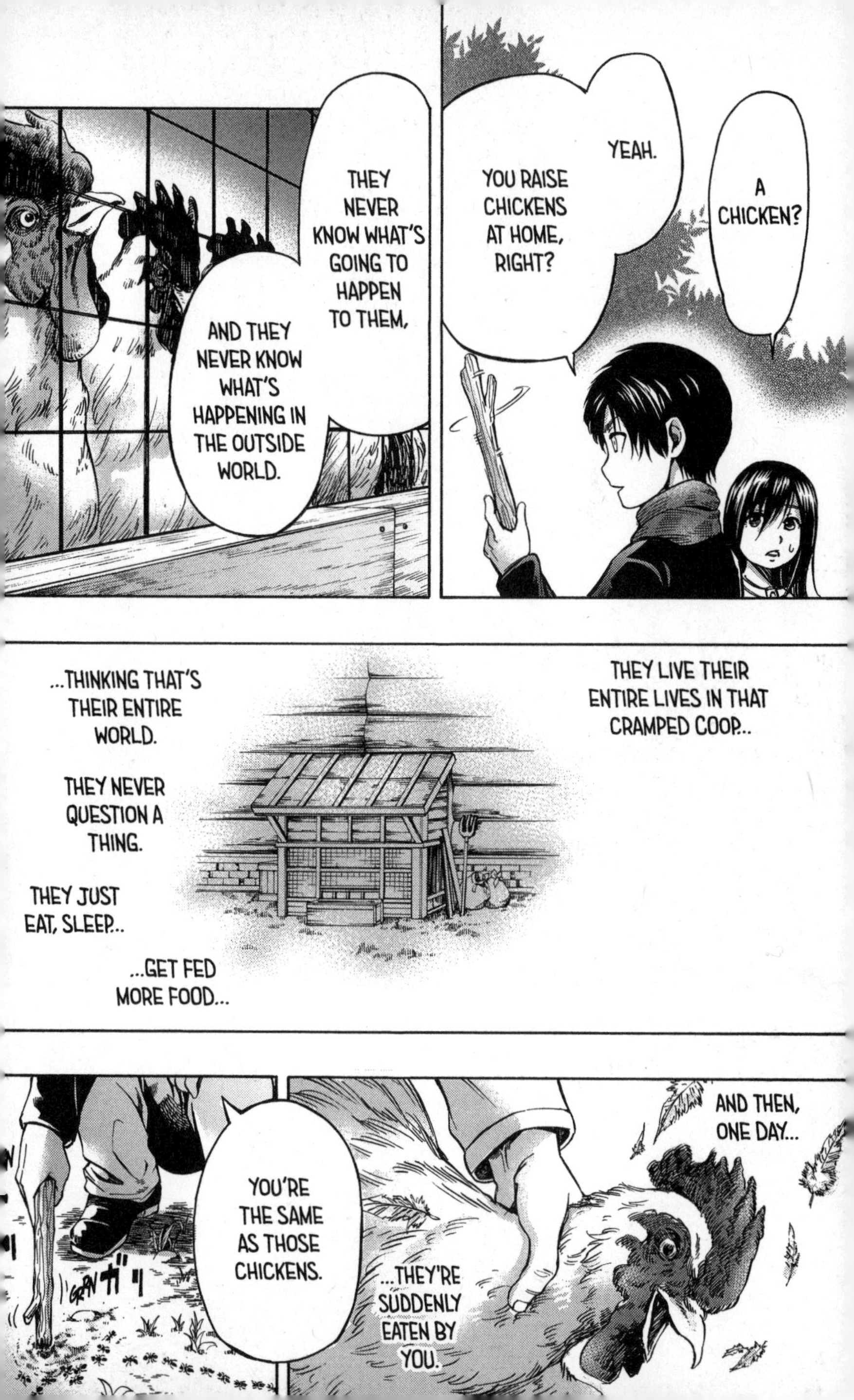
A CHICKEN?
YEAH.
YOU RAISE CHICKENS AT HOME, RIGHT?
THEY NEVER KNOW WHAT'S GOING TO HAPPEN TO THEM,
AND THEY NEVER KNOW WHAT'S HAPPENING IN THE OUTSIDE WORLD.
THEY LIVE THEIR ENTIRE LIVES IN THAT CRAMPED COOP...
...THINKING THAT'S THEIR ENTIRE WORLD.
THEY NEVER QUESTION A THING.
THEY JUST EAT, SLEEP...
...GET FED MORE FOOD...
AND THEN, ONE DAY...
...THEY'RE SUDDENLY EATEN BY YOU.
YOU'RE THE SAME AS THOSE CHICKENS.

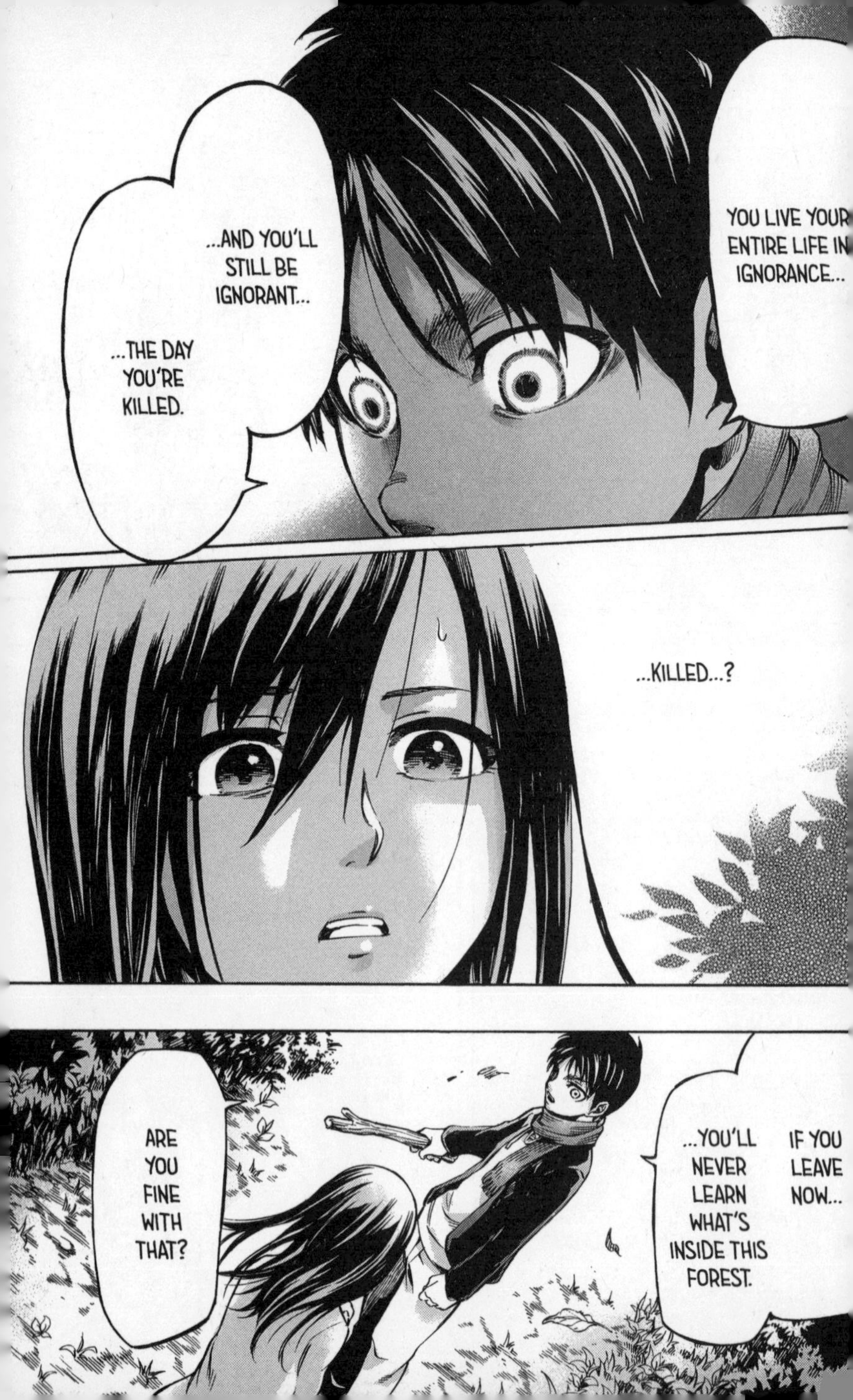
YOU LIVE YOUR ENTIRE LIFE IN IGNORANCE...
...AND YOU'LL STILL BE IGNORANT...
...THE DAY YOU'RE KILLED.
...KILLED...?
IF YOU LEAVE NOW...
...YOU'LL NEVER LEARN WHAT'S INSIDE THIS FOREST.
ARE YOU FINE WITH THAT?

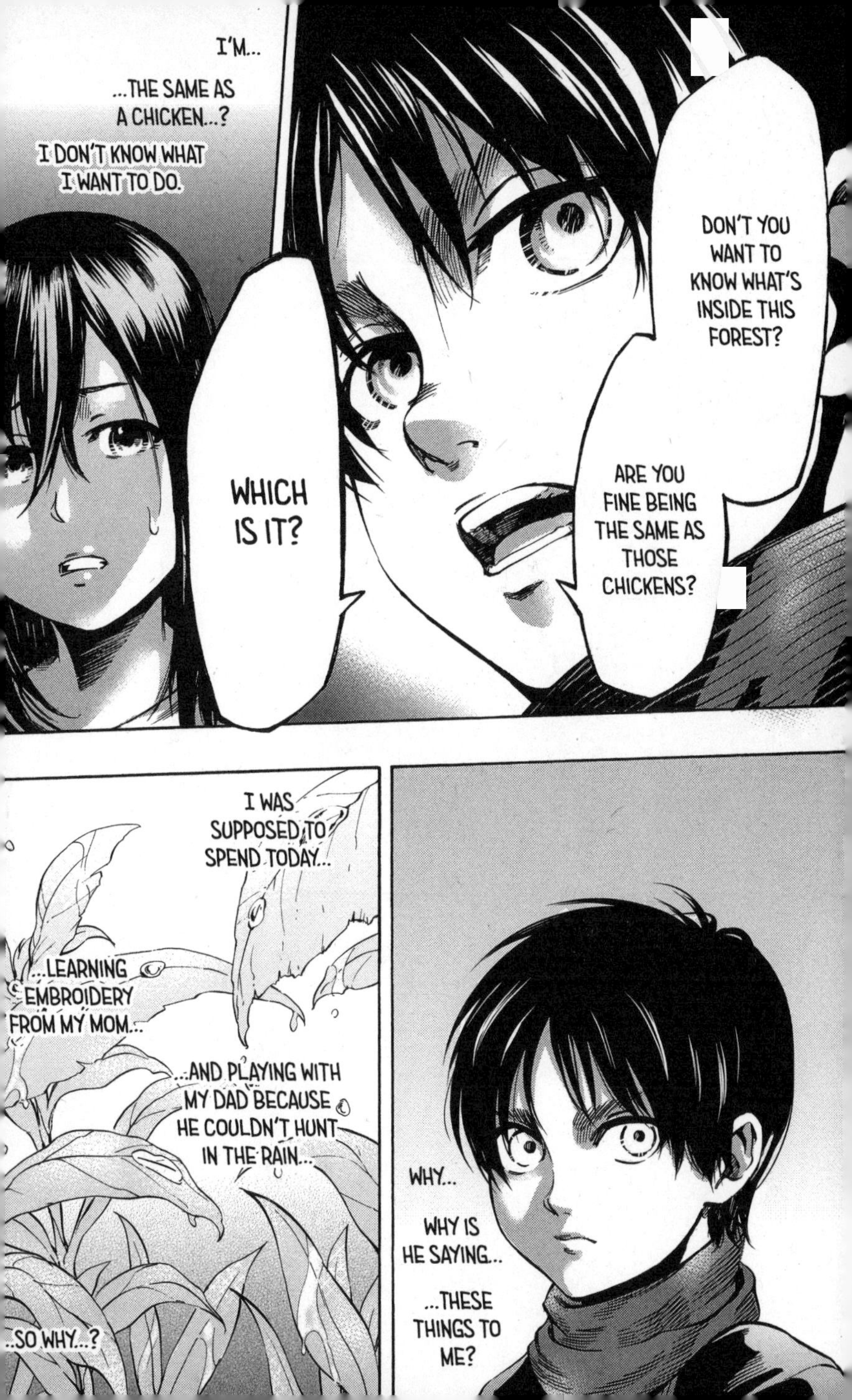
DON'T YOU WANT TO KNOW WHAT'S INSIDE THIS FOREST?
ARE YOU FINE BEING THE SAME AS THOSE CHICKENS?
WHICH IS IT?
I'M...
...THE SAME AS A CHICKEN...?
I DON'T KNOW WHAT I WANT TO DO.
WHY...
WHY IS HE SAYING...
...THESE THINGS TO ME?
I WAS SUPPOSED TO SPEND TODAY...
...LEARNING EMBROIDERY FROM MY MOM...
...AND PLAYING WITH MY DAD BECAUSE HE COULDN'T HUNT IN THE RAIN...
..SO WHY...?

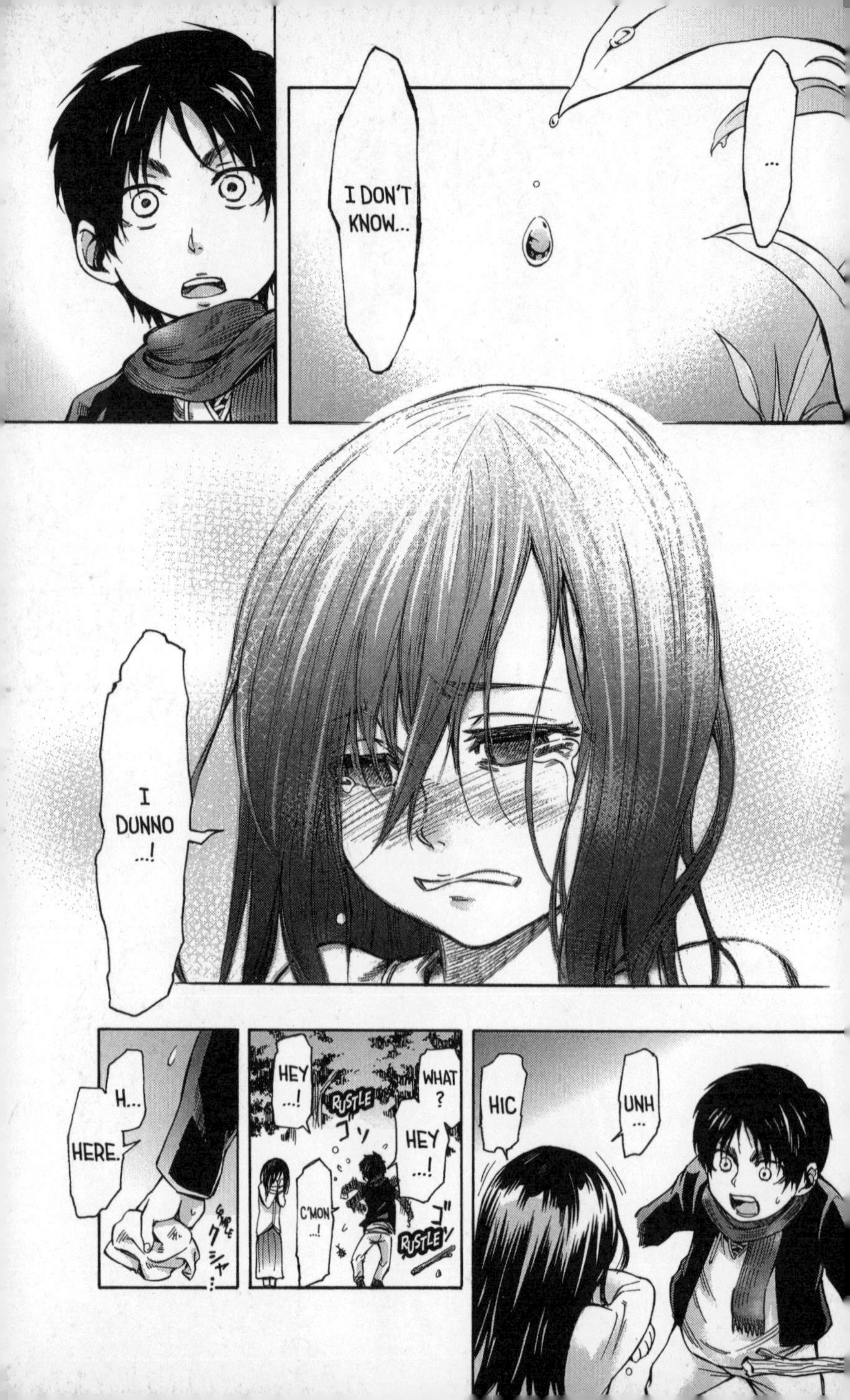
...
I DON'T KNOW...
I DUNNO ...!
UNH ...
HIC
WHAT ?
HEY ...!
RUSTLE
HEY ...!
C'MON ...!
RUSTLE
H...
HERE.

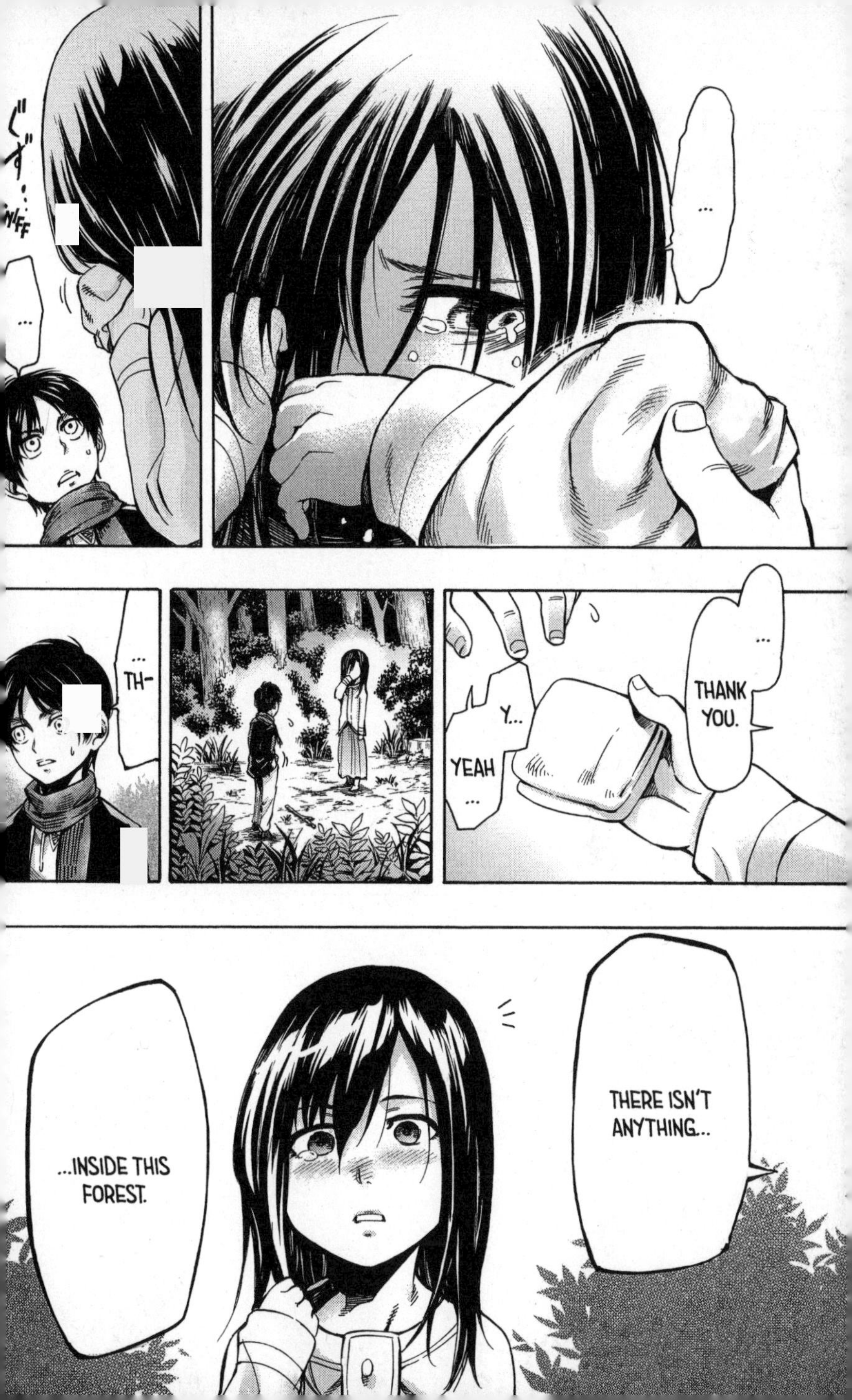
...
ぐず…
...
...
THANK YOU.
Y... YEAH ...
... TH-
THERE ISN'T ANYTHING...
...INSIDE THIS FOREST.

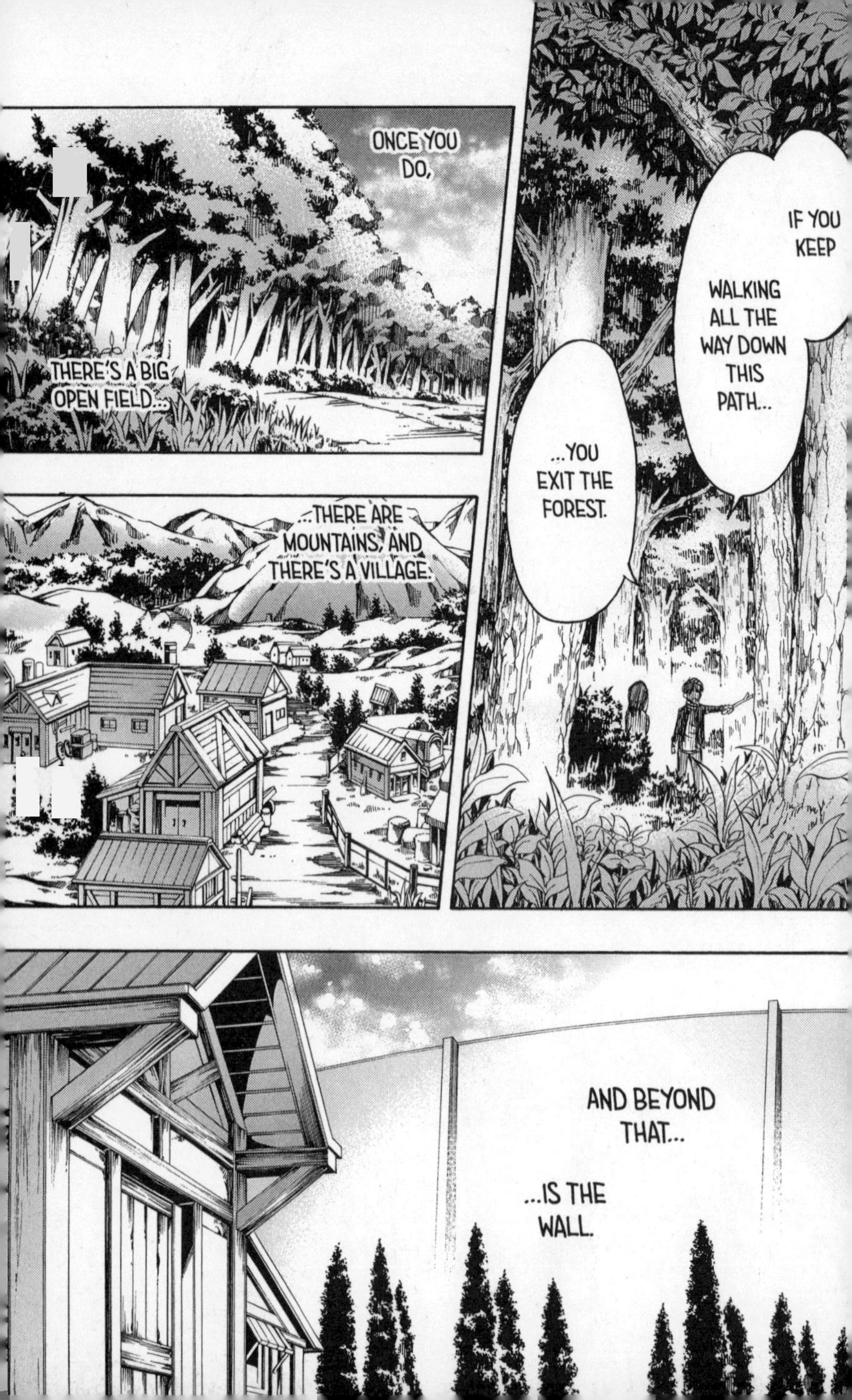
IF YOU KEEP WALKING ALL THE WAY DOWN THIS PATH...
...YOU EXIT THE FOREST.
ONCE YOU DO,
THERE'S A BIG OPEN FIELD...
...THERE ARE MOUNTAINS, AND THERE'S A VILLAGE.
AND BEYOND THAT...
...IS THE WALL.

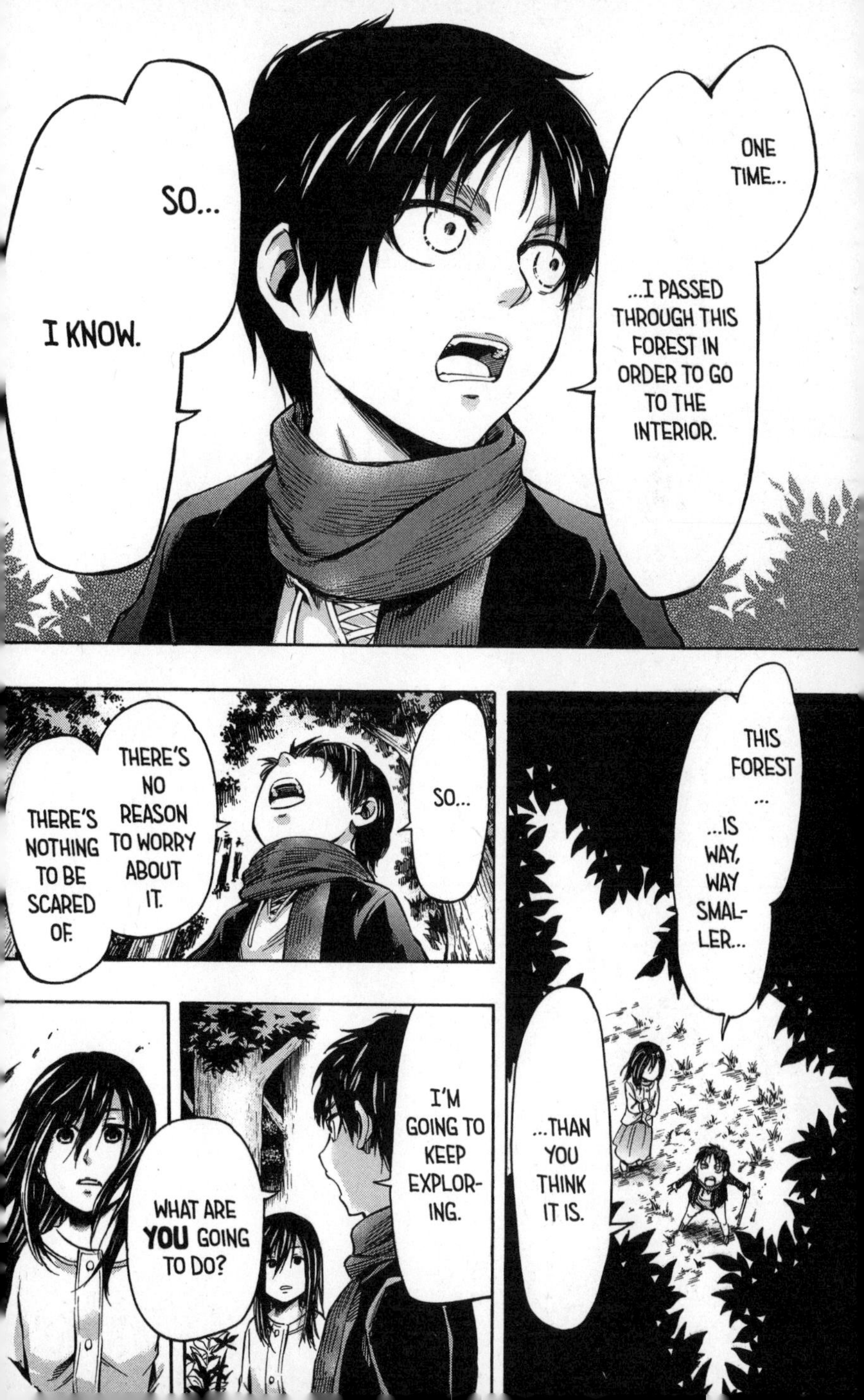
ONE TIME... ...I PASSED THROUGH THIS FOREST IN ORDER TO GO TO THE INTERIOR.
SO... I KNOW.
THIS FOREST... ...IS WAY, WAY SMAL-LER...
...THAN YOU THINK IT IS.
SO...
THERE'S NO REASON TO WORRY ABOUT IT.
THERE'S NOTHING TO BE SCARED OF.
I'M GOING TO KEEP EXPLOR-ING.
WHAT ARE **YOU** GOING TO DO?

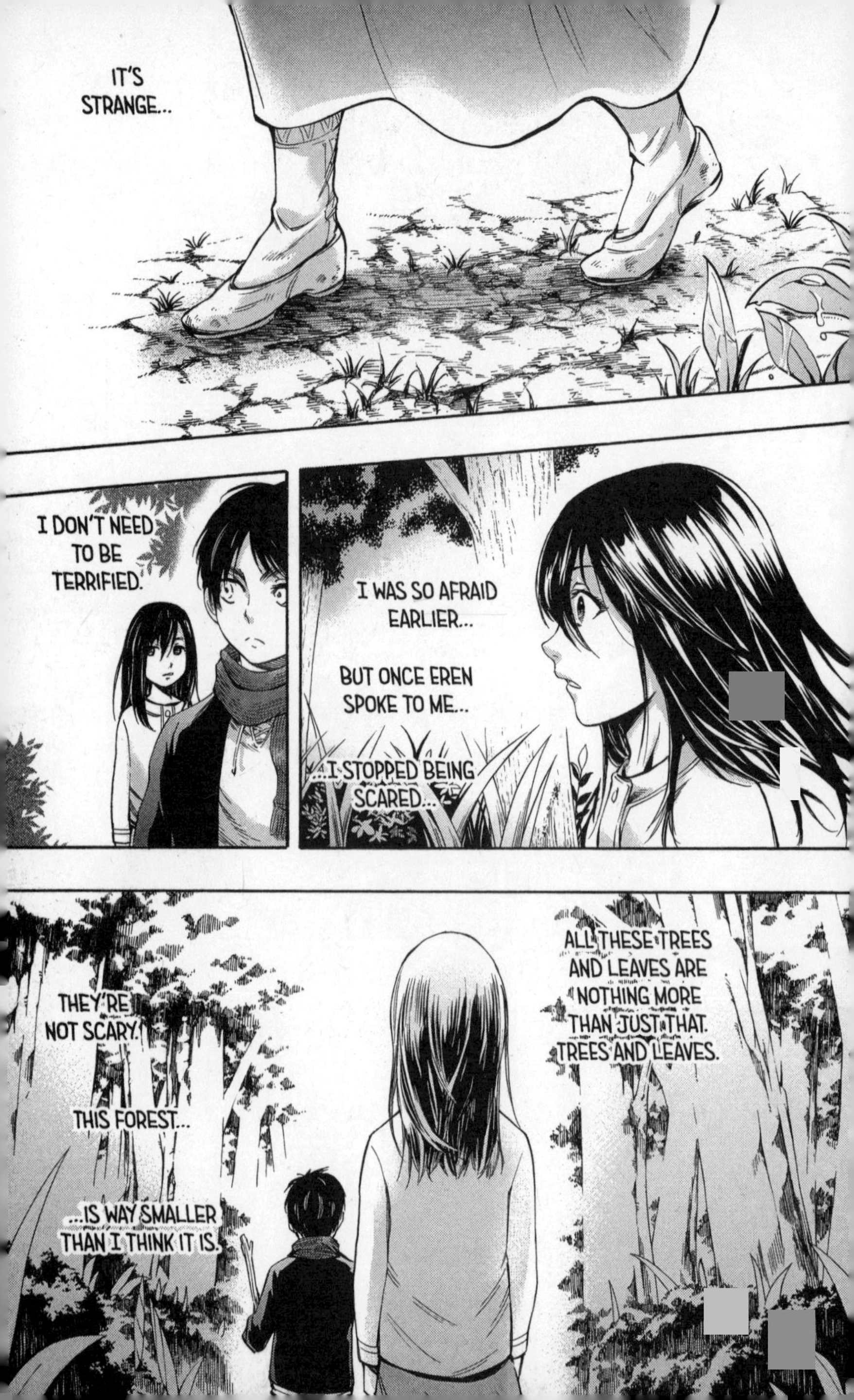
IT'S STRANGE...
I WAS SO AFRAID EARLIER...
BUT ONCE EREN SPOKE TO ME...
...I STOPPED BEING SCARED...
I DON'T NEED TO BE TERRIFIED.
ALL THESE TREES AND LEAVES ARE NOTHING MORE THAN JUST THAT. TREES AND LEAVES.
THEY'RE NOT SCARY.
THIS FOREST...
...IS WAY SMALLER THAN I THINK IT IS.

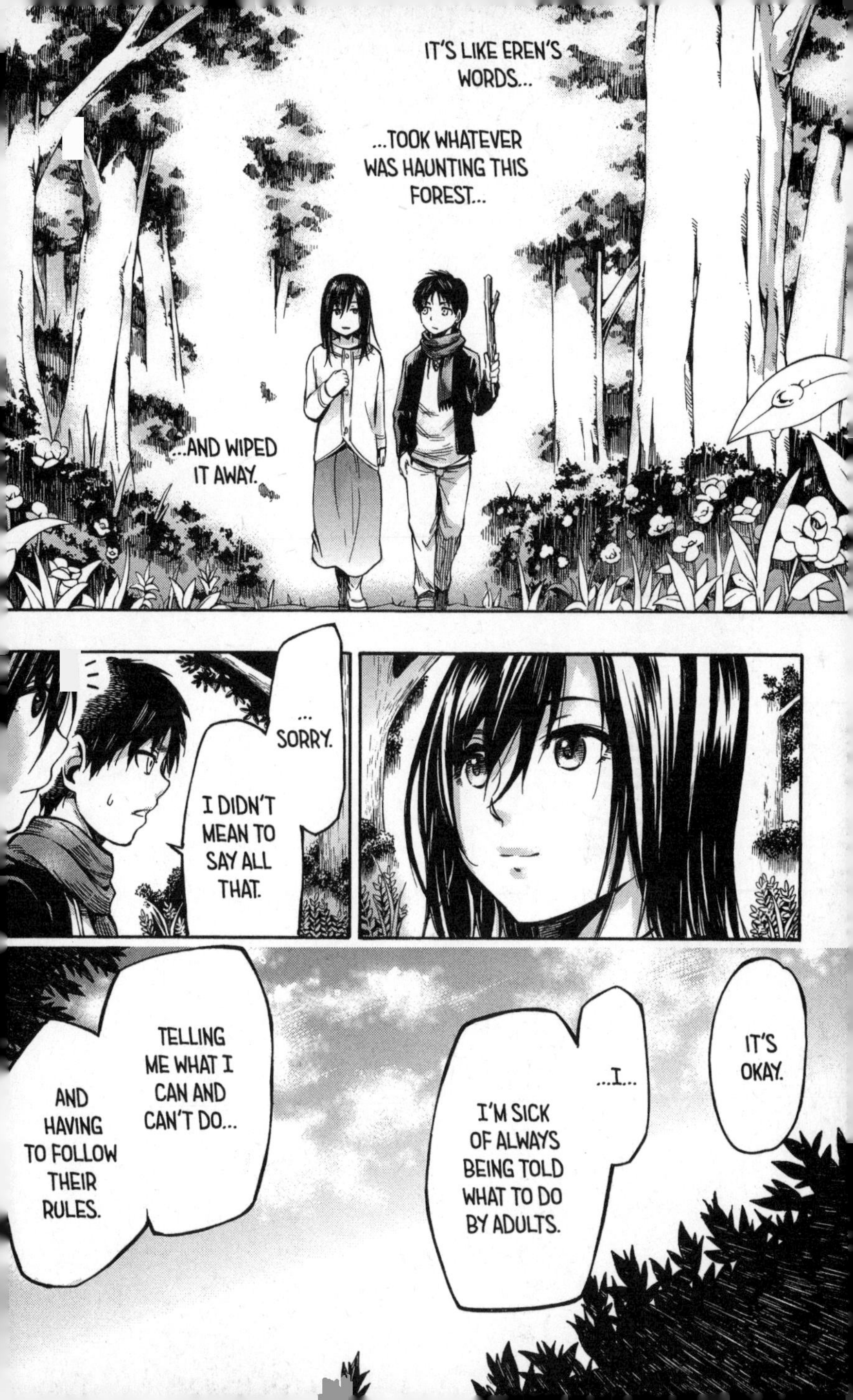
IT'S LIKE EREN'S WORDS...
...TOOK WHATEVER WAS HAUNTING THIS FOREST...
...AND WIPED IT AWAY.
... SORRY.
I DIDN'T MEAN TO SAY ALL THAT.
IT'S OKAY.
...I...
I'M SICK OF ALWAYS BEING TOLD WHAT TO DO BY ADULTS.
TELLING ME WHAT I CAN AND CAN'T DO...
AND HAVING TO FOLLOW THEIR RULES.

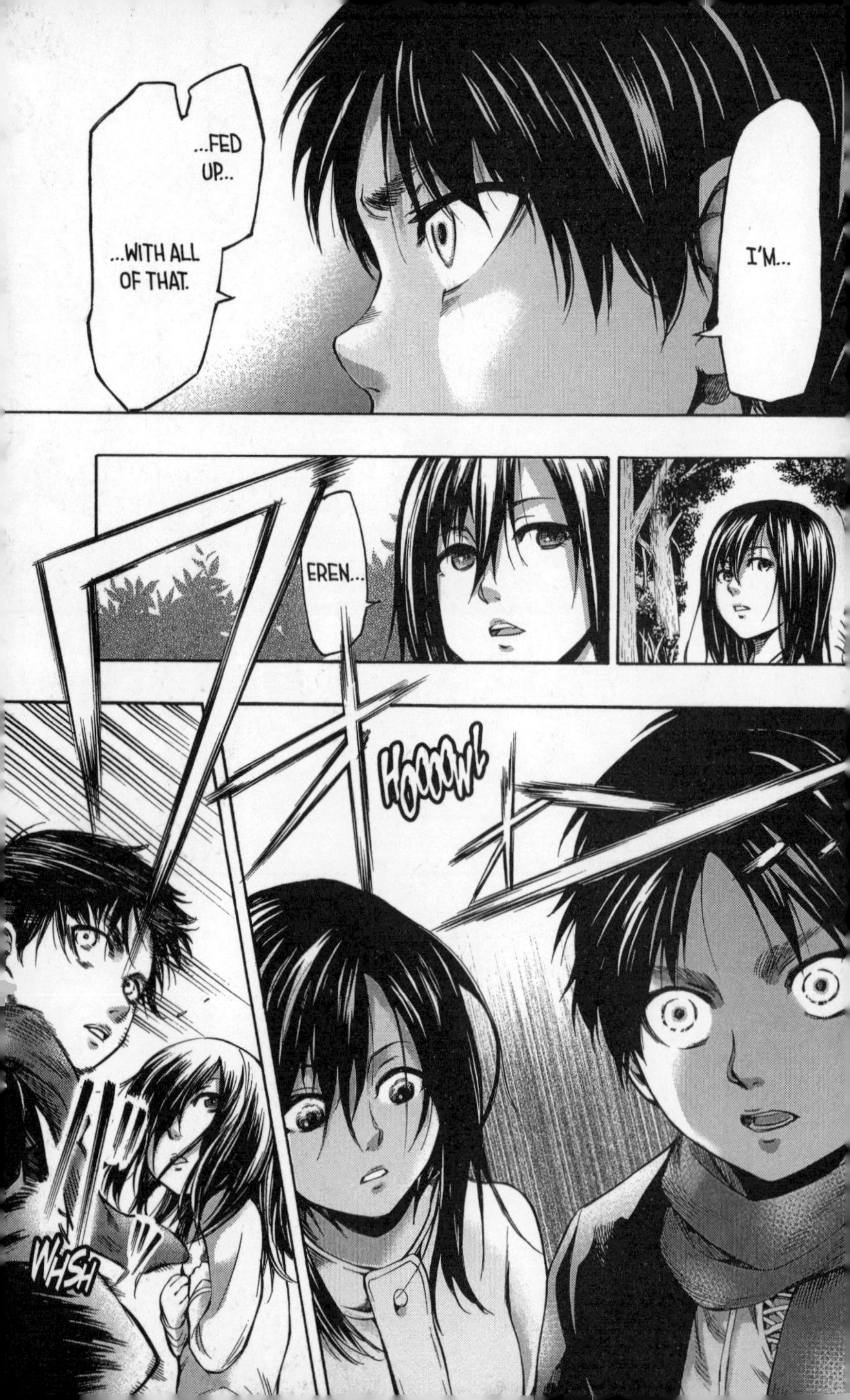
I'M...
...FED UP...
...WITH ALL OF THAT.
EREN...
HOOOOWL
WHSH

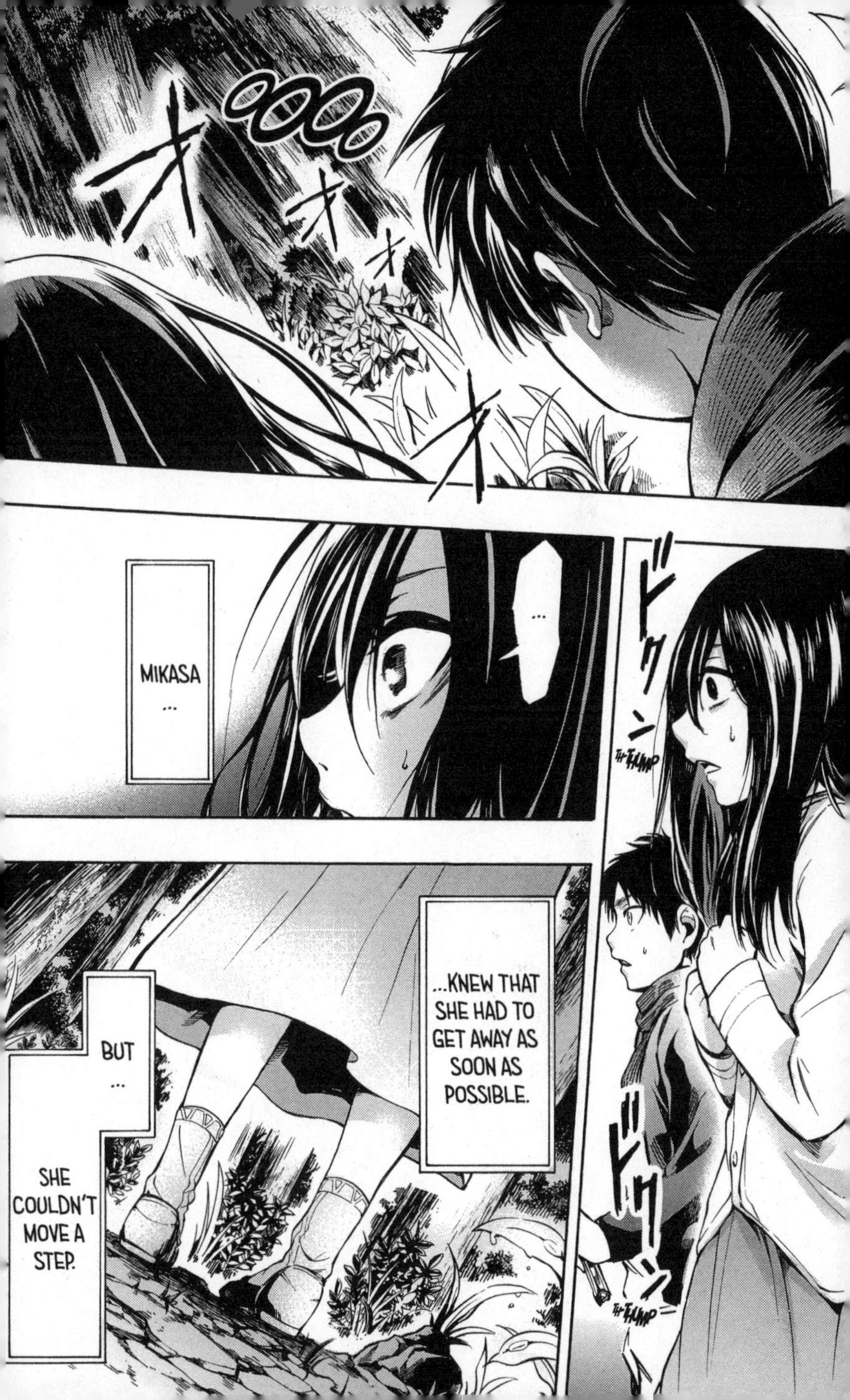
OOOO
TH-THUMP
TH-THUMP
...
MIKASA ...
...KNEW THAT SHE HAD TO GET AWAY AS SOON AS POSSIBLE.
BUT ...
SHE COULDN'T MOVE A STEP.

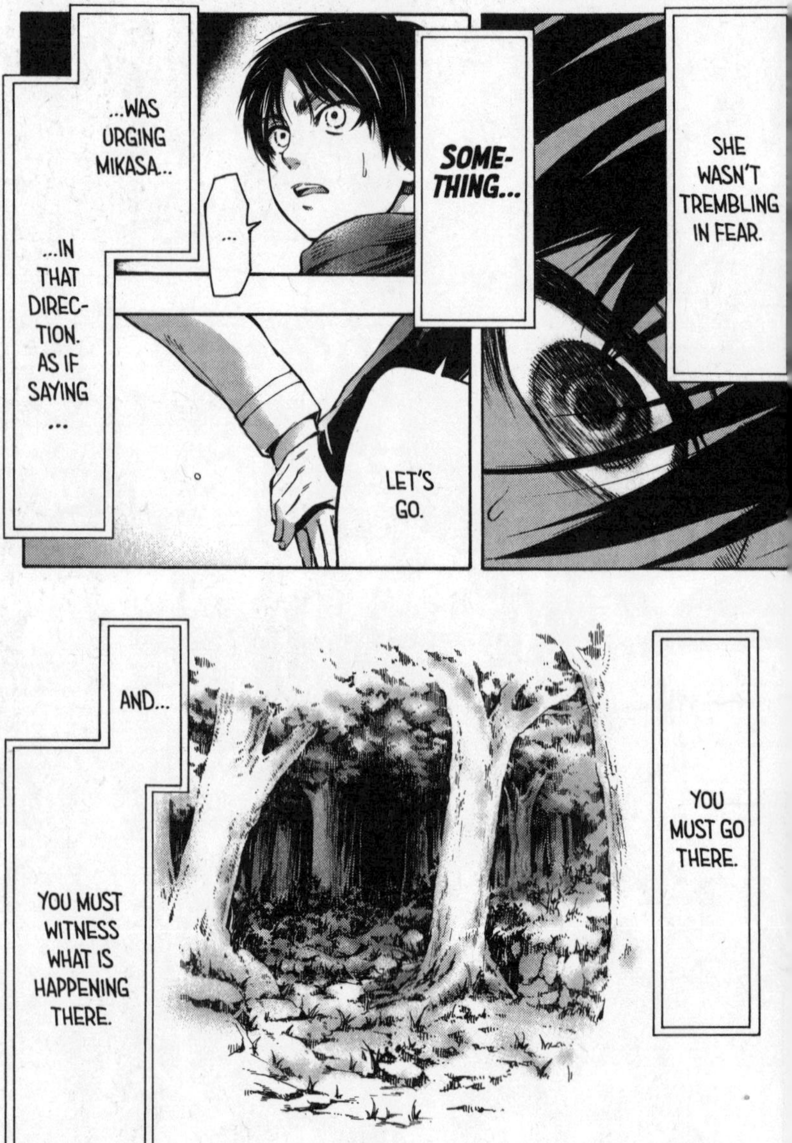
SHE WASN'T TREMBLING IN FEAR.
SOME-THING...
...
...WAS URGING MIKASA...
...IN THAT DIREC-TION. AS IF SAYING ...
LET'S GO.
YOU MUST GO THERE.
AND...
YOU MUST WITNESS WHAT IS HAPPENING THERE.

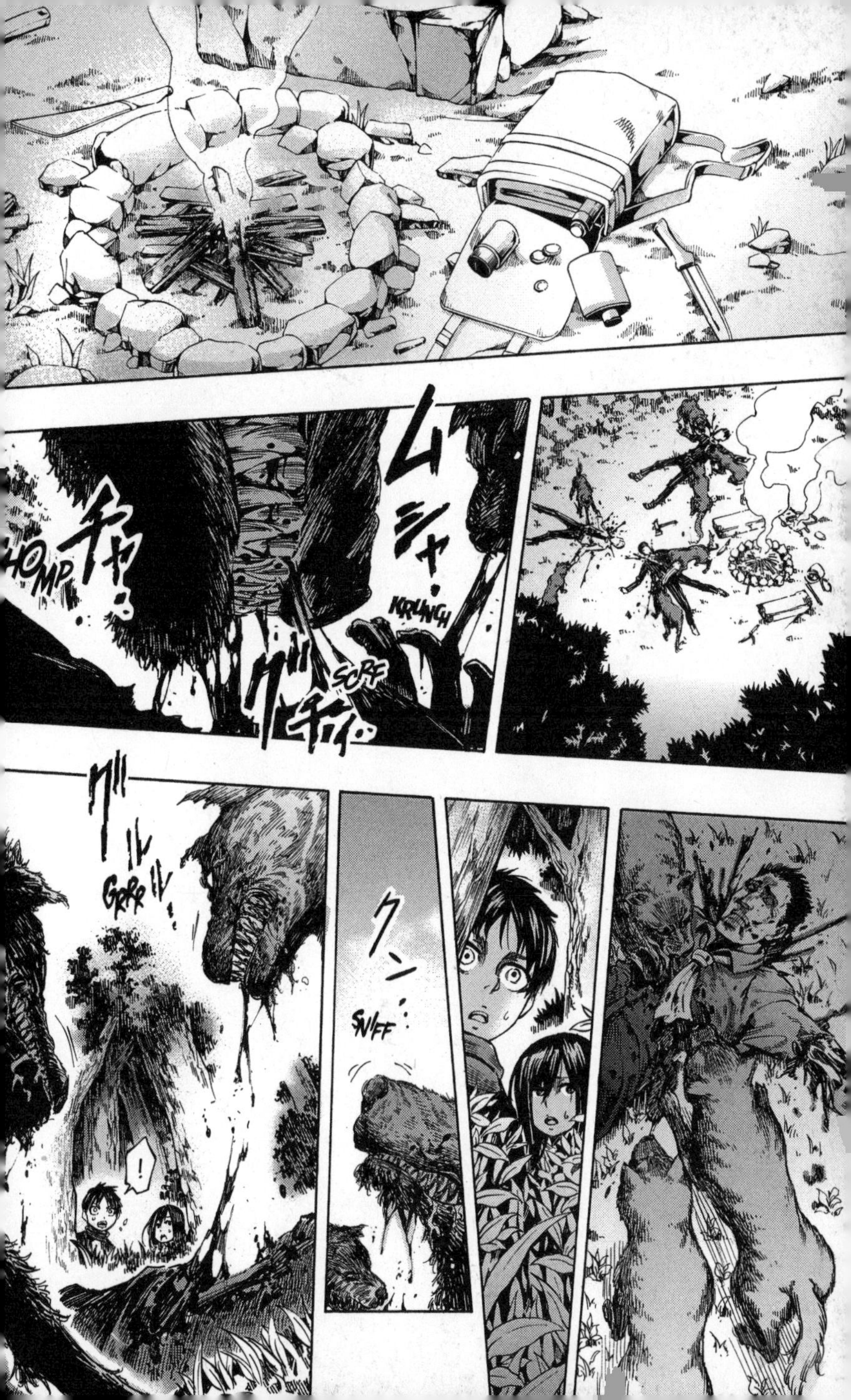
ムシャ・
KRUNCH
チャ・
CHOMP
SCRF
クン
SNIFF
GRRR
!

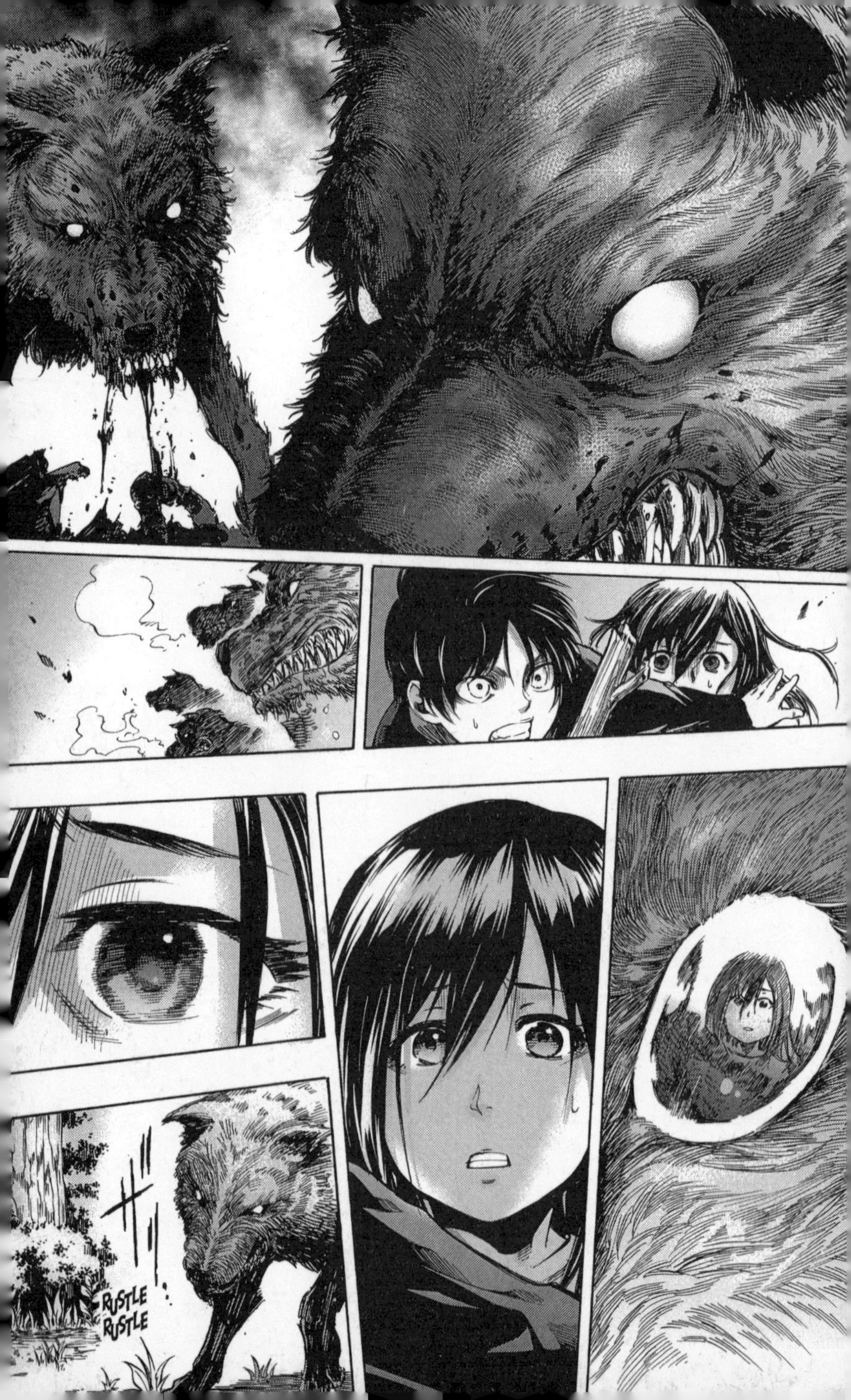
RUSTLE
RUSTLE

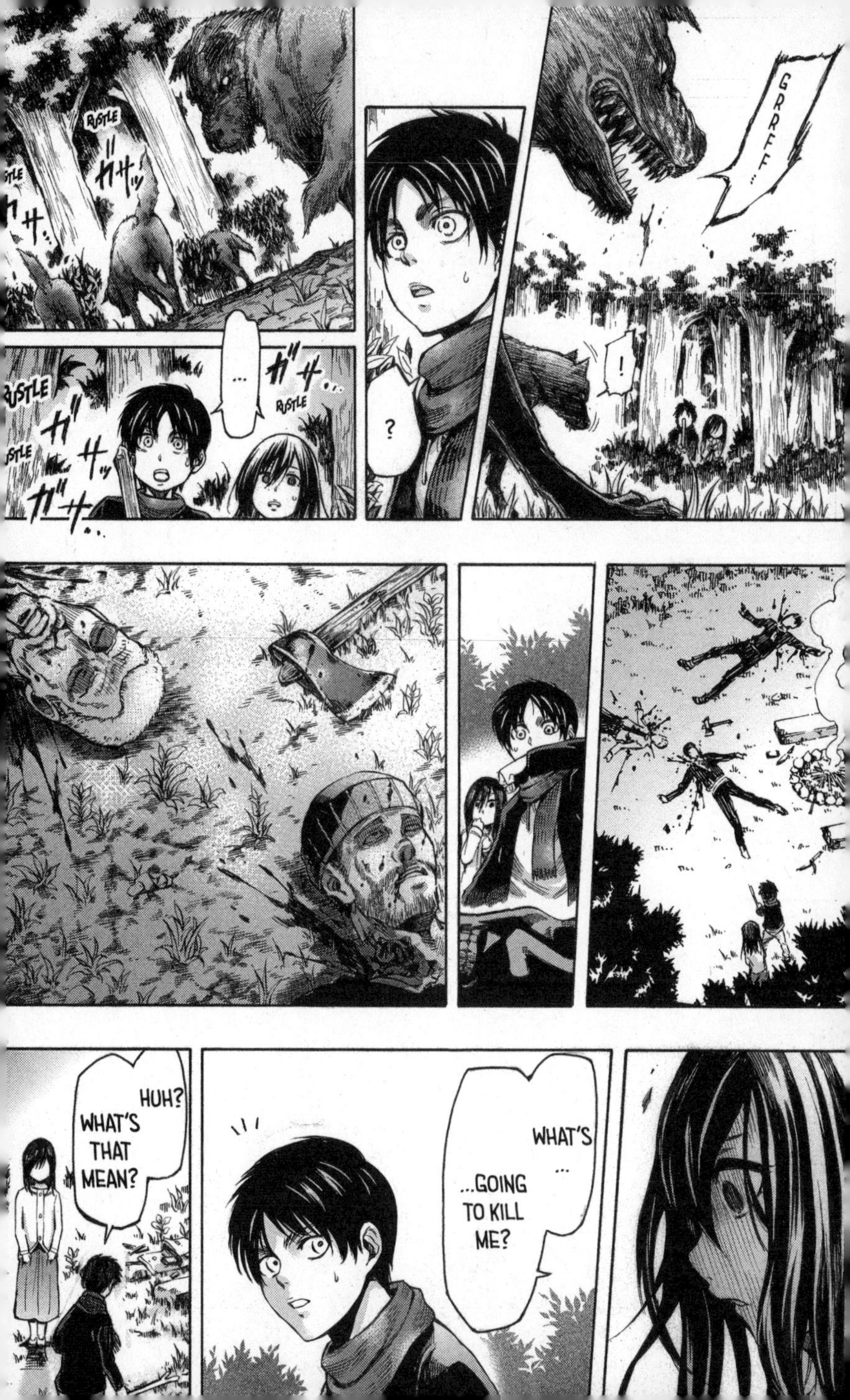
GRRFF...
!
?
RUSTLE
...
RUSTLE
RUSTLE
WHAT'S ...
...GOING TO KILL ME?
HUH? WHAT'S THAT MEAN?

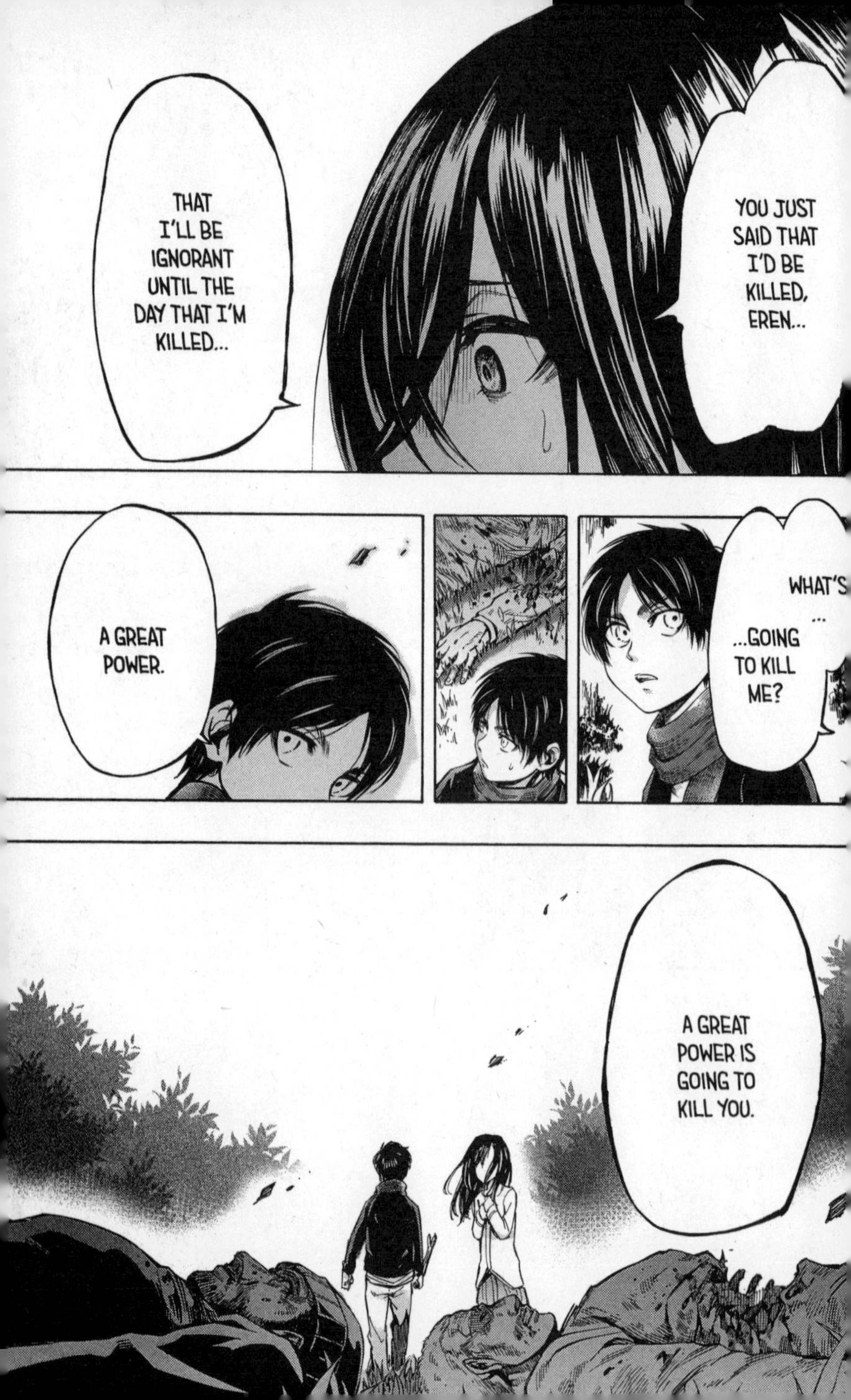
YOU JUST SAID THAT I'D BE KILLED, EREN...
THAT I'LL BE IGNORANT UNTIL THE DAY THAT I'M KILLED...
WHAT'S ... ...GOING TO KILL ME?
A GREAT POWER.
A GREAT POWER IS GOING TO KILL YOU.

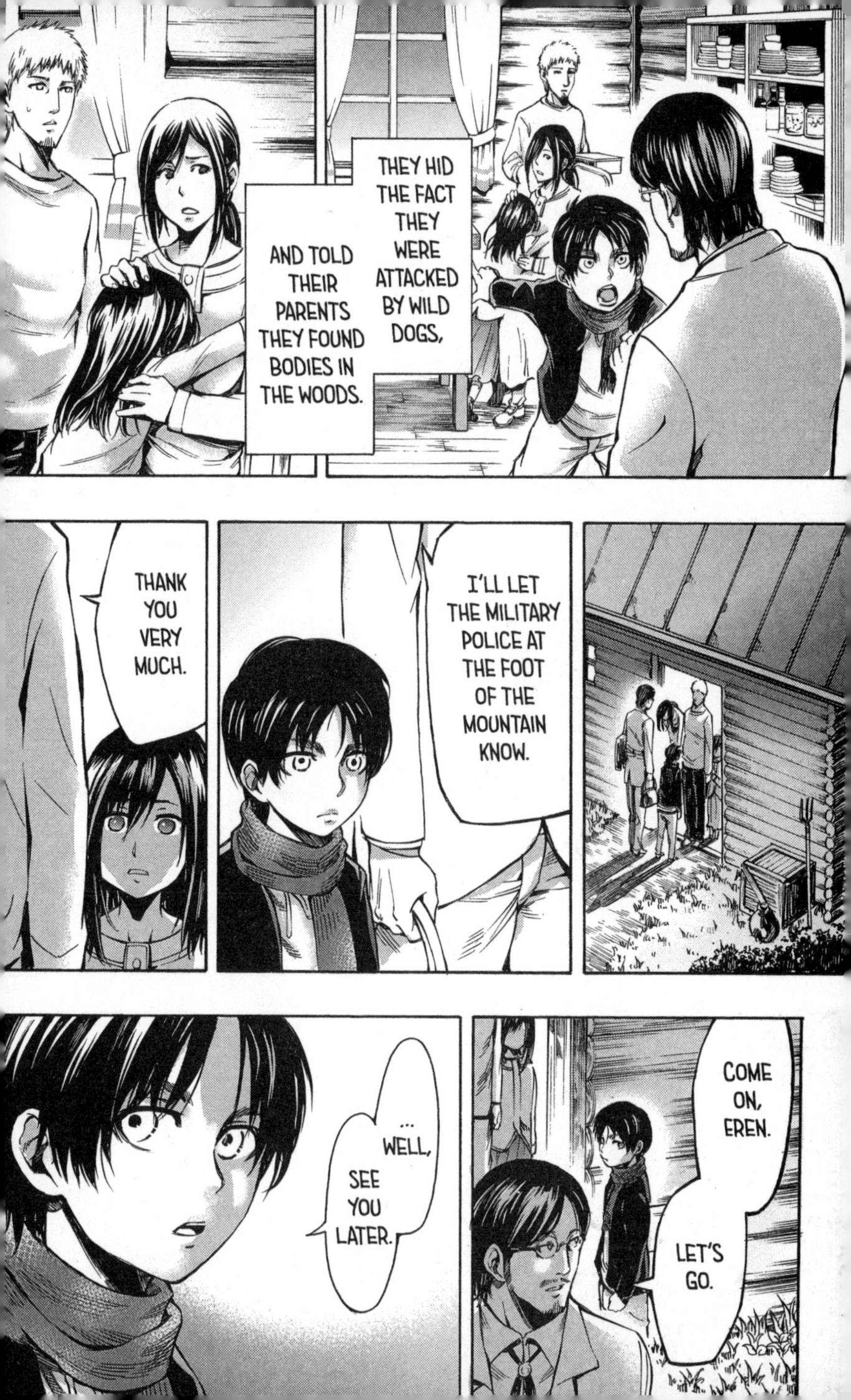
THEY HID THE FACT THEY WERE ATTACKED BY WILD DOGS,
AND TOLD THEIR PARENTS THEY FOUND BODIES IN THE WOODS.
I'LL LET THE MILITARY POLICE AT THE FOOT OF THE MOUNTAIN KNOW.
THANK YOU VERY MUCH.
COME ON, EREN.
LET'S GO.
... WELL, SEE YOU LATER.

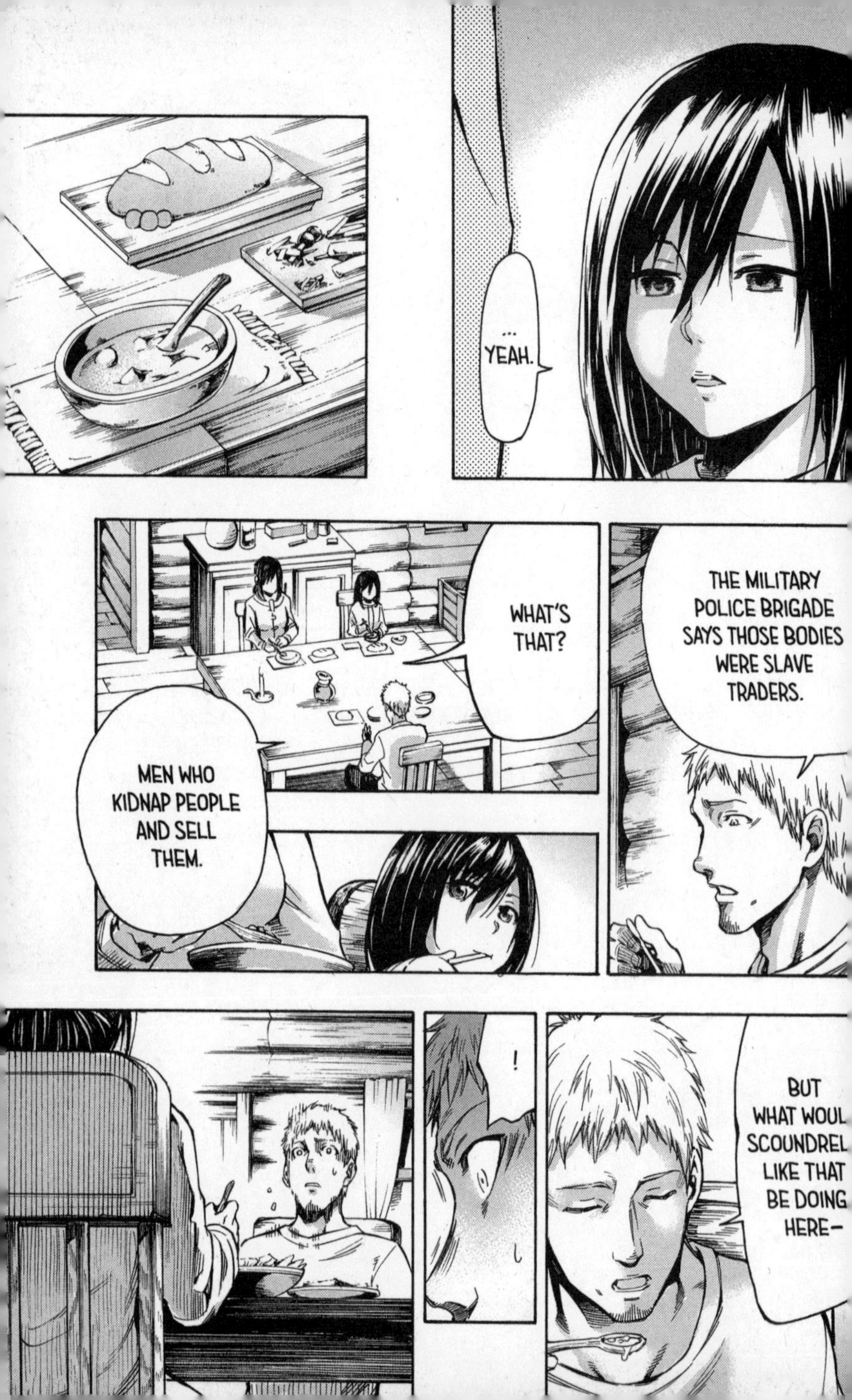
... YEAH.
THE MILITARY POLICE BRIGADE SAYS THOSE BODIES WERE SLAVE TRADERS.
WHAT'S THAT?
MEN WHO KIDNAP PEOPLE AND SELL THEM.
BUT WHAT WOUL SCOUNDREL LIKE THAT BE DOING HERE–
!

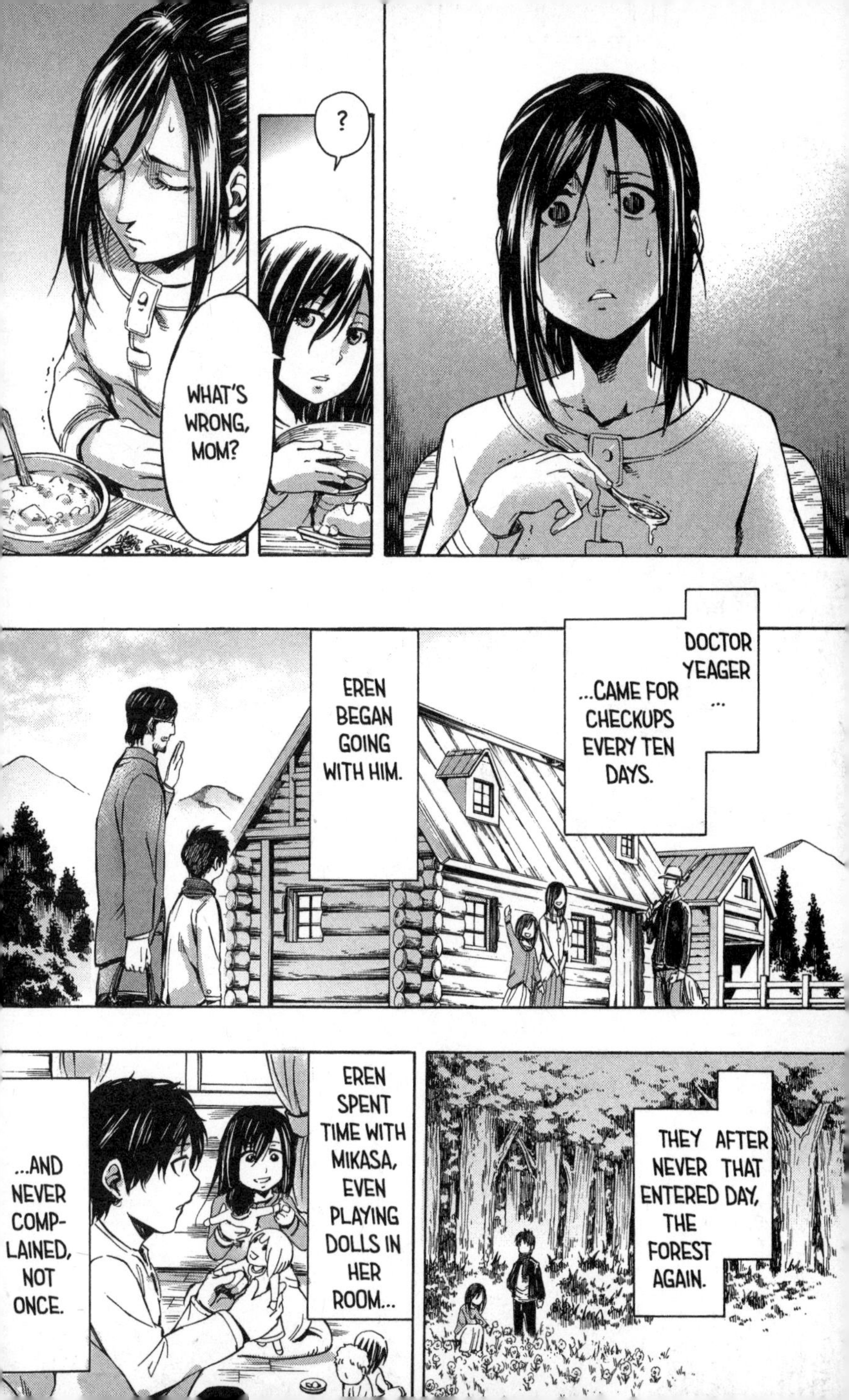
?
WHAT'S WRONG, MOM?
DOCTOR YEAGER ...
...CAME FOR CHECKUPS EVERY TEN DAYS.
EREN BEGAN GOING WITH HIM.
AFTER THAT DAY,
THEY NEVER ENTERED THE FOREST AGAIN.
EREN SPENT TIME WITH MIKASA, EVEN PLAYING DOLLS IN HER ROOM...
...AND NEVER COMP-LAINED, NOT ONCE.

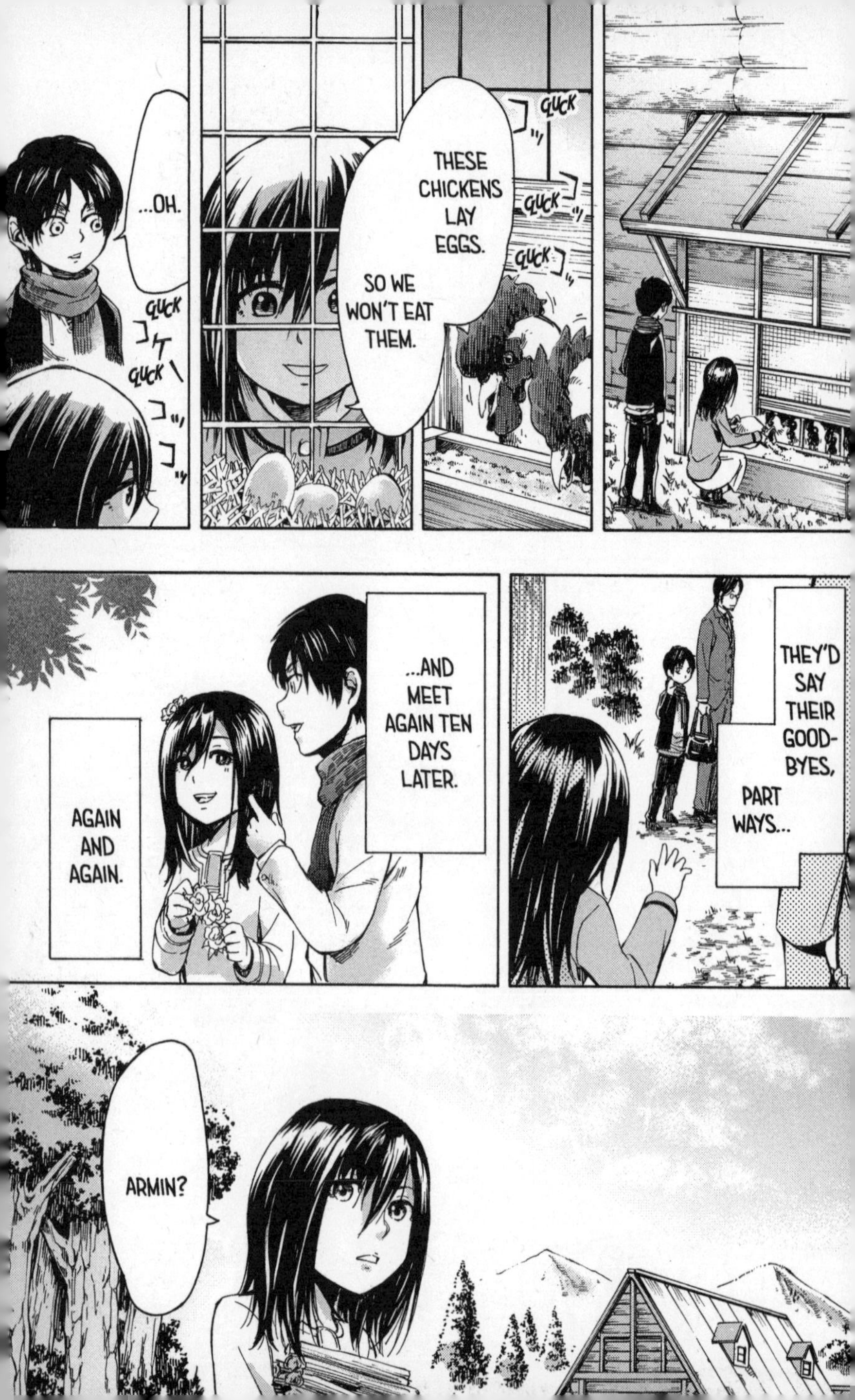
GLUCK
GLUCK
GLUCK
THESE CHICKENS LAY EGGS.
SO WE WON'T EAT THEM.
...OH.
GLUCK
GLUCK
THEY'D SAY THEIR GOOD-BYES,
PART WAYS...
...AND MEET AGAIN TEN DAYS LATER.
AGAIN AND AGAIN.
ARMIN?

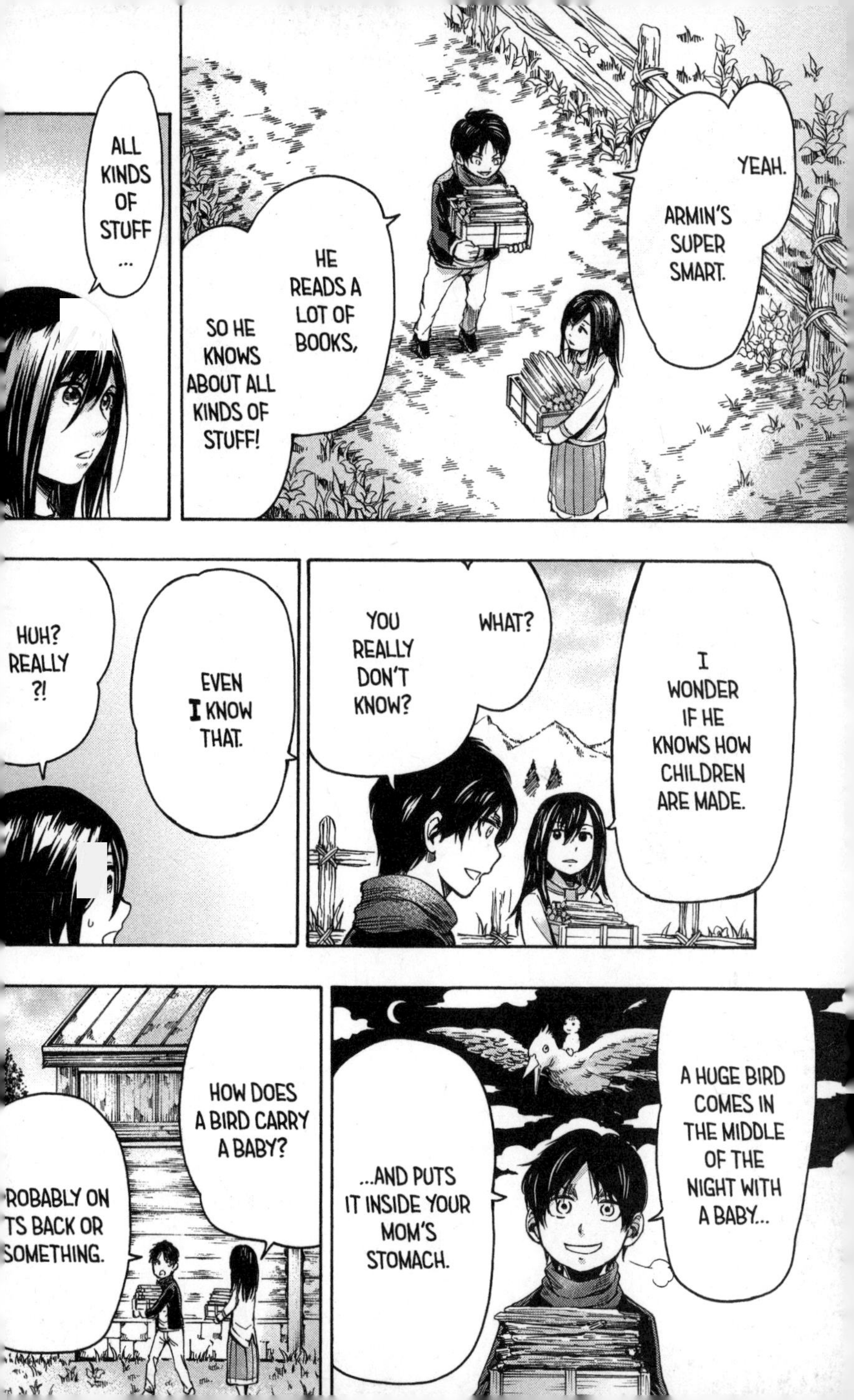
YEAH.
ARMIN'S SUPER SMART.
HE READS A LOT OF BOOKS,
SO HE KNOWS ABOUT ALL KINDS OF STUFF!
ALL KINDS OF STUFF ...
I WONDER IF HE KNOWS HOW CHILDREN ARE MADE.
WHAT?
YOU REALLY DON'T KNOW?
EVEN I KNOW THAT.
HUH? REALLY ?!
A HUGE BIRD COMES IN THE MIDDLE OF THE NIGHT WITH A BABY...
...AND PUTS IT INSIDE YOUR MOM'S STOMACH.
HOW DOES A BIRD CARRY A BABY?
ROBABLY ON TS BACK OR SOMETHING.

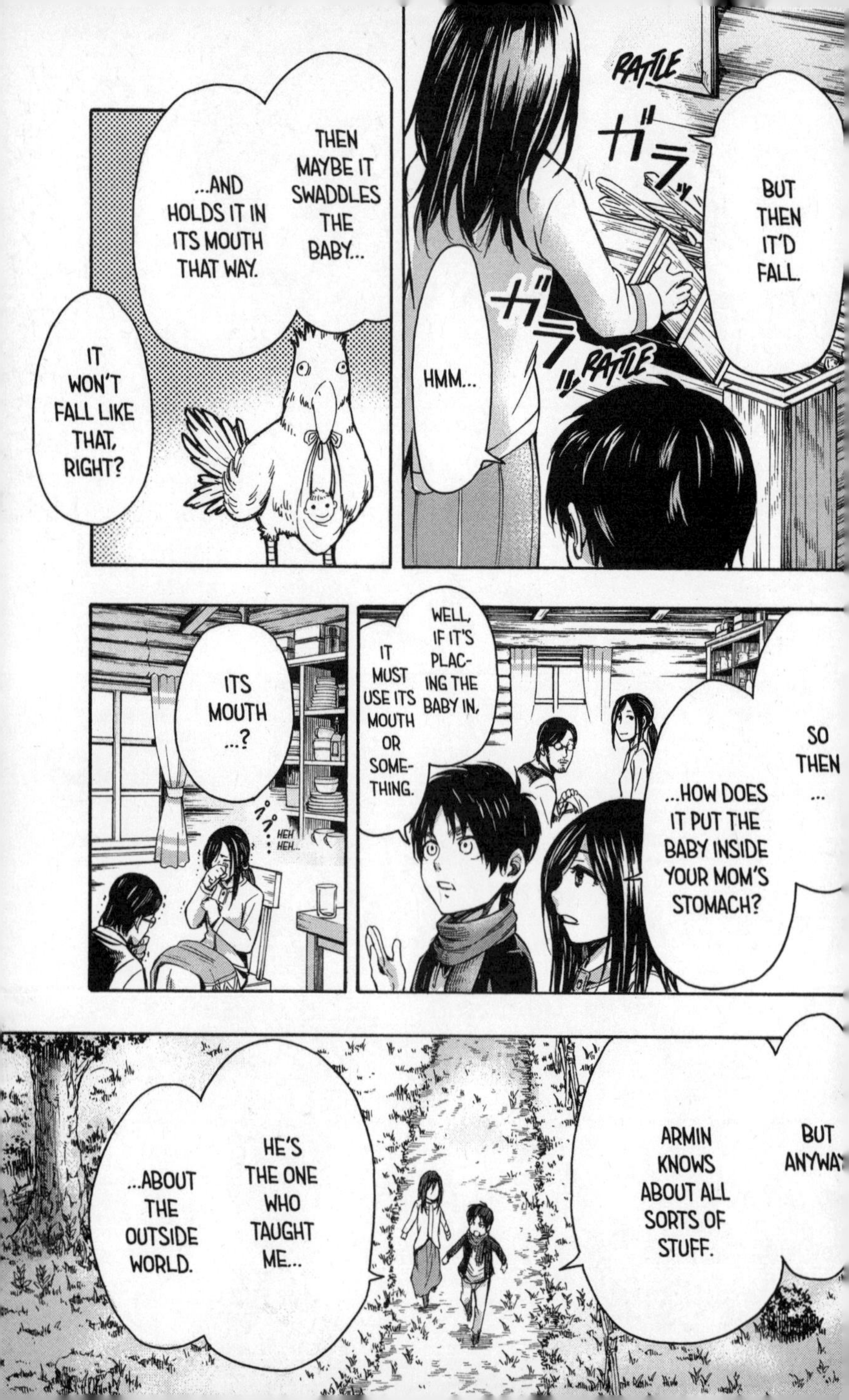
RATTLE
ガラッ
BUT THEN IT'D FALL.
ガラッ
RATTLE
HMM...
THEN MAYBE IT SWADDLES THE BABY...
...AND HOLDS IT IN ITS MOUTH THAT WAY.
IT WON'T FALL LIKE THAT, RIGHT?
SO THEN...
...HOW DOES IT PUT THE BABY INSIDE YOUR MOM'S STOMACH?
WELL, IF IT'S PLACING THE BABY IN,
IT MUST USE ITS MOUTH OR SOMETHING.
ITS MOUTH...?
HEH HEH...
BUT ANYWA
ARMIN KNOWS ABOUT ALL SORTS OF STUFF.
HE'S THE ONE WHO TAUGHT ME...
...ABOUT THE OUTSIDE WORLD.

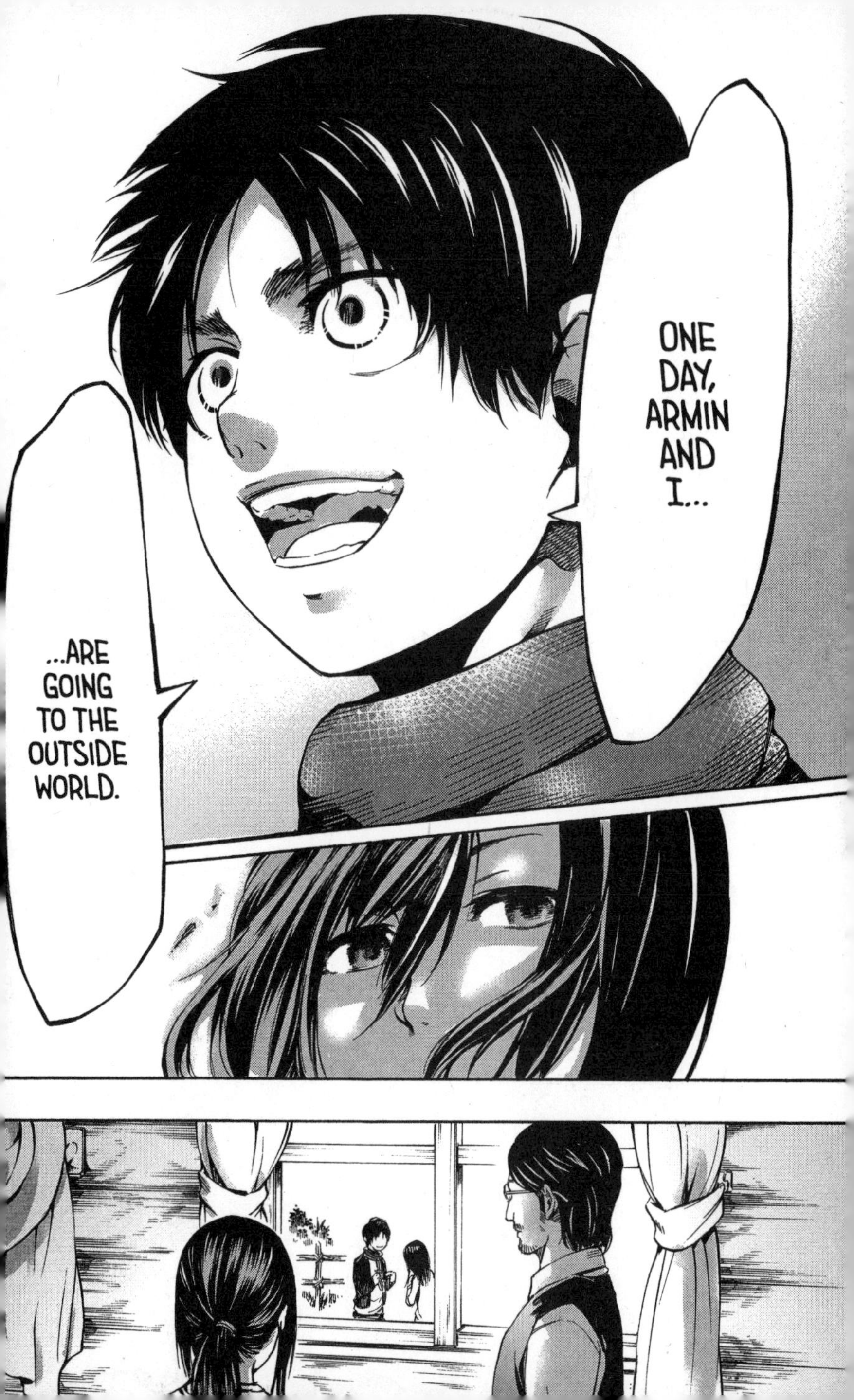
ONE DAY, ARMIN AND I...
...ARE GOING TO THE OUTSIDE WORLD.

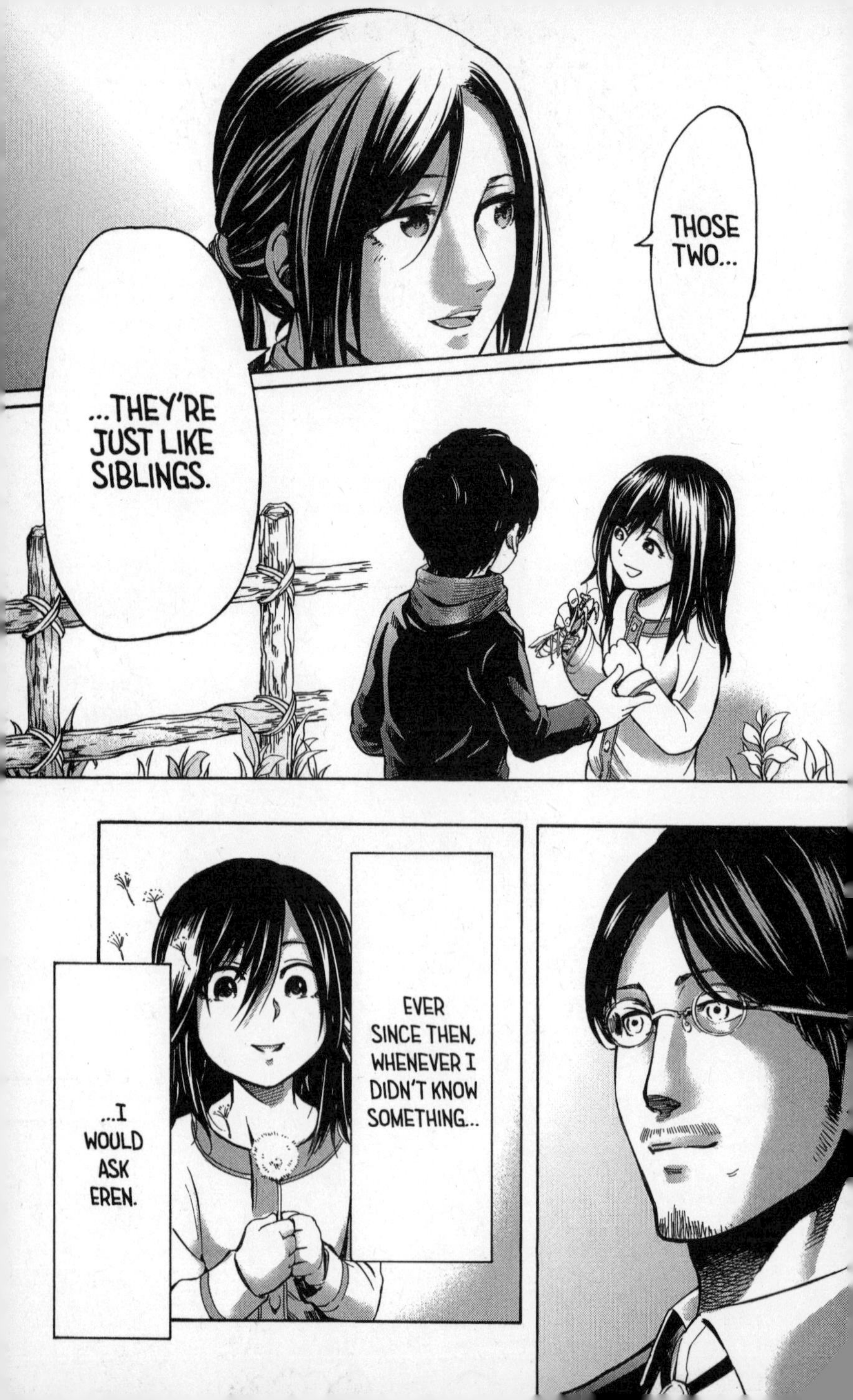
THOSE TWO...
...THEY'RE JUST LIKE SIBLINGS.
EVER SINCE THEN, WHENEVER I DIDN'T KNOW SOMETHING...
...I WOULD ASK EREN.

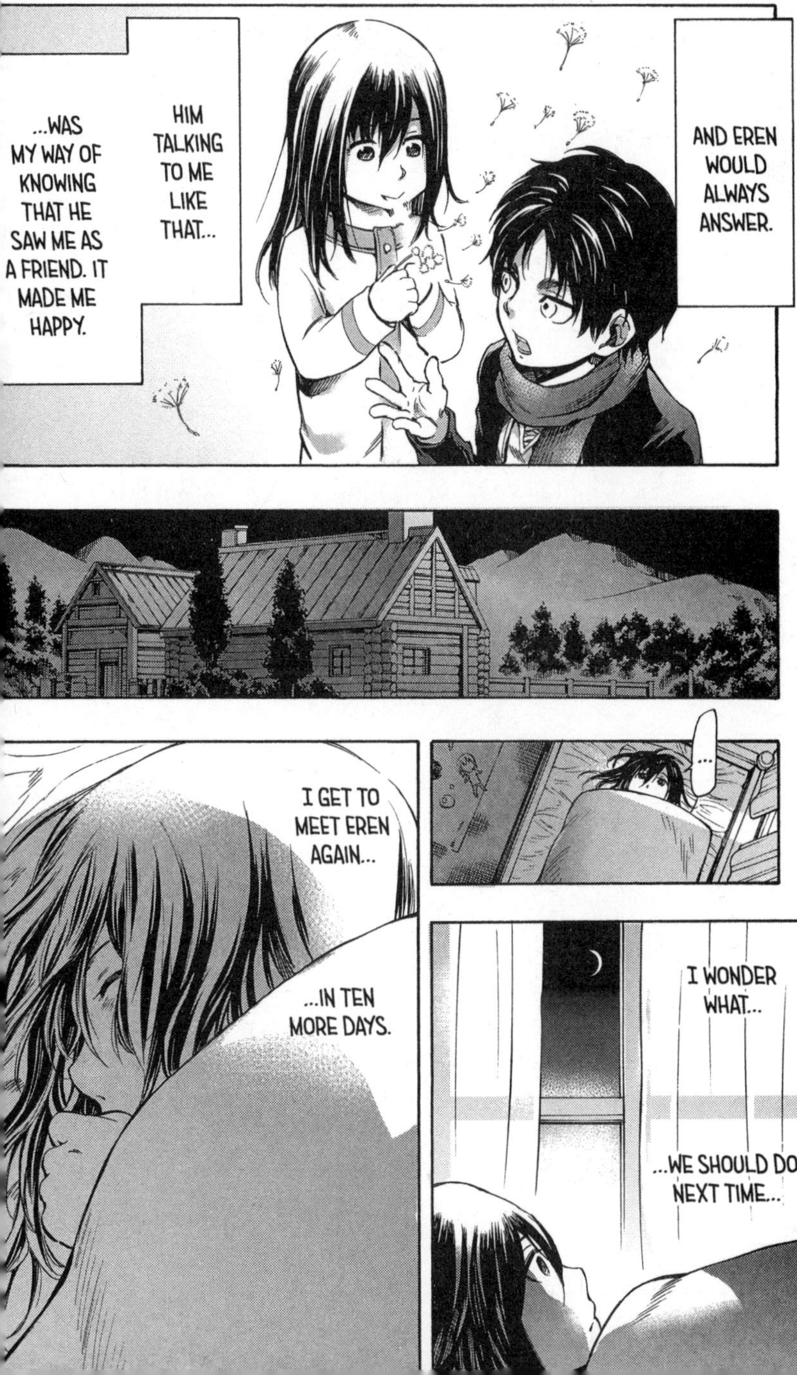
AND EREN WOULD ALWAYS ANSWER.
HIM TALKING TO ME LIKE THAT...
...WAS MY WAY OF KNOWING THAT HE SAW ME AS A FRIEND. IT MADE ME HAPPY.
...
I WONDER WHAT...
...WE SHOULD DO NEXT TIME...
I GET TO MEET EREN AGAIN...
...IN TEN MORE DAYS.

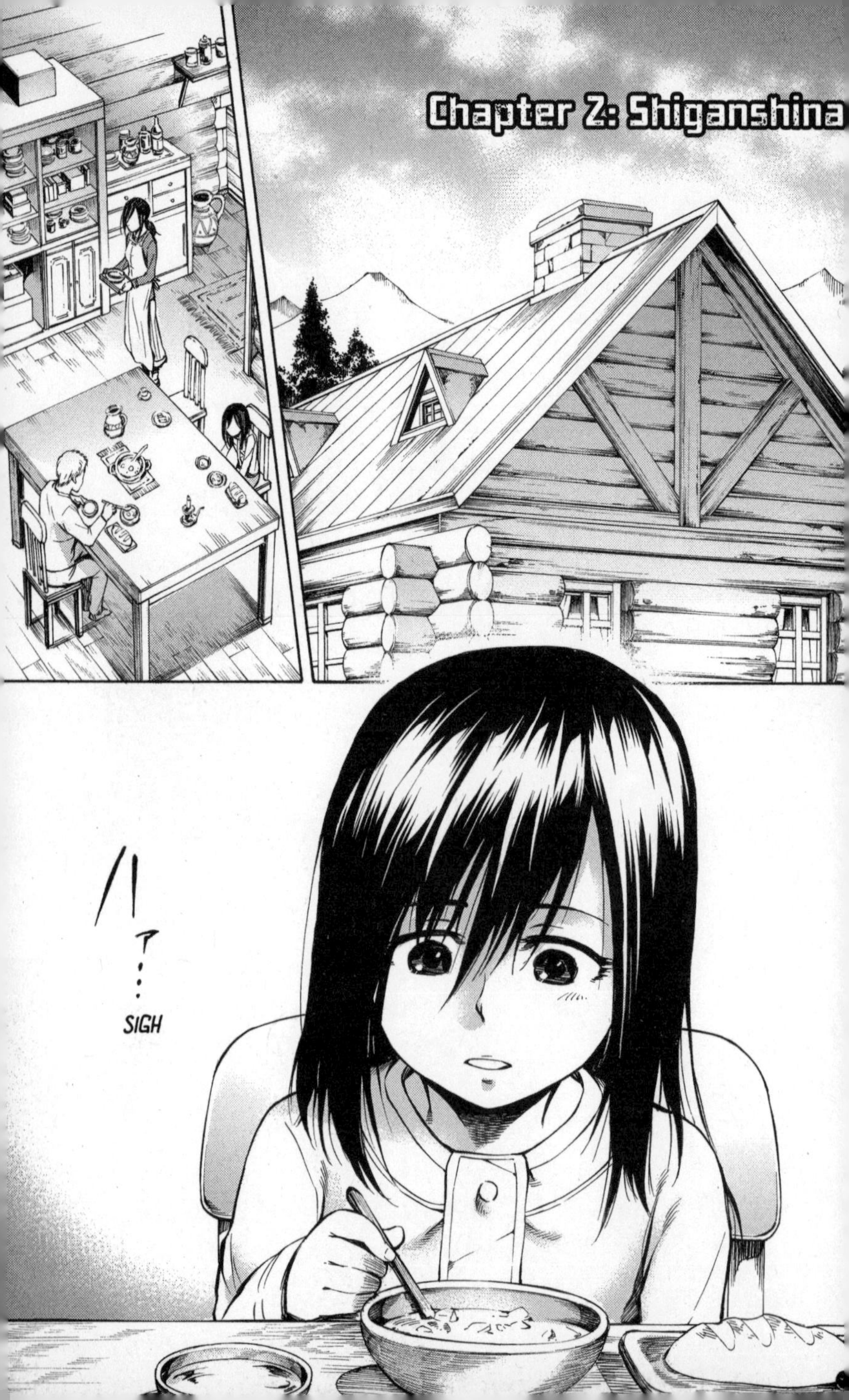
Chapter 2: Shiganshina
ハァ…
SIGH

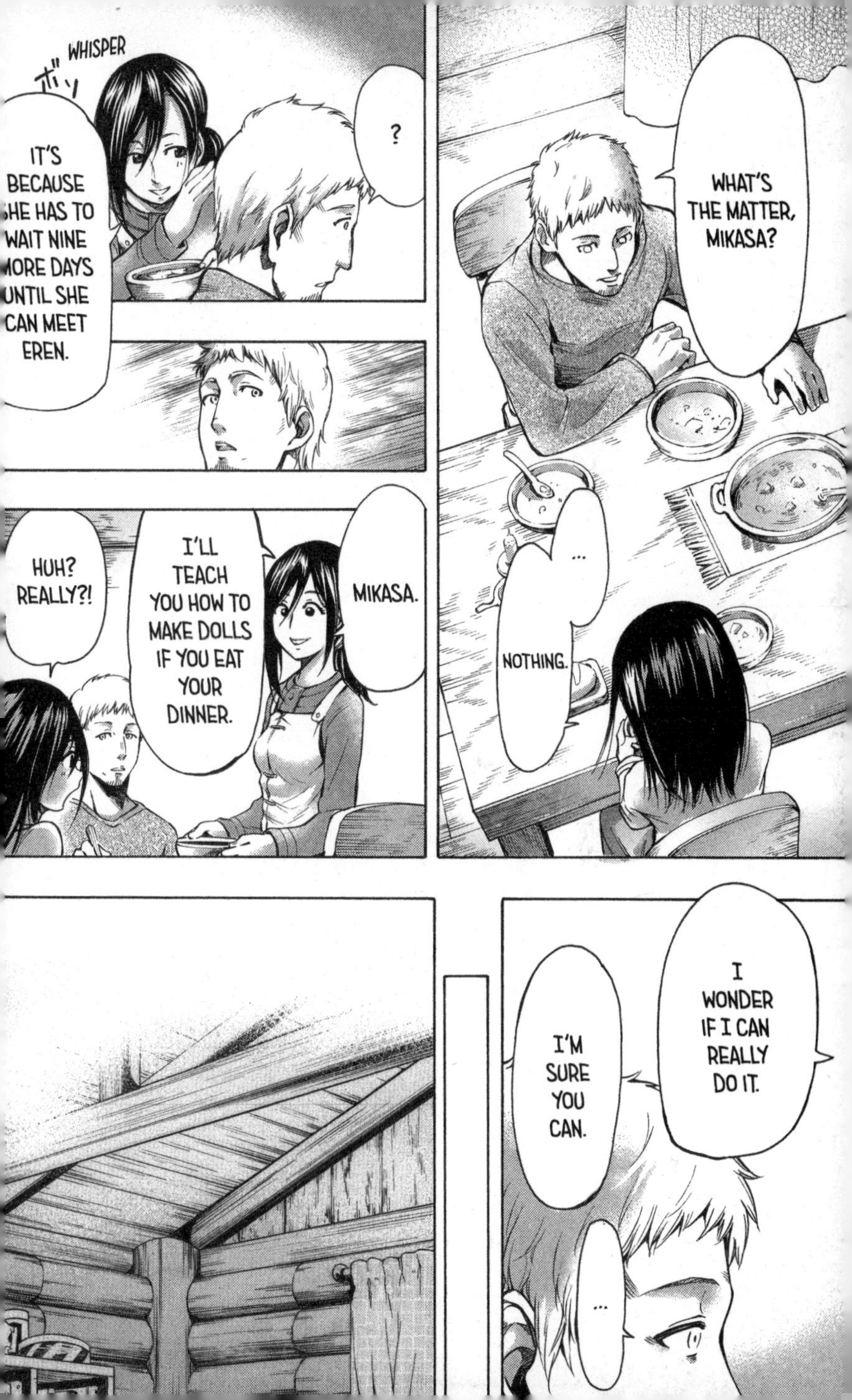
WHAT'S THE MATTER, MIKASA?
...
NOTHING.
?
WHISPER
ボソ
IT'S BECAUSE SHE HAS TO WAIT NINE MORE DAYS UNTIL SHE CAN MEET EREN.
MIKASA.
I'LL TEACH YOU HOW TO MAKE DOLLS IF YOU EAT YOUR DINNER.
HUH? REALLY?!
I WONDER IF I CAN REALLY DO IT.
I'M SURE YOU CAN.
...

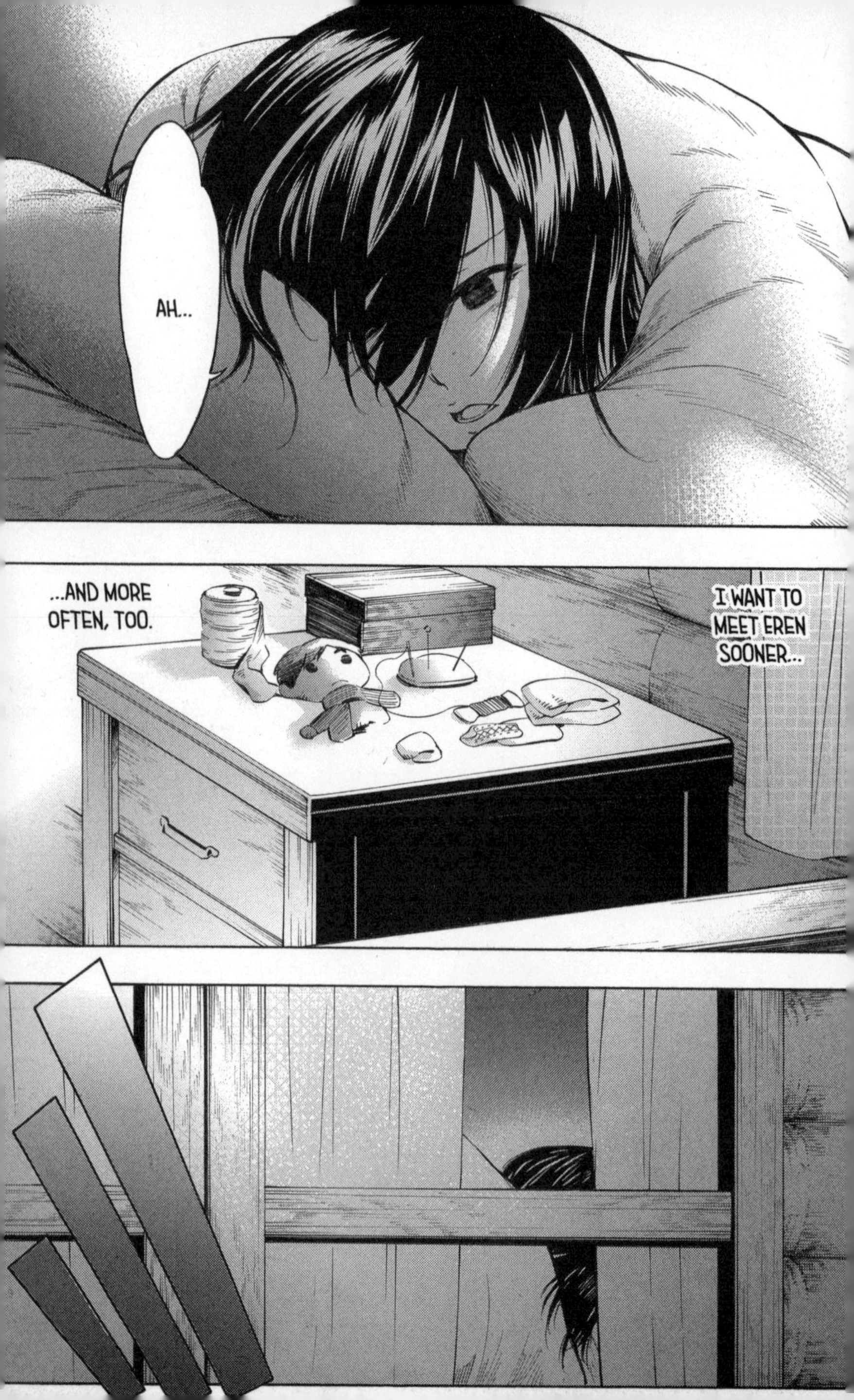
AH...
I WANT TO MEET EREN SOONER...
...AND MORE OFTEN, TOO.

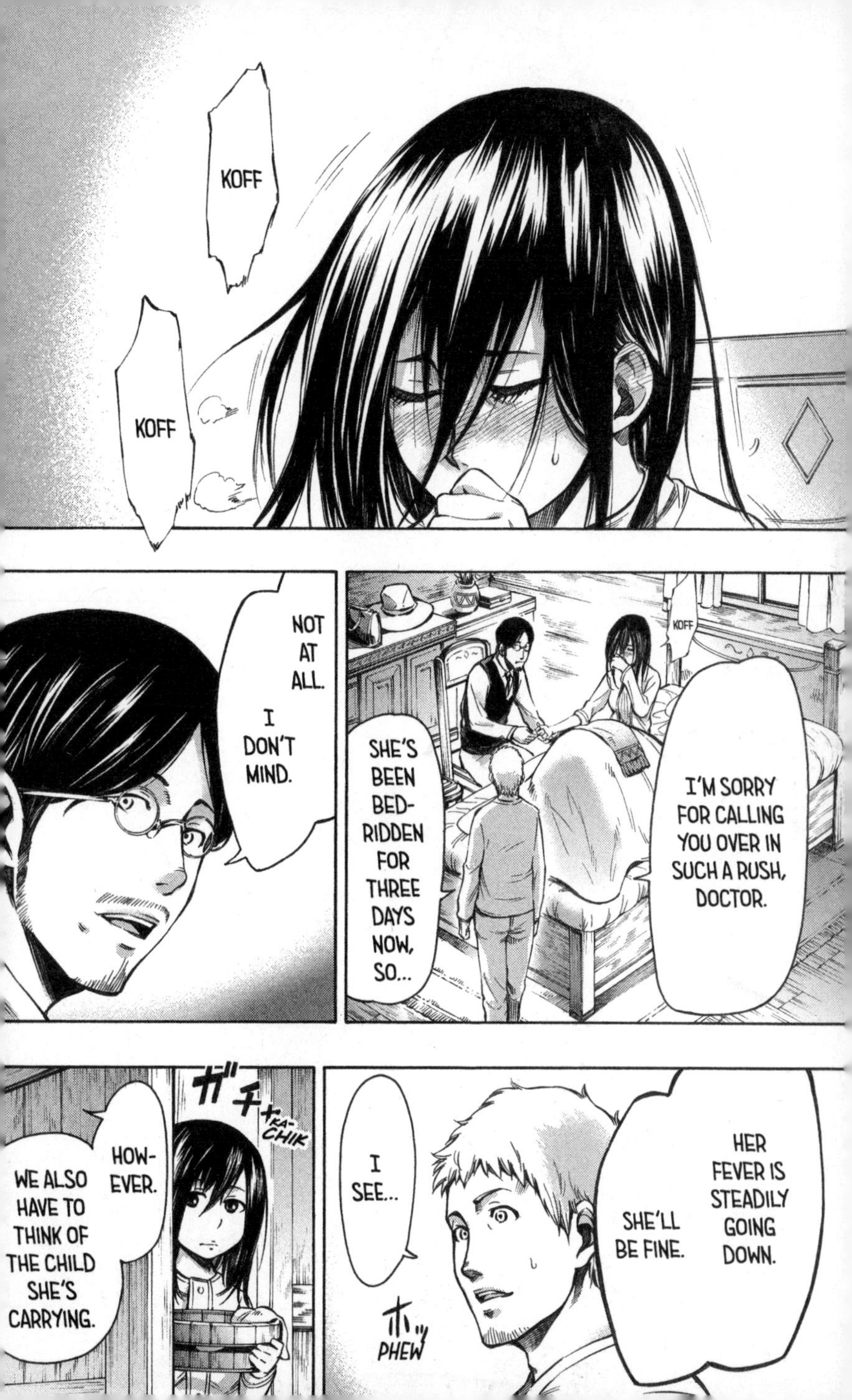
KOFF
KOFF
KOFF
I'M SORRY FOR CALLING YOU OVER IN SUCH A RUSH, DOCTOR.
SHE'S BEEN BED-RIDDEN FOR THREE DAYS NOW, SO...
NOT AT ALL.
I DON'T MIND.
HER FEVER IS STEADILY GOING DOWN.
SHE'LL BE FINE.
I SEE...
ホッ
PHEW
ガチャ
KA-CHIK
HOW-EVER.
WE ALSO HAVE TO THINK OF THE CHILD SHE'S CARRYING.

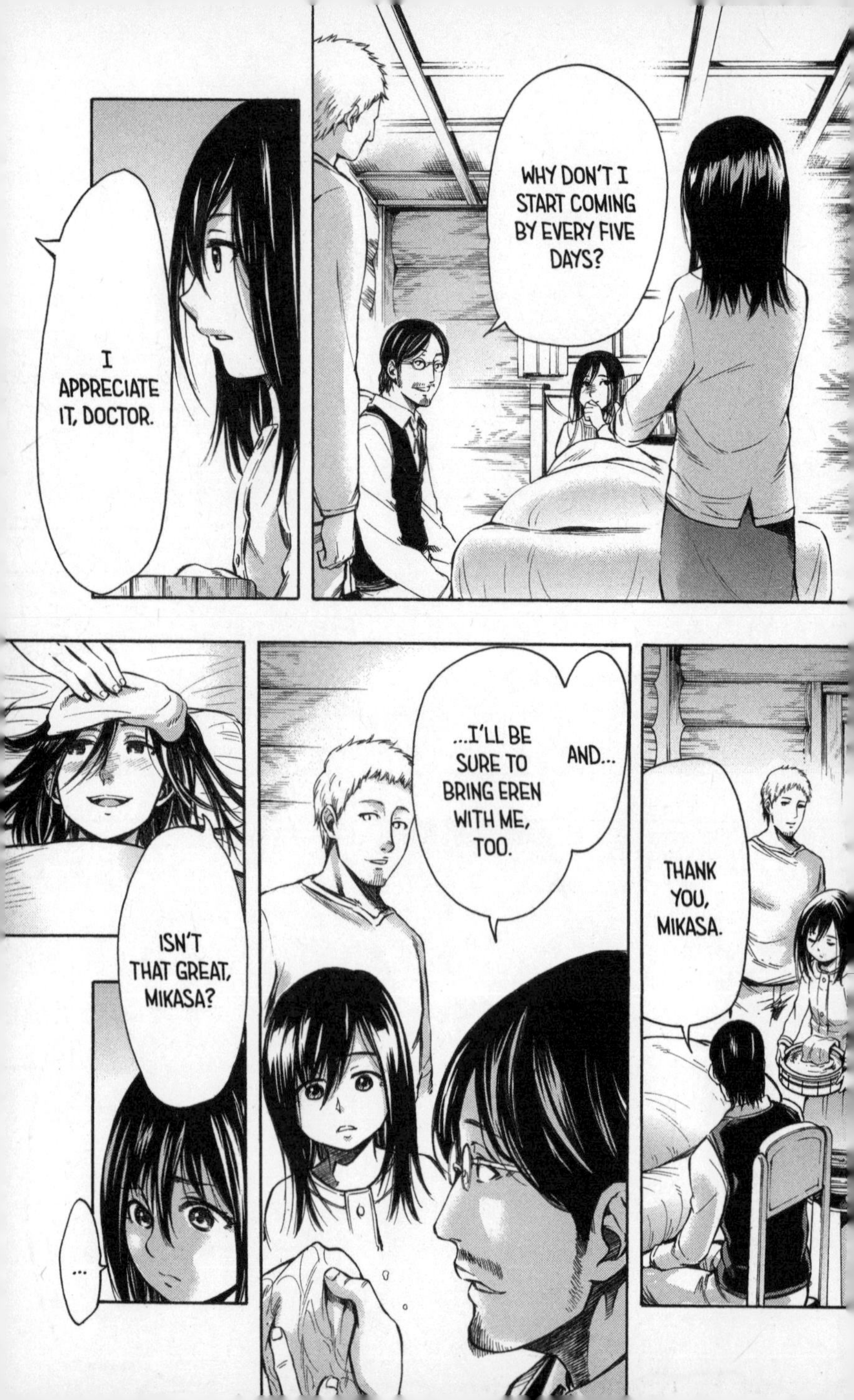
WHY DON'T I START COMING BY EVERY FIVE DAYS?
I APPRECIATE IT, DOCTOR.
THANK YOU, MIKASA.
AND...
...I'LL BE SURE TO BRING EREN WITH ME, TOO.
ISN'T THAT GREAT, MIKASA?
...

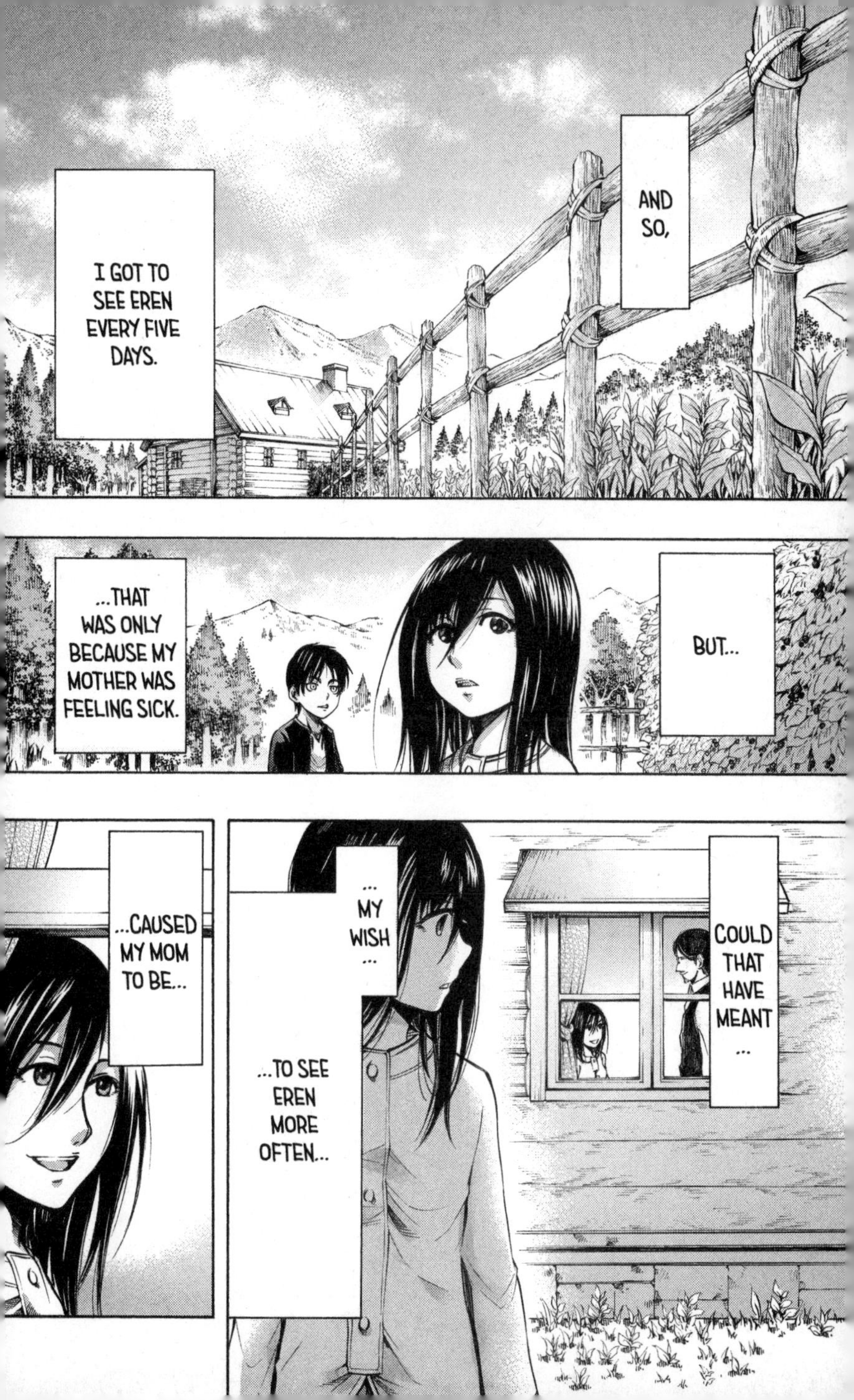
AND SO,
I GOT TO SEE EREN EVERY FIVE DAYS.
BUT...
...THAT WAS ONLY BECAUSE MY MOTHER WAS FEELING SICK.
COULD THAT HAVE MEANT...
...MY WISH...
...TO SEE EREN MORE OFTEN...
...CAUSED MY MOM TO BE...

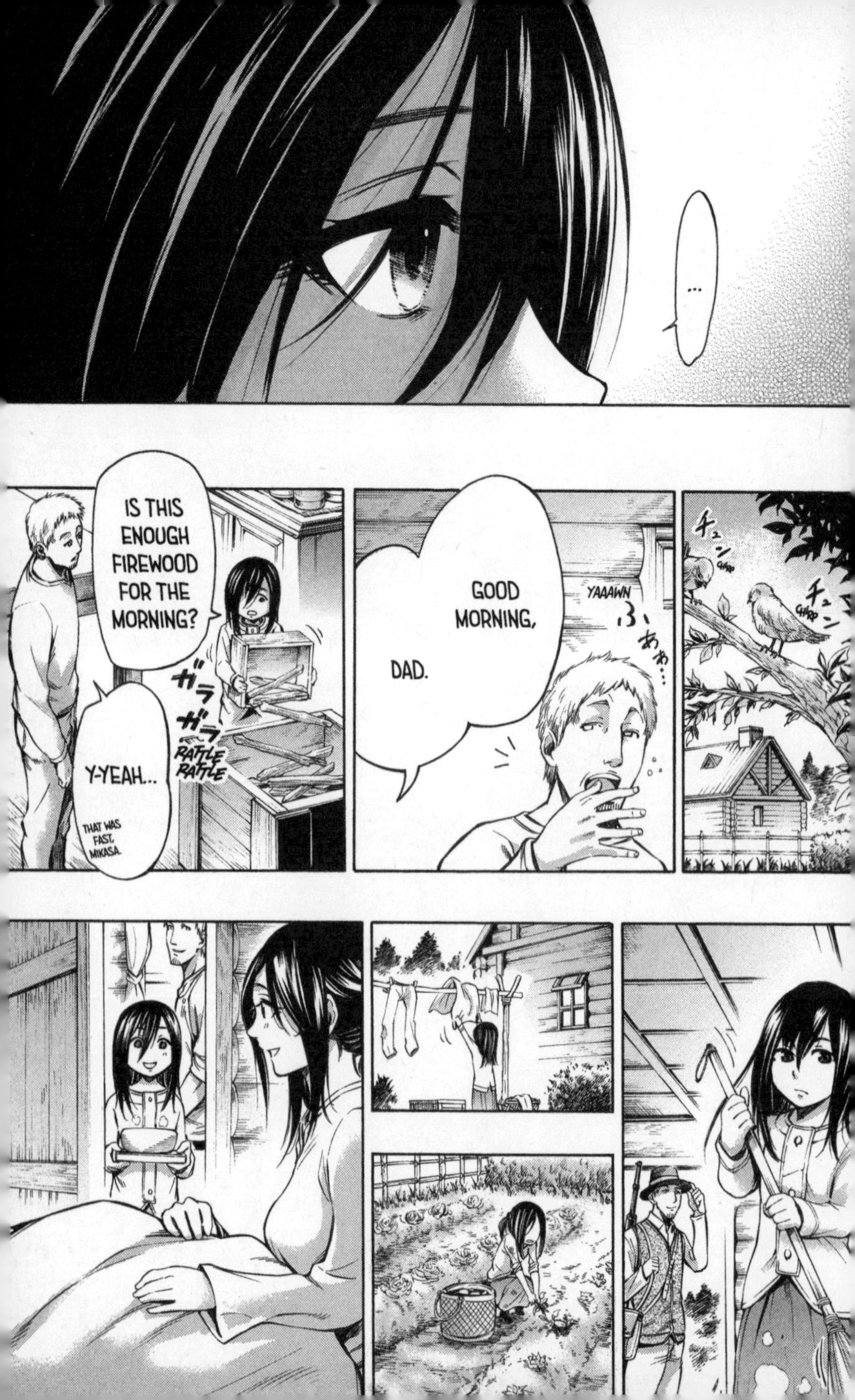
...
チュン
CHIRP
チュン
CHIRP
YAAAWN
ふあぁ…
GOOD MORNING, DAD.
IS THIS ENOUGH FIREWOOD FOR THE MORNING?
ガラガラ
RATTLE RATTLE
Y-YEAH...
THAT WAS FAST, MIKASA.

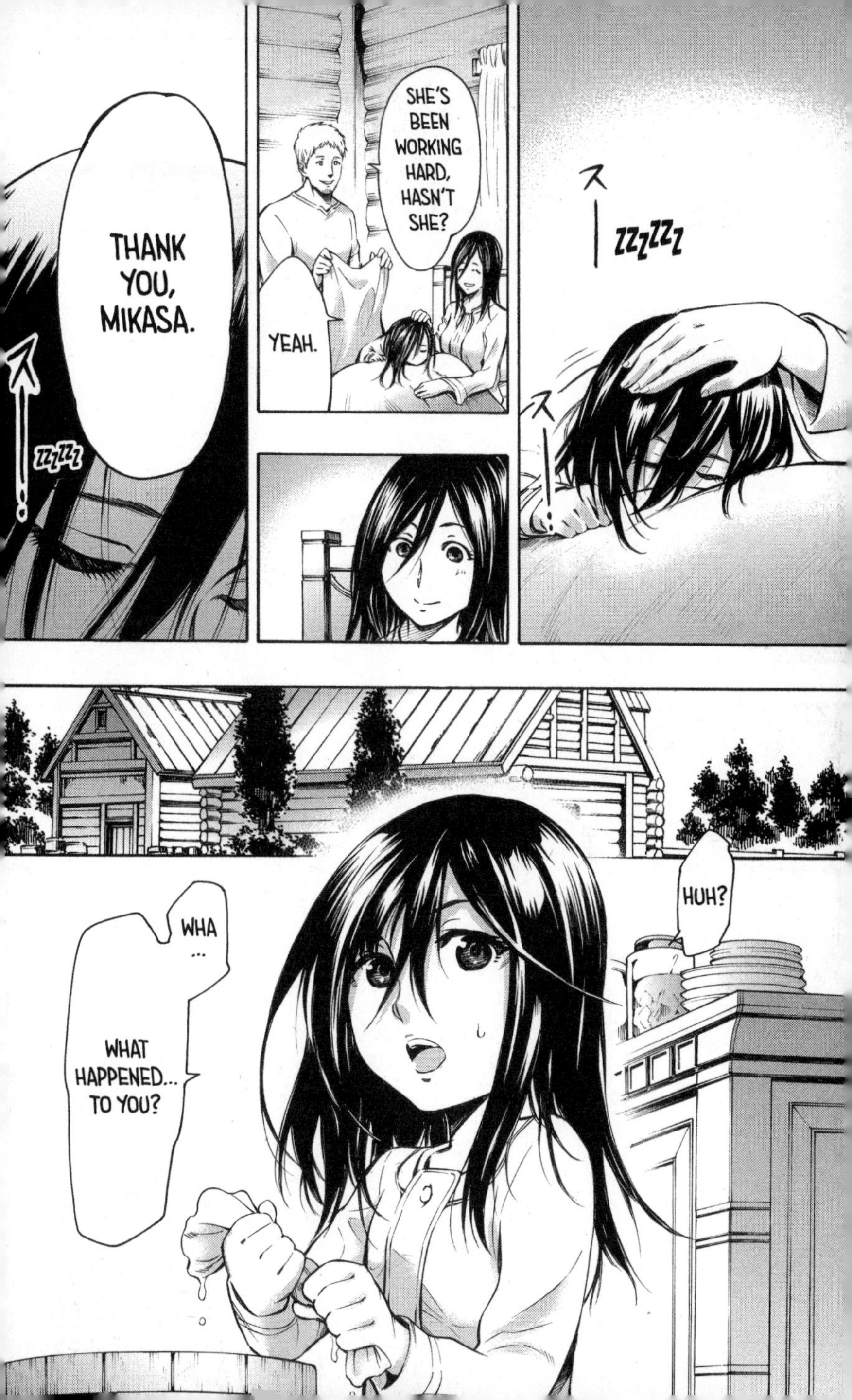

ス
ZZZZZZ
ス
SHE'S BEEN WORKING HARD, HASN'T SHE?
YEAH.
THANK YOU, MIKASA.
ス
ZZZZZ
HUH?
WHA ...
WHAT HAPPENED... TO YOU?

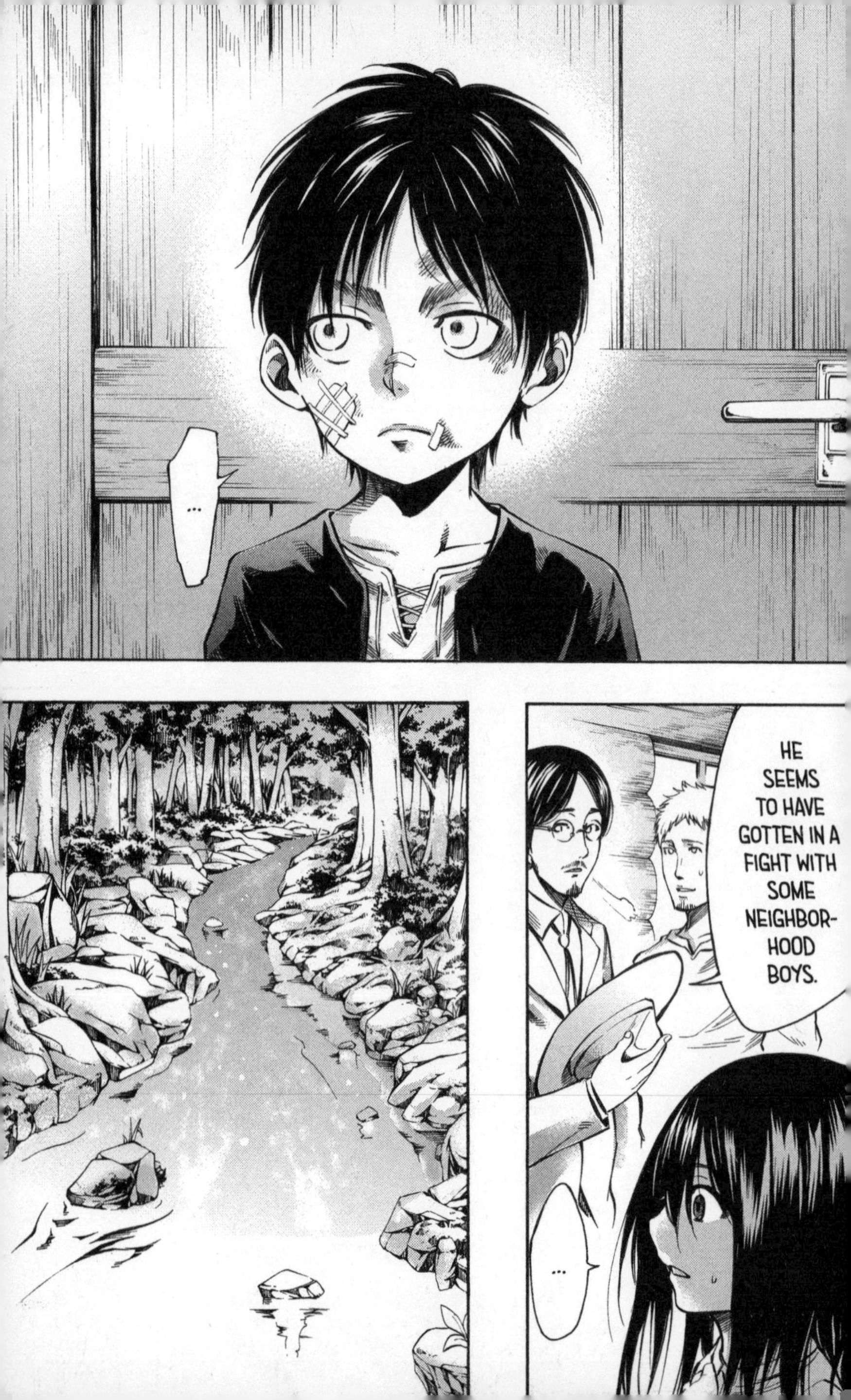
...
HE SEEMS TO HAVE GOTTEN IN A FIGHT WITH SOME NEIGHBOR-HOOD BOYS.
...

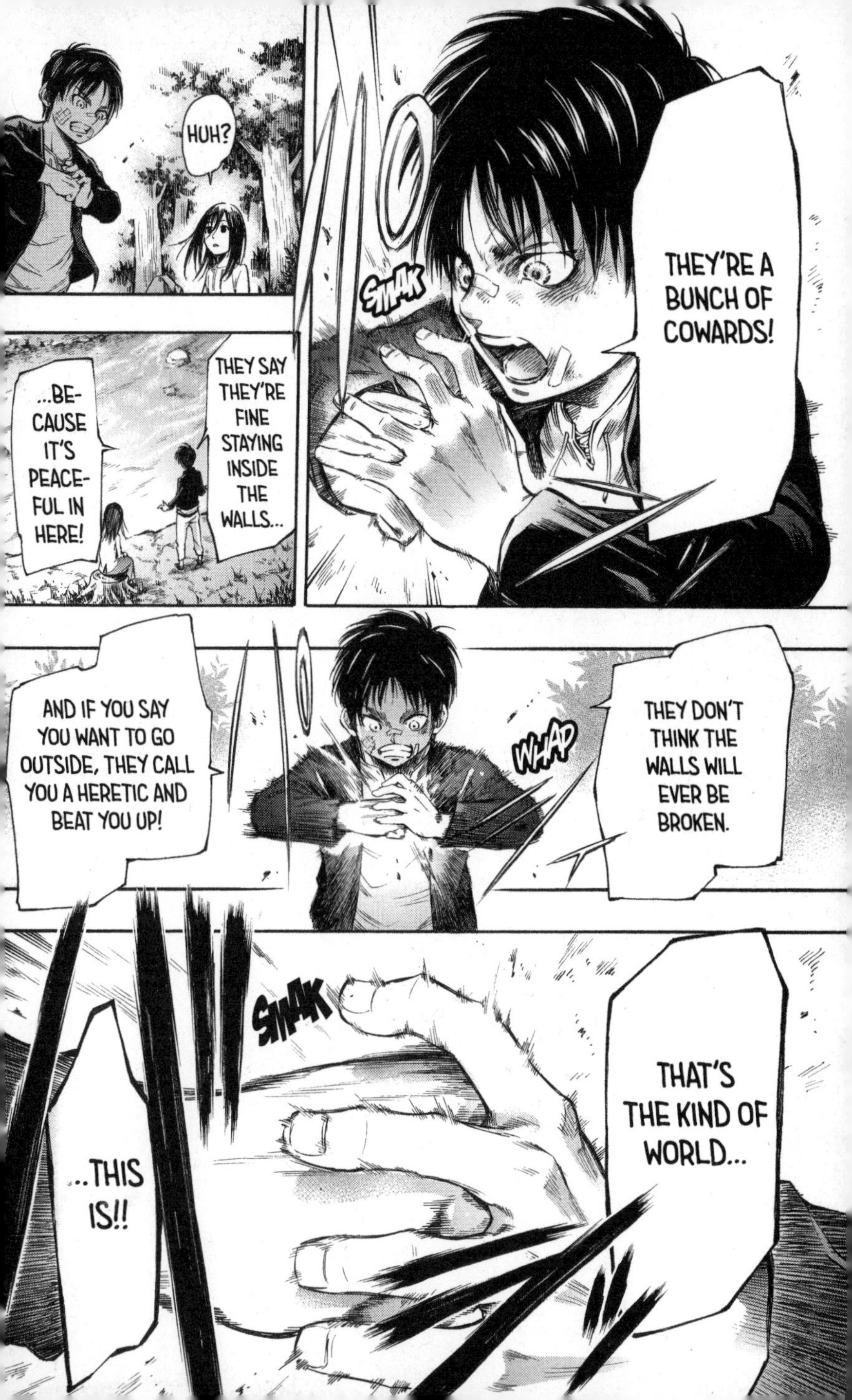
SMAK
THEY'RE A BUNCH OF COWARDS!
HUH?
THEY SAY THEY'RE FINE STAYING INSIDE THE WALLS...
...BE-CAUSE IT'S PEACE-FUL IN HERE!
THEY DON'T THINK THE WALLS WILL EVER BE BROKEN.
WHAP
AND IF YOU SAY YOU WANT TO GO OUTSIDE, THEY CALL YOU A HERETIC AND BEAT YOU UP!
THAT'S THE KIND OF WORLD...
SMAK
...THIS IS!!

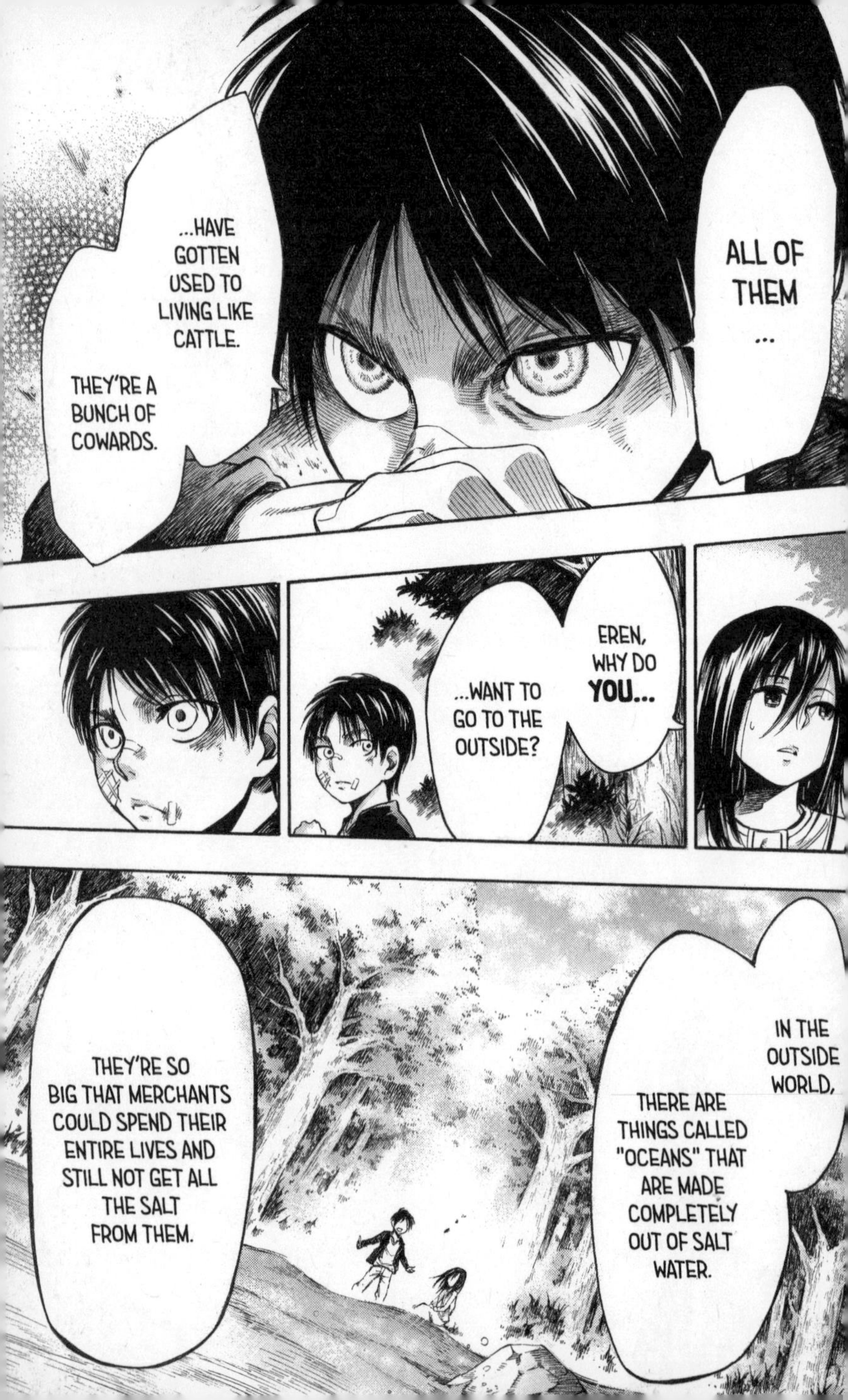
ALL OF THEM ...
...HAVE GOTTEN USED TO LIVING LIKE CATTLE.
THEY'RE A BUNCH OF COWARDS.
EREN, WHY DO **YOU...**
...WANT TO GO TO THE OUTSIDE?
IN THE OUTSIDE WORLD,
THERE ARE THINGS CALLED "OCEANS" THAT ARE MADE COMPLETELY OUT OF SALT WATER.
THEY'RE SO BIG THAT MERCHANTS COULD SPEND THEIR ENTIRE LIVES AND STILL NOT GET ALL THE SALT FROM THEM.

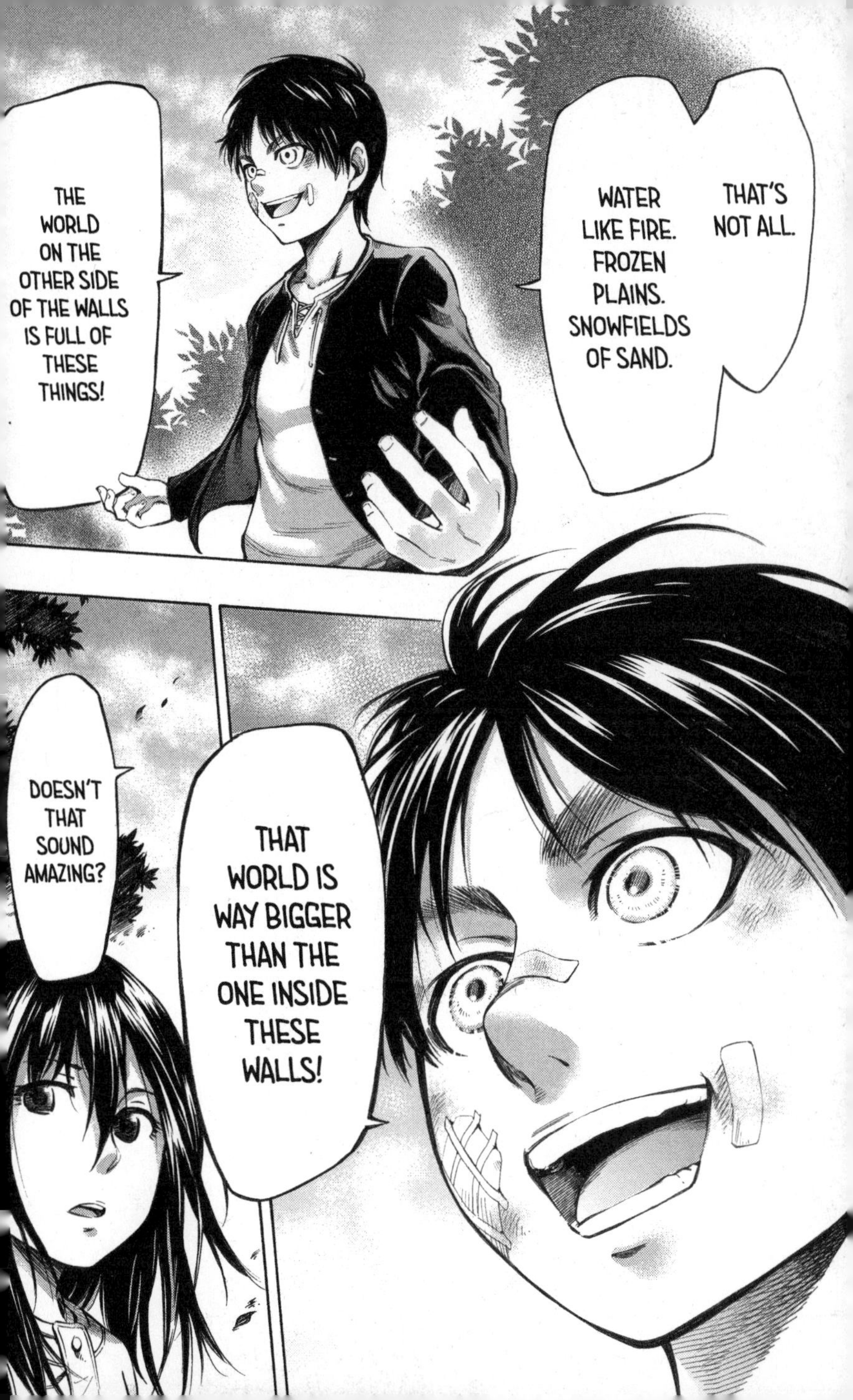
THAT'S NOT ALL.
WATER LIKE FIRE. FROZEN PLAINS. SNOWFIELDS OF SAND.
THE WORLD ON THE OTHER SIDE OF THE WALLS IS FULL OF THESE THINGS!
THAT WORLD IS WAY BIGGER THAN THE ONE INSIDE THESE WALLS!
DOESN'T THAT SOUND AMAZING?

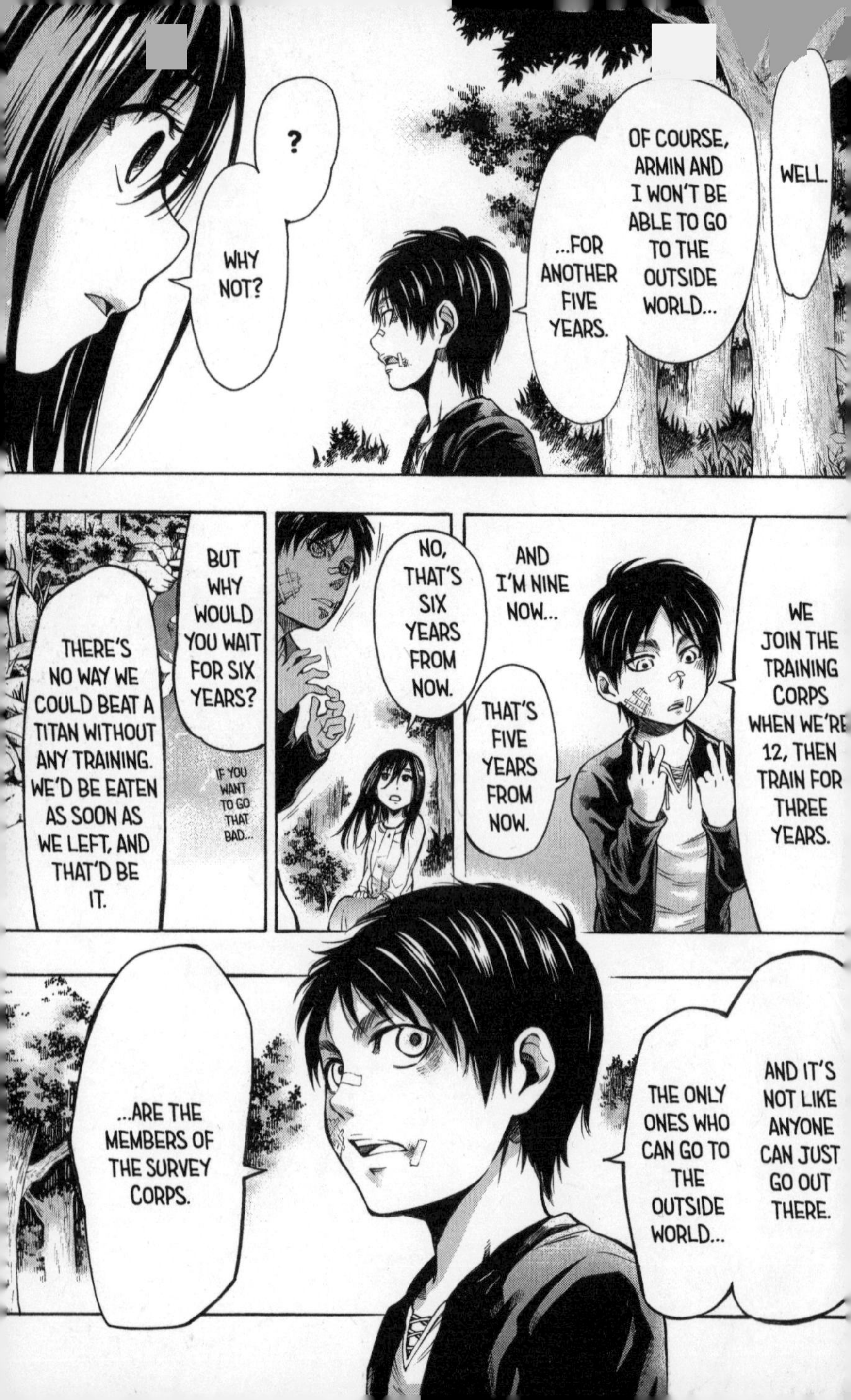
WELL.
OF COURSE, ARMIN AND I WON'T BE ABLE TO GO TO THE OUTSIDE WORLD...
...FOR ANOTHER FIVE YEARS.
?
WHY NOT?
WE JOIN THE TRAINING CORPS WHEN WE'RE 12, THEN TRAIN FOR THREE YEARS.
AND I'M NINE NOW...
THAT'S FIVE YEARS FROM NOW.
NO, THAT'S SIX YEARS FROM NOW.
BUT WHY WOULD YOU WAIT FOR SIX YEARS?
IF YOU WANT TO GO THAT BAD...
THERE'S NO WAY WE COULD BEAT A TITAN WITHOUT ANY TRAINING. WE'D BE EATEN AS SOON AS WE LEFT, AND THAT'D BE IT.
AND IT'S NOT LIKE ANYONE CAN JUST GO OUT THERE.
THE ONLY ONES WHO CAN GO TO THE OUTSIDE WORLD...
...ARE THE MEMBERS OF THE SURVEY CORPS.

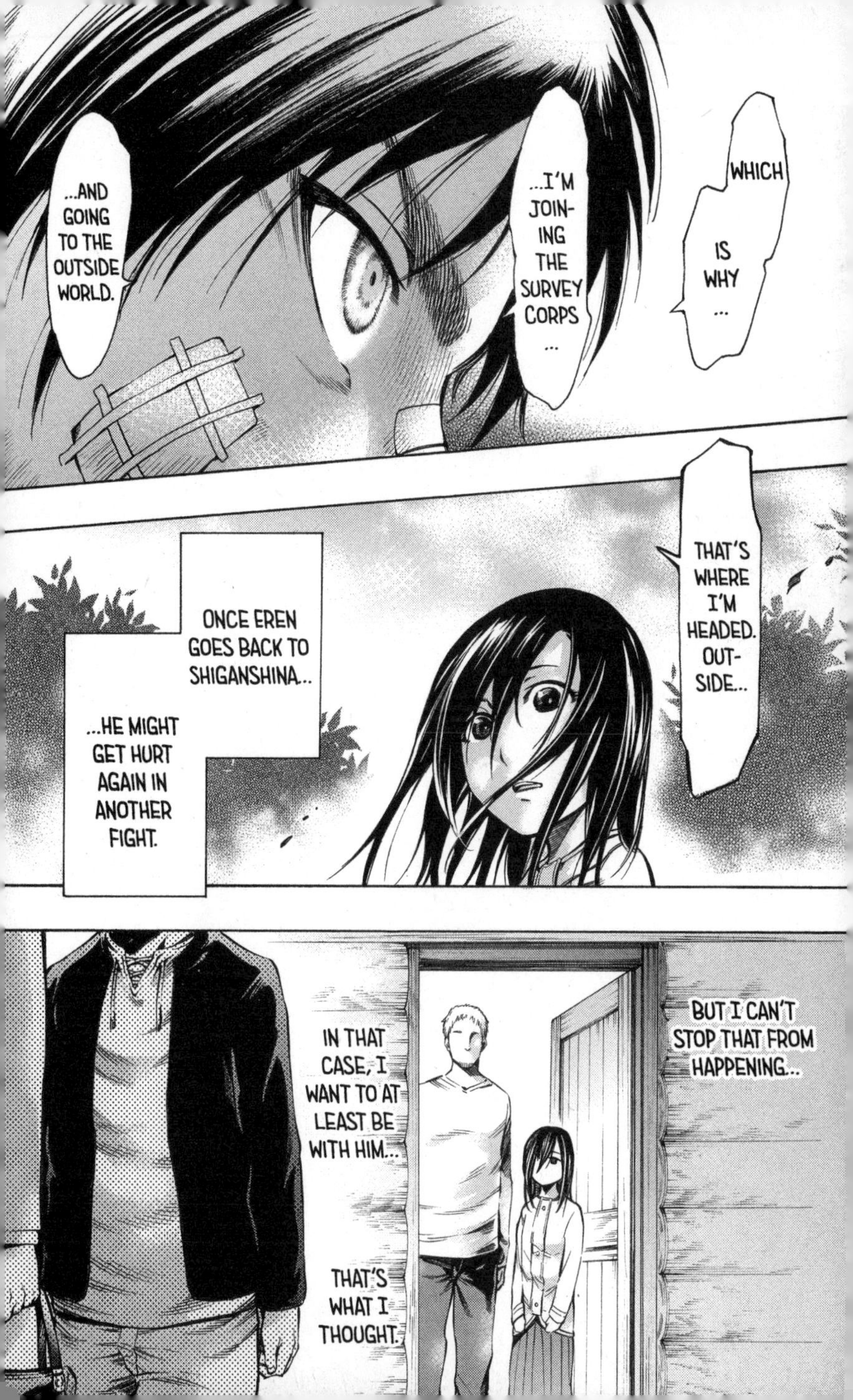
WHICH IS WHY ...
...I'M JOIN-ING THE SURVEY CORPS ...
...AND GOING TO THE OUTSIDE WORLD.
THAT'S WHERE I'M HEADED. OUT-SIDE...
ONCE EREN GOES BACK TO SHIGANSHINA...
...HE MIGHT GET HURT AGAIN IN ANOTHER FIGHT.
BUT I CAN'T STOP THAT FROM HAPPENING...
IN THAT CASE, I WANT TO AT LEAST BE WITH HIM...
THAT'S WHAT I THOUGHT.

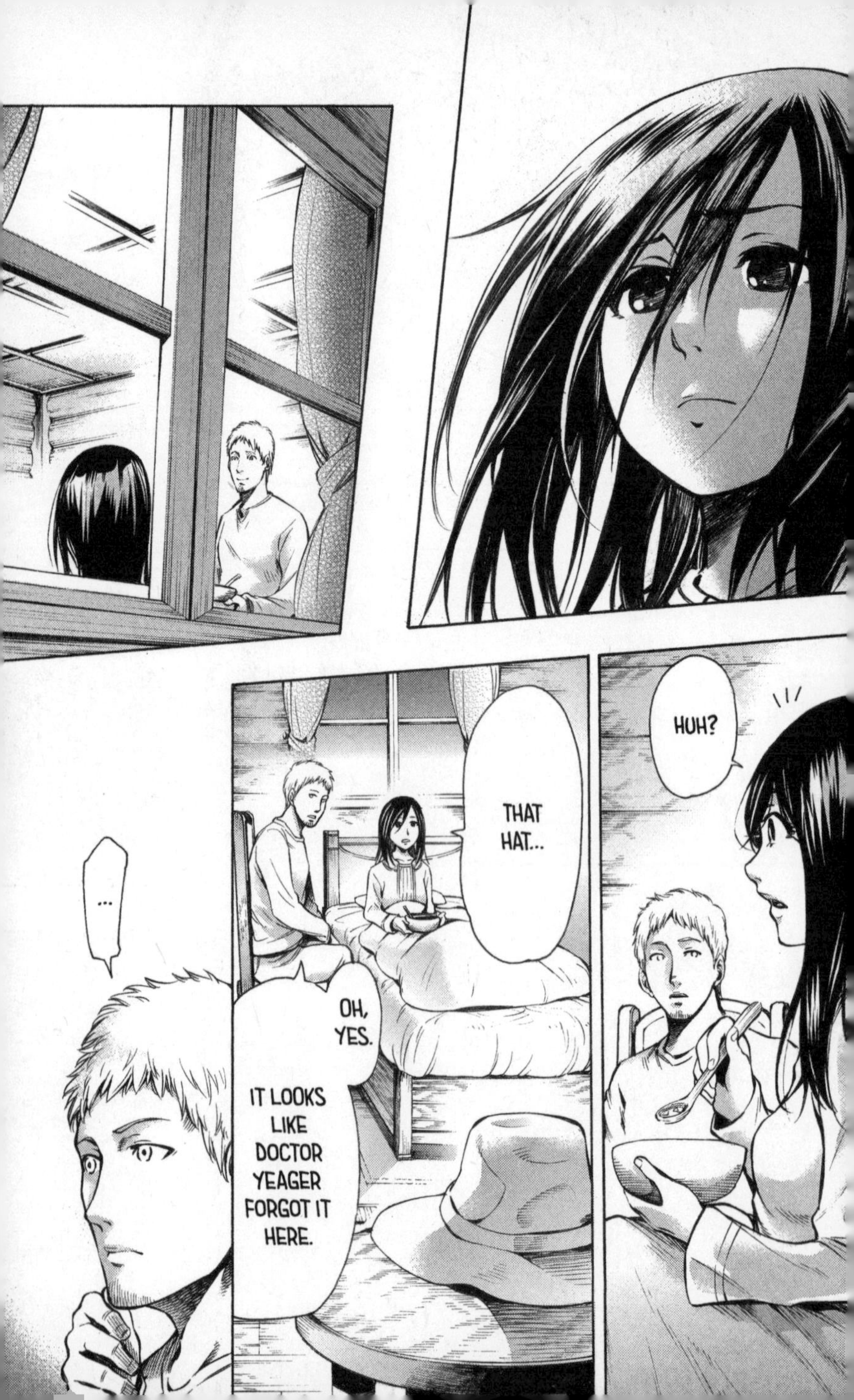
HUH?
THAT HAT...
OH, YES.
IT LOOKS LIKE DOCTOR YEAGER FORGOT IT HERE.
...

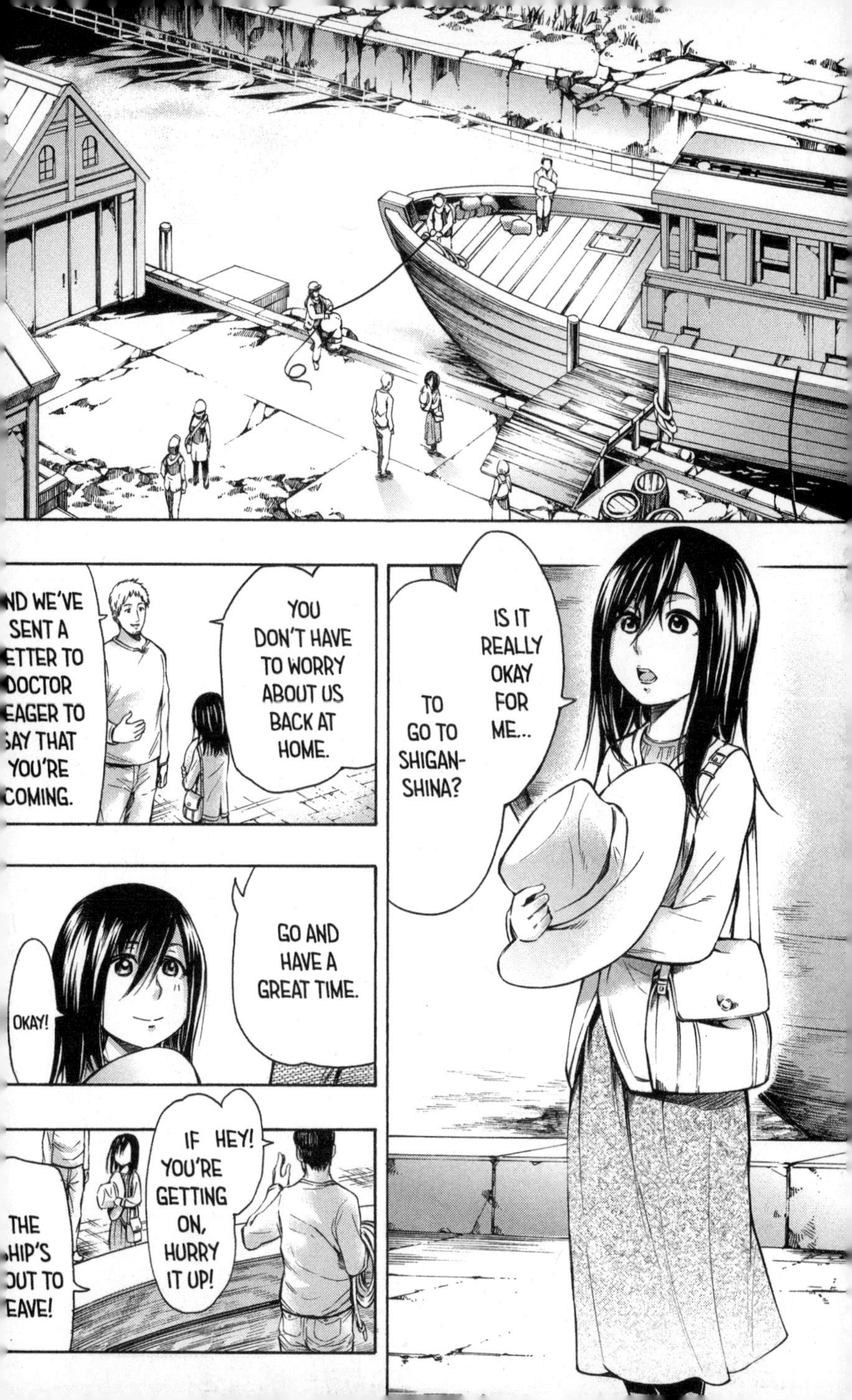
IS IT REALLY OKAY FOR ME... TO GO TO SHIGAN-SHINA?
YOU DON'T HAVE TO WORRY ABOUT US BACK AT HOME.
ND WE'VE SENT A ETTER TO DOCTOR EAGER TO SAY THAT YOU'RE COMING.
GO AND HAVE A GREAT TIME.
OKAY!
HEY! IF YOU'RE GETTING ON, HURRY IT UP!
THE HIP'S OUT TO EAVE!

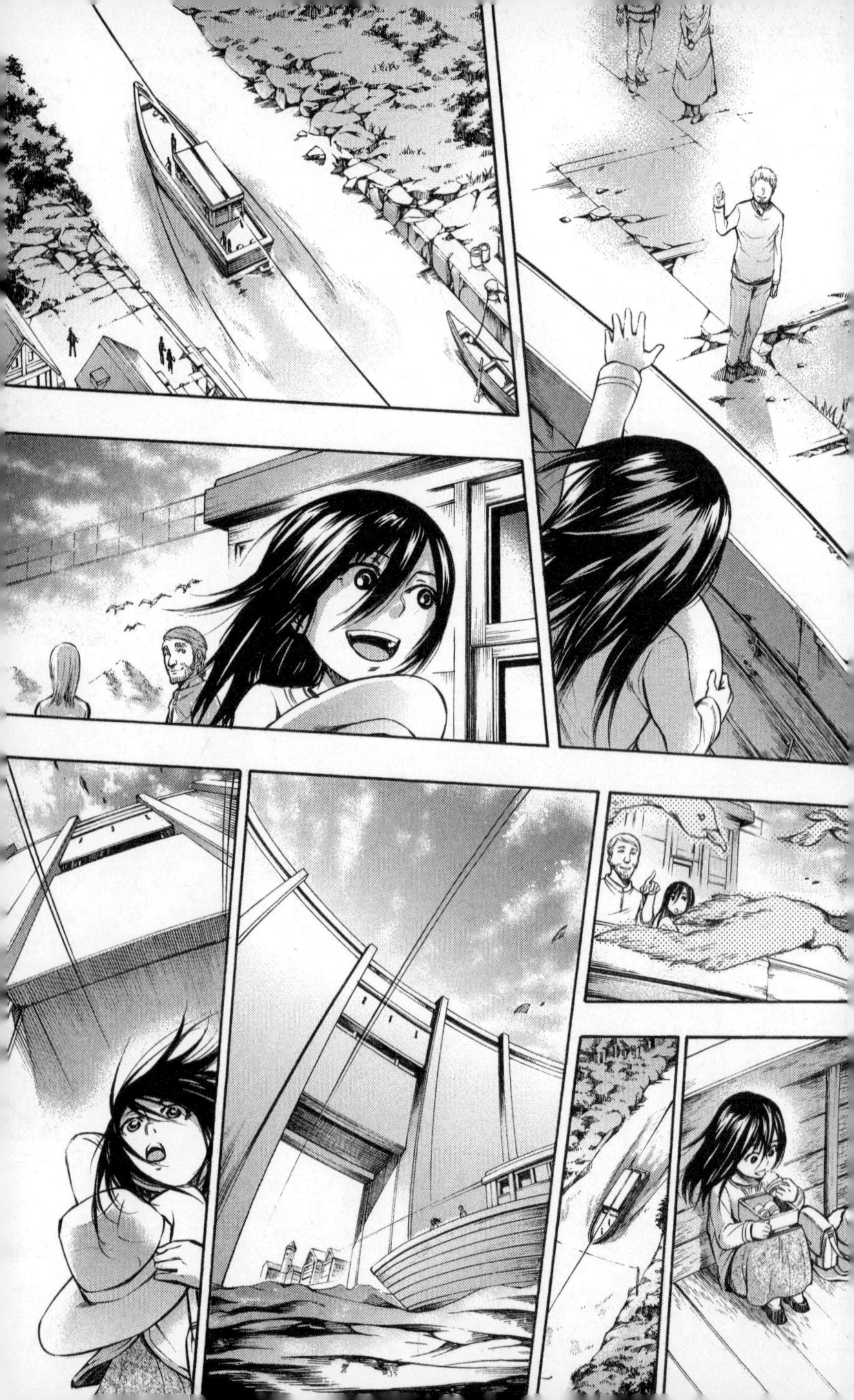

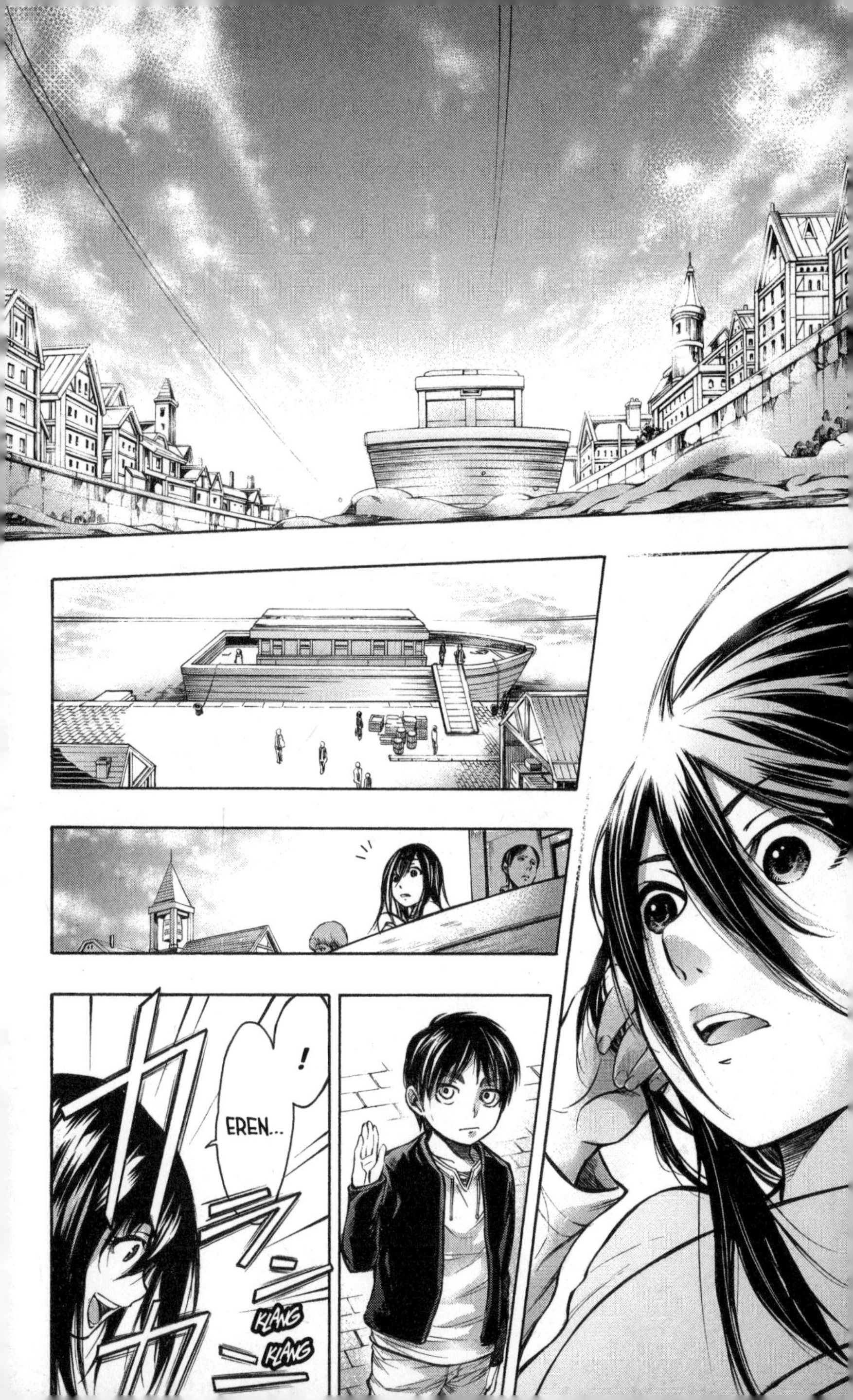
!
EREN...
KLANG
KLANG

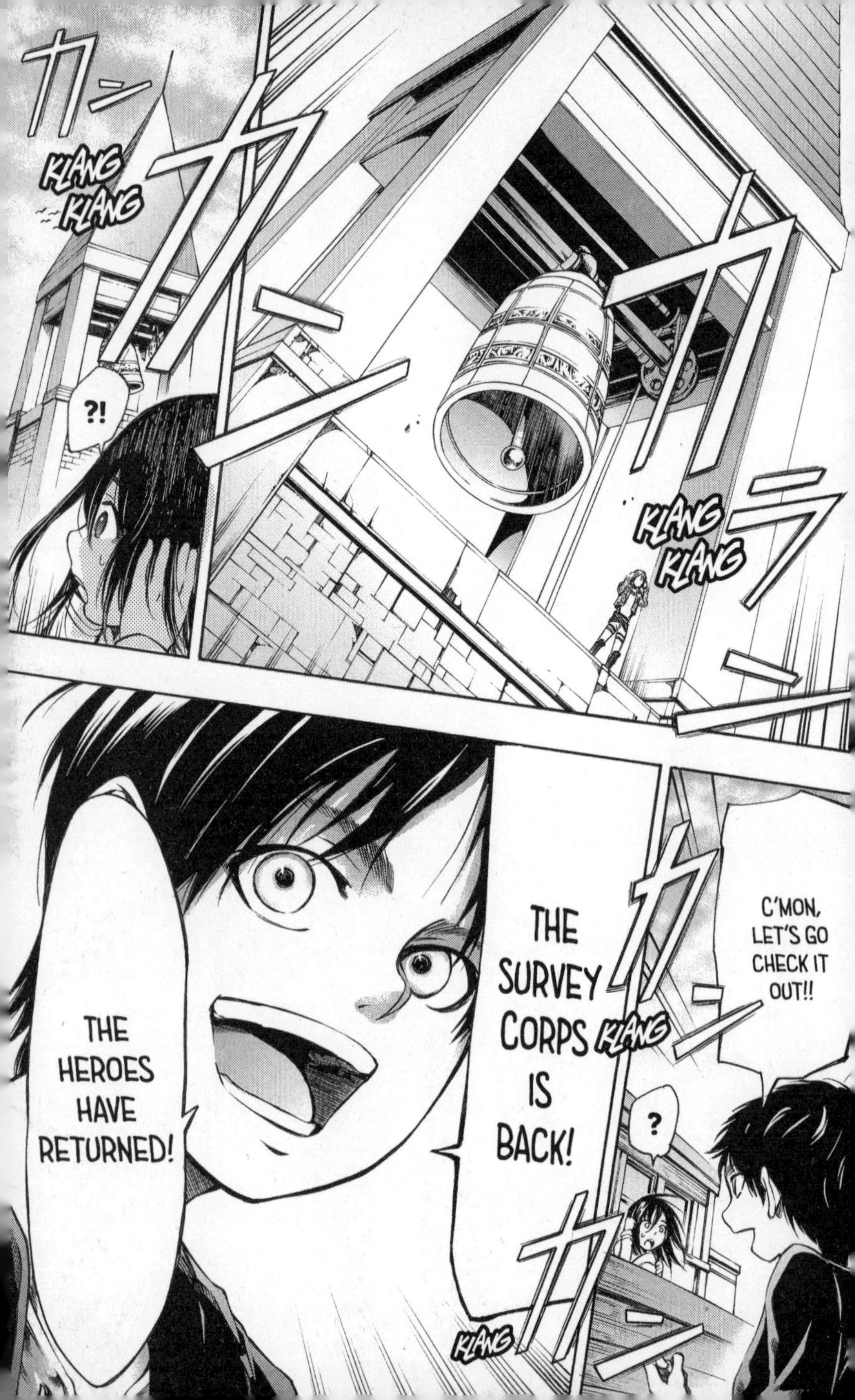
KLANG KLANG
?!
KLANG KLANG
C'MON, LET'S GO CHECK IT OUT!!
?
THE SURVEY CORPS IS BACK!
KLANG
THE HEROES HAVE RETURNED!
KLANG

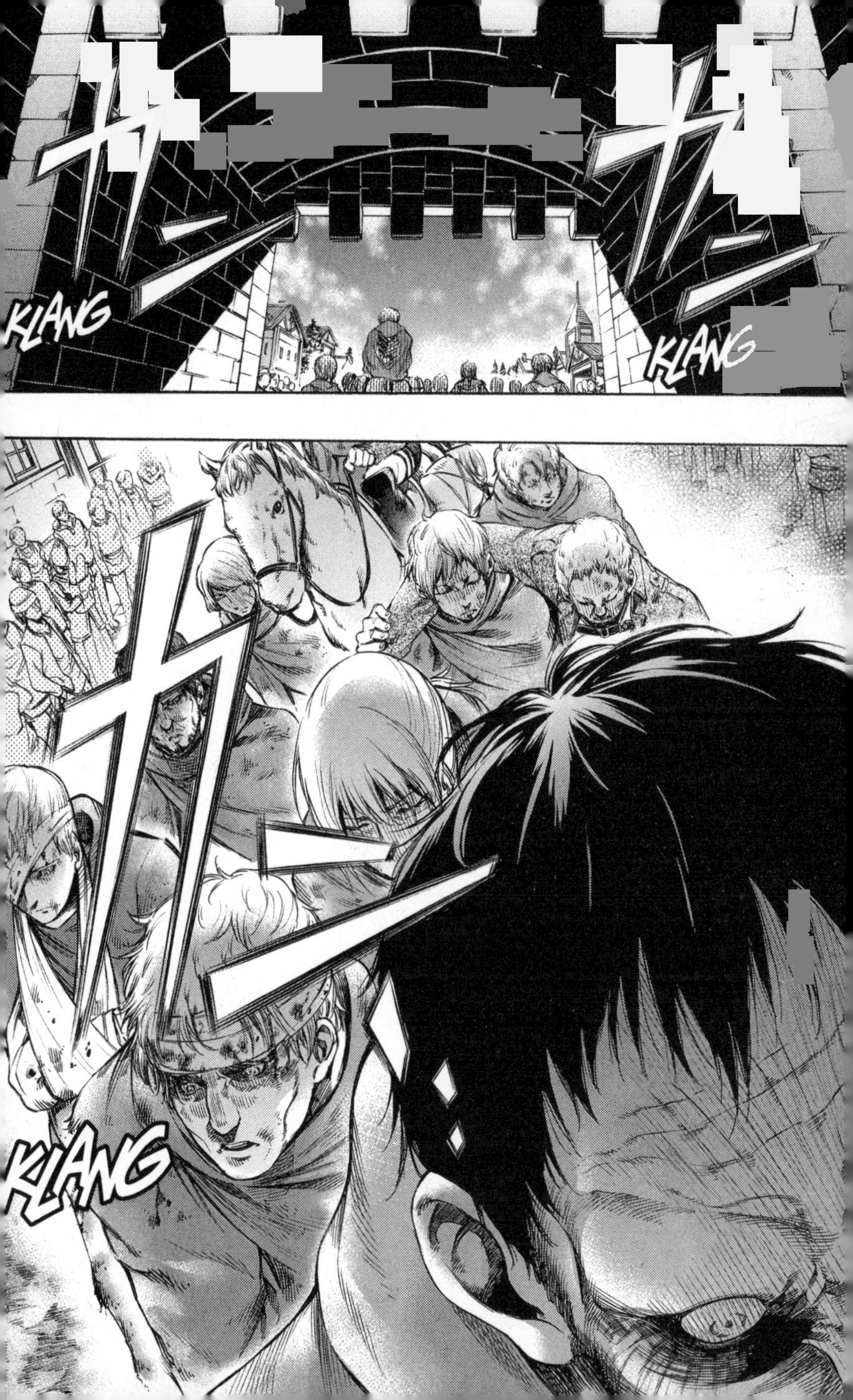
KLANG
KLANG
KLANG

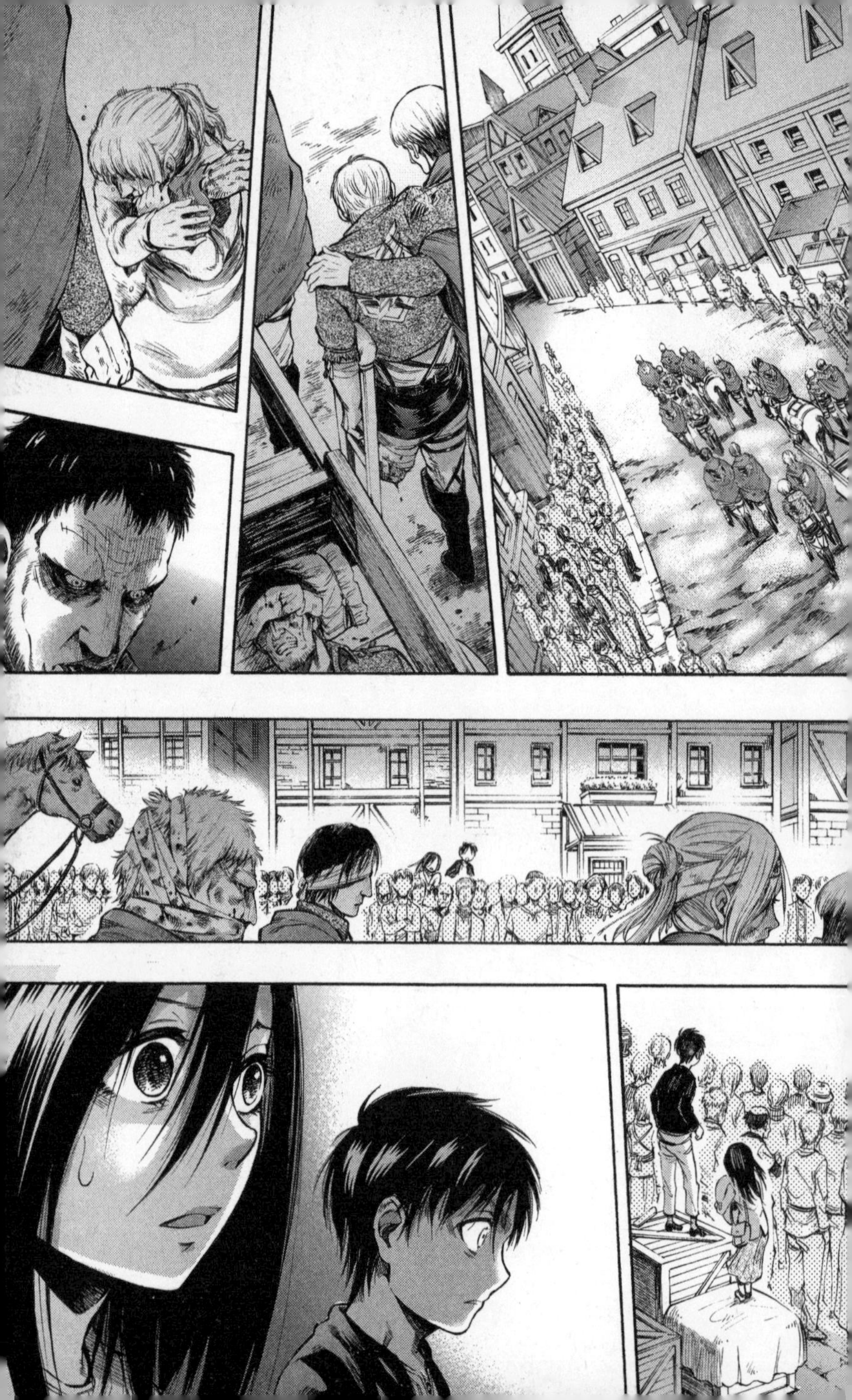

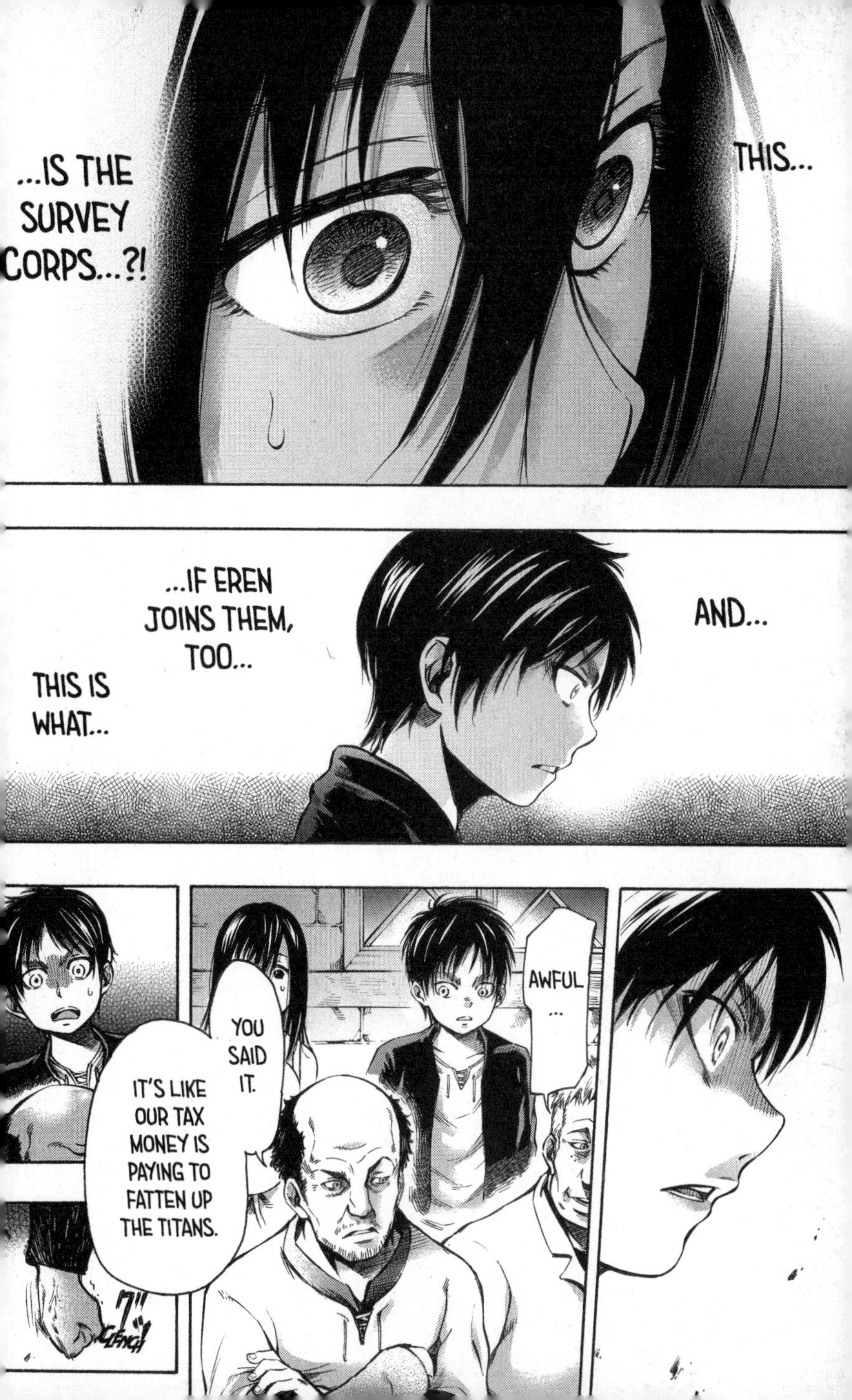
THIS...
...IS THE SURVEY CORPS...?!
AND...
...IF EREN JOINS THEM, TOO...
THIS IS WHAT...
AWFUL ...
YOU SAID IT.
IT'S LIKE OUR TAX MONEY IS PAYING TO FATTEN UP THE TITANS.
CLENCH

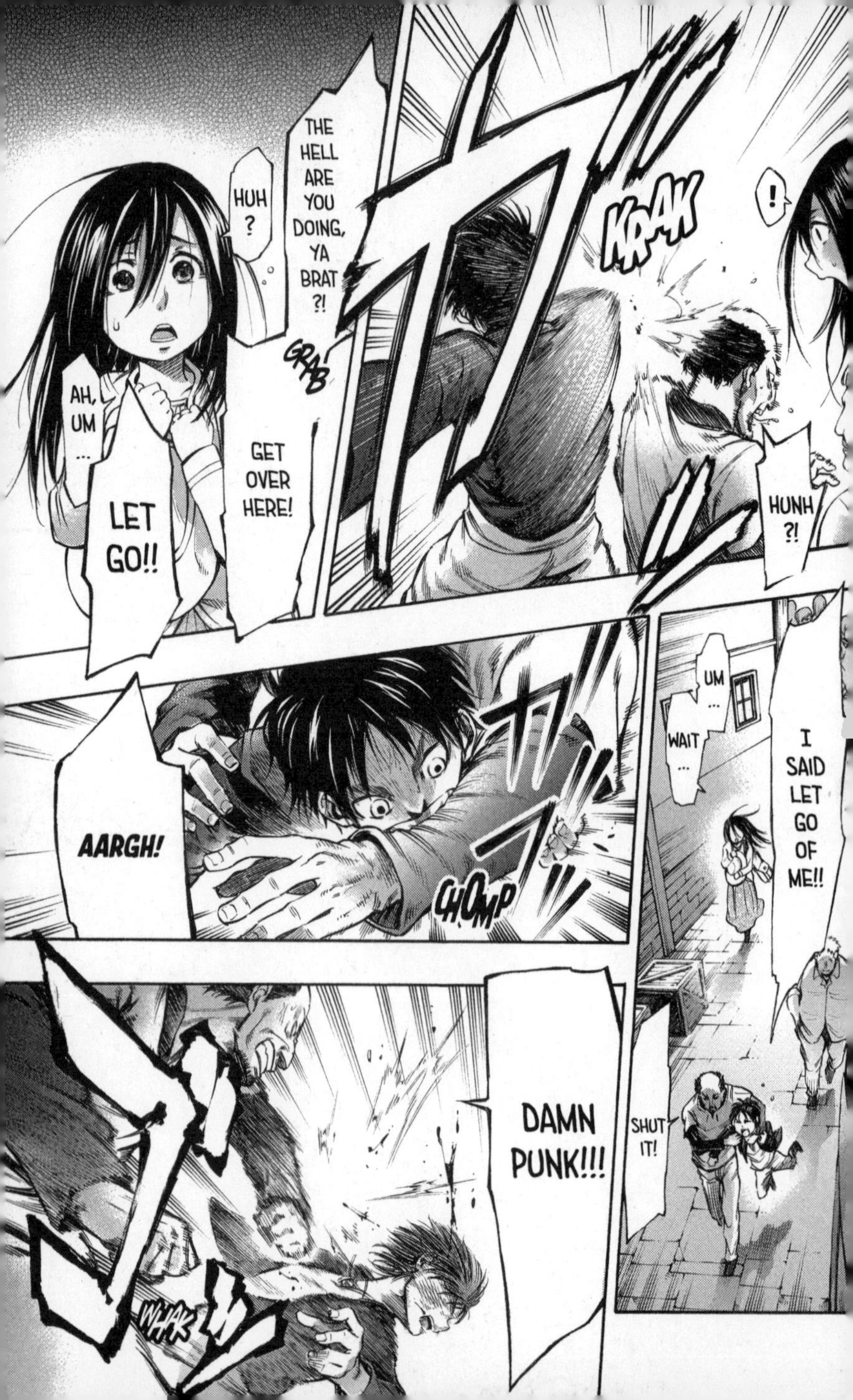
!
KRAK
HUNH?!
GRAB
THE HELL ARE YOU DOING, YA BRAT?!
HUH?
GET OVER HERE!
AH, UM...
LET GO!!
I SAID LET GO OF ME!!
UM... WAIT...
SHUT IT!
CHOMP
AARGH!
DAMN PUNK!!!
WHAK

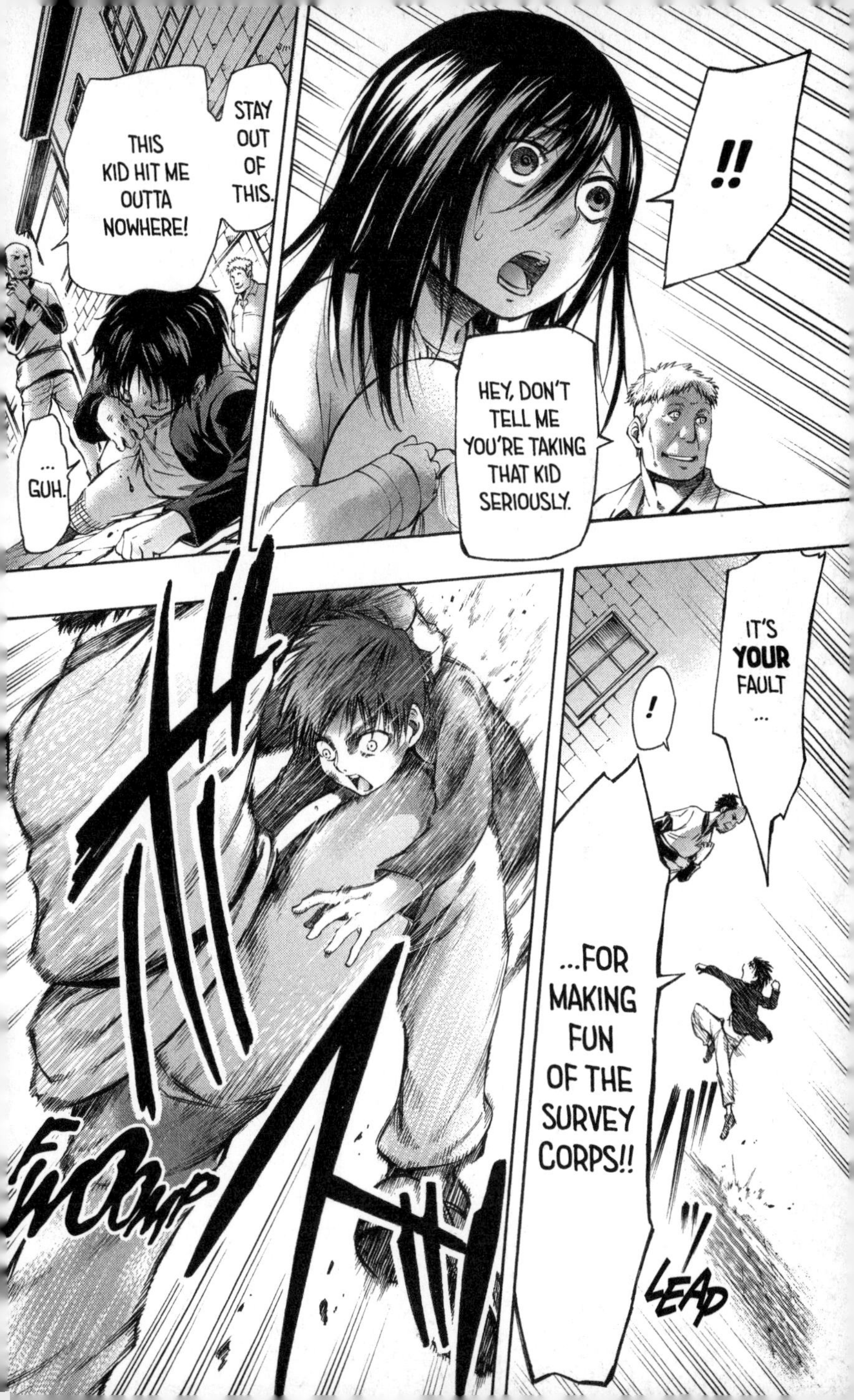
!!
HEY, DON'T TELL ME YOU'RE TAKING THAT KID SERIOUSLY.
STAY OUT OF THIS.
THIS KID HIT ME OUTTA NOWHERE!
... GUH.
IT'S YOUR FAULT ...
!
...FOR MAKING FUN OF THE SURVEY CORPS!!
LEAP
FWOOMP

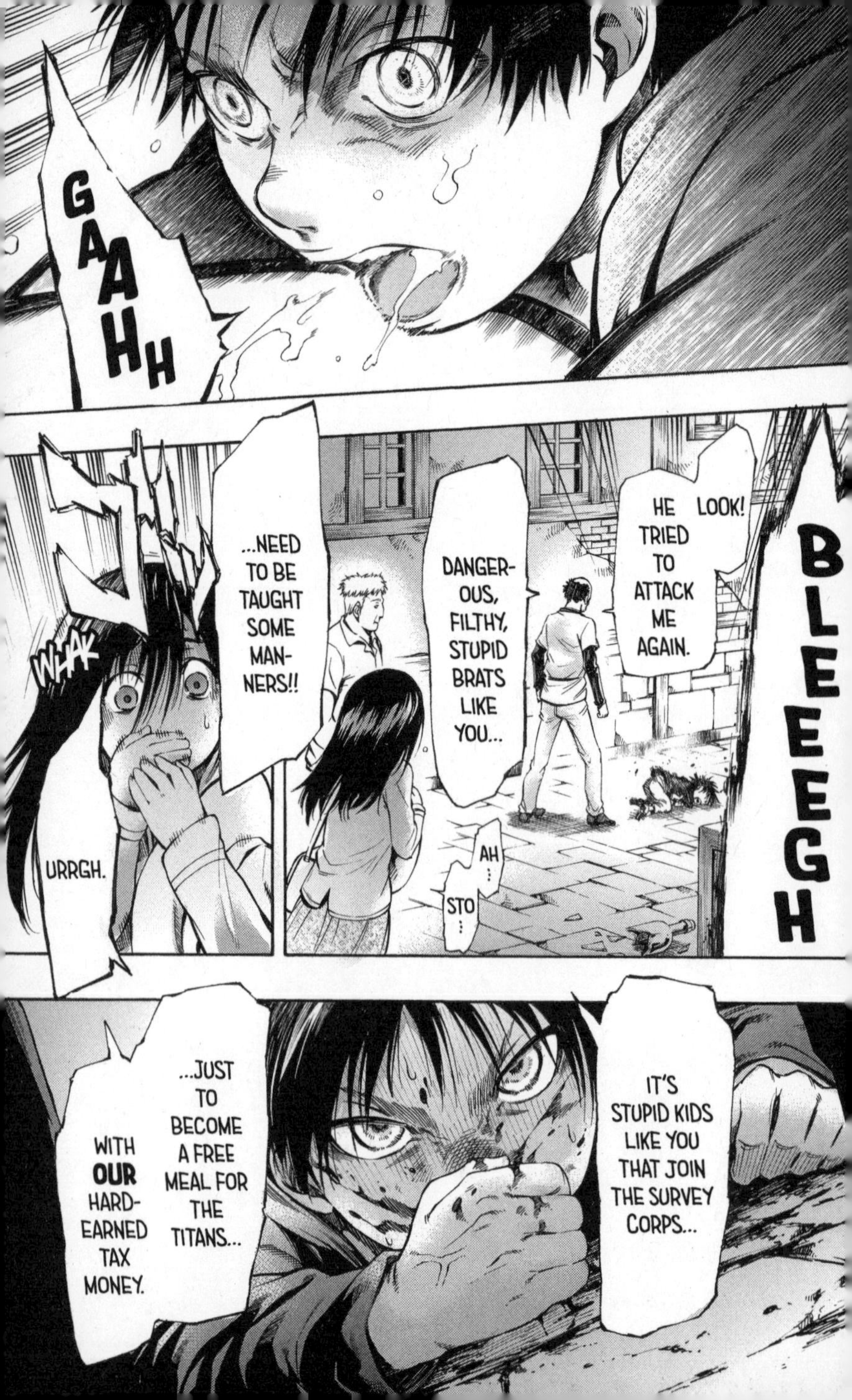
GAAHH
BLEEGH
LOOK! HE TRIED TO ATTACK ME AGAIN.
DANGER-OUS, FILTHY, STUPID BRATS LIKE YOU...
AH...
STO...
...NEED TO BE TAUGHT SOME MAN-NERS!!
WHAK
URRGH.
IT'S STUPID KIDS LIKE YOU THAT JOIN THE SURVEY CORPS...
...JUST TO BECOME A FREE MEAL FOR THE TITANS...
WITH **OUR** HARD-EARNED TAX MONEY.

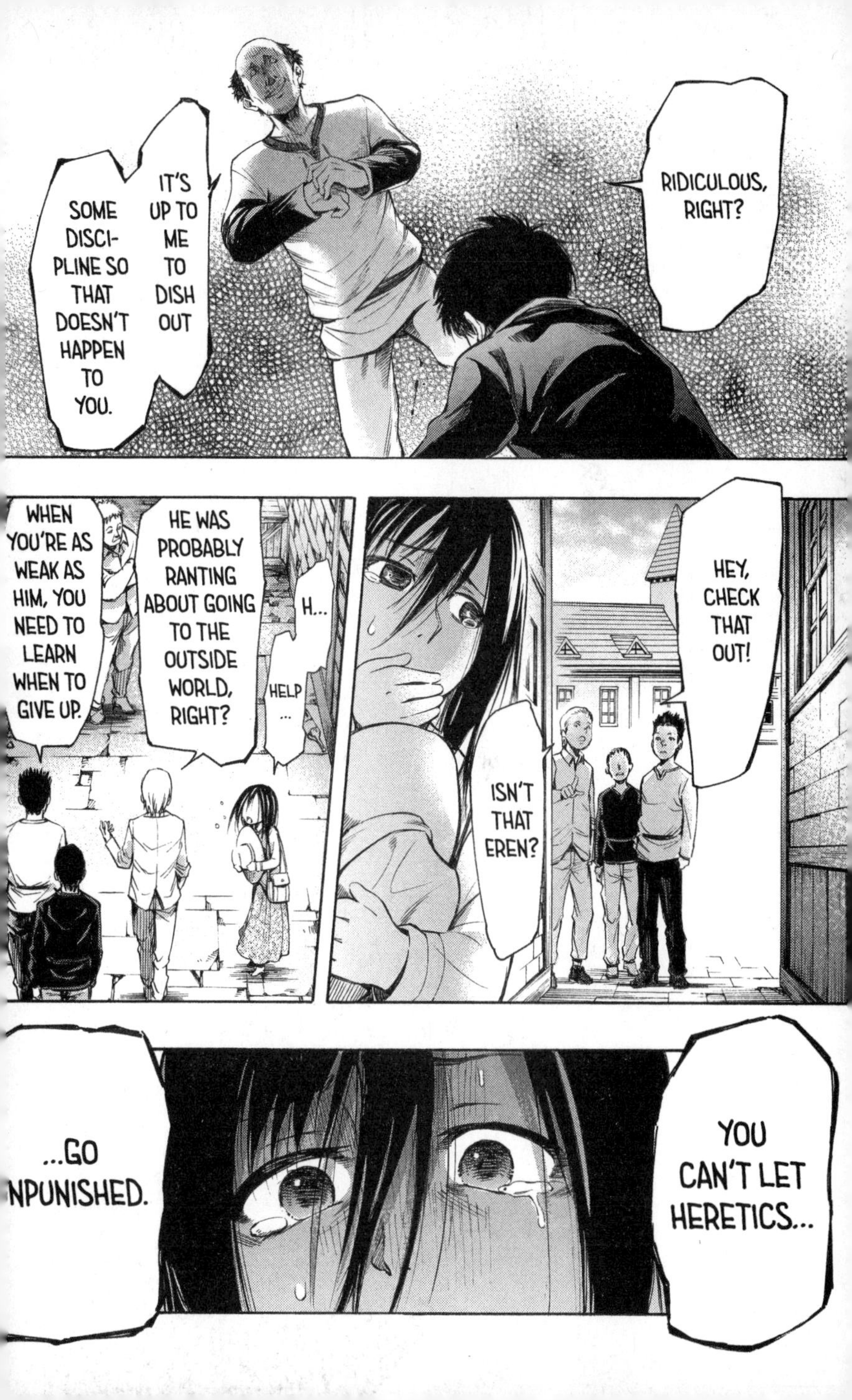
RIDICULOUS, RIGHT?
IT'S UP TO ME TO DISH OUT
SOME DISCI-PLINE SO THAT DOESN'T HAPPEN TO YOU.
HEY, CHECK THAT OUT!
ISN'T THAT EREN?
H...
HELP ...
HE WAS PROBABLY RANTING ABOUT GOING TO THE OUTSIDE WORLD, RIGHT?
WHEN YOU'RE AS WEAK AS HIM, YOU NEED TO LEARN WHEN TO GIVE UP.
YOU CAN'T LET HERETICS...
...GO NPUNISHED.

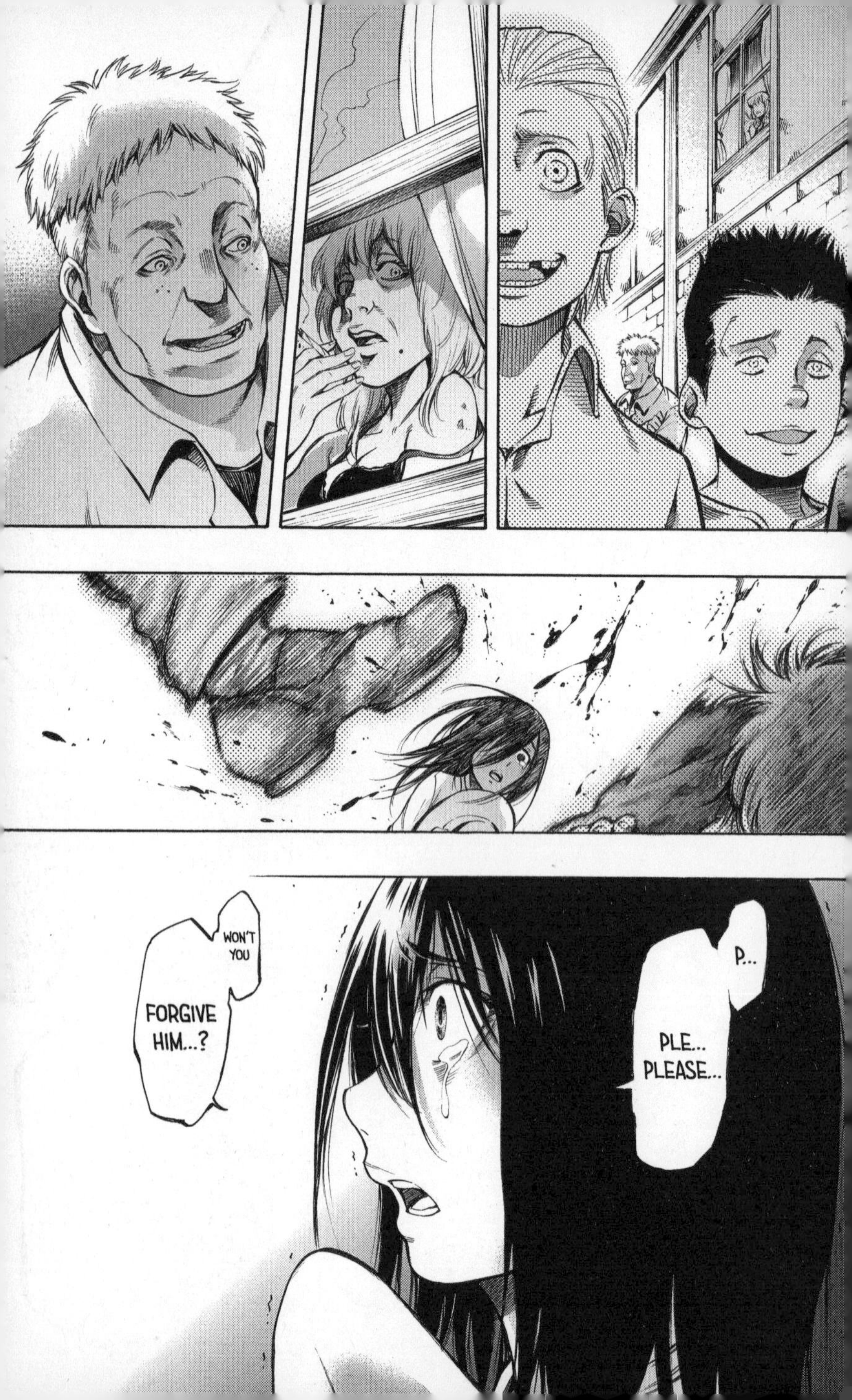
P...
PLE... PLEASE...
WON'T YOU FORGIVE HIM...?

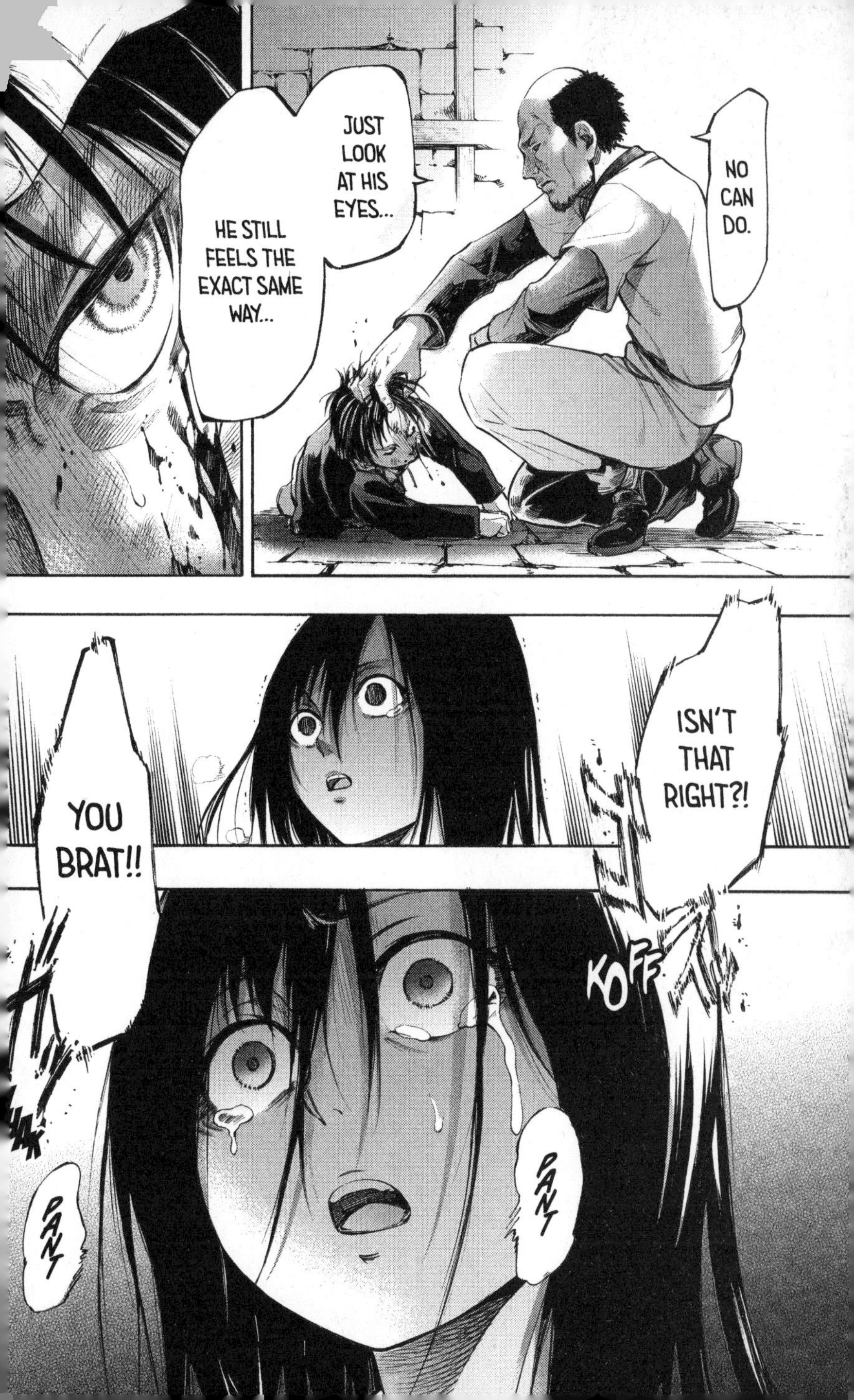
NO CAN DO.
JUST LOOK AT HIS EYES...
HE STILL FEELS THE EXACT SAME WAY...
ISN'T THAT RIGHT?!
YOU BRAT!!
KOFF
PANT
PANT

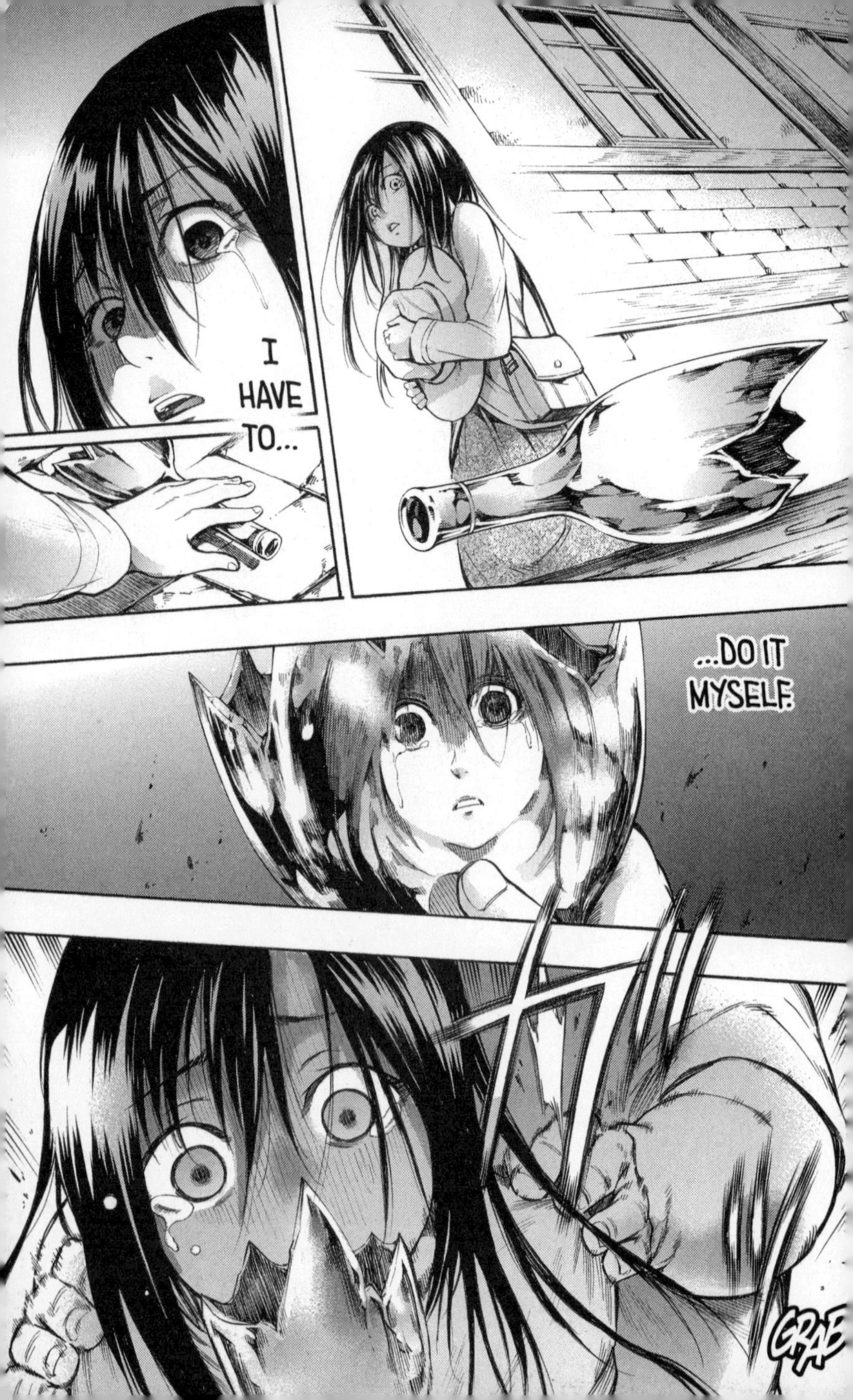
I HAVE TO...
...DO IT MYSELF.
GRAB

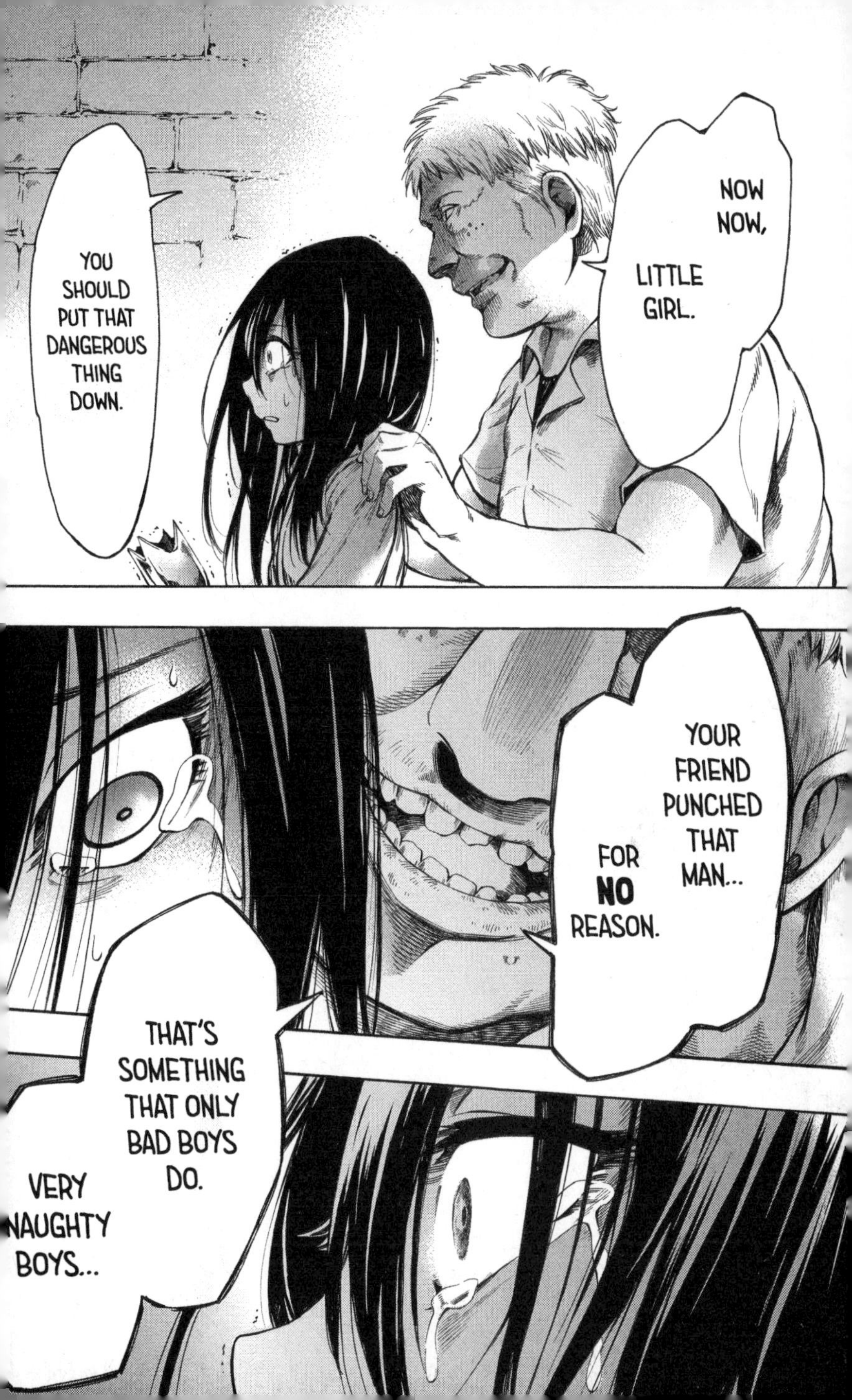
NOW NOW, LITTLE GIRL.
YOU SHOULD PUT THAT DANGEROUS THING DOWN.
YOUR FRIEND PUNCHED THAT MAN... FOR **NO** REASON.
THAT'S SOMETHING THAT ONLY BAD BOYS DO.
VERY NAUGHTY BOYS...

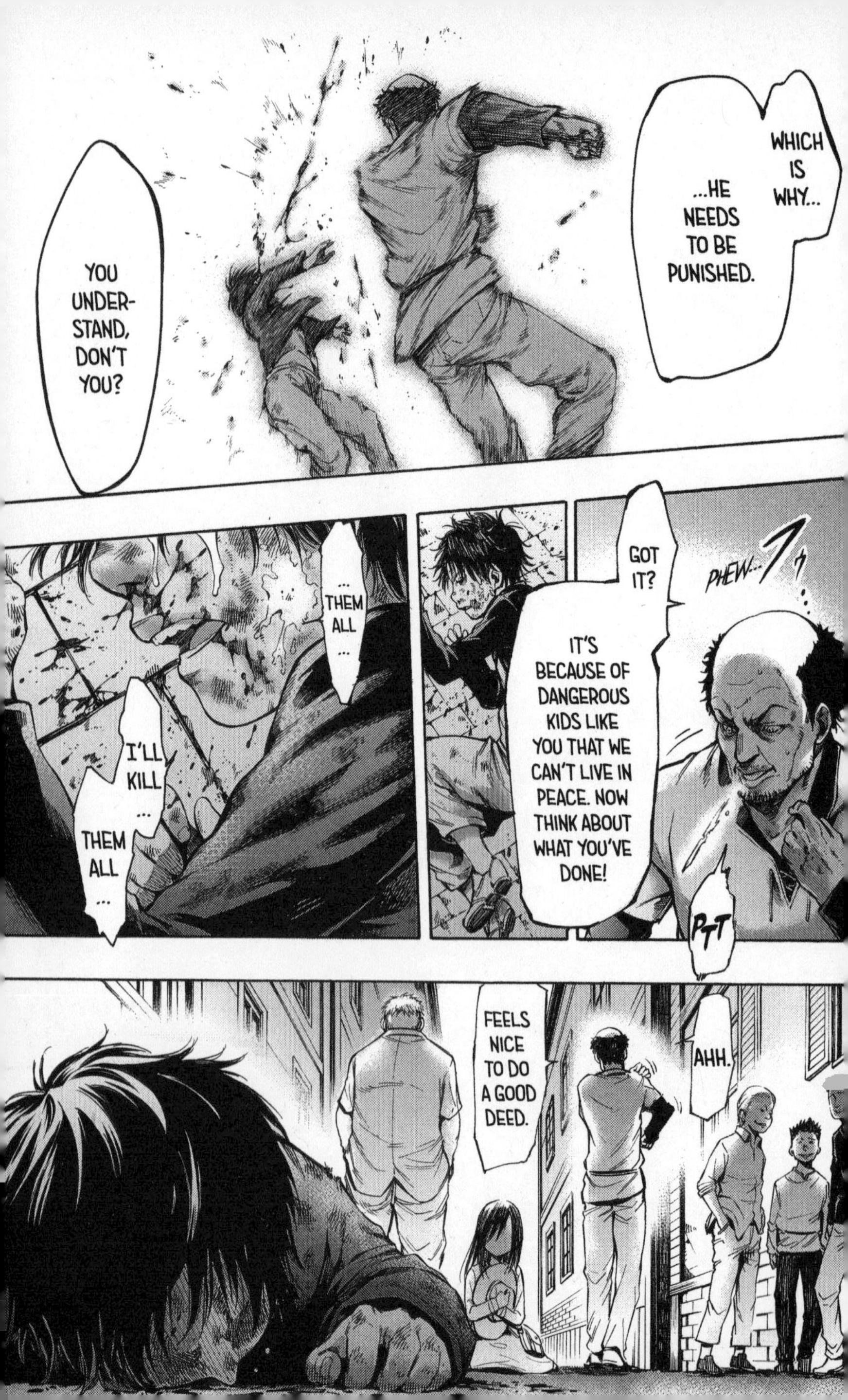
WHICH IS WHY...
...HE NEEDS TO BE PUNISHED.
YOU UNDER-STAND, DON'T YOU?
PHEW...
GOT IT?
IT'S BECAUSE OF DANGEROUS KIDS LIKE YOU THAT WE CAN'T LIVE IN PEACE. NOW THINK ABOUT WHAT YOU'VE DONE!
PTT
... THEM ALL ...
I'LL KILL ... THEM ALL ...
AHH.
FEELS NICE TO DO A GOOD DEED.

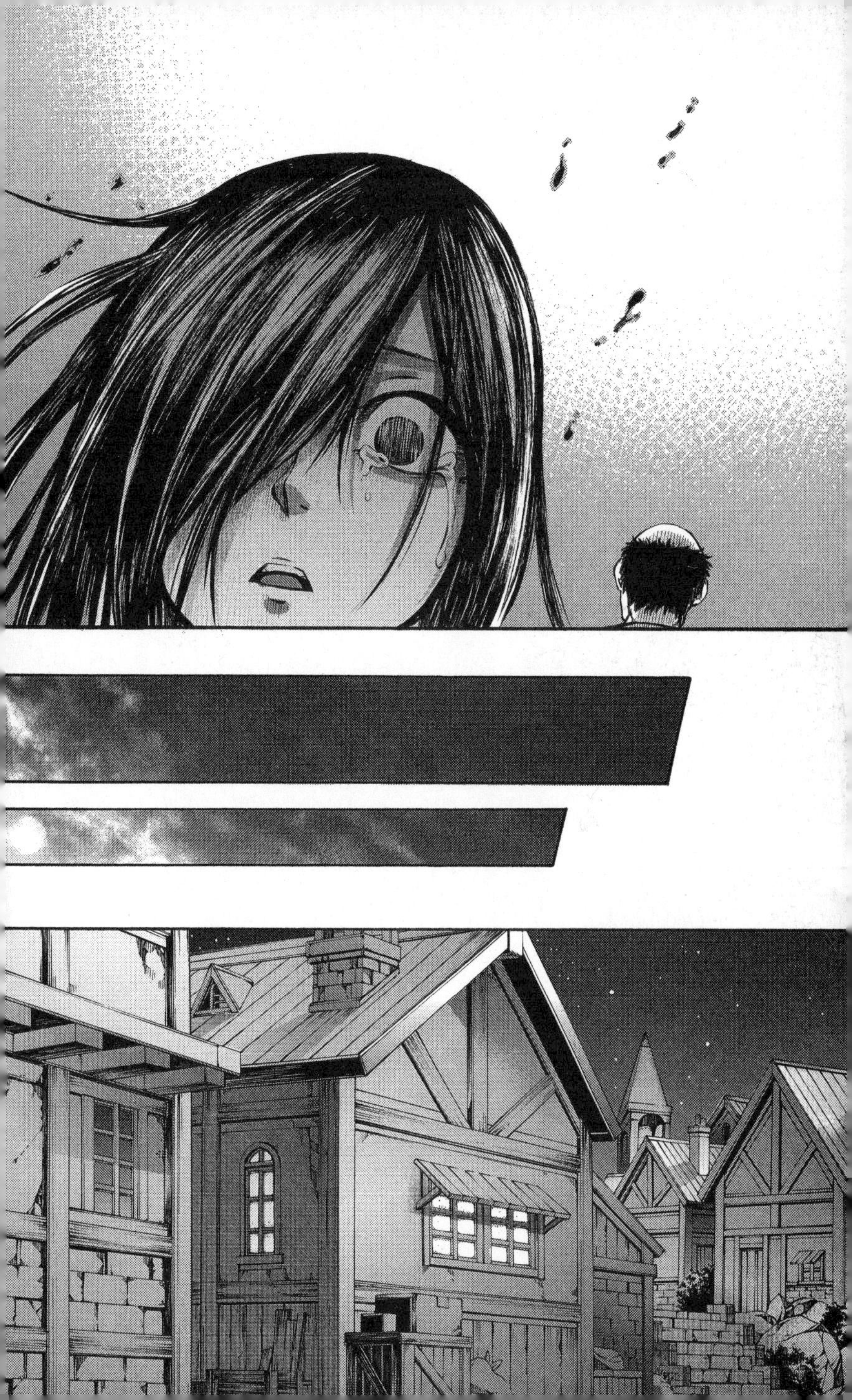

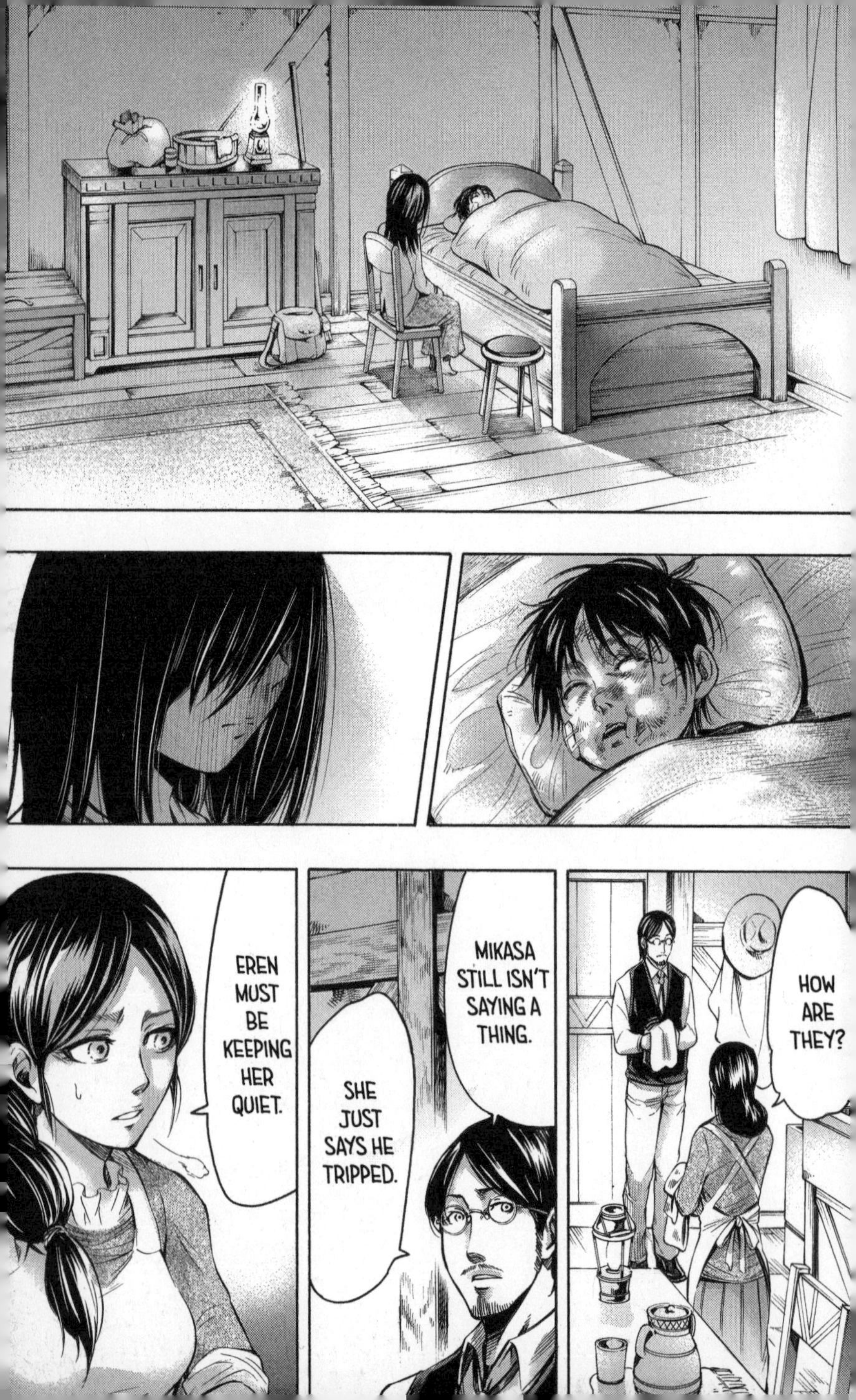
HOW ARE THEY?
MIKASA STILL ISN'T SAYING A THING.
SHE JUST SAYS HE TRIPPED.
EREN MUST BE KEEPING HER QUIET.

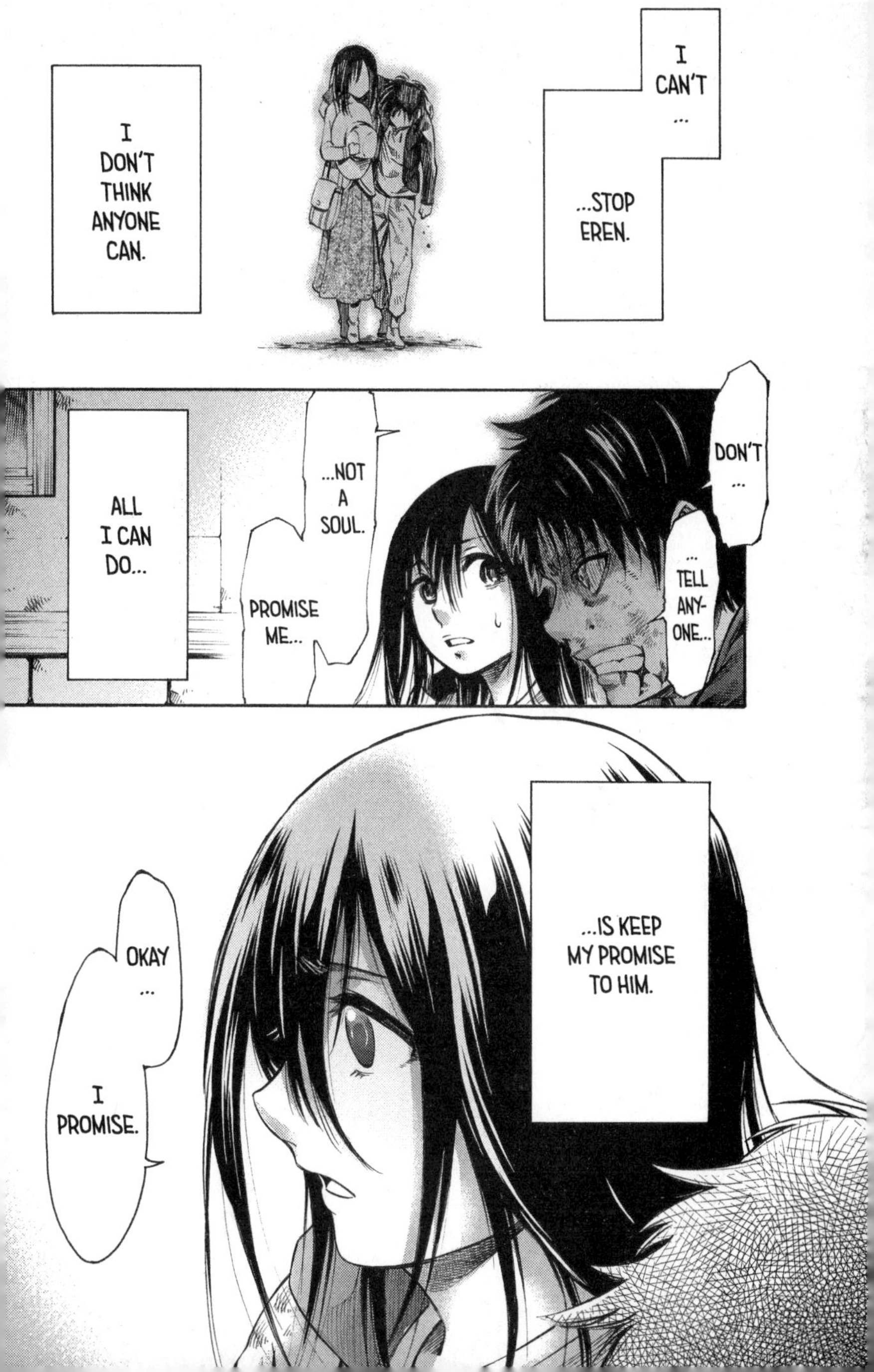
I CAN'T...
...STOP EREN.
I DON'T THINK ANYONE CAN.
DON'T...
...TELL ANYONE...
...NOT A SOUL.
PROMISE ME...
ALL I CAN DO...
...IS KEEP MY PROMISE TO HIM.
OKAY...
I PROMISE.

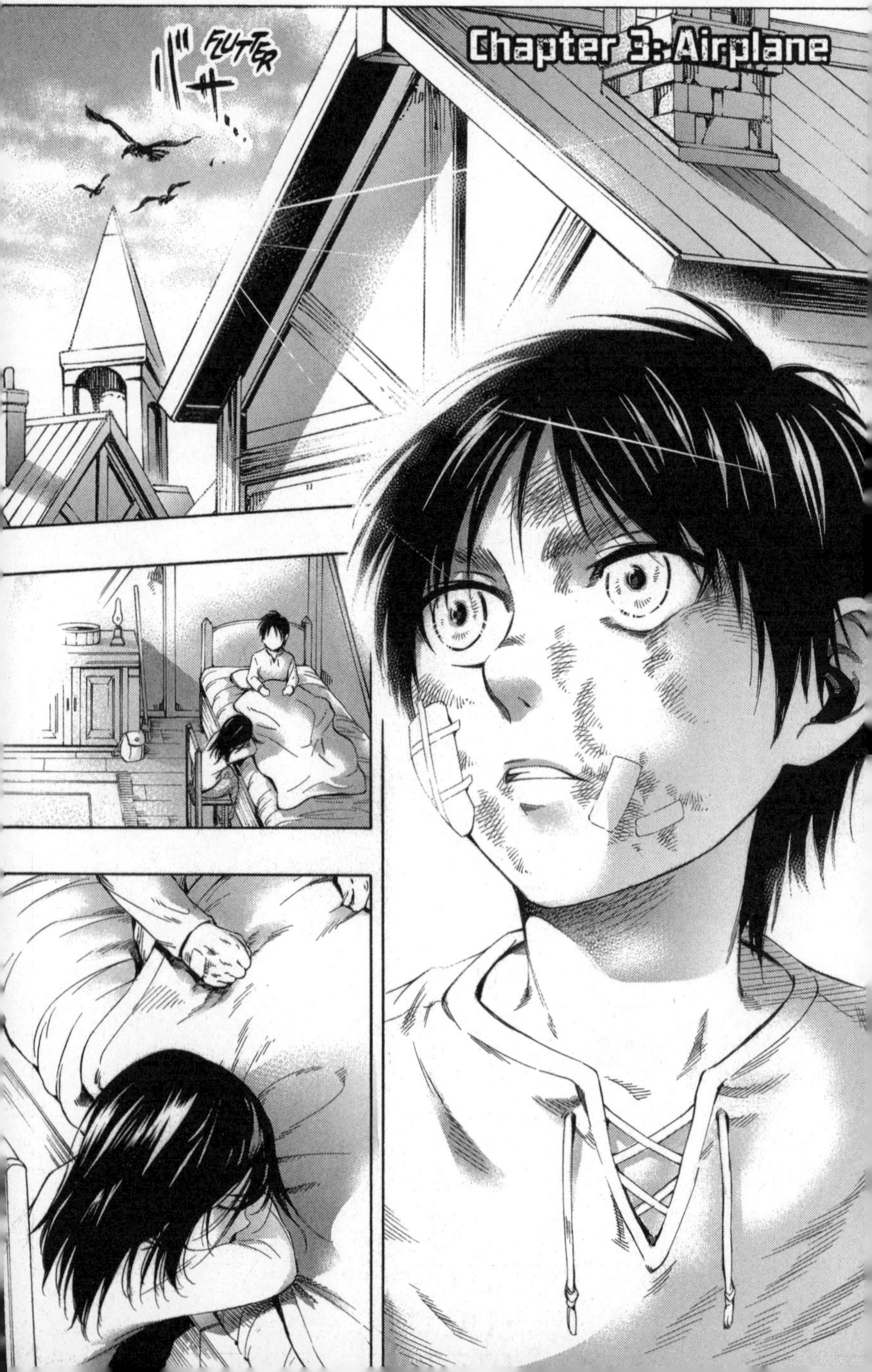
Chapter 3: Airplane
バサ
FLUTTER

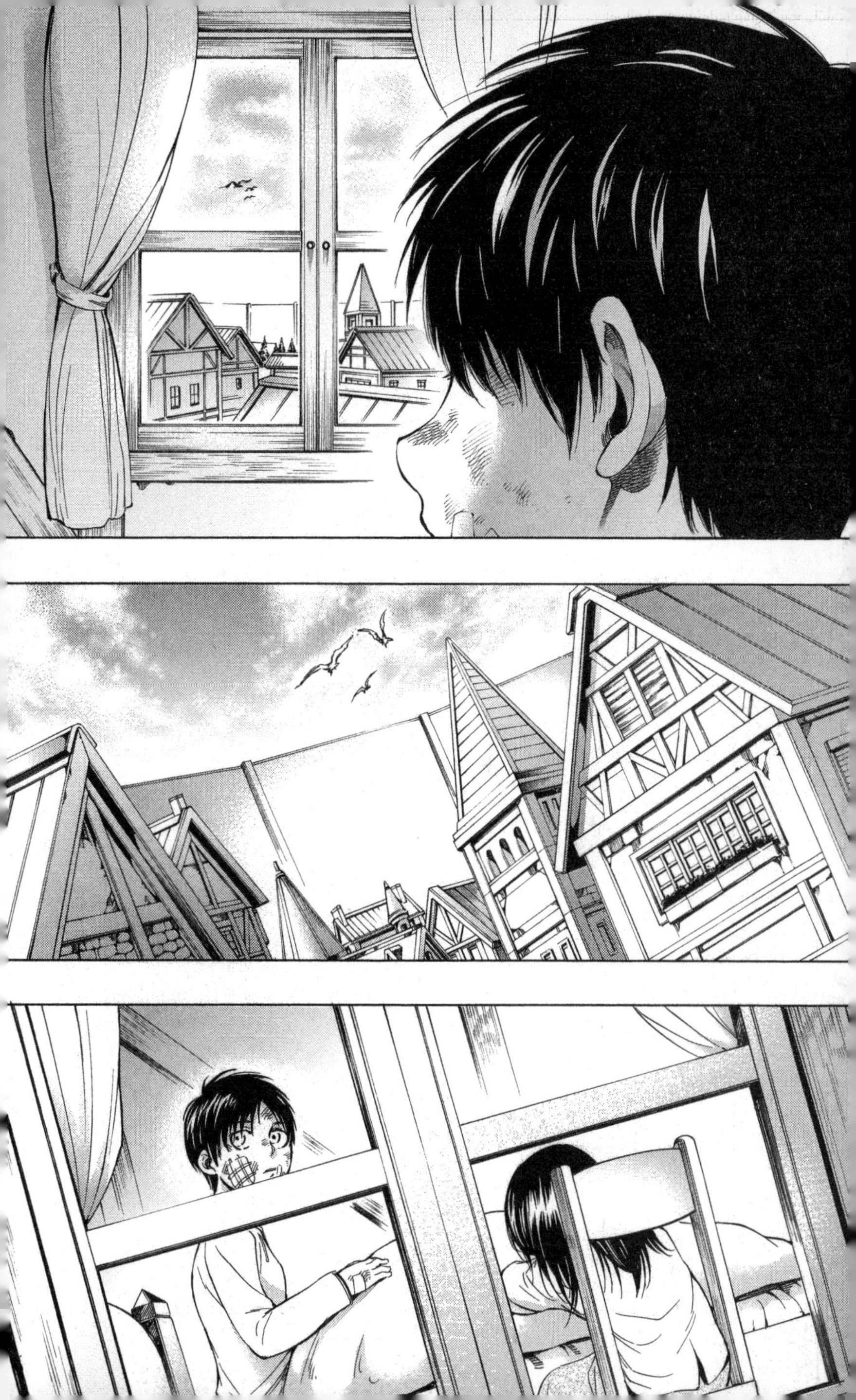

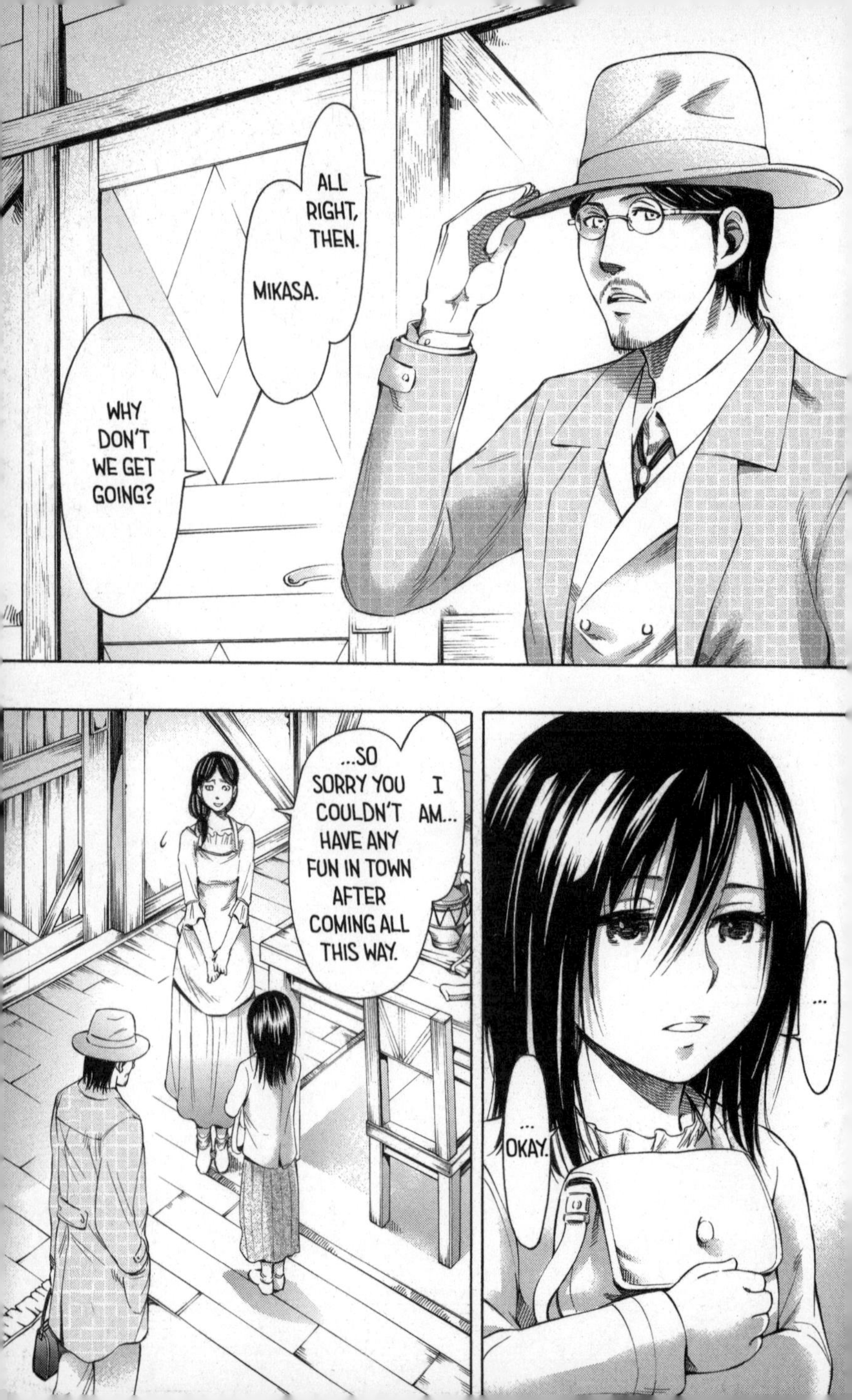
ALL RIGHT, THEN.
MIKASA.
WHY DON'T WE GET GOING?
...
... OKAY.
I AM... ...SO SORRY YOU COULDN'T HAVE ANY FUN IN TOWN AFTER COMING ALL THIS WAY.

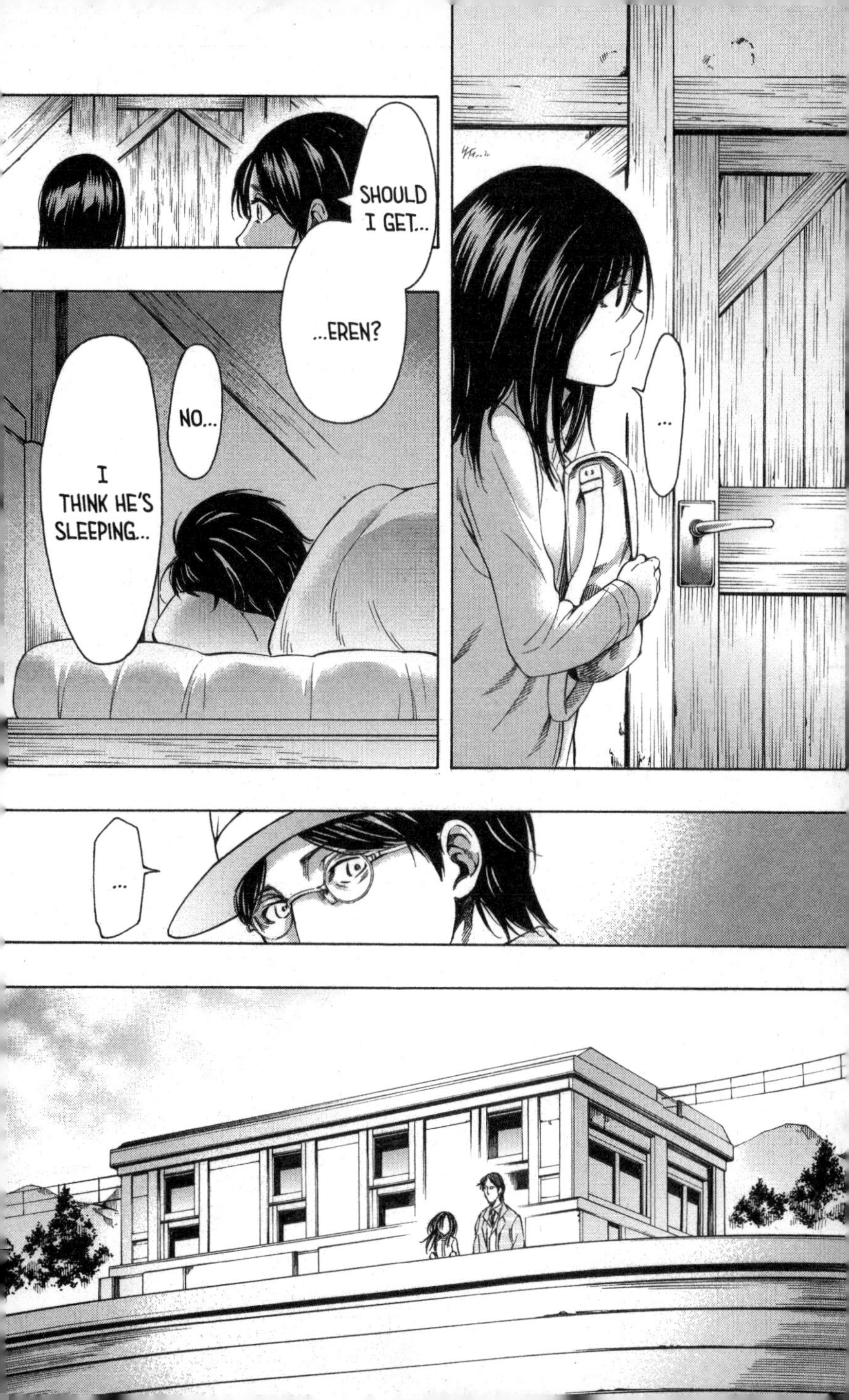
...
SHOULD I GET...
...EREN?
NO...
I THINK HE'S SLEEPING...
...

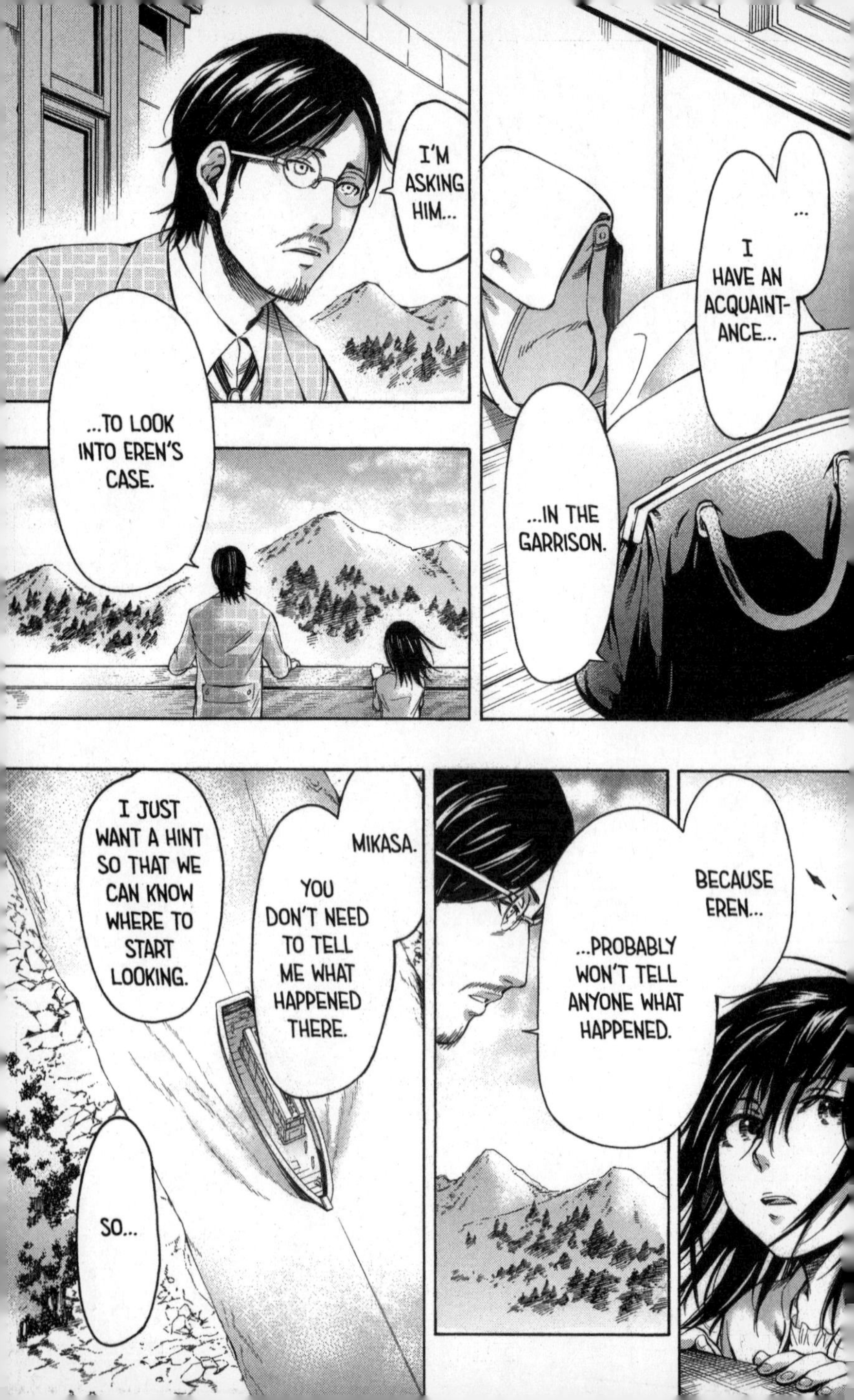
...
I HAVE AN ACQUAINTANCE...
...IN THE GARRISON.
I'M ASKING HIM...
...TO LOOK INTO EREN'S CASE.
BECAUSE EREN...
...PROBABLY WON'T TELL ANYONE WHAT HAPPENED.
MIKASA.
YOU DON'T NEED TO TELL ME WHAT HAPPENED THERE.
I JUST WANT A HINT SO THAT WE CAN KNOW WHERE TO START LOOKING.
SO...

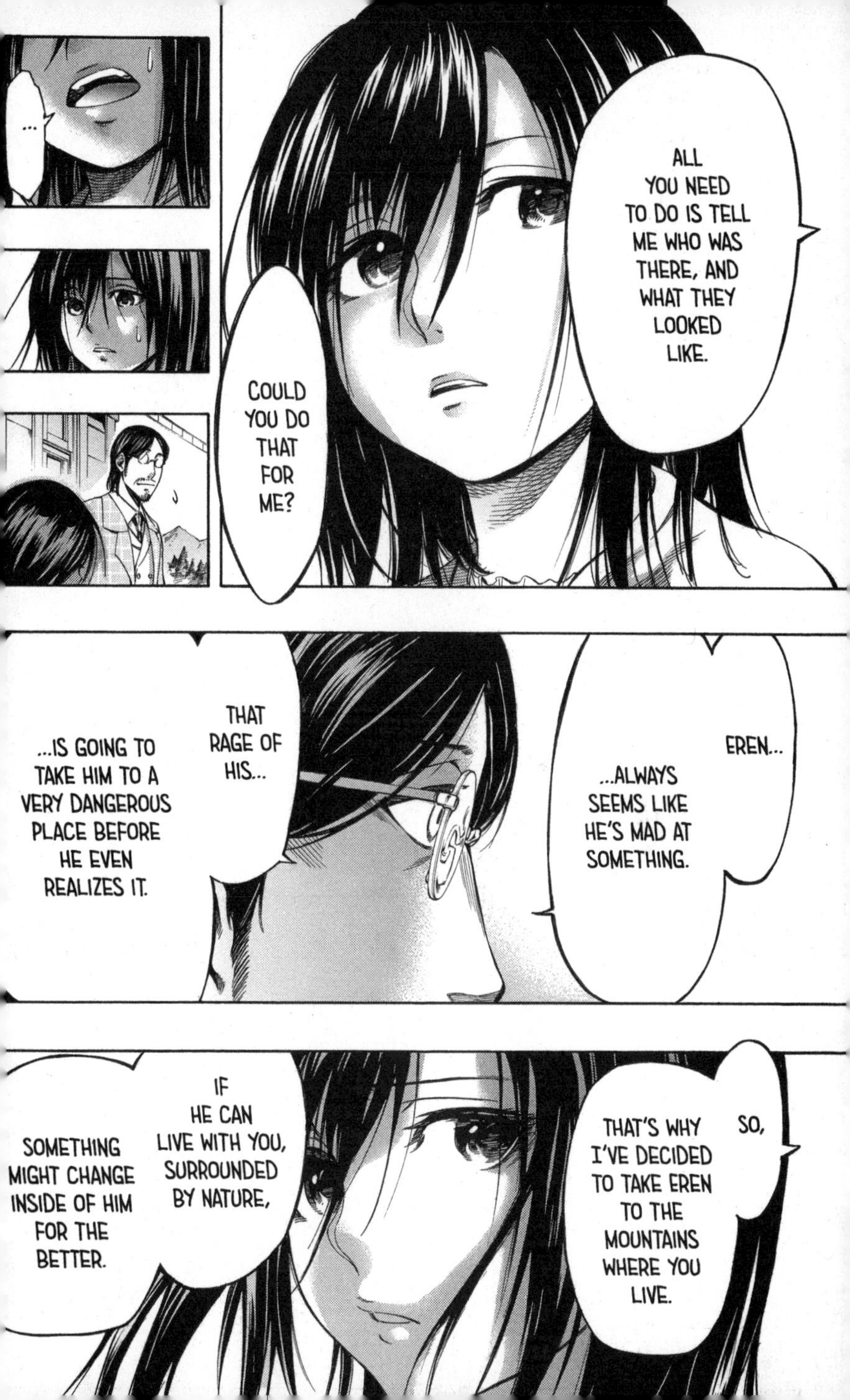
ALL YOU NEED TO DO IS TELL ME WHO WAS THERE, AND WHAT THEY LOOKED LIKE.
COULD YOU DO THAT FOR ME?
...
EREN...
...ALWAYS SEEMS LIKE HE'S MAD AT SOMETHING.
THAT RAGE OF HIS...
...IS GOING TO TAKE HIM TO A VERY DANGEROUS PLACE BEFORE HE EVEN REALIZES IT.
SO,
THAT'S WHY I'VE DECIDED TO TAKE EREN TO THE MOUNTAINS WHERE YOU LIVE.
IF HE CAN LIVE WITH YOU, SURROUNDED BY NATURE,
SOMETHING MIGHT CHANGE INSIDE OF HIM FOR THE BETTER.

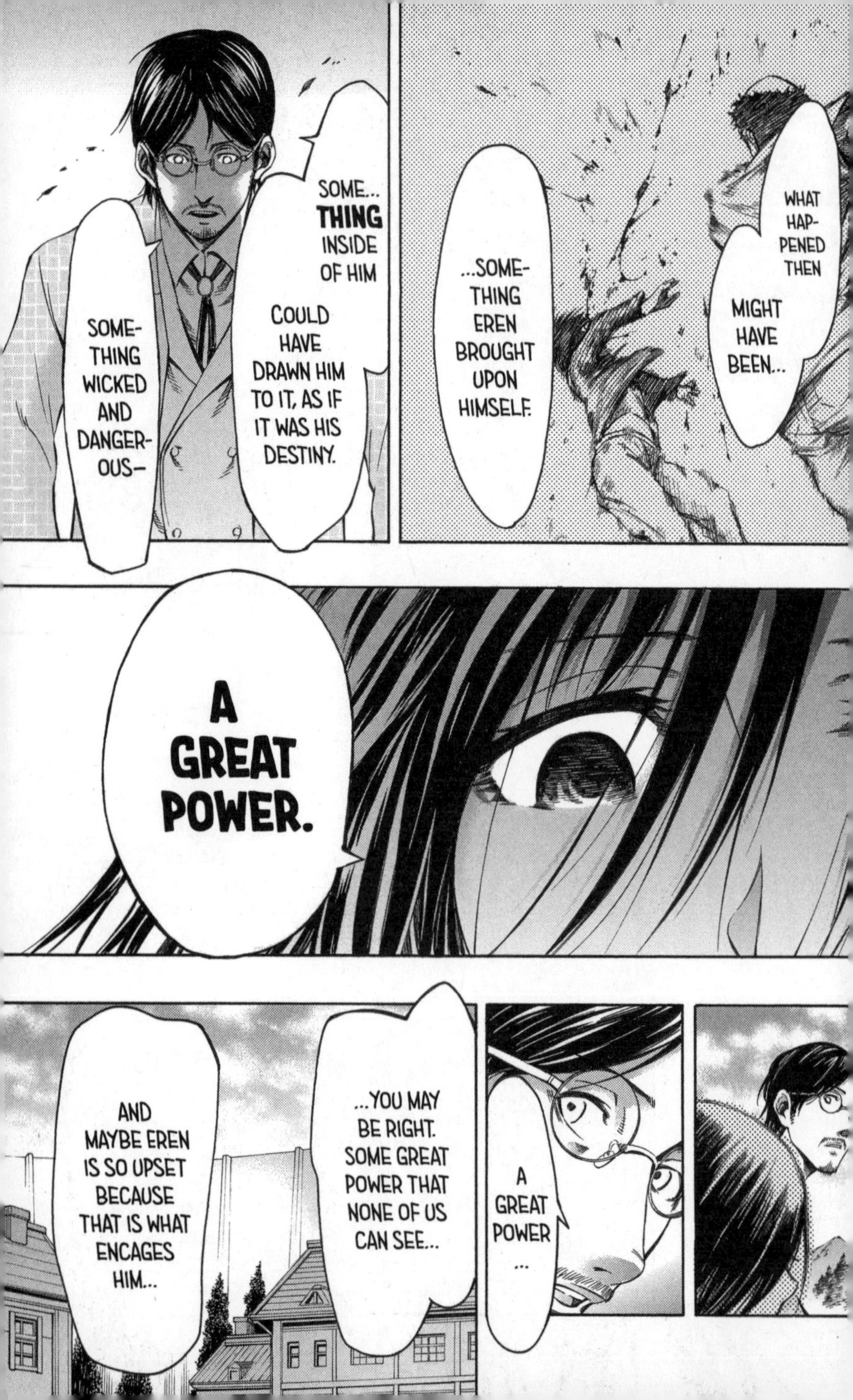

WHAT HAPPENED THEN MIGHT HAVE BEEN...
...SOMETHING EREN BROUGHT UPON HIMSELF.
SOME... THING INSIDE OF HIM COULD HAVE DRAWN HIM TO IT, AS IF IT WAS HIS DESTINY.
SOMETHING WICKED AND DANGEROUS—
A GREAT POWER.
A GREAT POWER...
...YOU MAY BE RIGHT. SOME GREAT POWER THAT NONE OF US CAN SEE...
AND MAYBE EREN IS SO UPSET BECAUSE THAT IS WHAT ENCAGES HIM...

PERHAPS YOU...

...ARE THE ONLY ONE ABLE TO PROTECT EREN FROM THAT GREAT POWER.

M-ME...?

...?

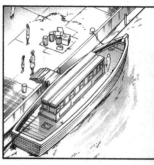

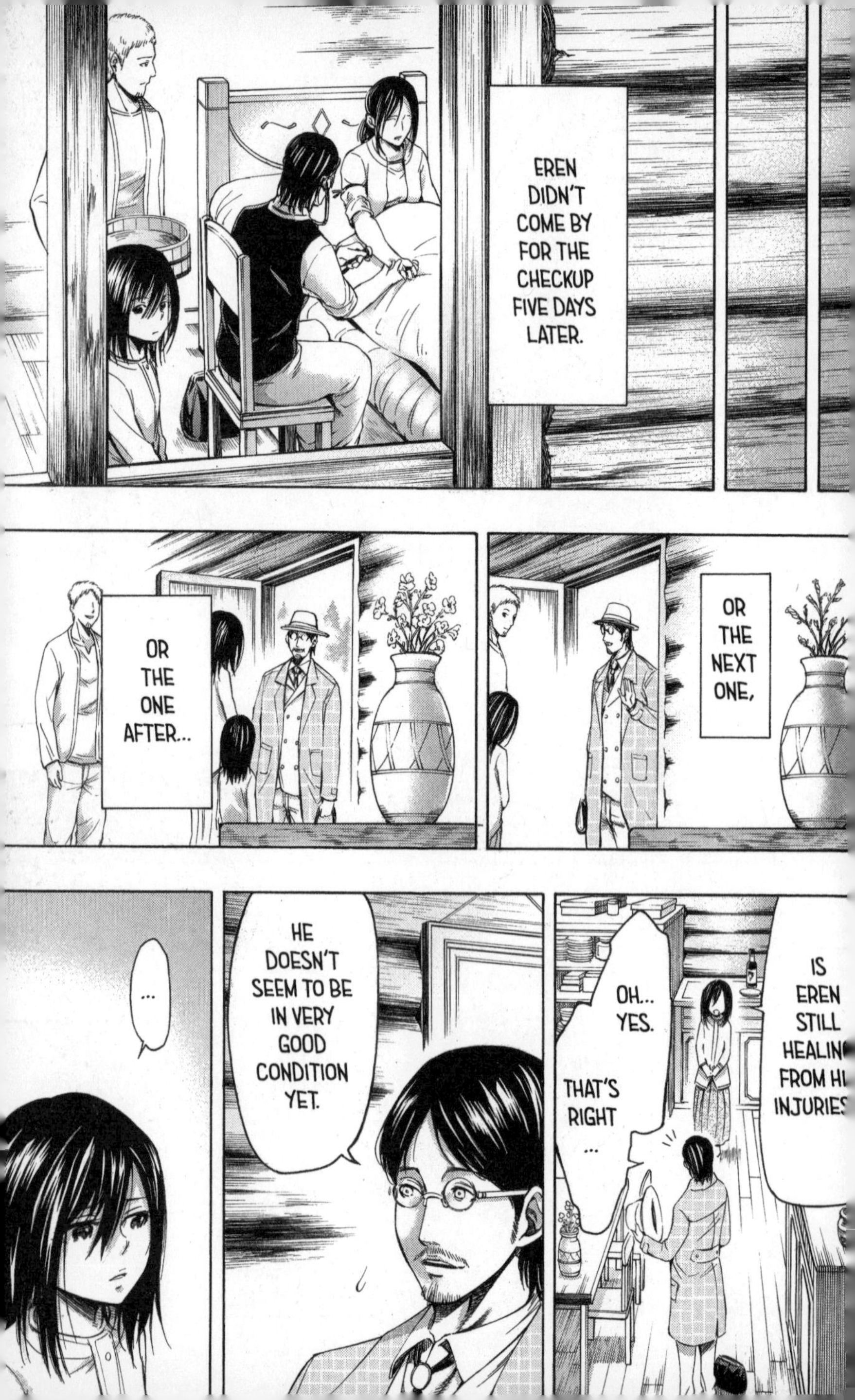
EREN DIDN'T COME BY FOR THE CHECKUP FIVE DAYS LATER.
OR THE NEXT ONE,
OR THE ONE AFTER...
IS EREN STILL HEALIN FROM HI INJURIES
OH... YES.
THAT'S RIGHT ...
HE DOESN'T SEEM TO BE IN VERY GOOD CONDITION YET.
...

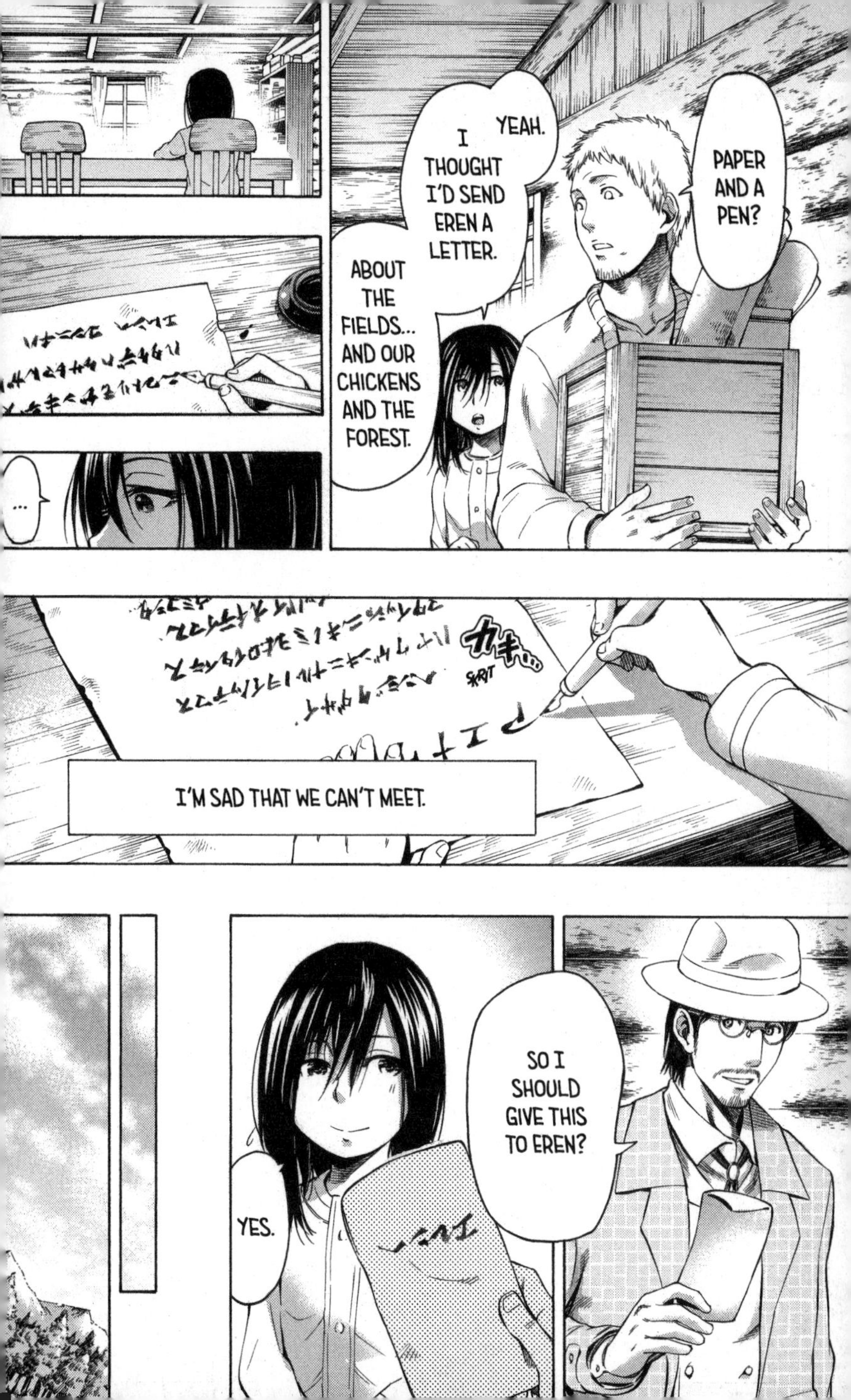

PAPER AND A PEN?
YEAH.
I THOUGHT I'D SEND EREN A LETTER.
ABOUT THE FIELDS... AND OUR CHICKENS AND THE FOREST.
...
SKRIT
I'M SAD THAT WE CAN'T MEET.
SO I SHOULD GIVE THIS TO EREN?
YES.

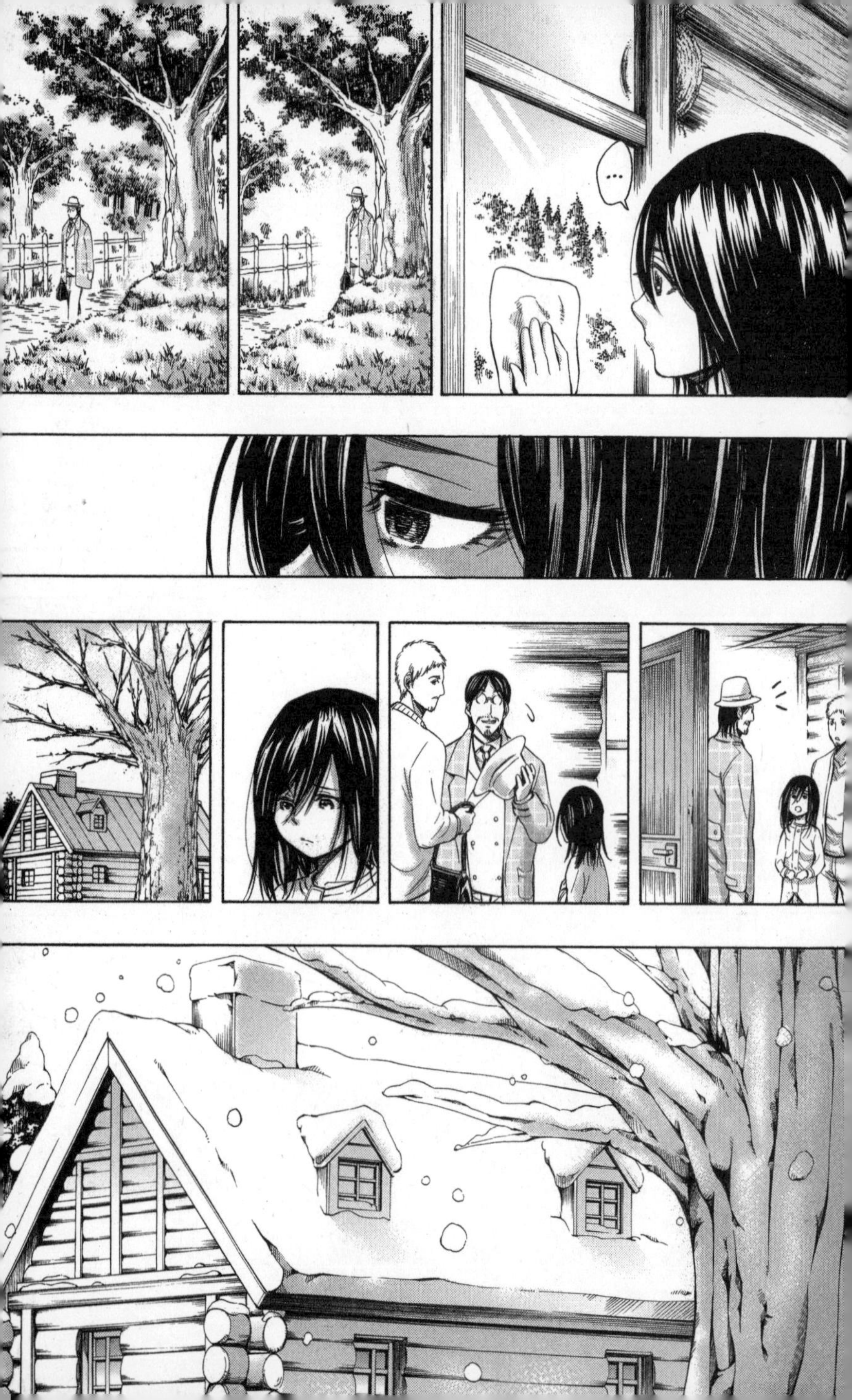
...

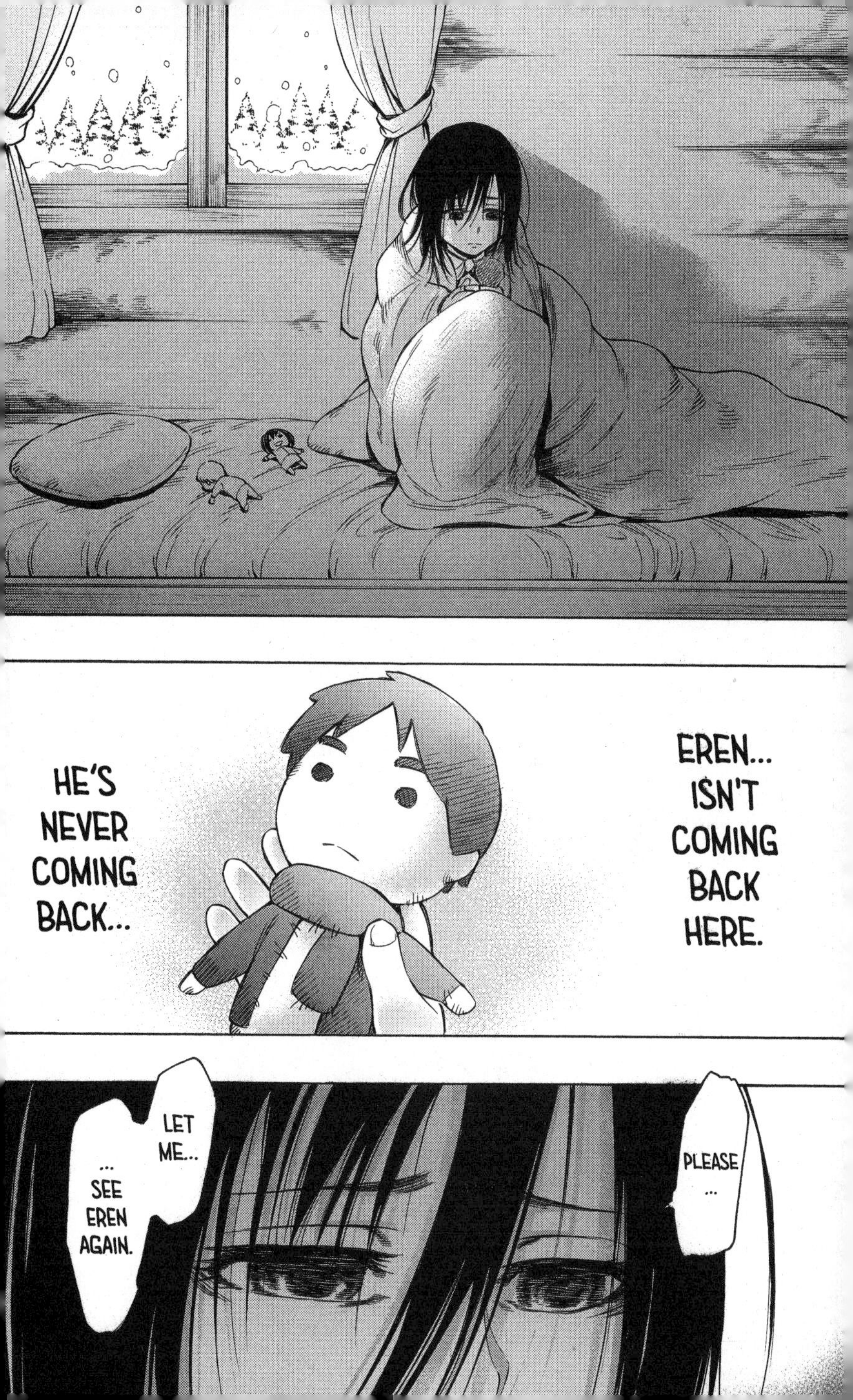
EREN... ISN'T COMING BACK HERE.
HE'S NEVER COMING BACK...
PLEASE ...
LET ME...
... SEE EREN AGAIN.

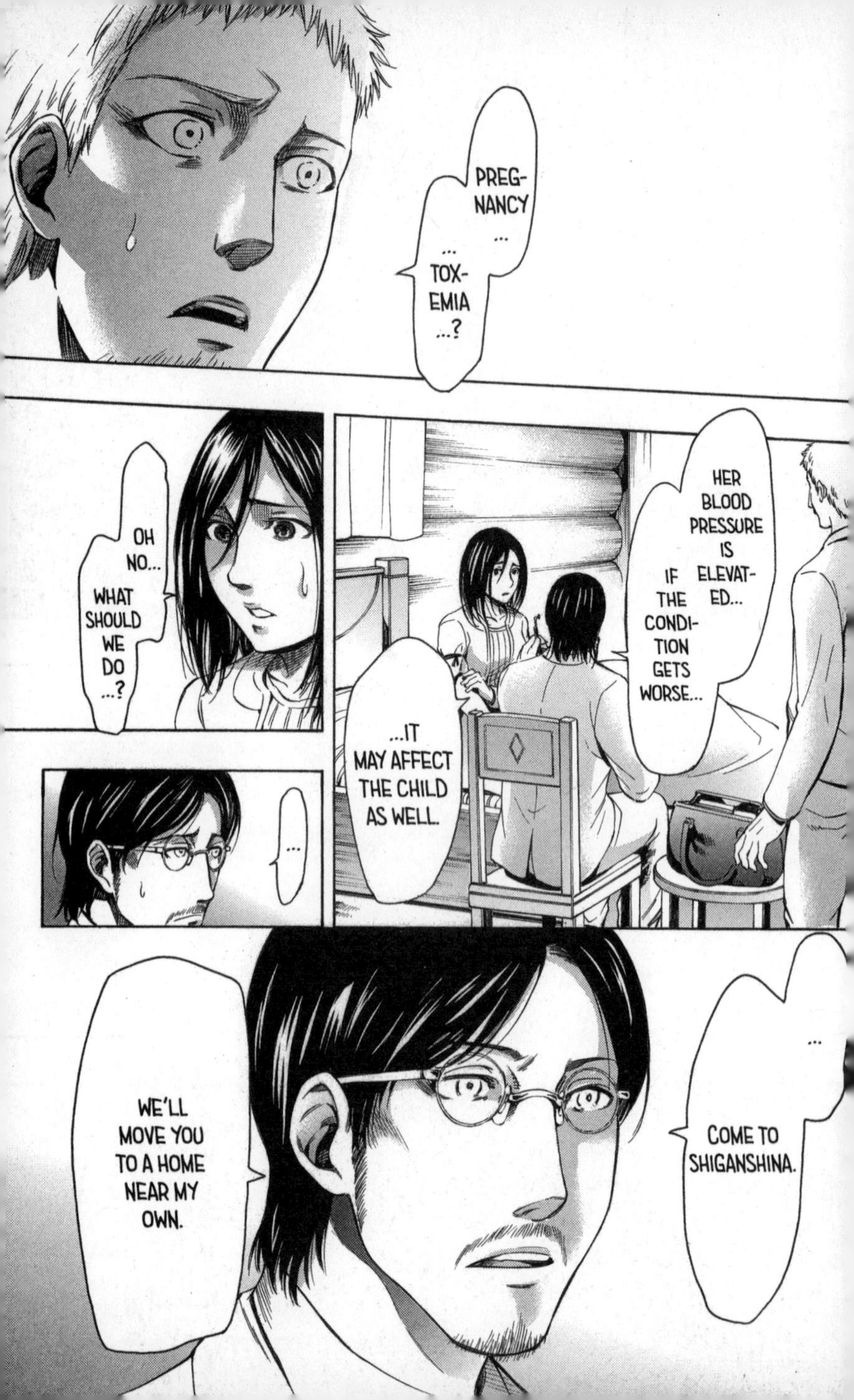
PREGNANCY ...
... TOXEMIA ...?
HER BLOOD PRESSURE IS ELEVATED...
IF THE CONDITION GETS WORSE...
...IT MAY AFFECT THE CHILD AS WELL.
OH NO... WHAT SHOULD WE DO ...?
...
...
COME TO SHIGANSHINA.
WE'LL MOVE YOU TO A HOME NEAR MY OWN.

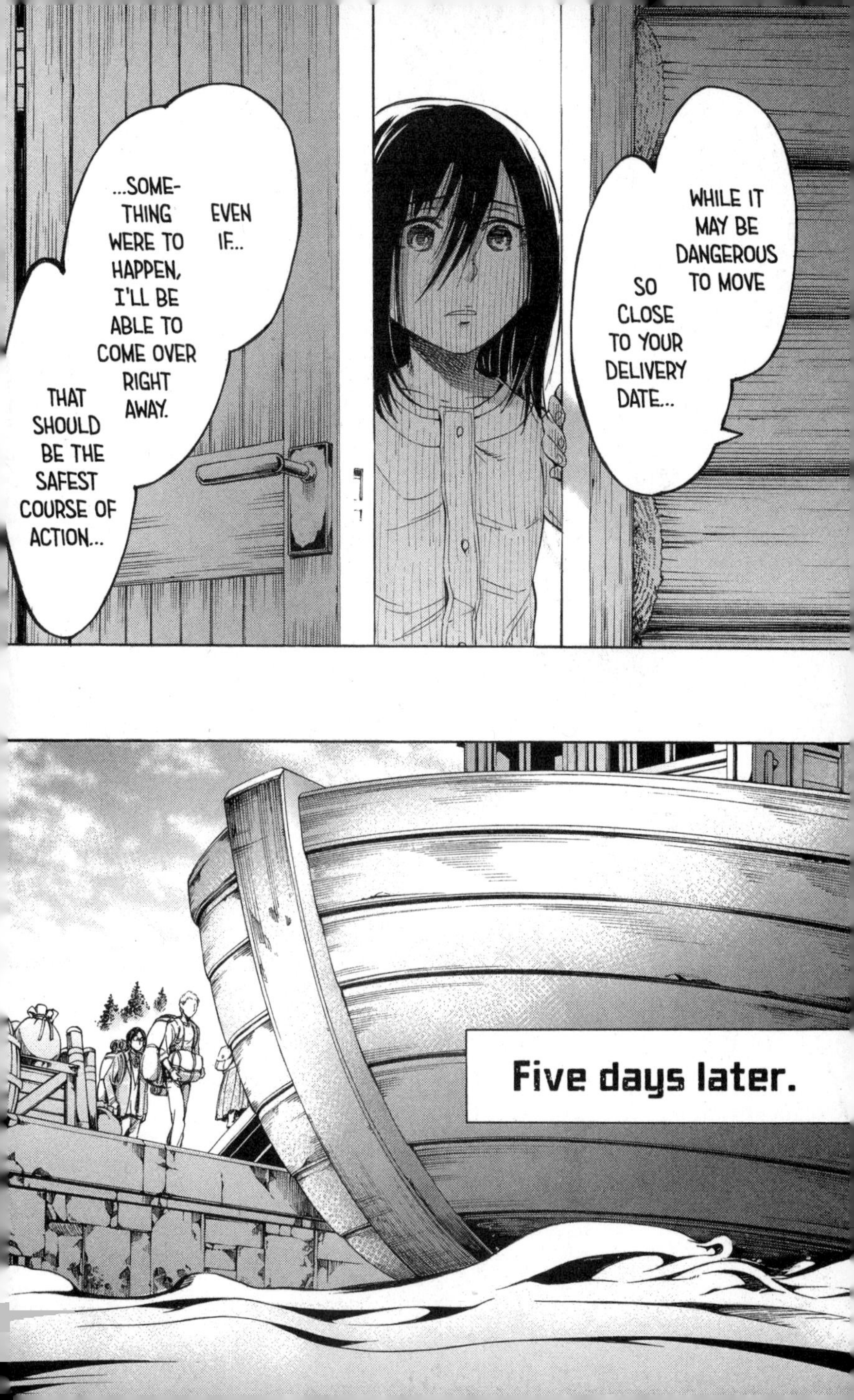
WHILE IT MAY BE DANGEROUS TO MOVE
SO CLOSE TO YOUR DELIVERY DATE...
EVEN IF...
...SOME-THING WERE TO HAPPEN, I'LL BE ABLE TO COME OVER RIGHT AWAY.
THAT SHOULD BE THE SAFEST COURSE OF ACTION...
Five days later.

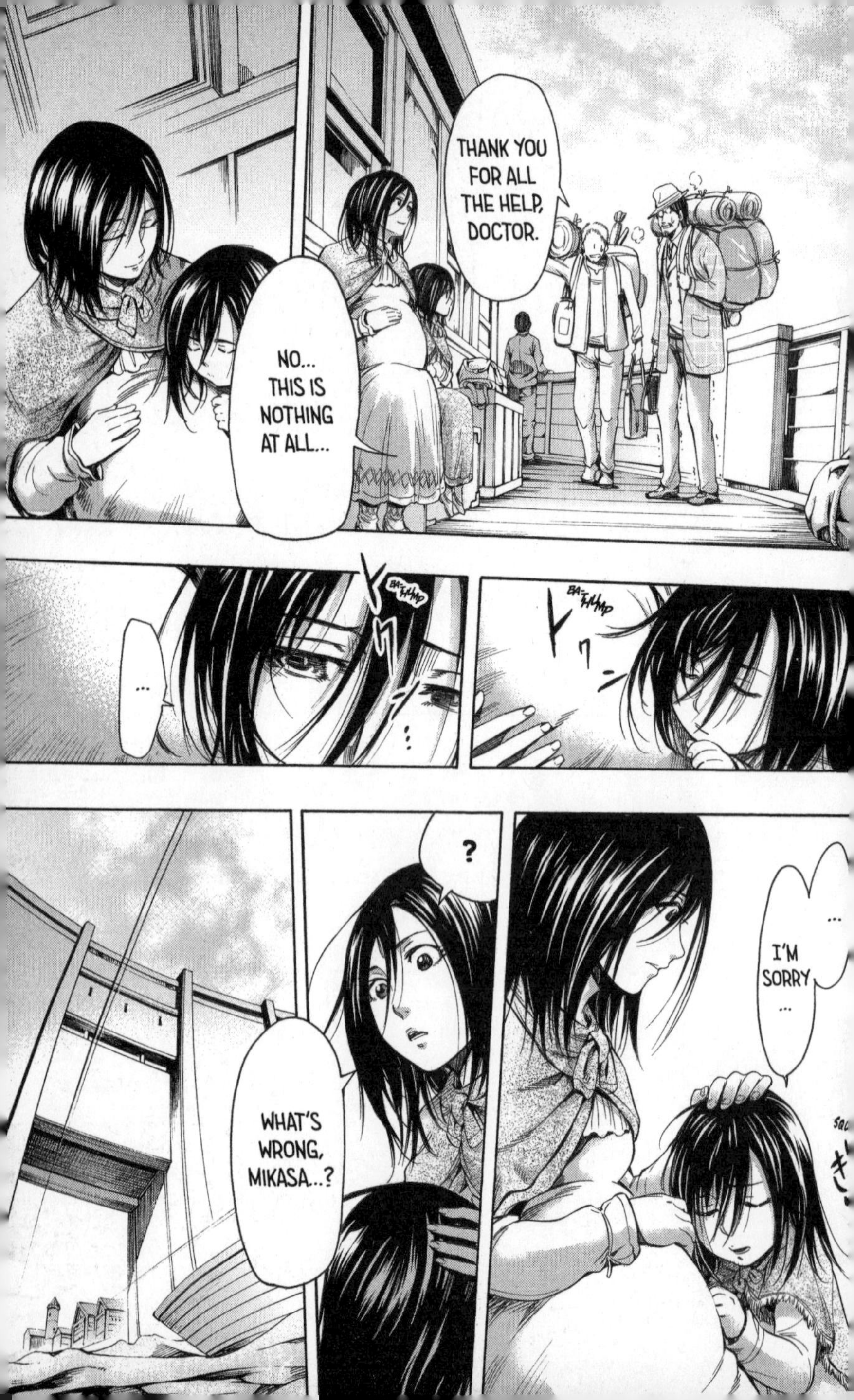
THANK YOU FOR ALL THE HELP, DOCTOR.
NO... THIS IS NOTHING AT ALL...
BA-THUMP
BA-THUMP
...
...
I'M SORRY ...
?
WHAT'S WRONG, MIKASA...?

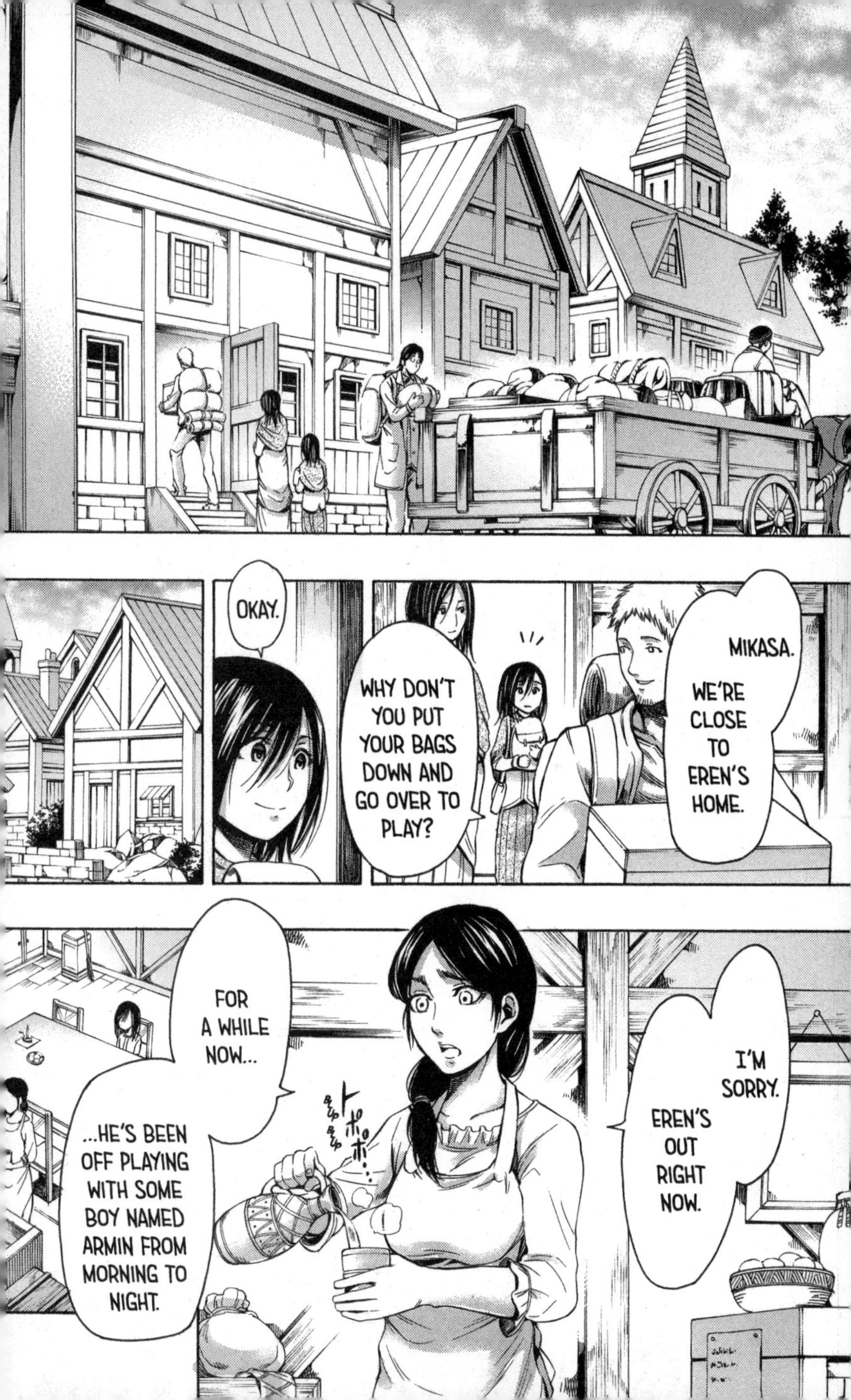
MIKASA.
WE'RE CLOSE TO EREN'S HOME.
WHY DON'T YOU PUT YOUR BAGS DOWN AND GO OVER TO PLAY?
OKAY.
I'M SORRY.
EREN'S OUT RIGHT NOW.
FOR A WHILE NOW...
BLUP BLUP
...HE'S BEEN OFF PLAYING WITH SOME BOY NAMED ARMIN FROM MORNING TO NIGHT.

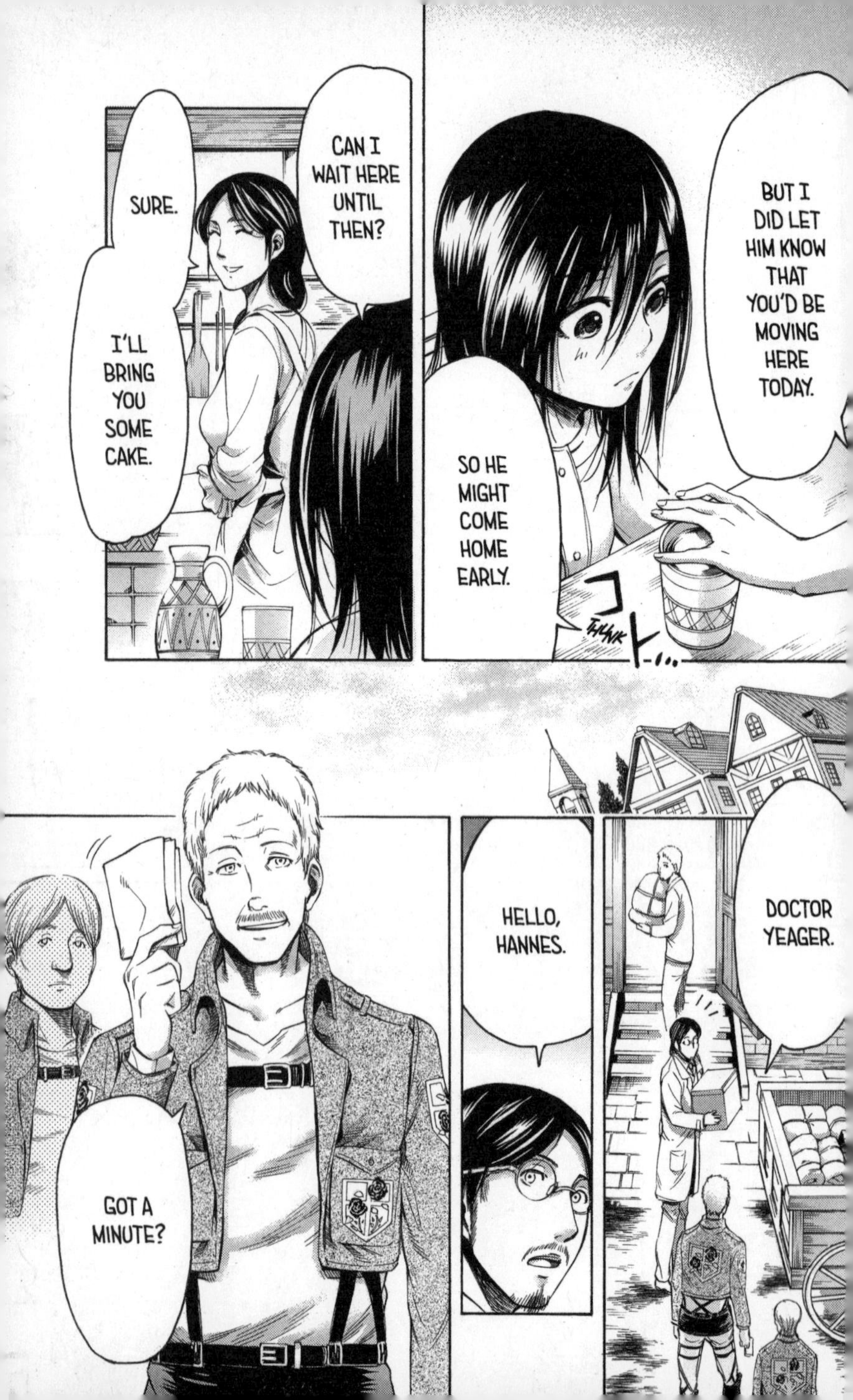
BUT I DID LET HIM KNOW THAT YOU'D BE MOVING HERE TODAY.
SO HE MIGHT COME HOME EARLY.
THUNK
CAN I WAIT HERE UNTIL THEN?
SURE.
I'LL BRING YOU SOME CAKE.
DOCTOR YEAGER.
HELLO, HANNES.
GOT A MINUTE?

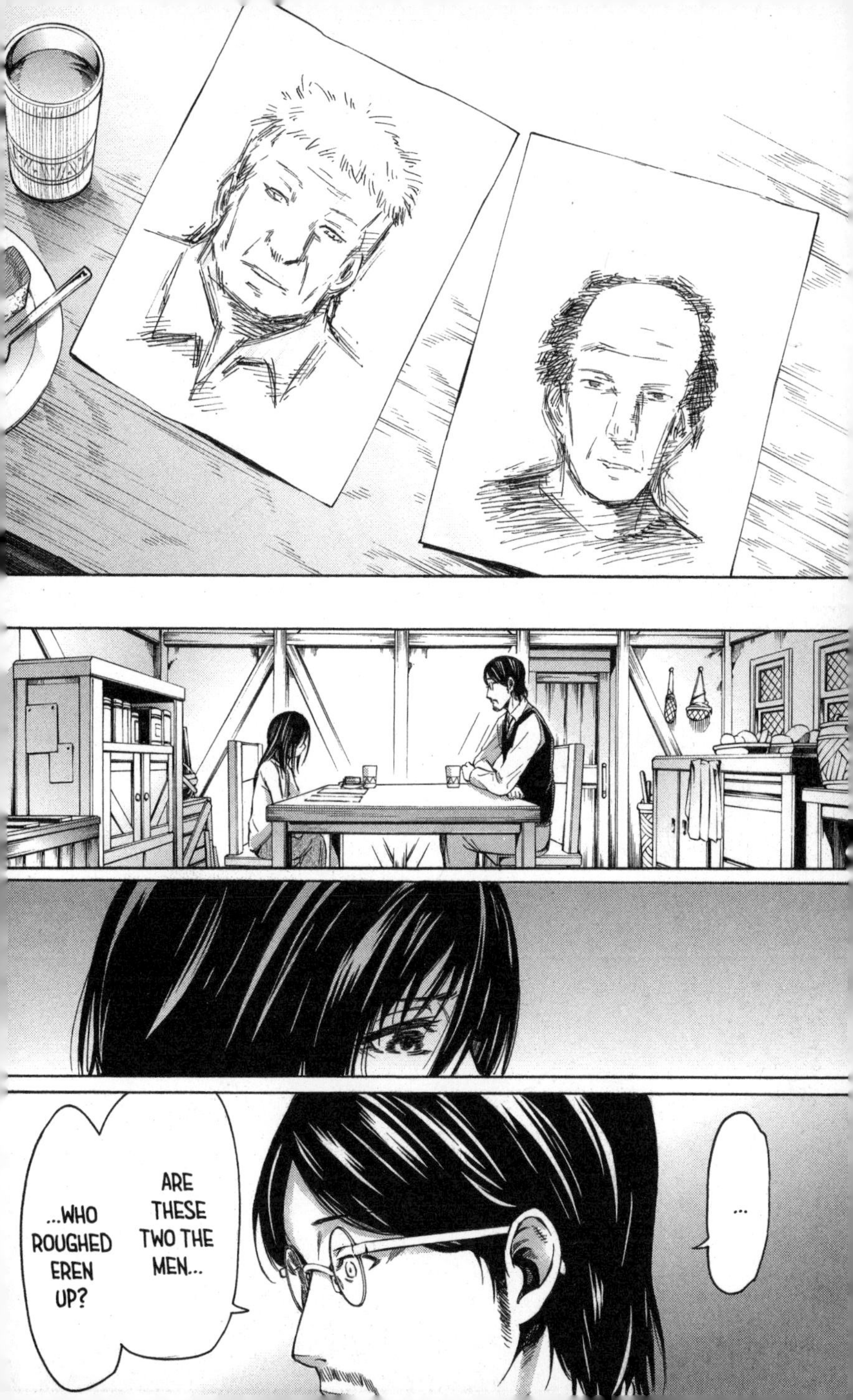
...
ARE THESE TWO THE MEN...
...WHO ROUGHED EREN UP?

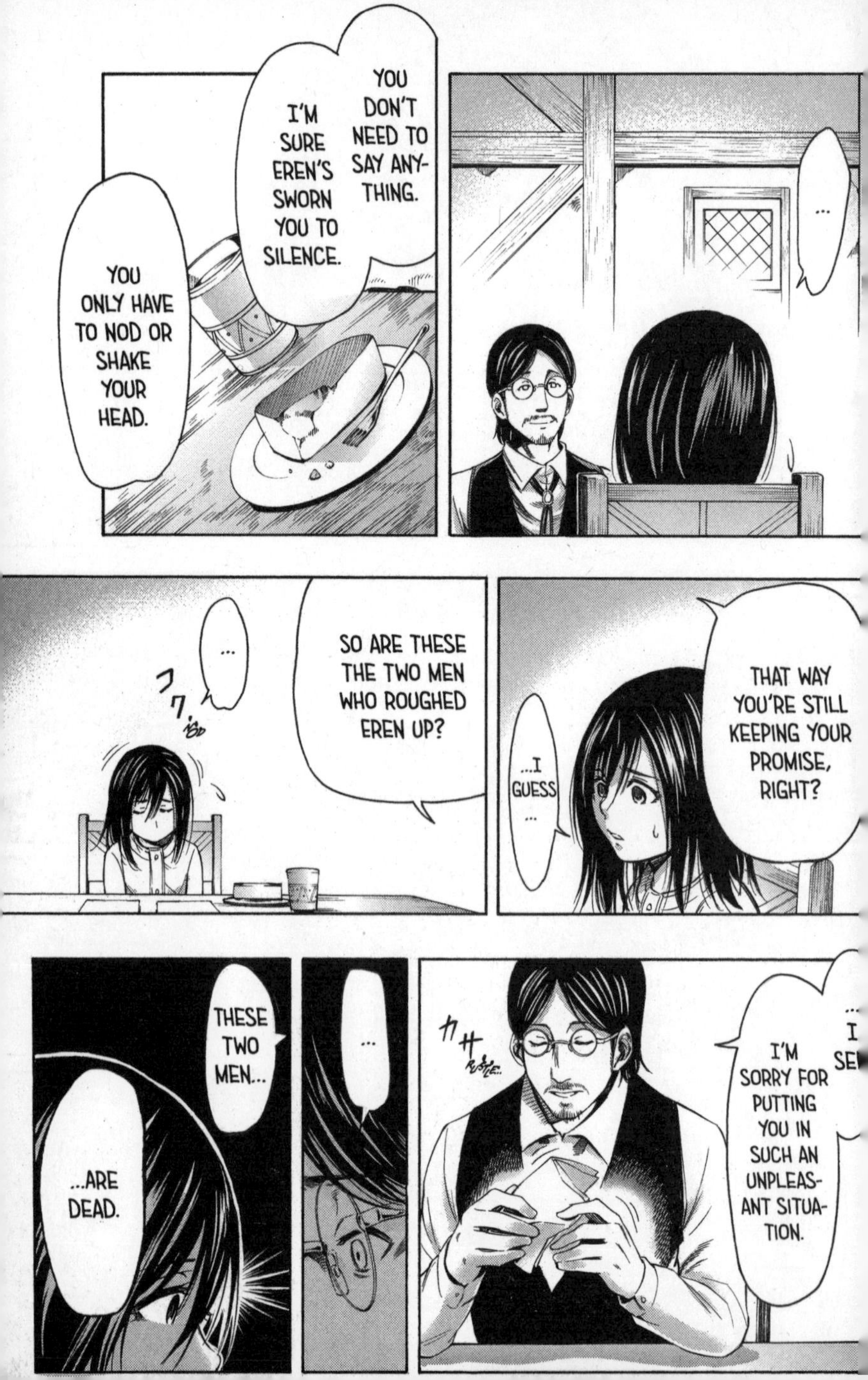
...
YOU DON'T NEED TO SAY ANYTHING.
I'M SURE EREN'S SWORN YOU TO SILENCE.
YOU ONLY HAVE TO NOD OR SHAKE YOUR HEAD.
THAT WAY YOU'RE STILL KEEPING YOUR PROMISE, RIGHT?
...I GUESS...
SO ARE THESE THE TWO MEN WHO ROUGHED EREN UP?
...
... I SE
I'M SORRY FOR PUTTING YOU IN SUCH AN UNPLEASANT SITUATION.
カサ
RUSTLE
...
THESE TWO MEN...
...ARE DEAD.

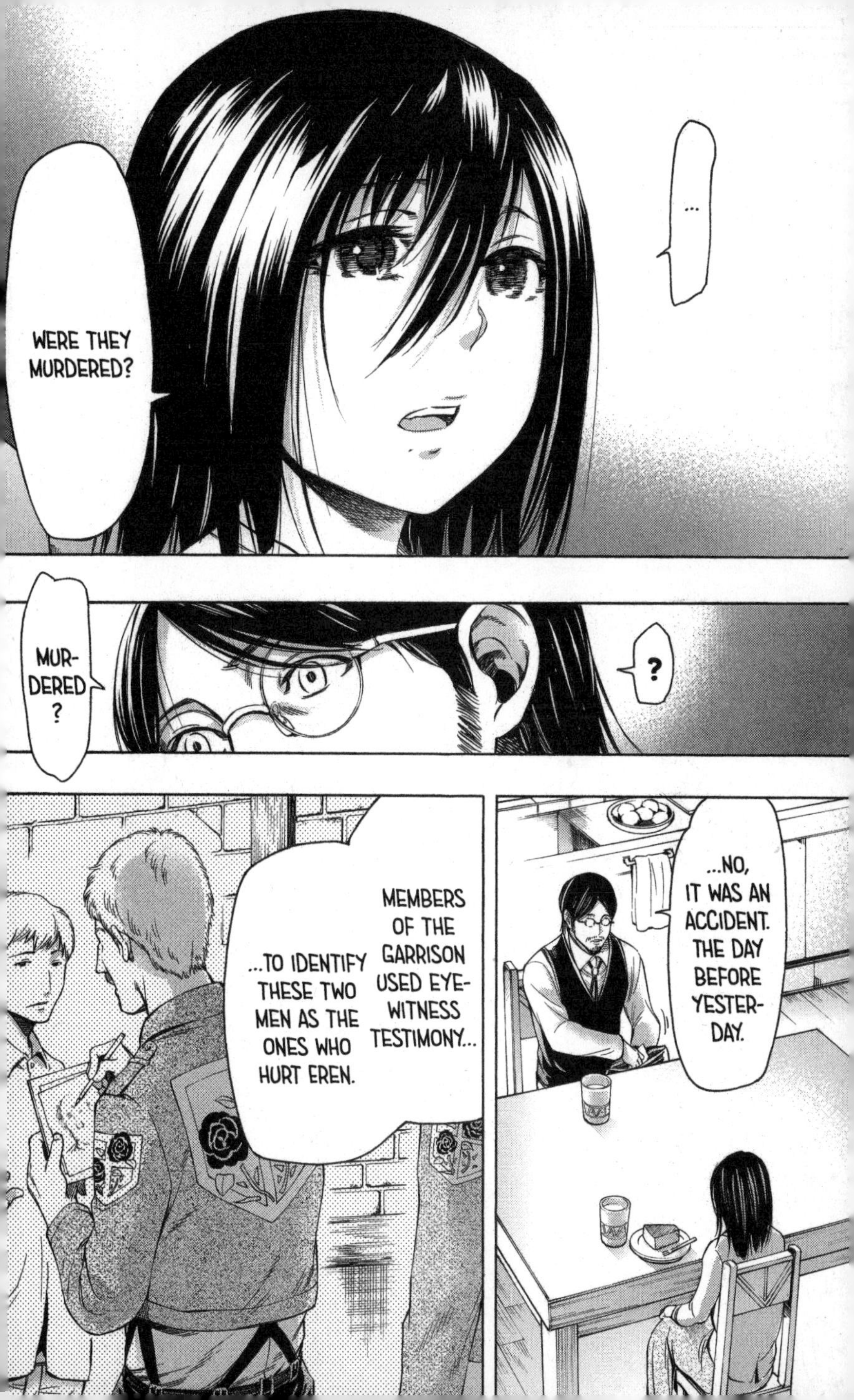
...
WERE THEY MURDERED?
?
MUR-DERED?
...NO, IT WAS AN ACCIDENT. THE DAY BEFORE YESTER-DAY.
MEMBERS OF THE GARRISON USED EYE-WITNESS TESTIMONY...
...TO IDENTIFY THESE TWO MEN AS THE ONES WHO HURT EREN.

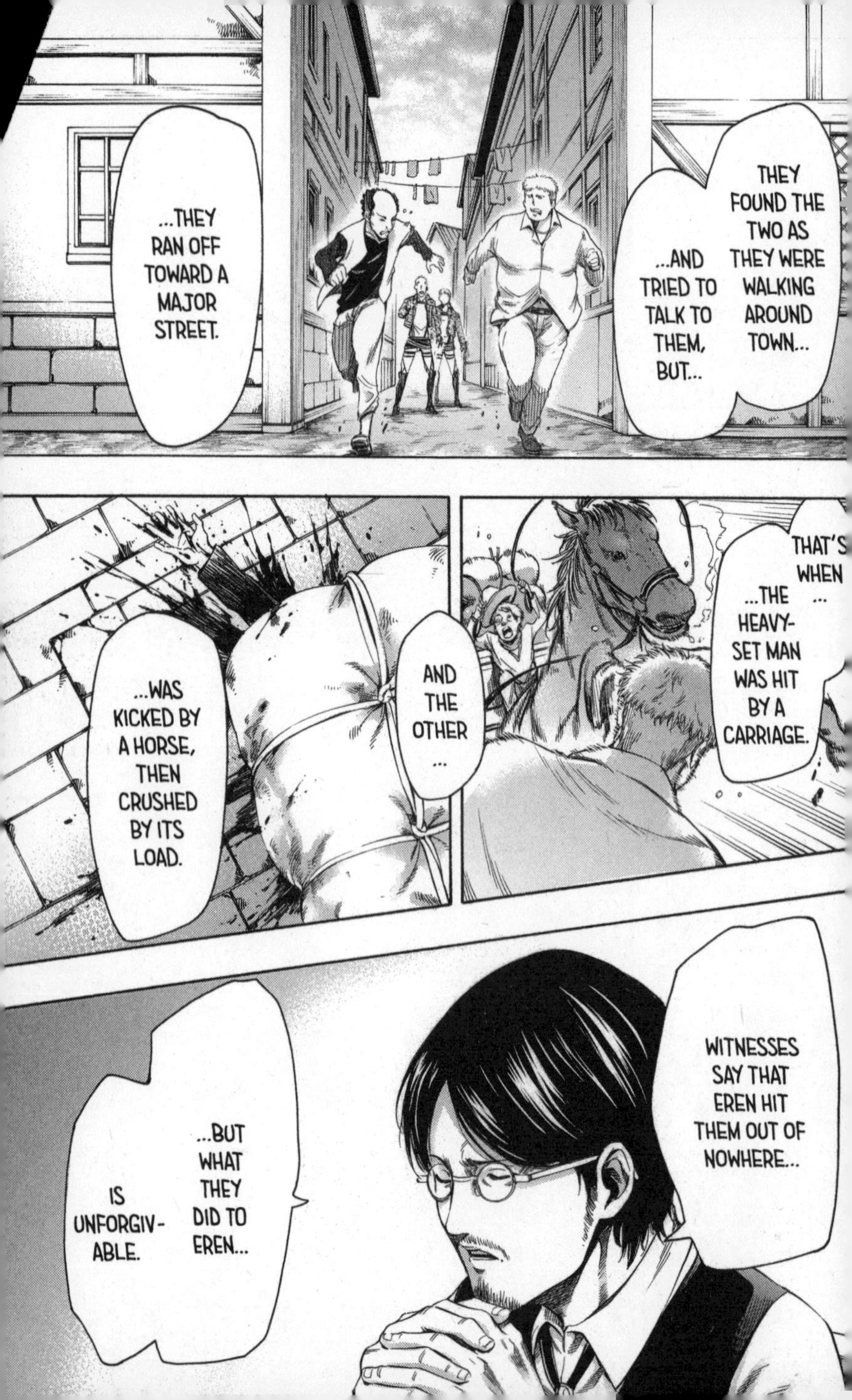
THEY FOUND THE TWO AS THEY WERE WALKING AROUND TOWN...
...AND TRIED TO TALK TO THEM, BUT...
...THEY RAN OFF TOWARD A MAJOR STREET.
THAT'S WHEN ...
...THE HEAVY-SET MAN WAS HIT BY A CARRIAGE.
AND THE OTHER ...
...WAS KICKED BY A HORSE, THEN CRUSHED BY ITS LOAD.
WITNESSES SAY THAT EREN HIT THEM OUT OF NOWHERE...
...BUT WHAT THEY DID TO EREN...
IS UNFORGIV-ABLE.

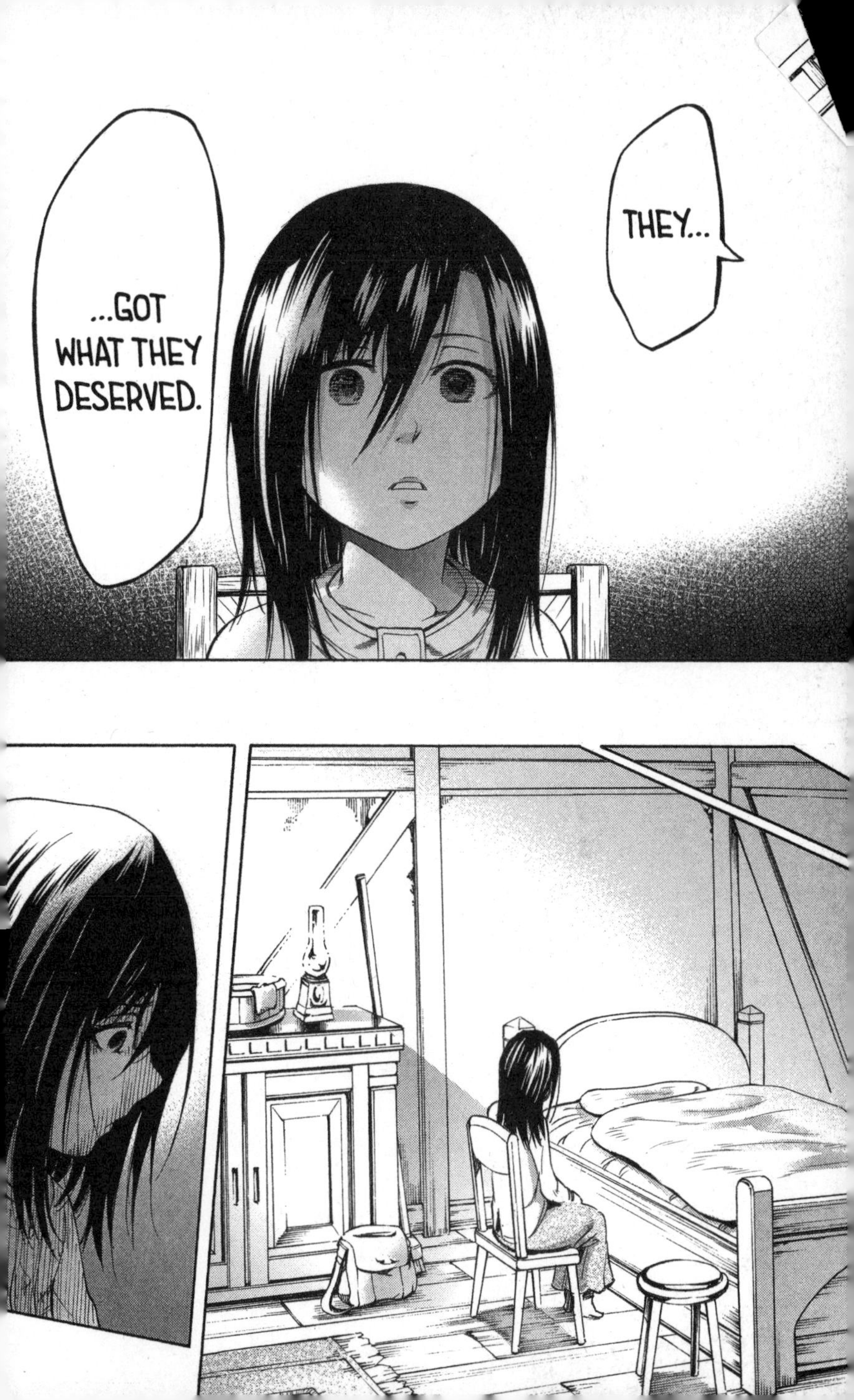
THEY...
...GOT WHAT THEY DESERVED.

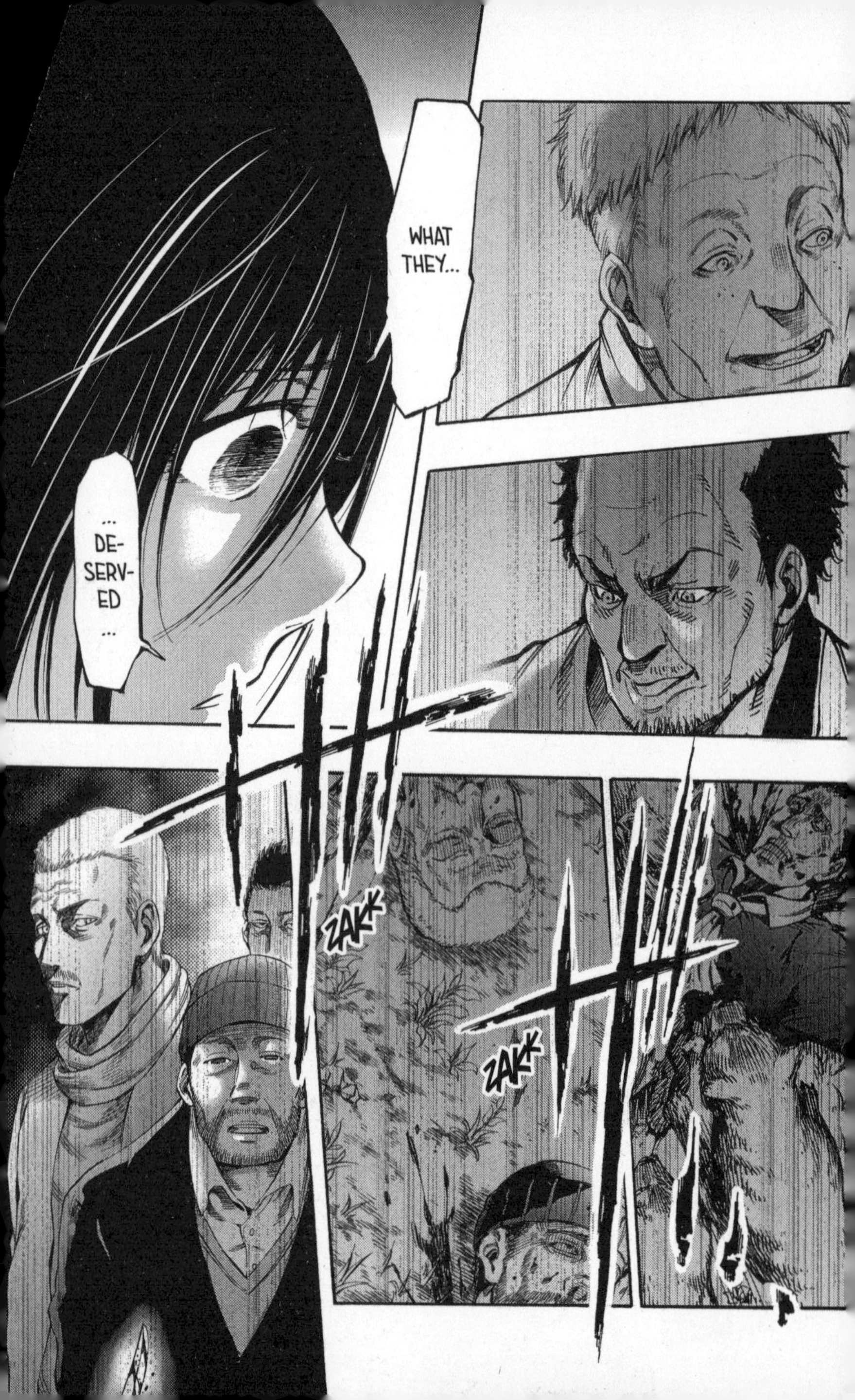
WHAT THEY...
... DE-SERV-ED ...
ZAKK
ZAKK

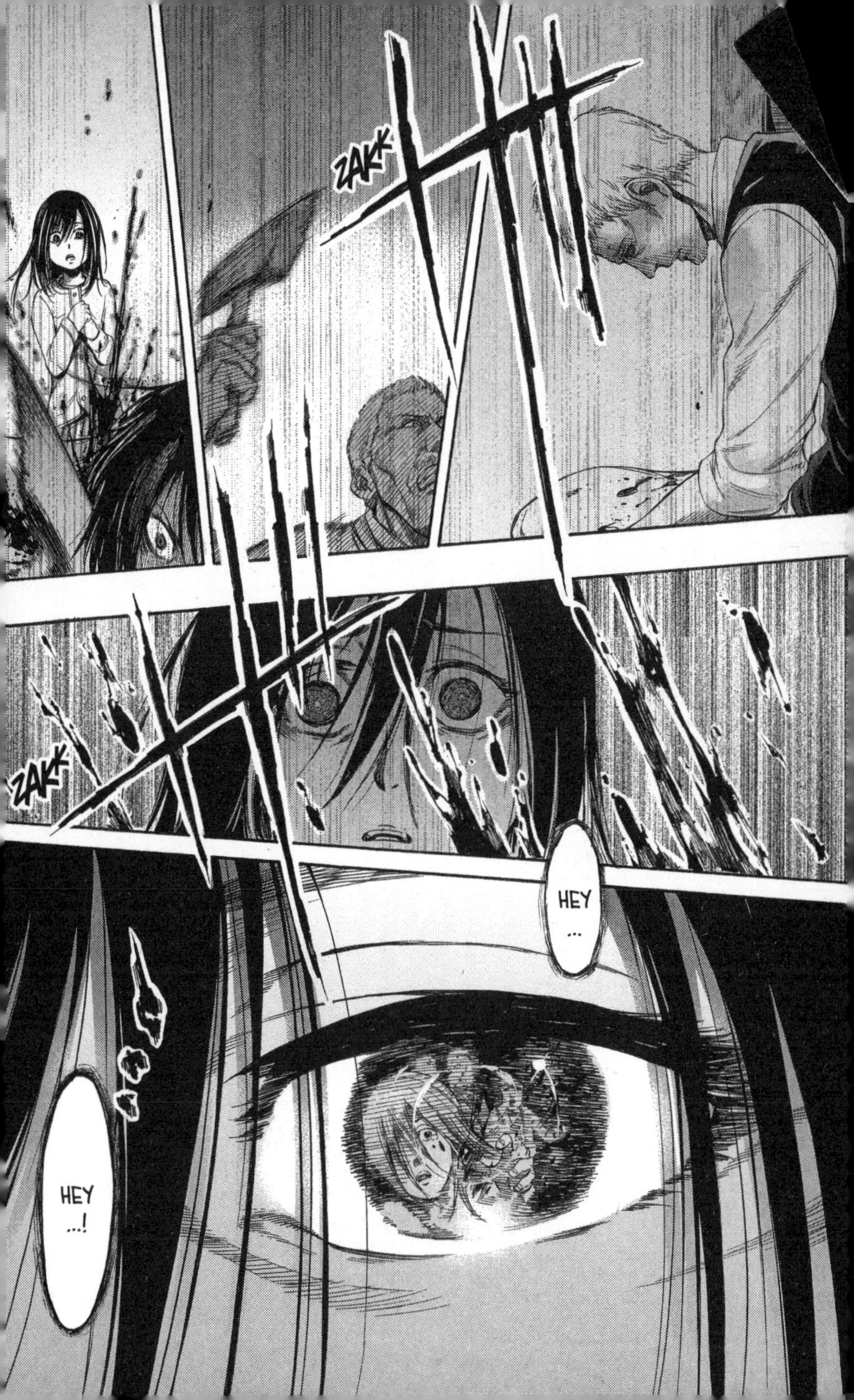
ZAKK
ZAKK
HEY ...
HEY ...!

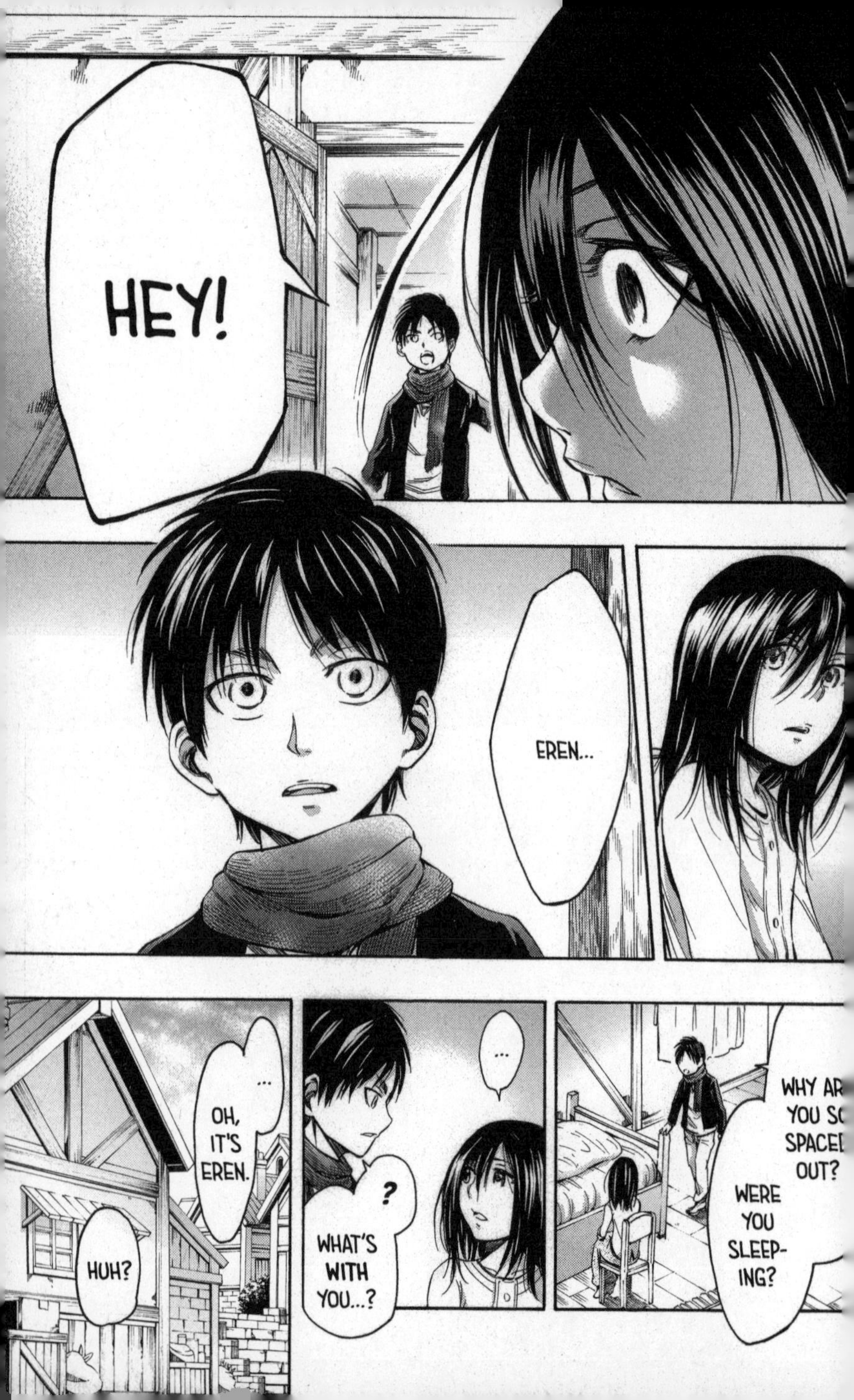
HEY!
EREN...
WHY AR YOU SO SPACED OUT?
WERE YOU SLEEPING?
...
?
WHAT'S WITH YOU...?
...
OH, IT'S EREN.
HUH?

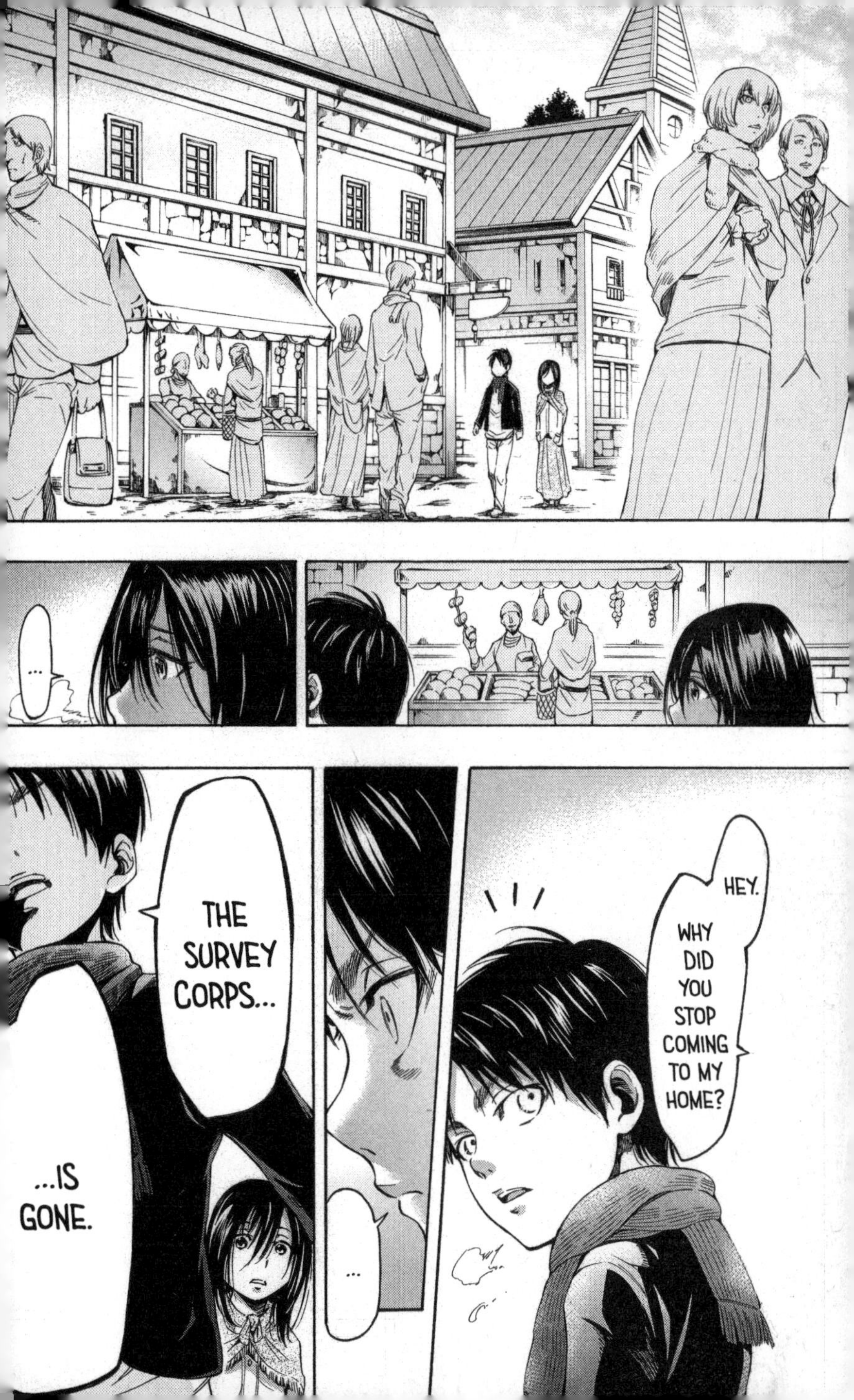
...
HEY.
WHY DID YOU STOP COMING TO MY HOME?
...
THE SURVEY CORPS...
...IS GONE.

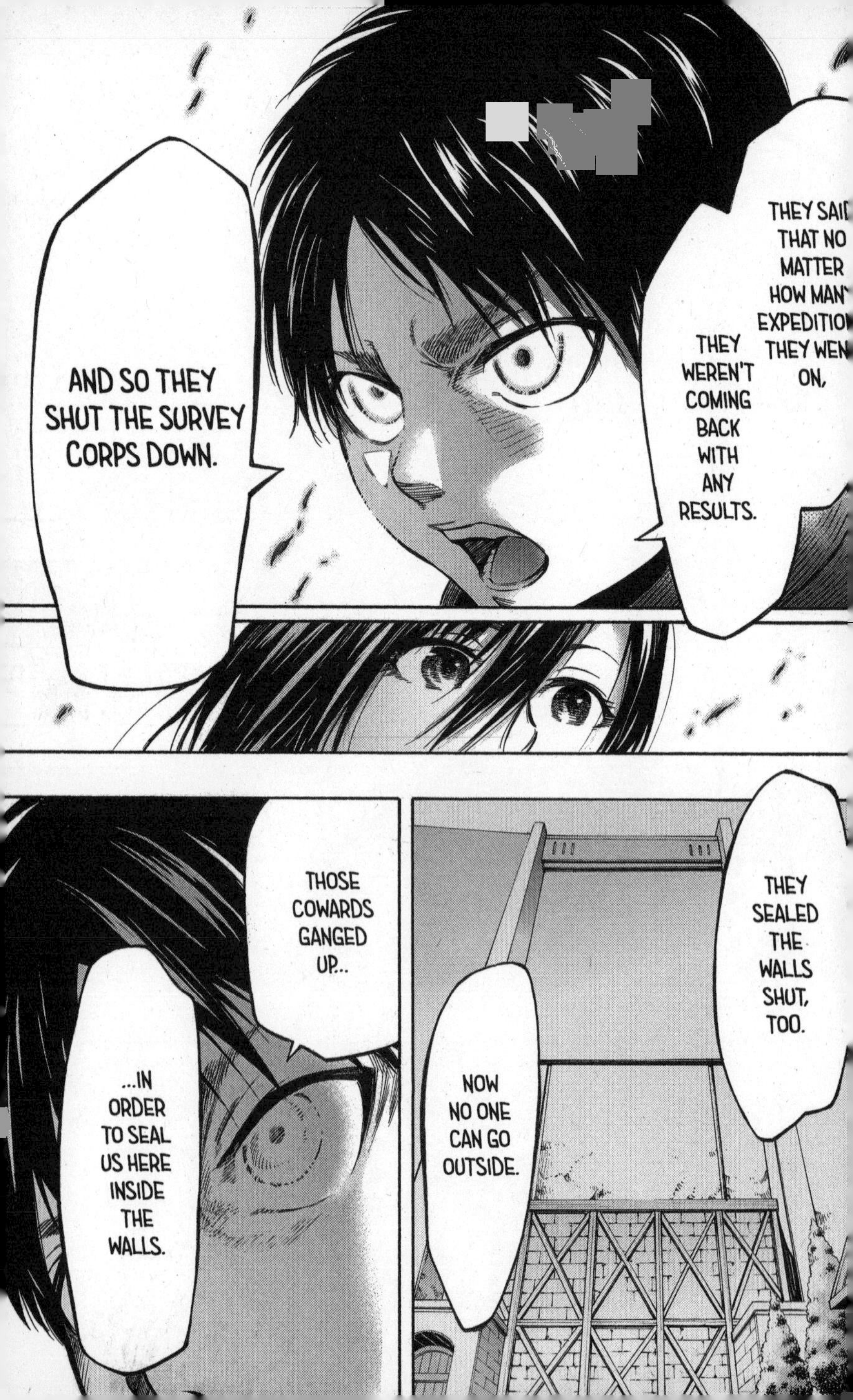
THEY SAI THAT NO MATTER HOW MAN EXPEDITIO THEY WEN ON,
THEY WEREN'T COMING BACK WITH ANY RESULTS.
AND SO THEY SHUT THE SURVEY CORPS DOWN.
THEY SEALED THE WALLS SHUT, TOO.
NOW NO ONE CAN GO OUTSIDE.
THOSE COWARDS GANGED UP...
...IN ORDER TO SEAL US HERE INSIDE THE WALLS.

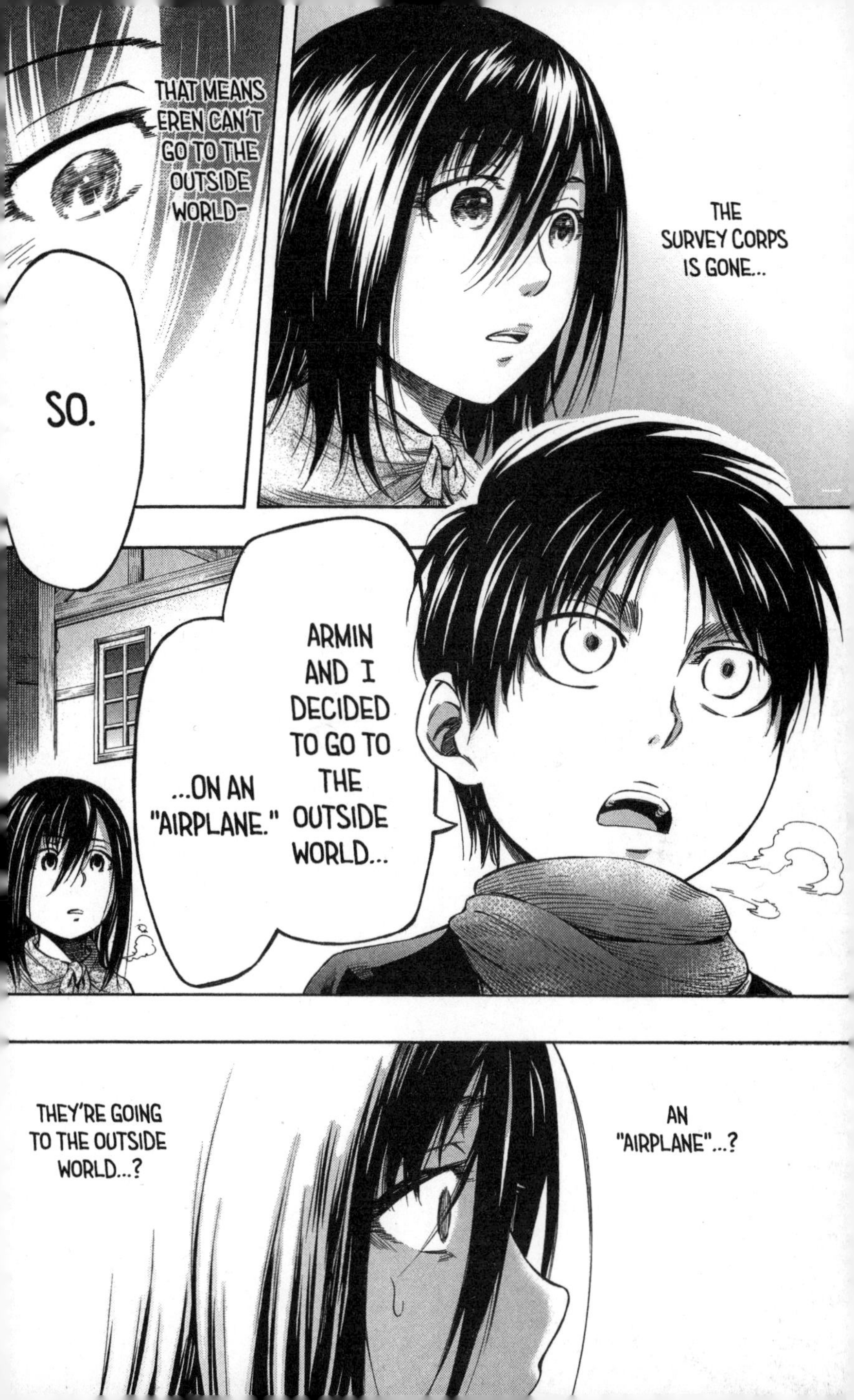
THE SURVEY CORPS IS GONE...
THAT MEANS EREN CAN'T GO TO THE OUTSIDE WORLD-
SO.
ARMIN AND I DECIDED TO GO TO THE OUTSIDE WORLD...
...ON AN "AIRPLANE."
AN "AIRPLANE"...?
THEY'RE GOING TO THE OUTSIDE WORLD...?

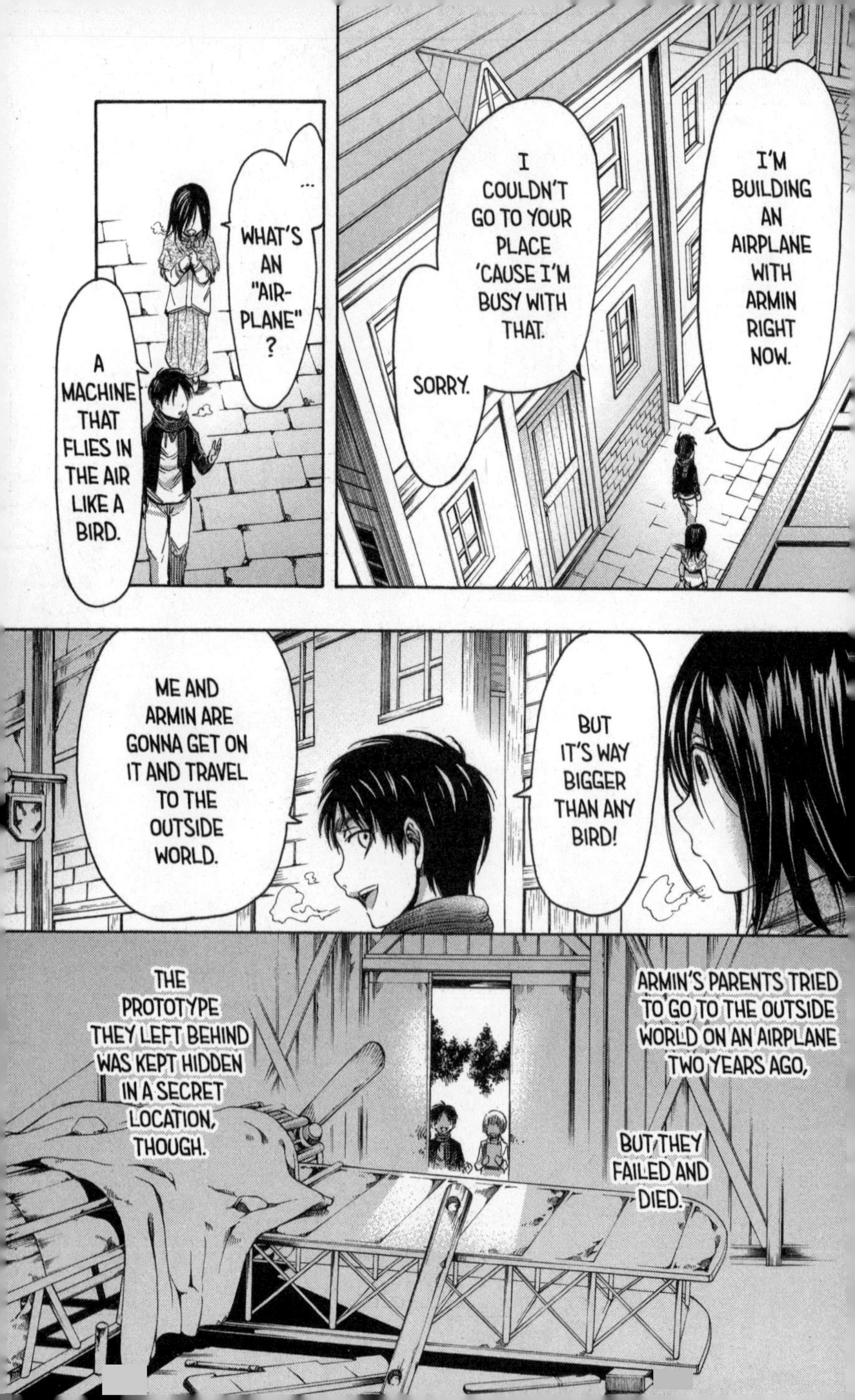
I'M BUILDING AN AIRPLANE WITH ARMIN RIGHT NOW.
I COULDN'T GO TO YOUR PLACE 'CAUSE I'M BUSY WITH THAT.
SORRY.
...
WHAT'S AN "AIR-PLANE"?
A MACHINE THAT FLIES IN THE AIR LIKE A BIRD.
BUT IT'S WAY BIGGER THAN ANY BIRD!
ME AND ARMIN ARE GONNA GET ON IT AND TRAVEL TO THE OUTSIDE WORLD.
ARMIN'S PARENTS TRIED TO GO TO THE OUTSIDE WORLD ON AN AIRPLANE TWO YEARS AGO,
BUT THEY FAILED AND DIED.
THE PROTOTYPE THEY LEFT BEHIND WAS KEPT HIDDEN IN A SECRET LOCATION, THOUGH.

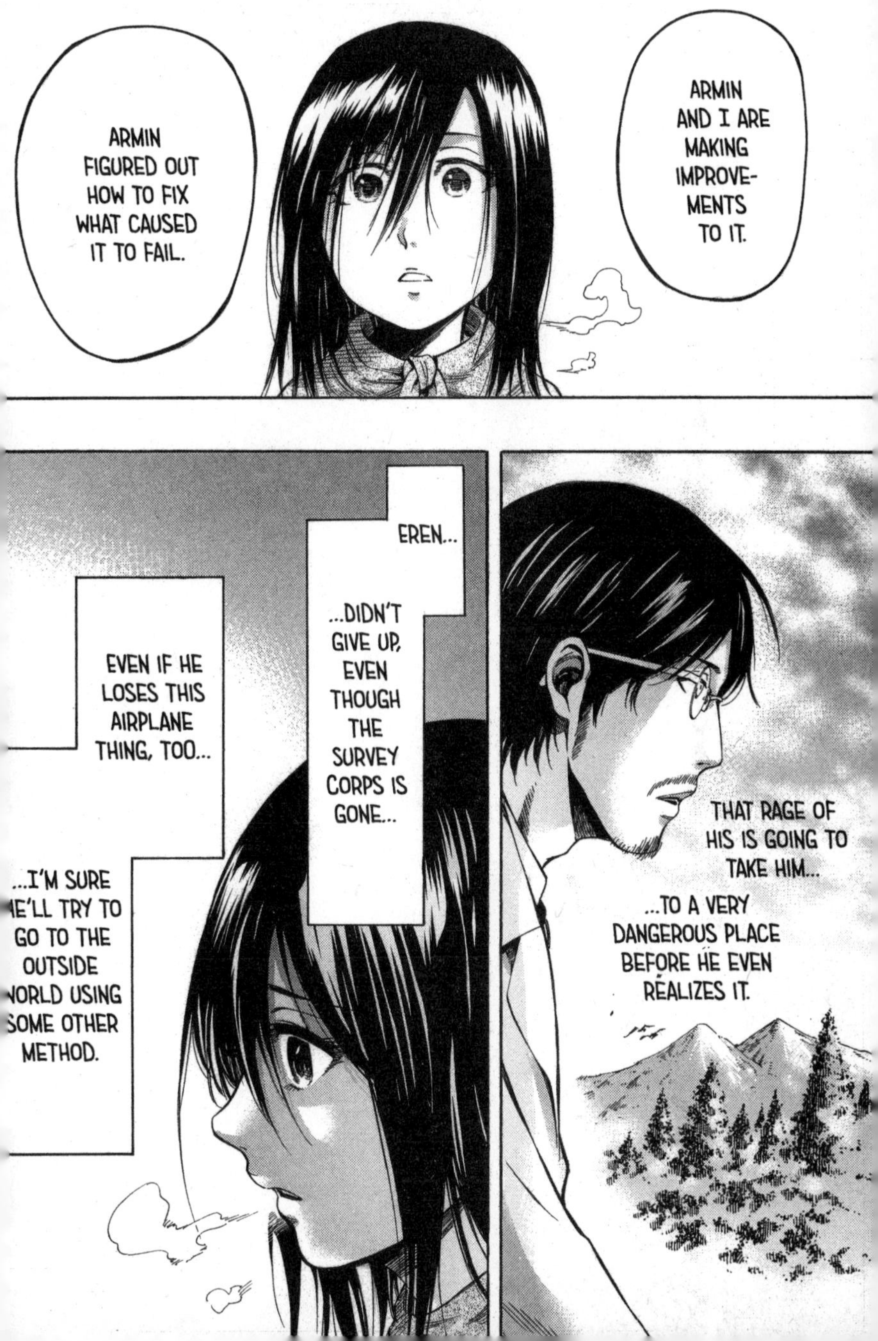

ARMIN AND I ARE MAKING IMPROVEMENTS TO IT.
ARMIN FIGURED OUT HOW TO FIX WHAT CAUSED IT TO FAIL.
THAT RAGE OF HIS IS GOING TO TAKE HIM...
...TO A VERY DANGEROUS PLACE BEFORE HE EVEN REALIZES IT.
EREN...
...DIDN'T GIVE UP, EVEN THOUGH THE SURVEY CORPS IS GONE...
EVEN IF HE LOSES THIS AIRPLANE THING, TOO...
...I'M SURE HE'LL TRY TO GO TO THE OUTSIDE WORLD USING SOME OTHER METHOD.

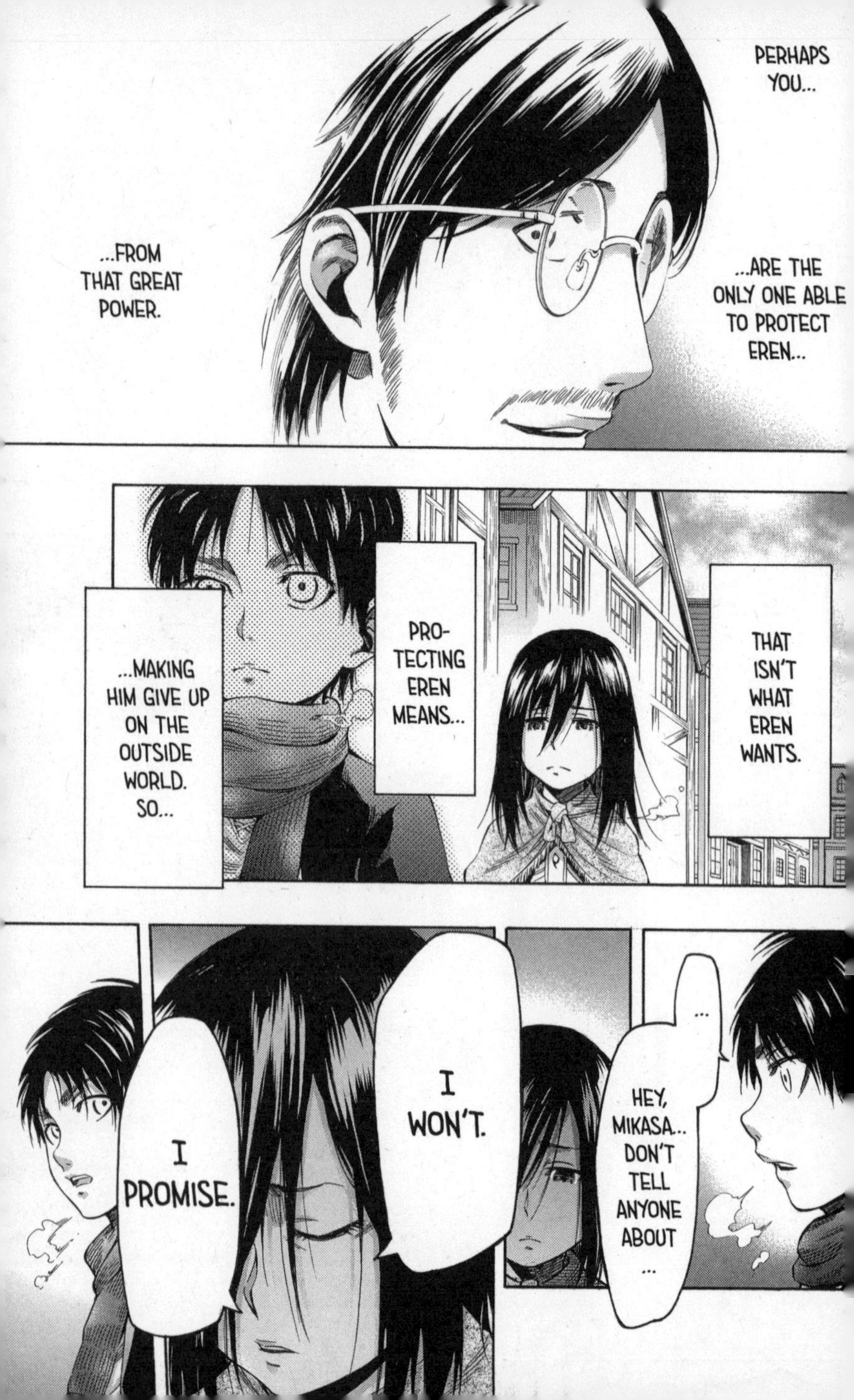
PERHAPS YOU...
...ARE THE ONLY ONE ABLE TO PROTECT EREN...
...FROM THAT GREAT POWER.
THAT ISN'T WHAT EREN WANTS.
PRO-TECTING EREN MEANS...
...MAKING HIM GIVE UP ON THE OUTSIDE WORLD. SO...
...
HEY, MIKASA... DON'T TELL ANYONE ABOUT ...
I WON'T.
I PROMISE.

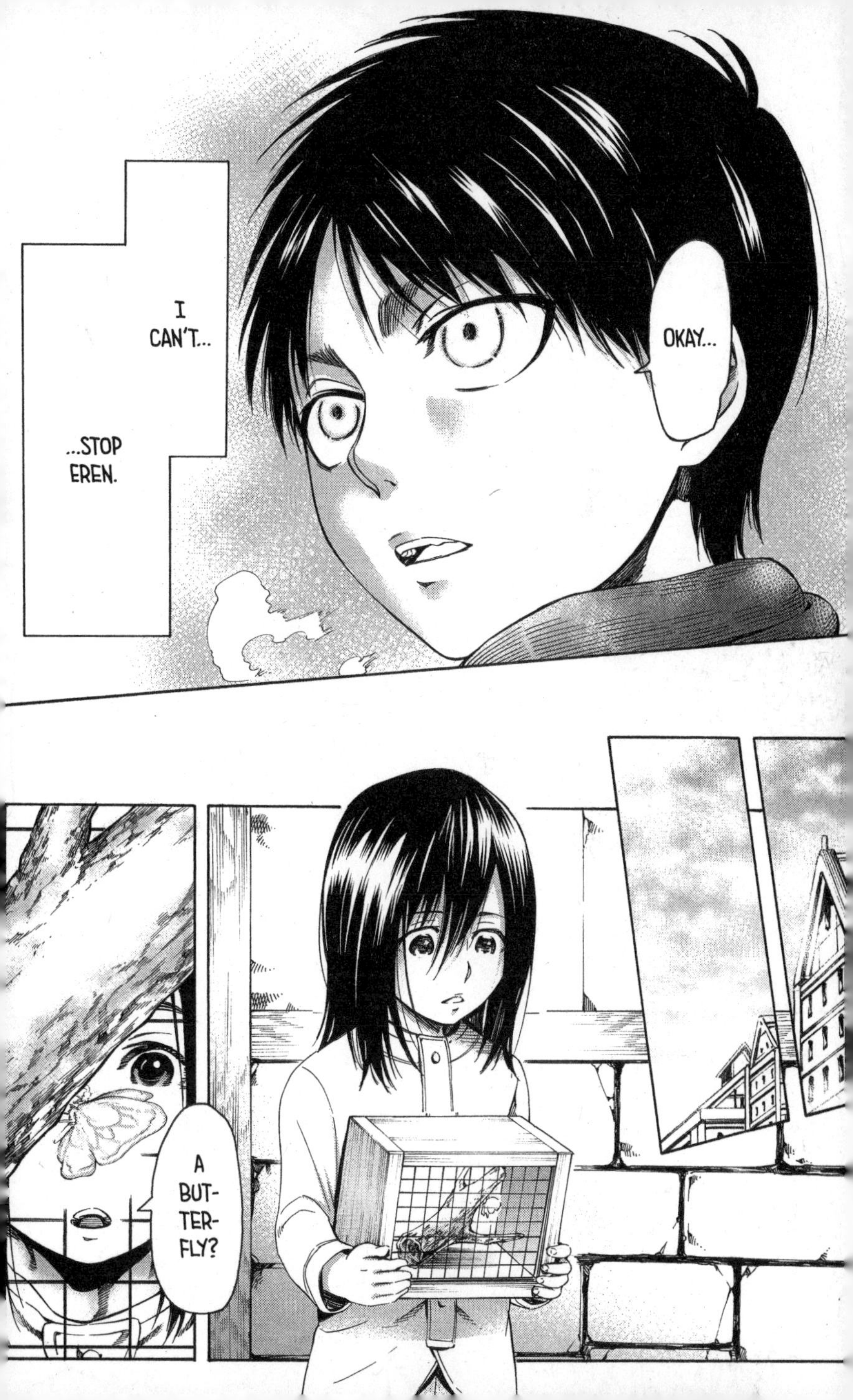
OKAY...
I CAN'T...
...STOP EREN.
A BUT-TER-FLY?

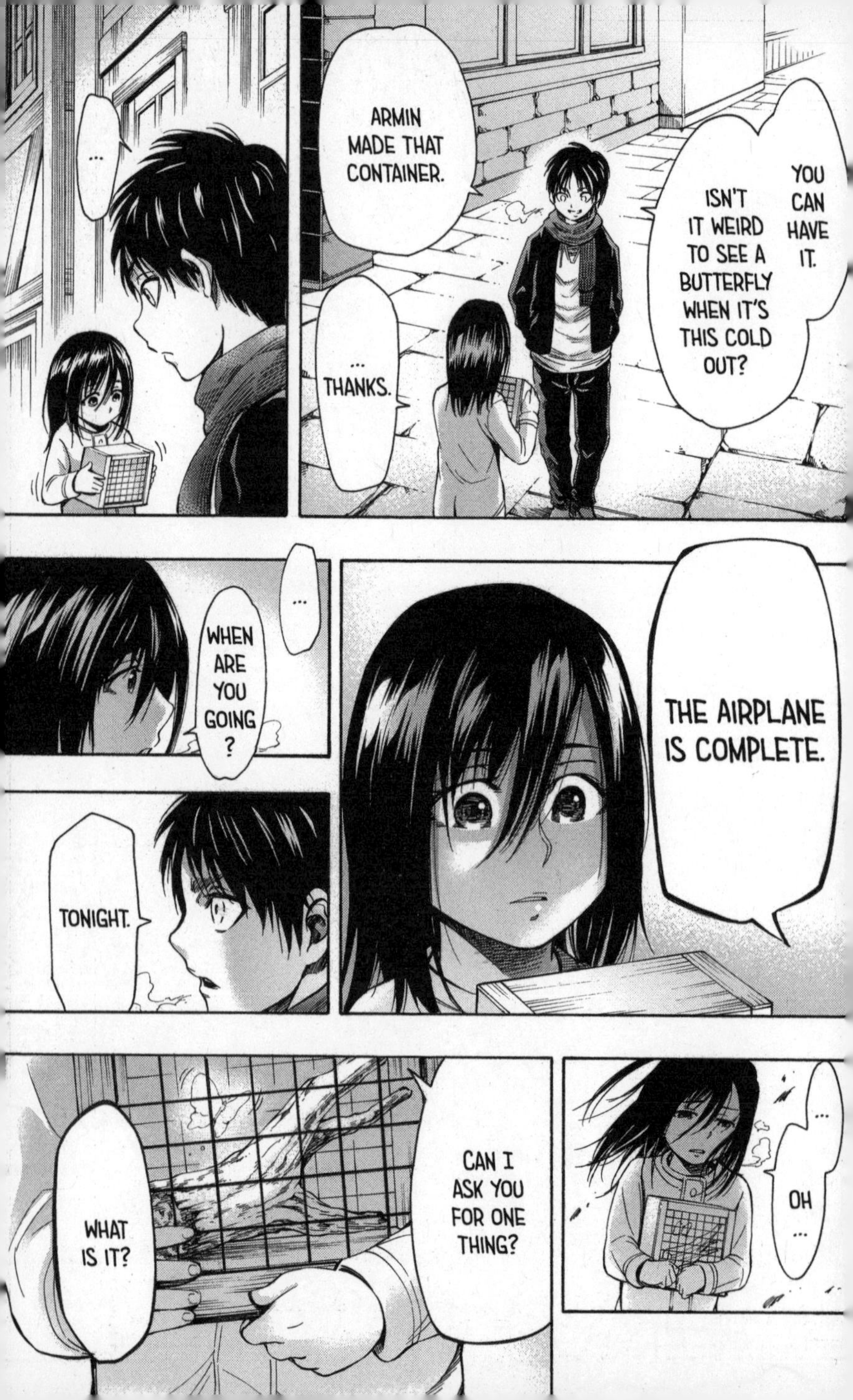
YOU CAN HAVE IT.
ISN'T IT WEIRD TO SEE A BUTTERFLY WHEN IT'S THIS COLD OUT?
ARMIN MADE THAT CONTAINER.
... THANKS.
...
THE AIRPLANE IS COMPLETE.
...
WHEN ARE YOU GOING?
TONIGHT.
...
OH ...
CAN I ASK YOU FOR ONE THING?
WHAT IS IT?

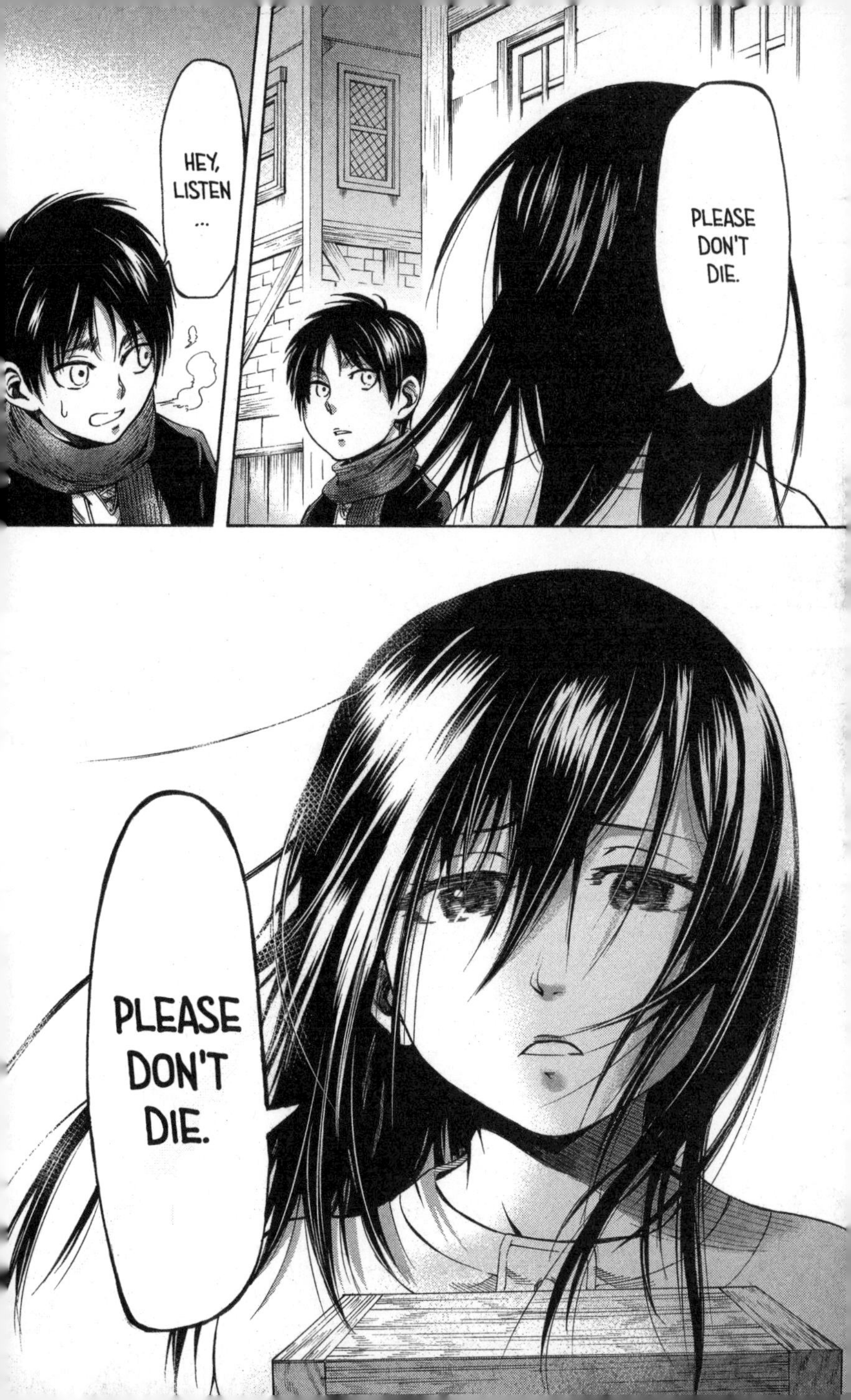
PLEASE DON'T DIE.
HEY, LISTEN ...
PLEASE DON'T DIE.

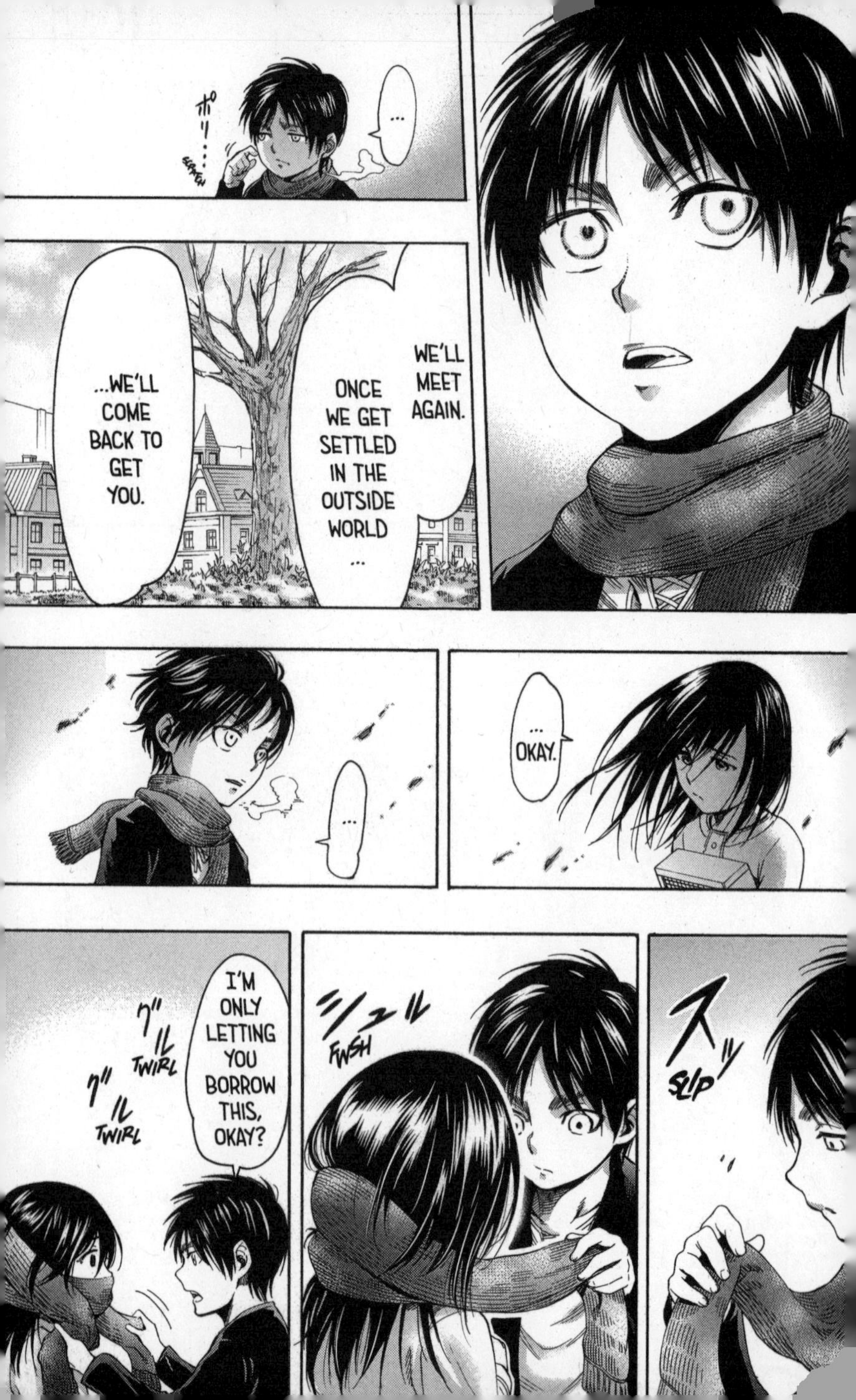

ポリ…
SCRATCH
...
WE'LL MEET AGAIN.
ONCE WE GET SETTLED IN THE OUTSIDE WORLD ...
...WE'LL COME BACK TO GET YOU.
... OKAY.
...
スッ
SLIP
シュル
FWSH
グル
TWIRL
グル
TWIRL
I'M ONLY LETTING YOU BORROW THIS, OKAY?

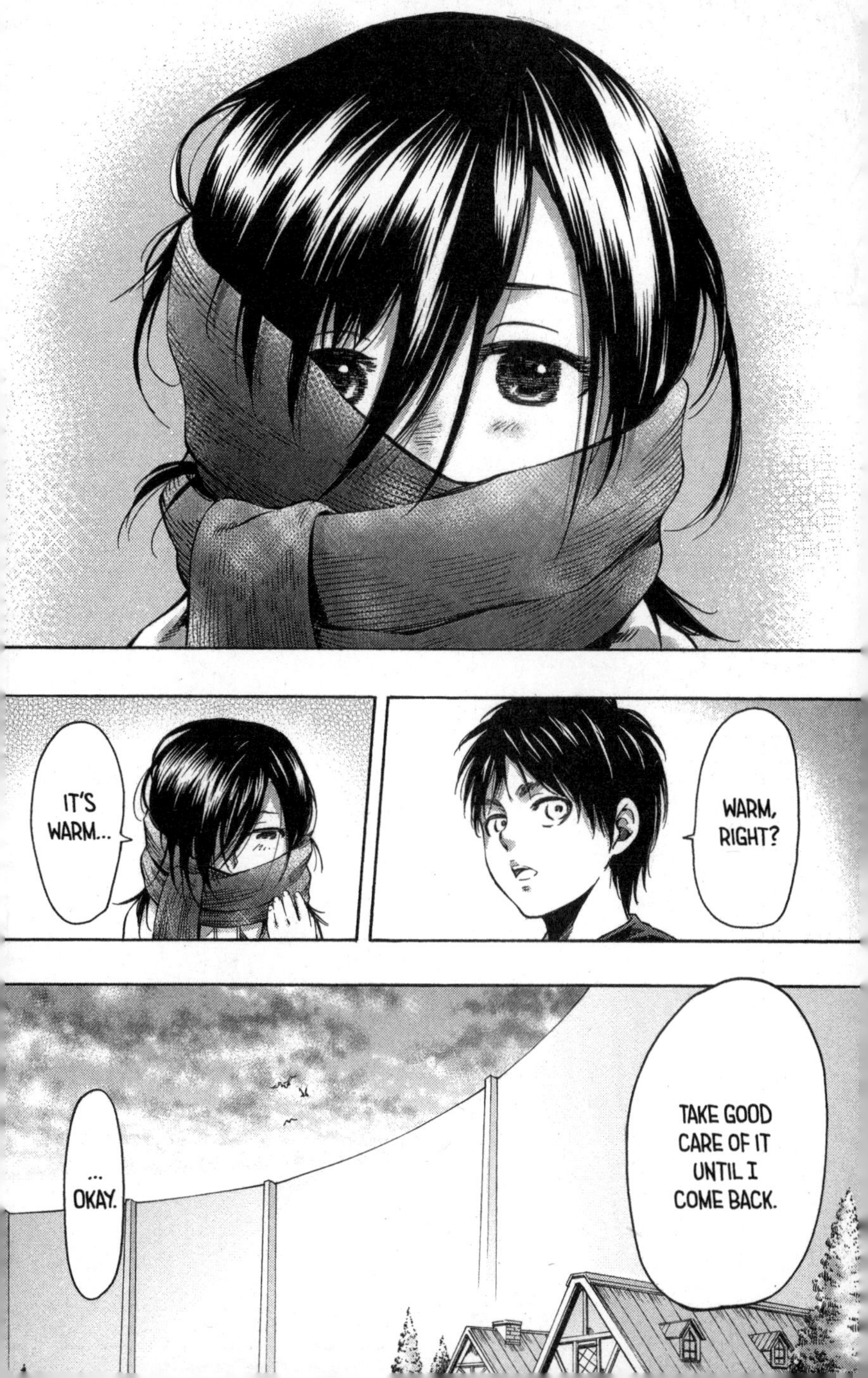
WARM, RIGHT?
IT'S WARM...
TAKE GOOD CARE OF IT UNTIL I COME BACK.
... OKAY.

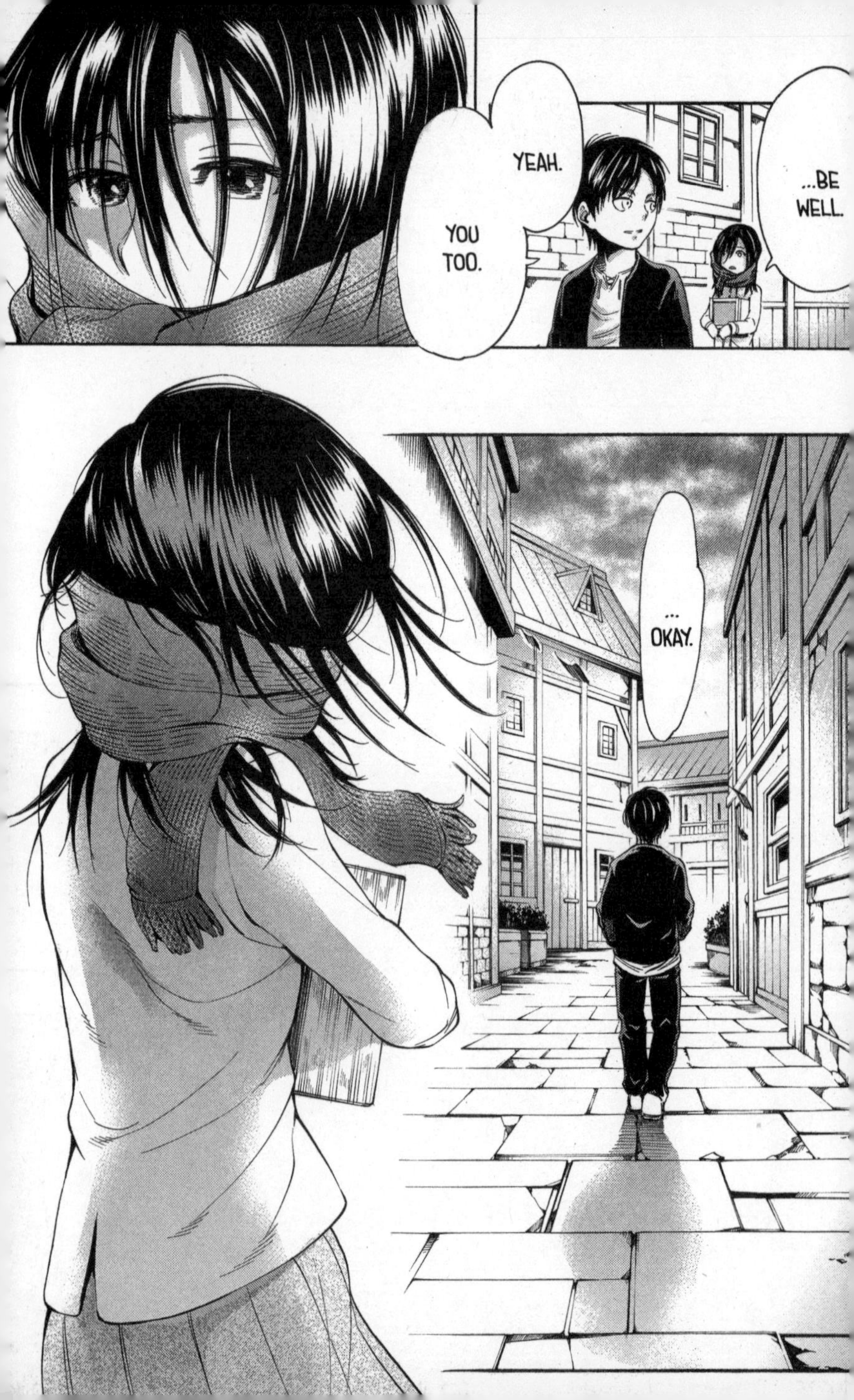
...BE WELL.
YEAH.
YOU TOO.
... OKAY.

ATTACK ON TITAN

LOST GIRLS

Chapter 4: Mirror Man

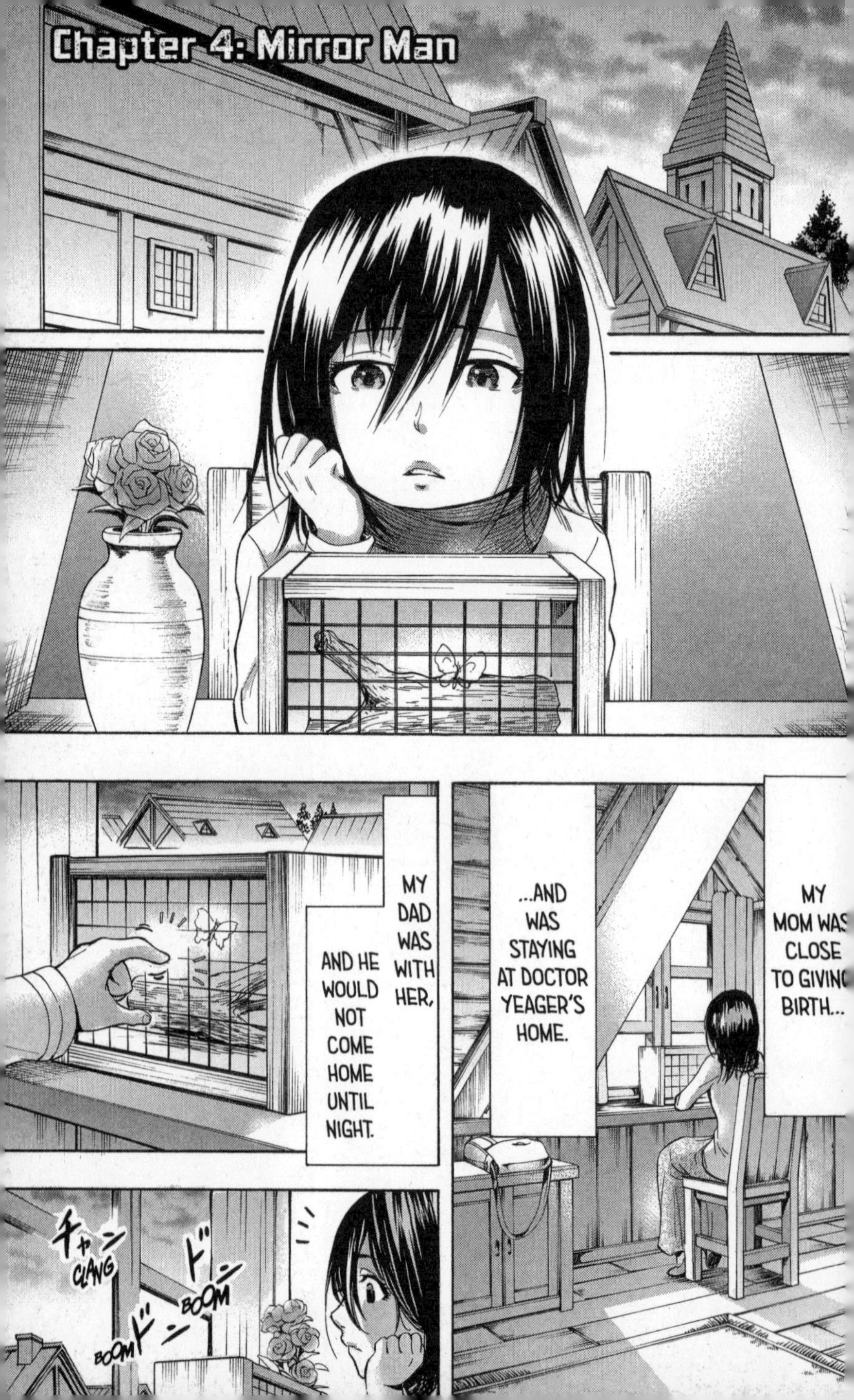

MY MOM WAS CLOSE TO GIVING BIRTH...
...AND WAS STAYING AT DOCTOR YEAGER'S HOME.
MY DAD WAS WITH HER,
AND HE WOULD NOT COME HOME UNTIL NIGHT.
チャン CLANG
ドン BOOM
ドン BOOM

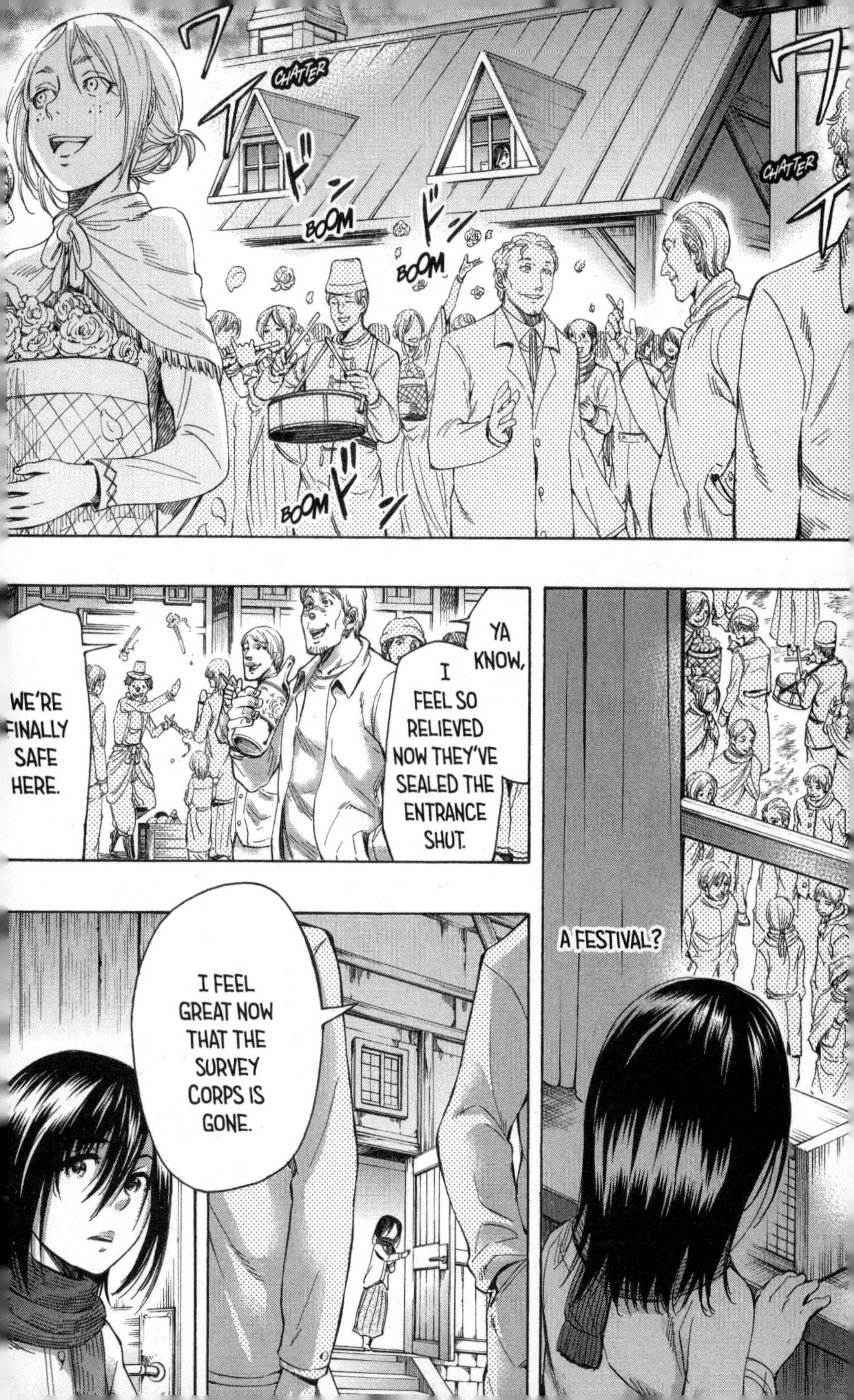
CHATTER
CHATTER
BOOM
BOOM
BOOM
A FESTIVAL?
YA KNOW, I FEEL SO RELIEVED NOW THEY'VE SEALED THE ENTRANCE SHUT.
WE'RE FINALLY SAFE HERE.
I FEEL GREAT NOW THAT THE SURVEY CORPS IS GONE.

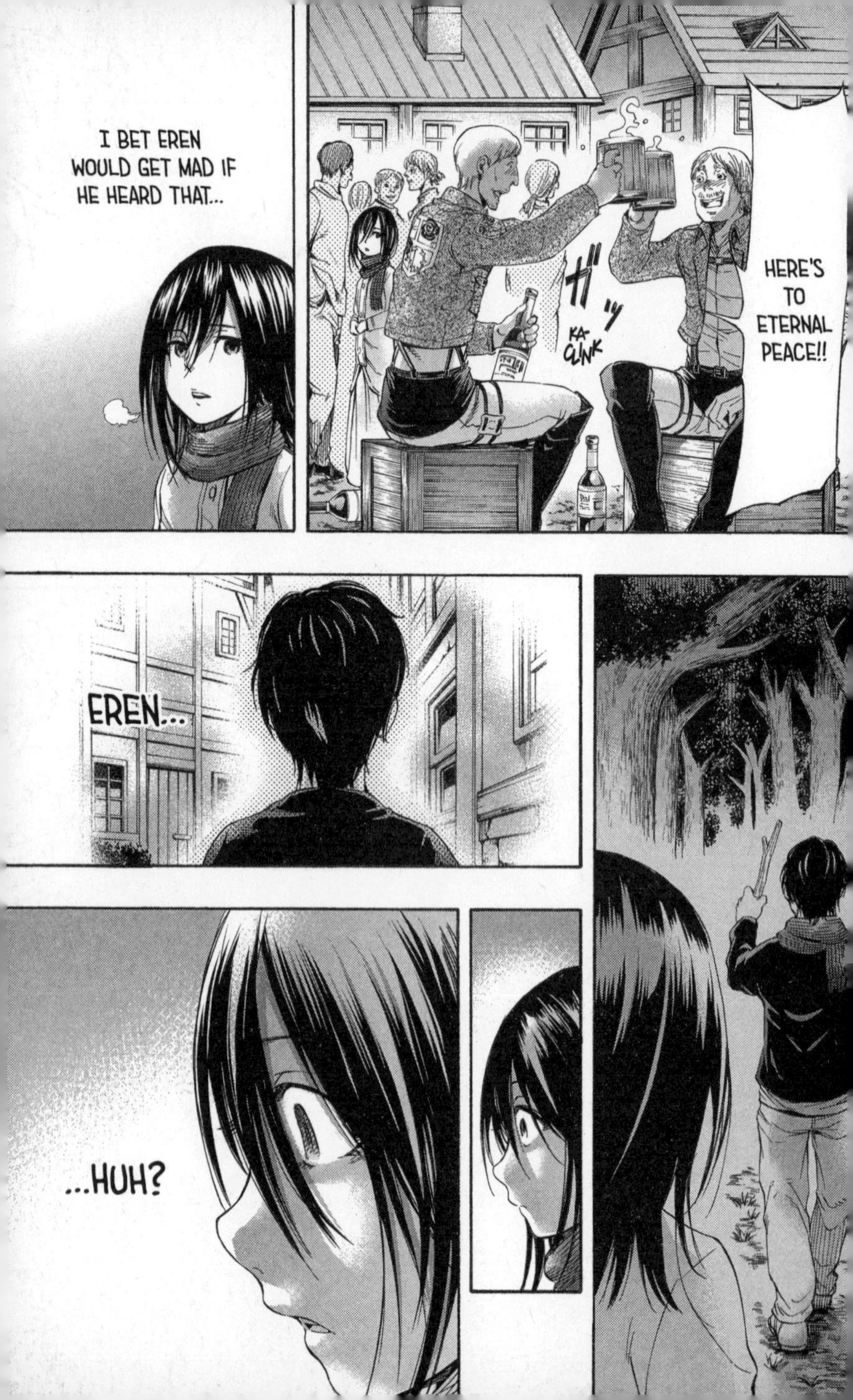
HERE'S TO ETERNAL PEACE!!
ガッ
KA-CLINK
I BET EREN WOULD GET MAD IF HE HEARD THAT...
EREN...
...HUH?

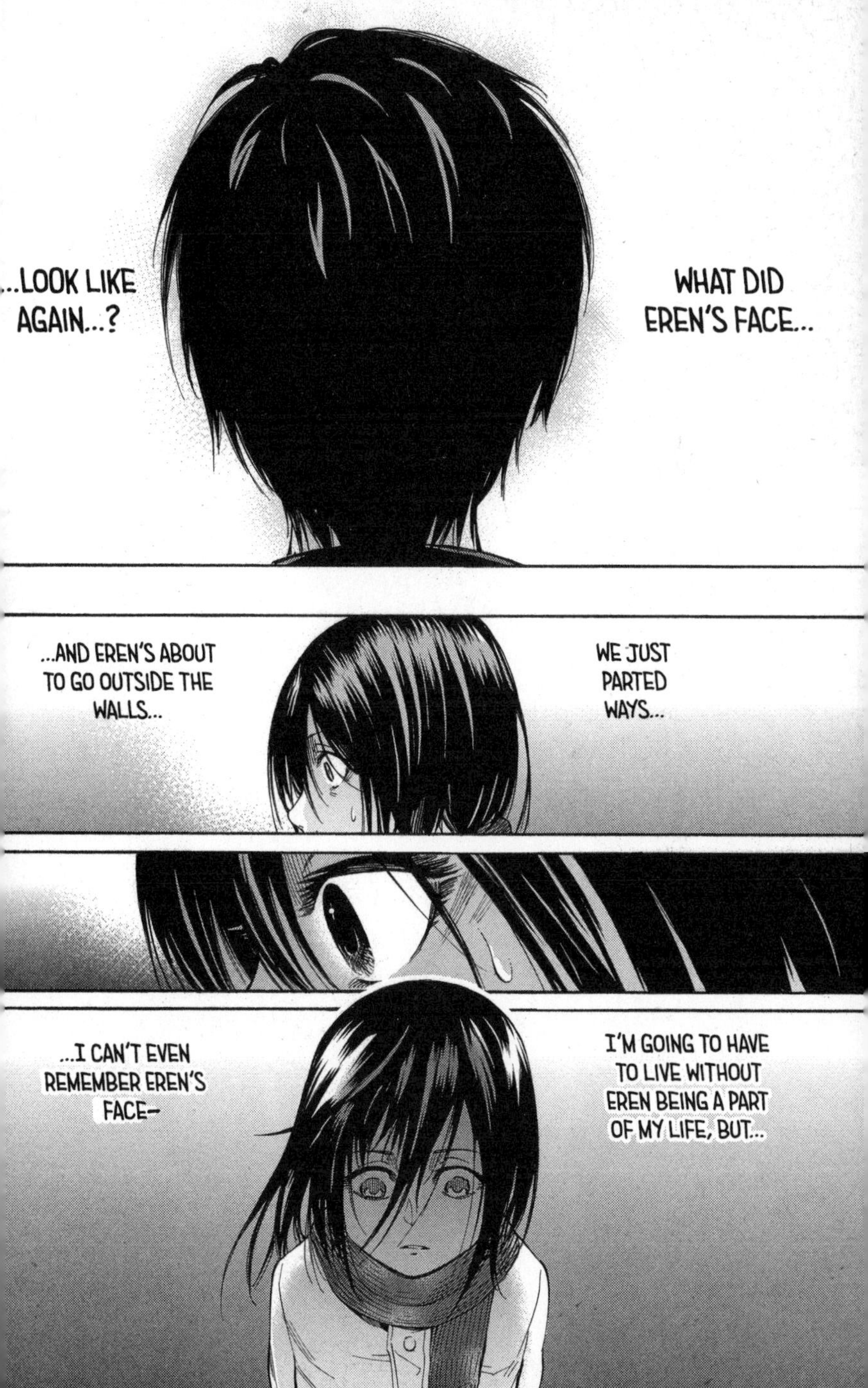
WHAT DID EREN'S FACE...
...LOOK LIKE AGAIN...?
WE JUST PARTED WAYS...
...AND EREN'S ABOUT TO GO OUTSIDE THE WALLS...
I'M GOING TO HAVE TO LIVE WITHOUT EREN BEING A PART OF MY LIFE, BUT...
...I CAN'T EVEN REMEMBER EREN'S FACE—

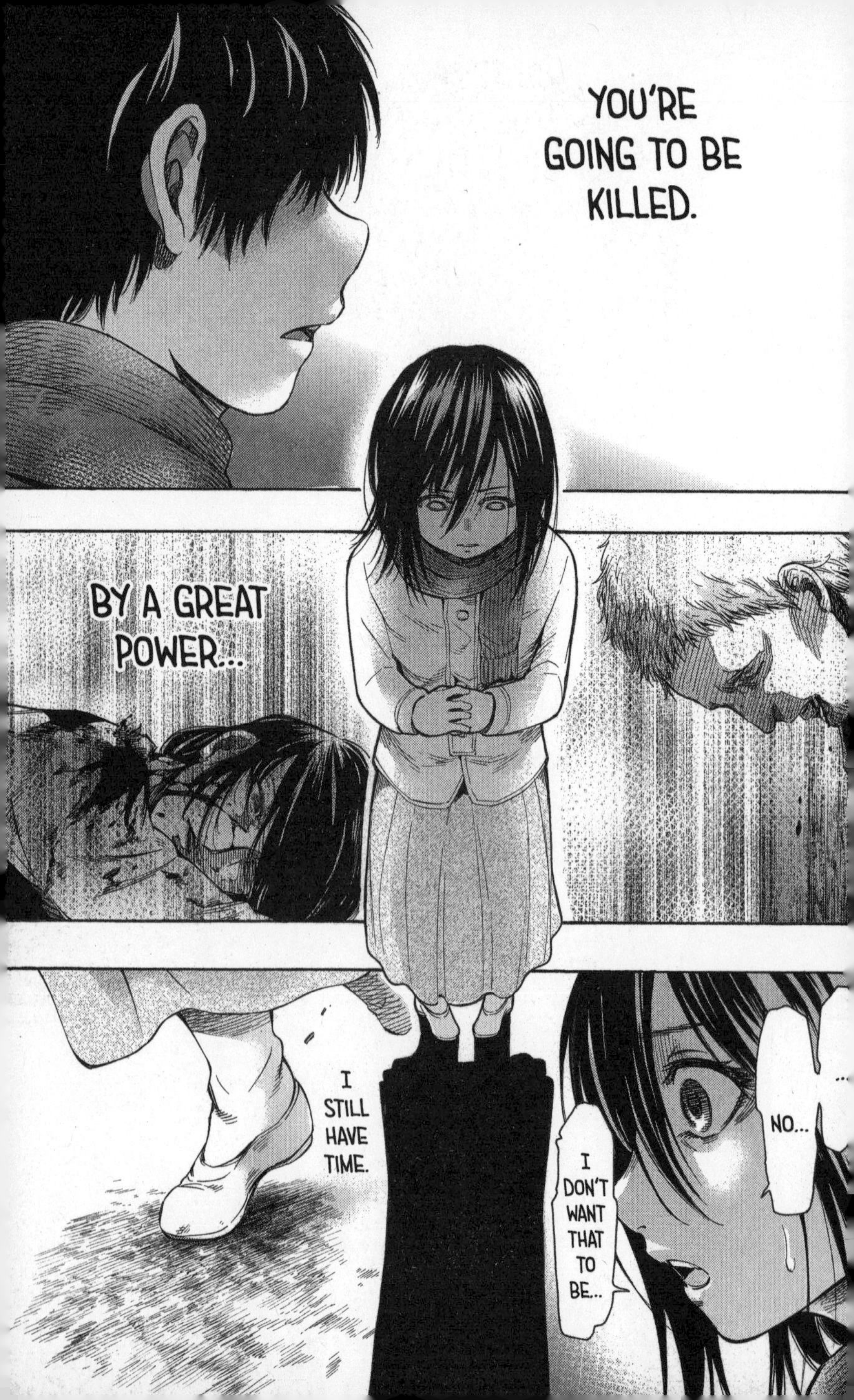
YOU'RE GOING TO BE KILLED.
BY A GREAT POWER...
...
NO...
I DON'T WANT THAT TO BE...
I STILL HAVE TIME.

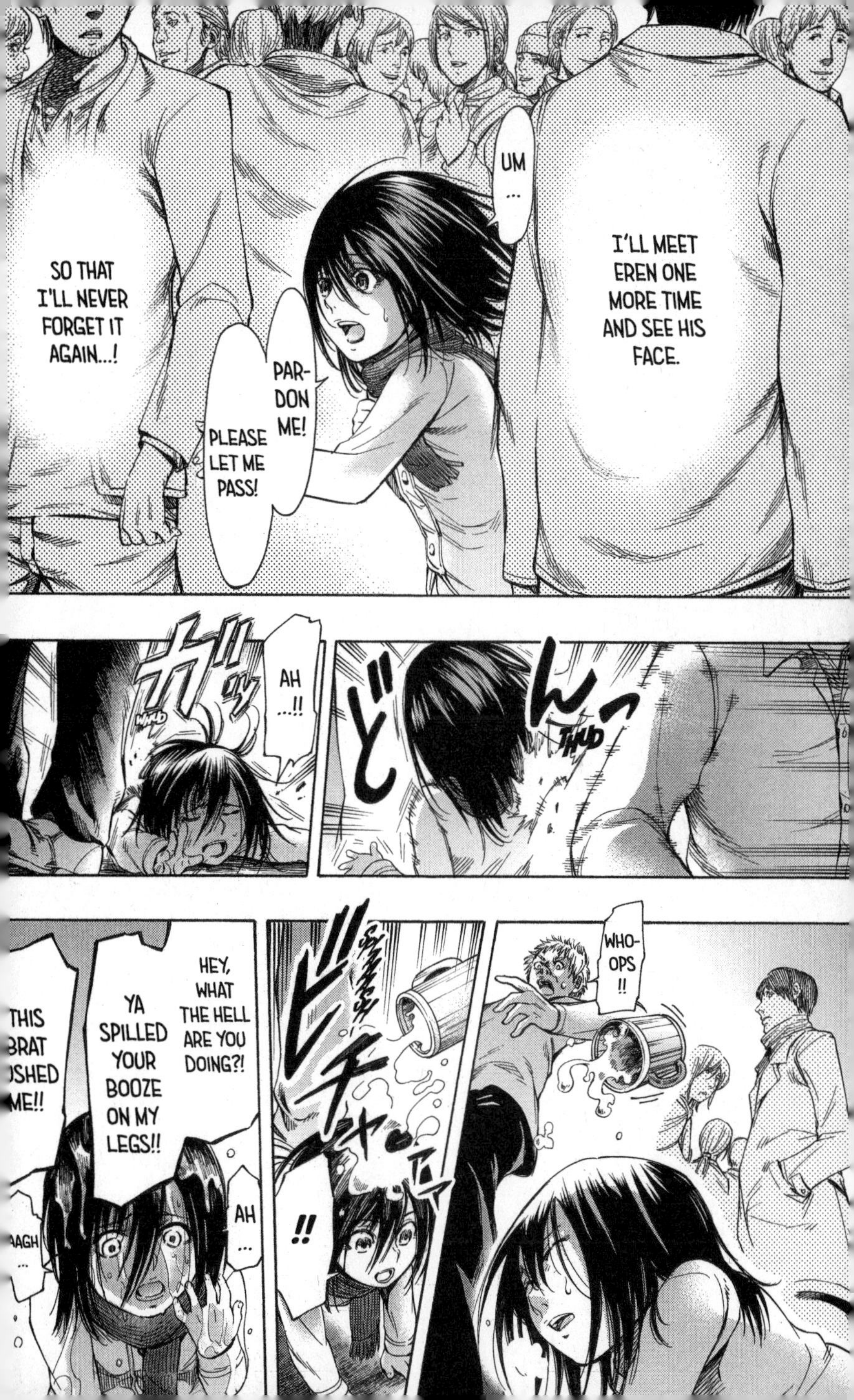
UM ...
I'LL MEET EREN ONE MORE TIME AND SEE HIS FACE.
PAR-DON ME!
PLEASE LET ME PASS!
SO THAT I'LL NEVER FORGET IT AGAIN...!
THUD
AH ...!!
WHUD
WHO-OPS !!
!!
HEY, WHAT THE HELL ARE YOU DOING?!
YA SPILLED YOUR BOOZE ON MY LEGS!!
THIS BRAT USHED ME!!
AH ...
AAGH ...

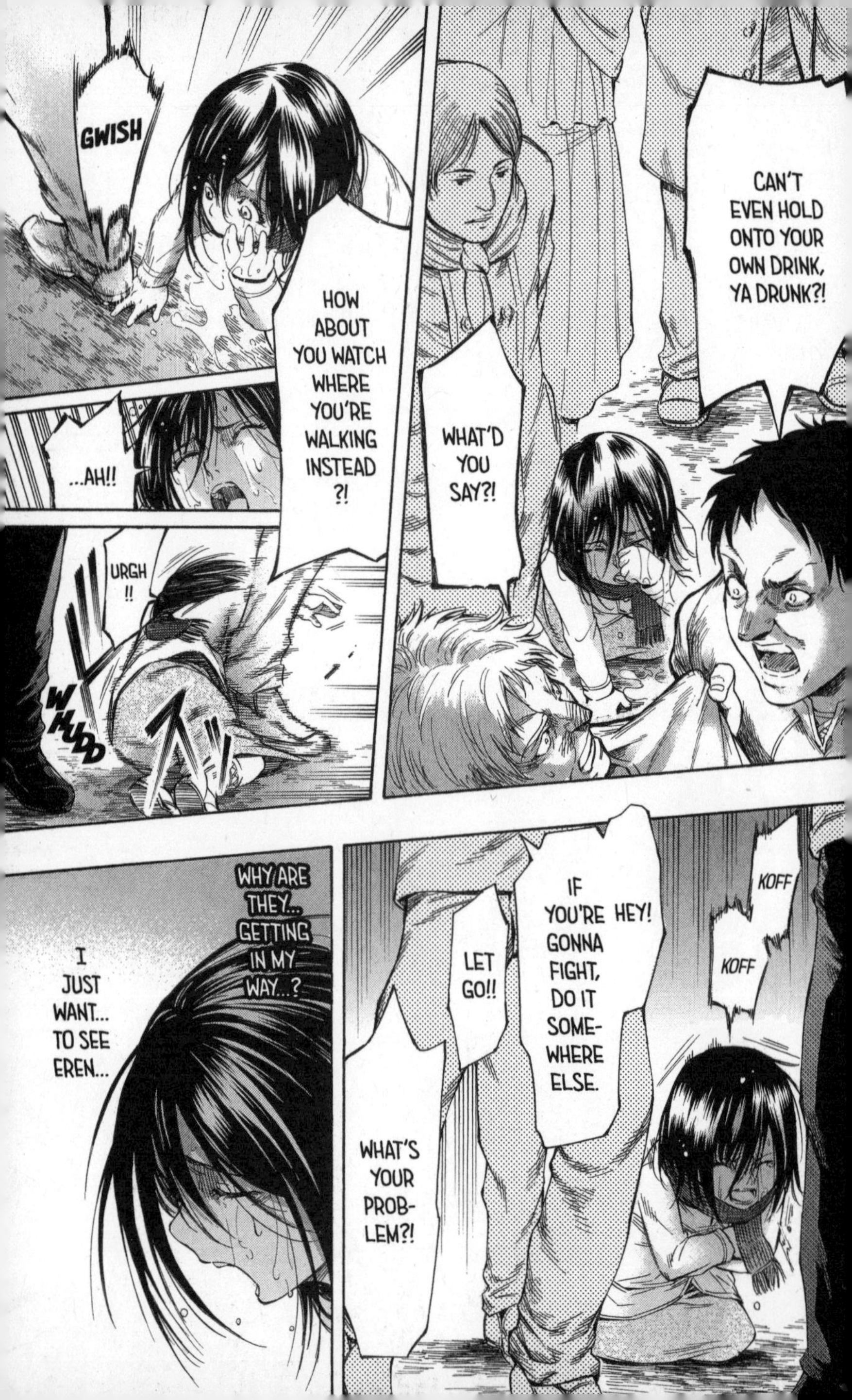

CAN'T EVEN HOLD ONTO YOUR OWN DRINK, YA DRUNK?!
WHAT'D YOU SAY?!
GWISH
HOW ABOUT YOU WATCH WHERE YOU'RE WALKING INSTEAD?!
...AH!!
URGH!!
WHUDD
KOFF
KOFF
HEY!
IF YOU'RE GONNA FIGHT, DO IT SOME-WHERE ELSE.
LET GO!!
WHAT'S YOUR PROB-LEM?!
WHY ARE THEY... GETTING IN MY WAY...?
I JUST WANT... TO SEE EREN...

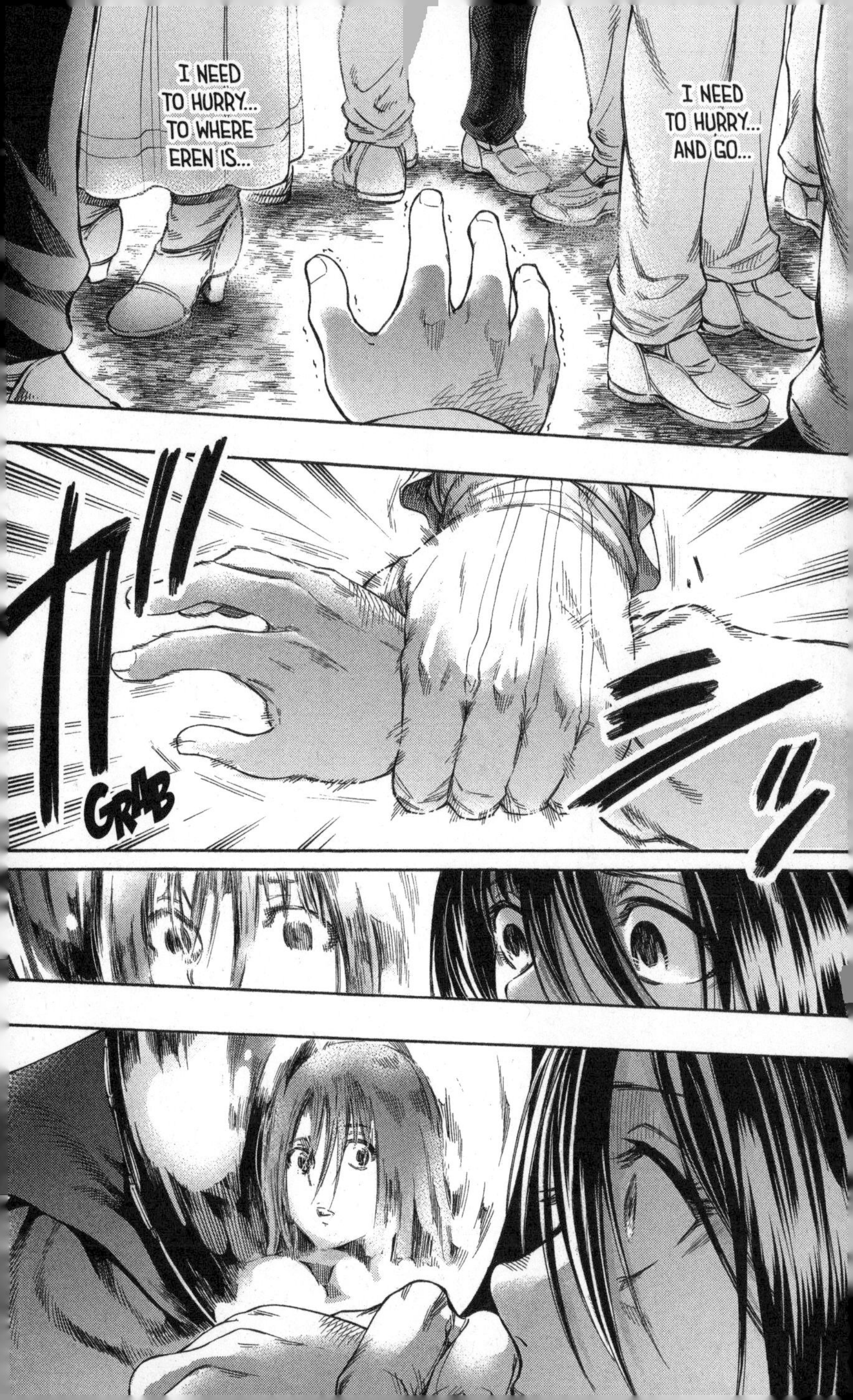
I NEED TO HURRY... AND GO...
I NEED TO HURRY... TO WHERE EREN IS...
GRAB

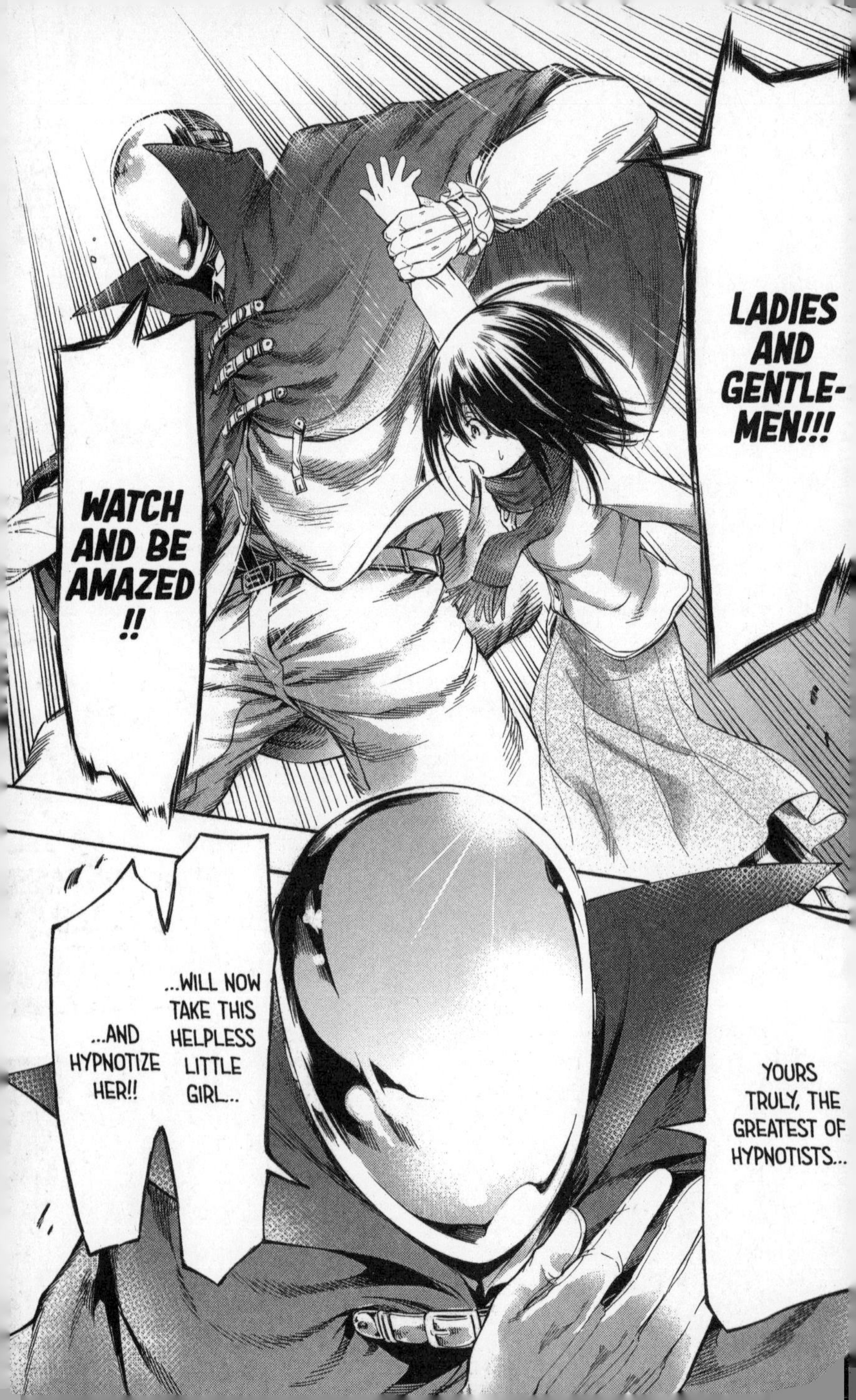
LADIES AND GENTLE-MEN!!!
WATCH AND BE AMAZED!!
YOURS TRULY, THE GREATEST OF HYPNOTISTS...
...WILL NOW TAKE THIS HELPLESS LITTLE GIRL...
...AND HYPNOTIZE HER!!

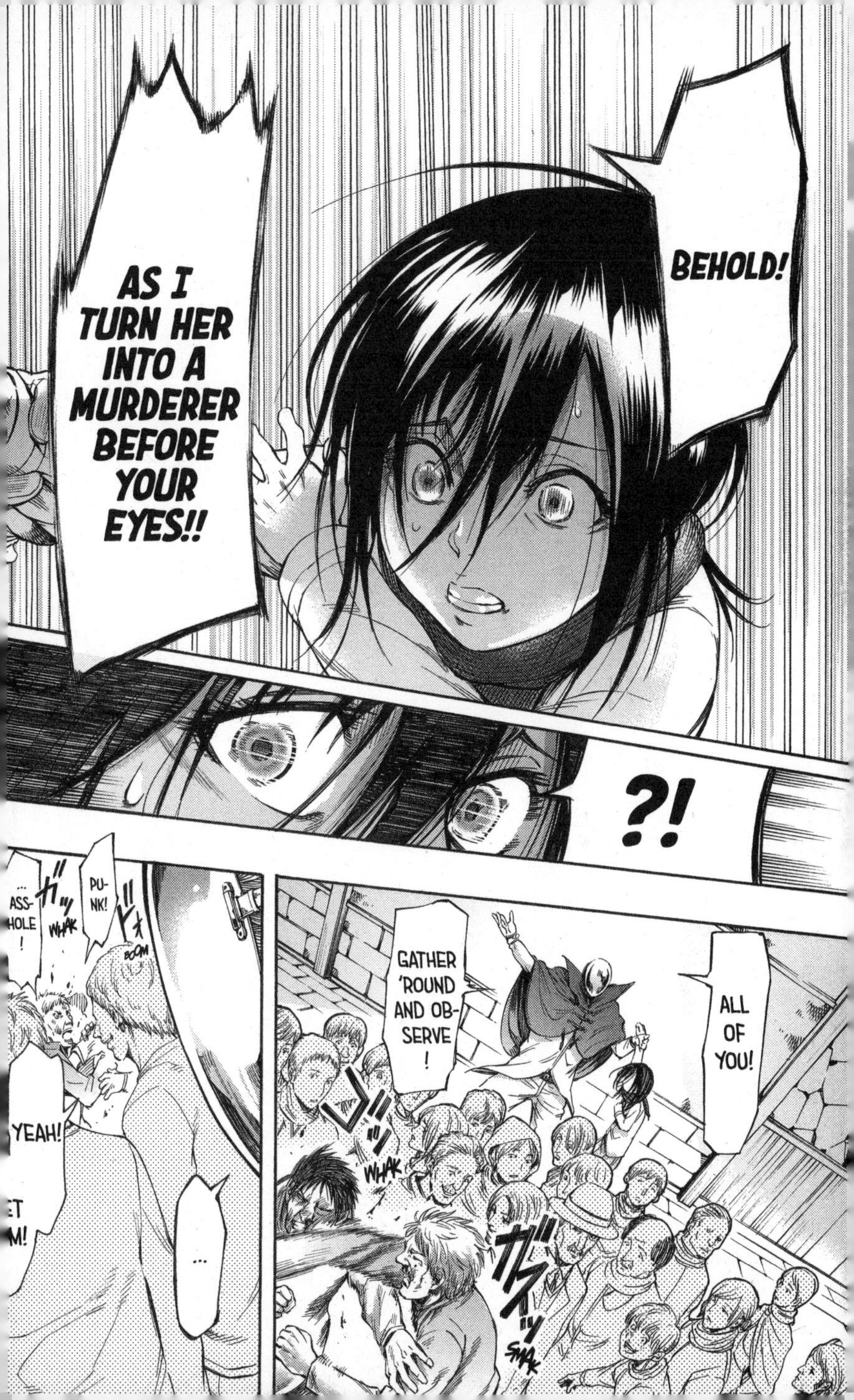
BEHOLD!
AS I TURN HER INTO A MURDERER BEFORE YOUR EYES!!
?!
ALL OF YOU!
GATHER 'ROUND AND OB-SERVE!
WHAK
SMAK
PU-NK!
BOOM
WHAK
... ASS-HOLE!
YEAH!
...

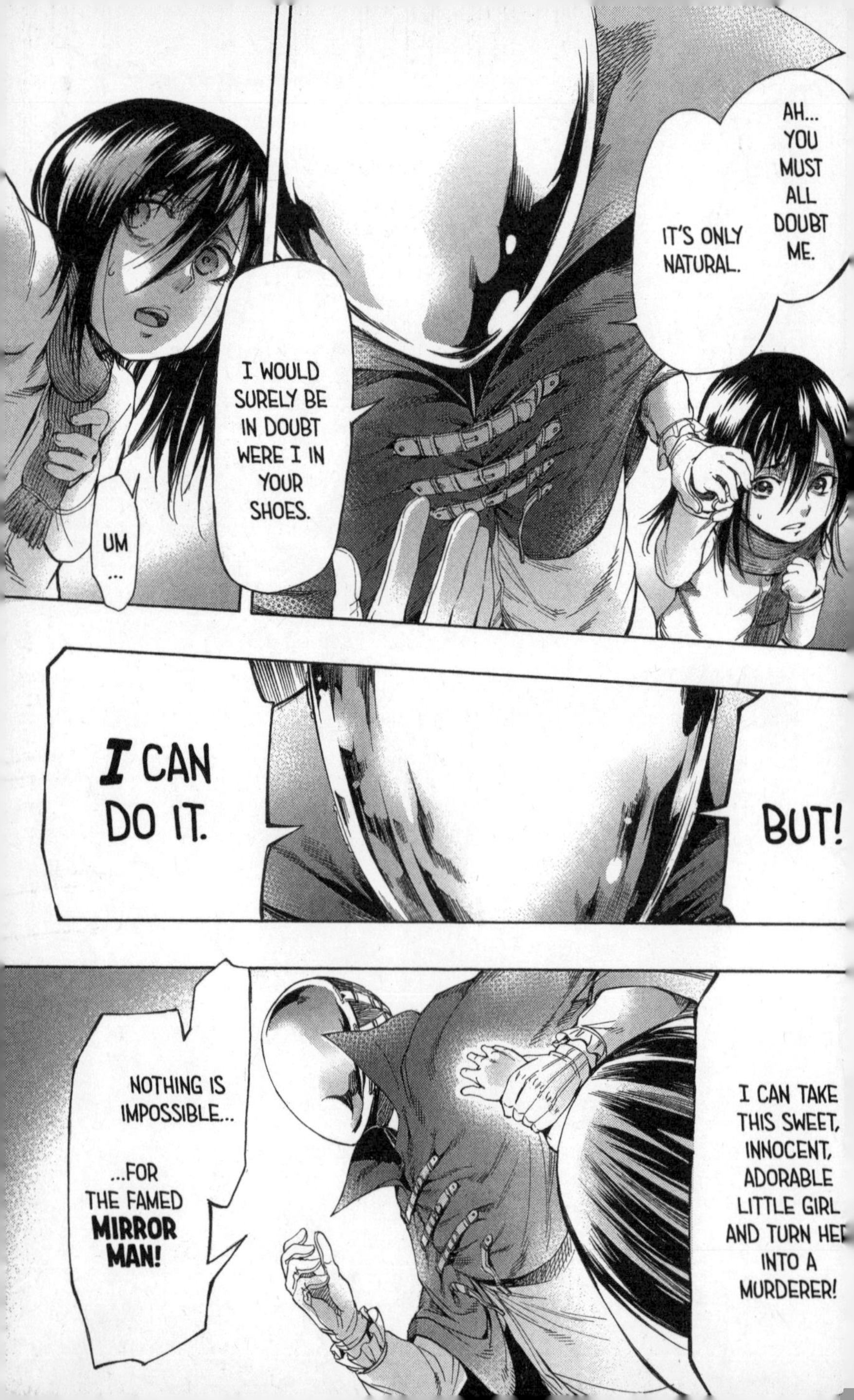
AH... YOU MUST ALL DOUBT ME.
IT'S ONLY NATURAL.
I WOULD SURELY BE IN DOUBT WERE I IN YOUR SHOES.
UM ...
BUT!
I CAN DO IT.
I CAN TAKE THIS SWEET, INNOCENT, ADORABLE LITTLE GIRL AND TURN HE
INTO A MURDERER!
NOTHING IS IMPOSSIBLE...
...FOR THE FAMED MIRROR MAN!

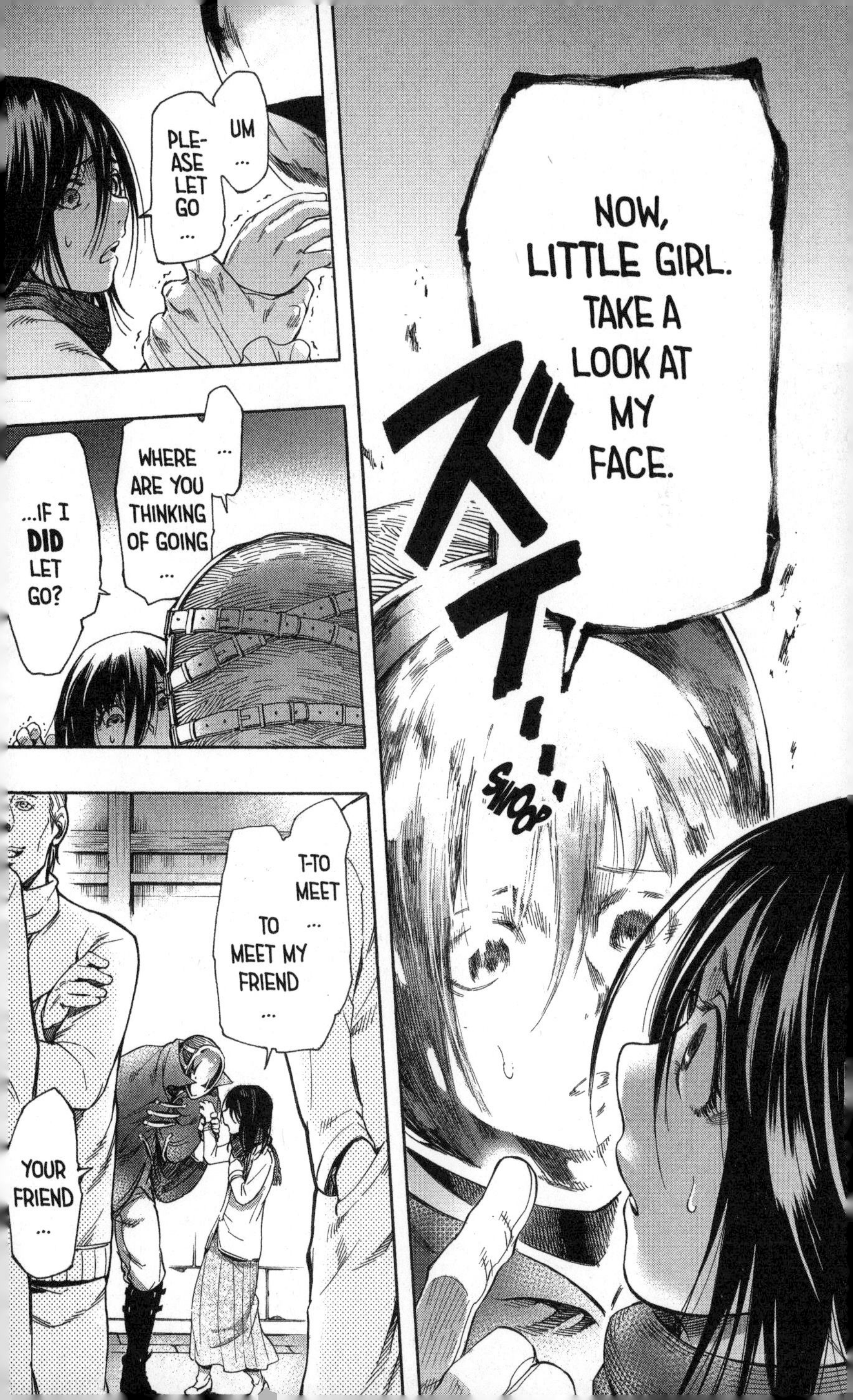
NOW, LITTLE GIRL. TAKE A LOOK AT MY FACE.
ズイ
SWOOP
UM ...
PLE-ASE LET GO ...
WHERE ARE YOU THINKING OF GOING ...
...IF I **DID** LET GO?
T-TO MEET ...
TO MEET MY FRIEND ...
YOUR FRIEND ...

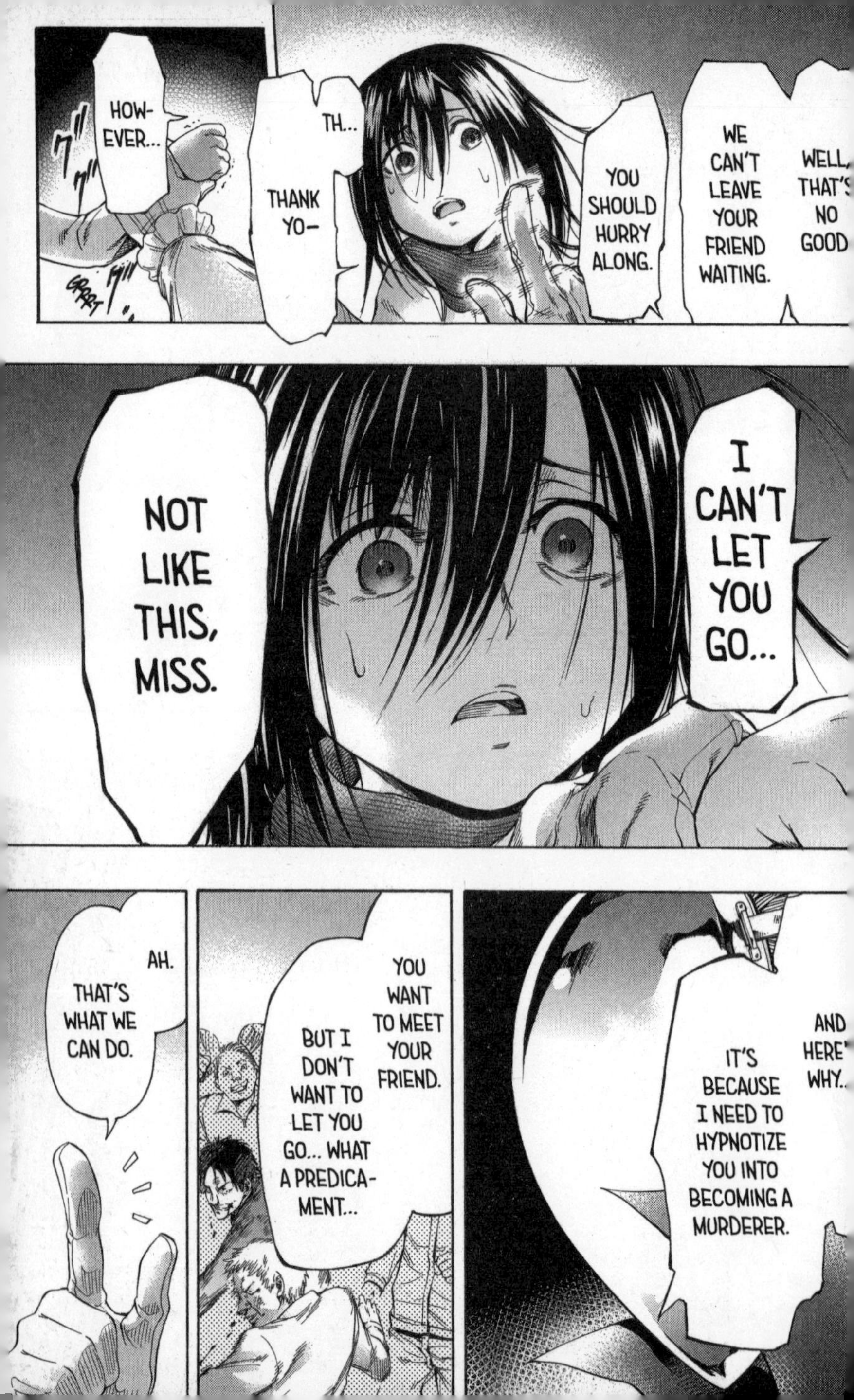
WELL, THAT'S NO GOOD
WE CAN'T LEAVE YOUR FRIEND WAITING.
YOU SHOULD HURRY ALONG.
TH...
THANK YO—
HOW-EVER...
GRRRT
I CAN'T LET YOU GO...
NOT LIKE THIS, MISS.
AND HERE' WHY...
IT'S BECAUSE I NEED TO HYPNOTIZE YOU INTO BECOMING A MURDERER.
YOU WANT TO MEET YOUR FRIEND.
BUT I DON'T WANT TO LET YOU GO... WHAT A PREDICA-MENT...
AH.
THAT'S WHAT WE CAN DO.

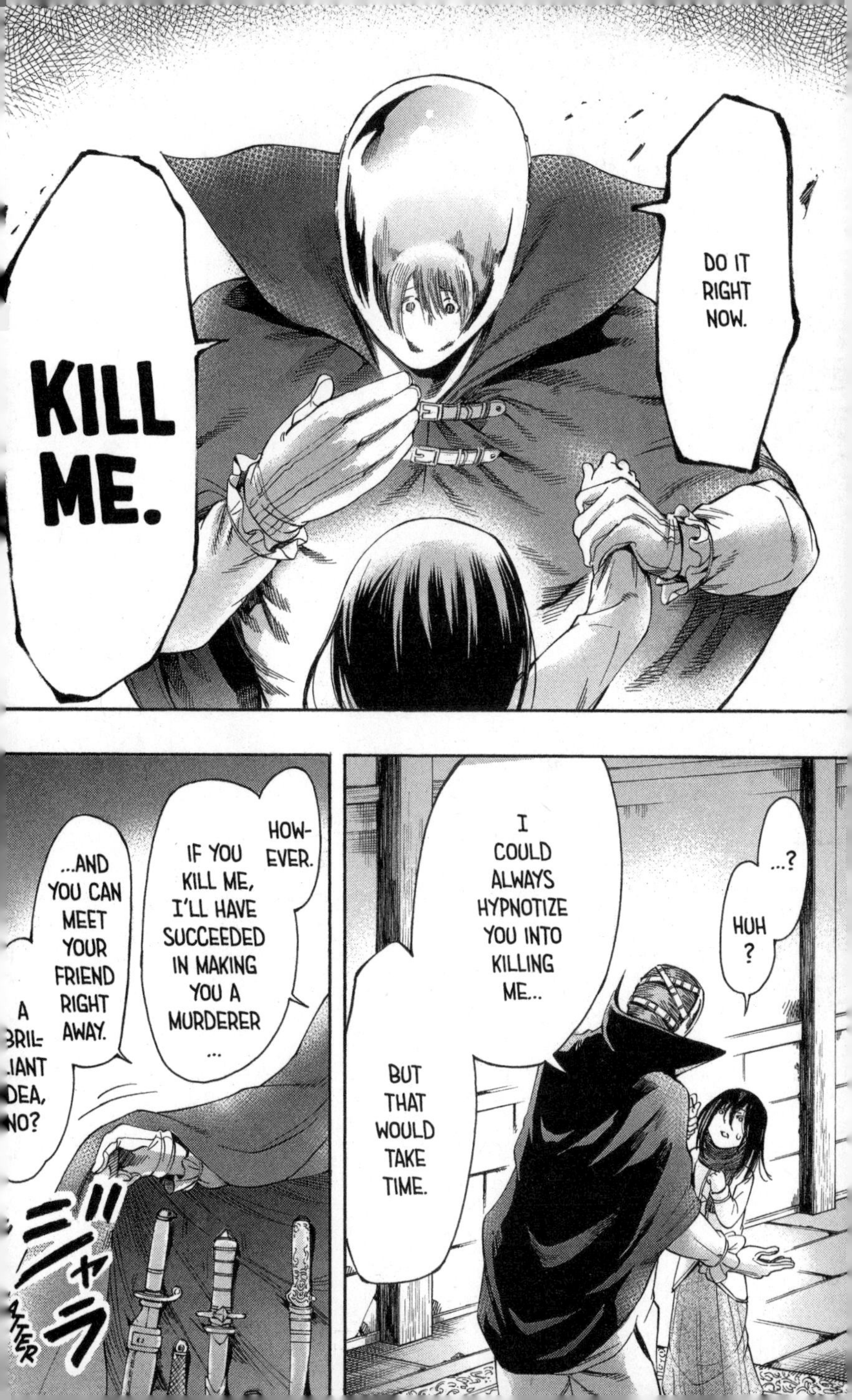
DO IT RIGHT NOW.
KILL ME.
...?
HUH?
I COULD ALWAYS HYPNOTIZE YOU INTO KILLING ME...
BUT THAT WOULD TAKE TIME.
HOW-EVER.
IF YOU KILL ME, I'LL HAVE SUCCEEDED IN MAKING YOU A MURDERER ...
...AND YOU CAN MEET YOUR FRIEND RIGHT AWAY.
A BRIL- IANT DEA, NO?
ジャラ

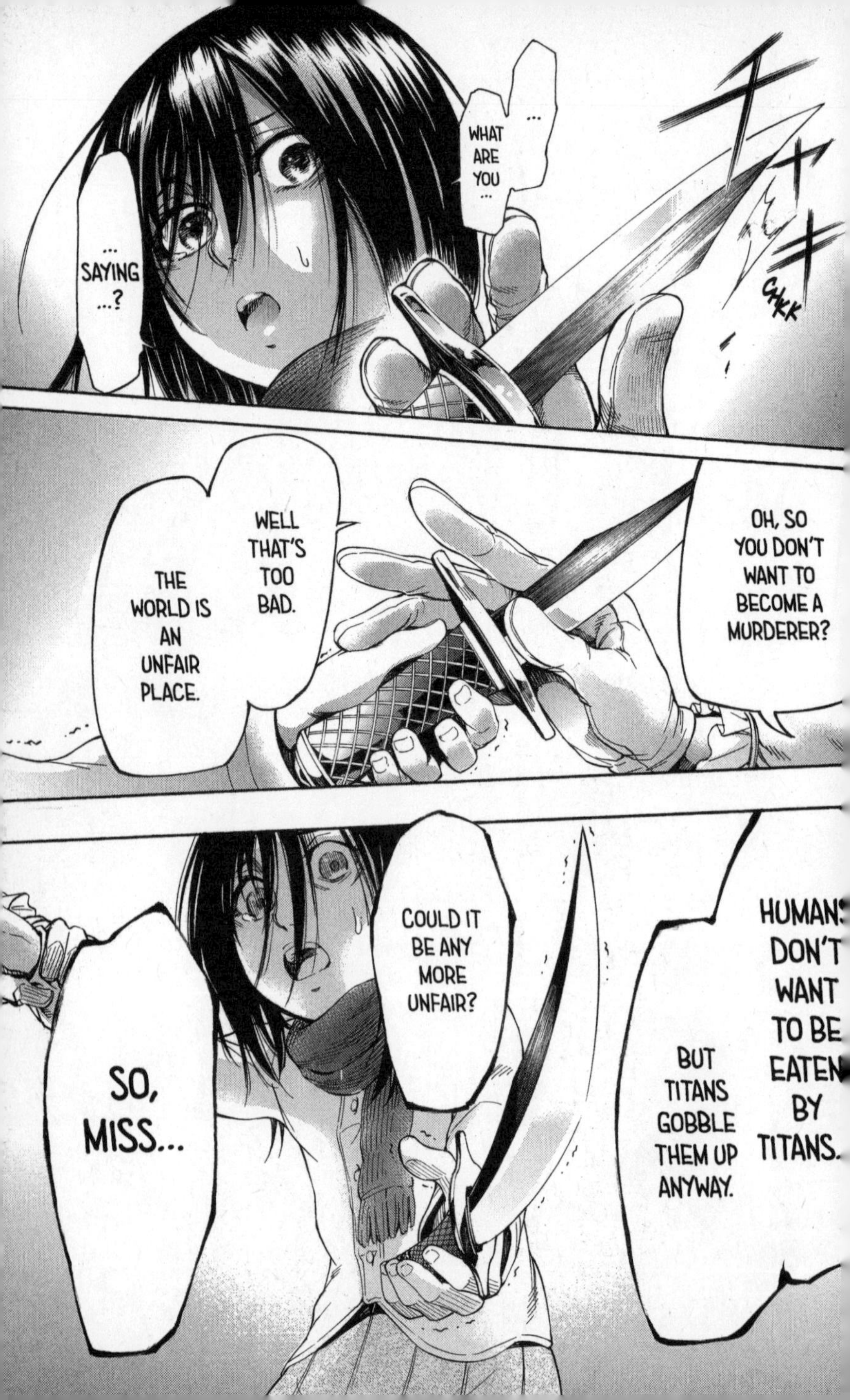
CHKK
... WHAT ARE YOU ...
... SAYING ...?
OH, SO YOU DON'T WANT TO BECOME A MURDERER?
WELL THAT'S TOO BAD.
THE WORLD IS AN UNFAIR PLACE.
HUMANS DON'T WANT TO BE EATEN BY TITANS.
BUT TITANS GOBBLE THEM UP ANYWAY.
COULD IT BE ANY MORE UNFAIR?
SO, MISS...

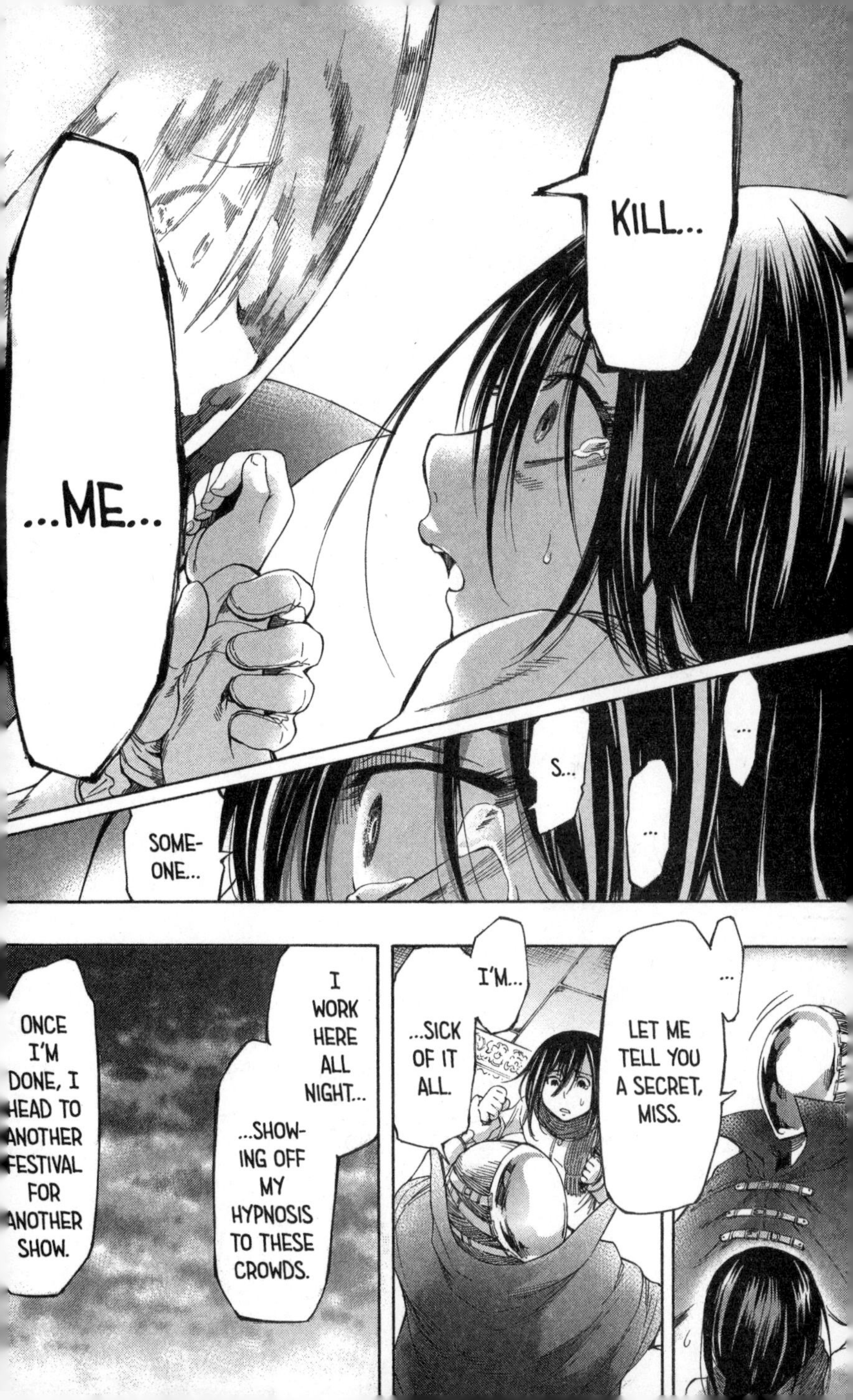
KILL...
...ME...
...
S...
...
SOME-ONE...
...
LET ME TELL YOU A SECRET, MISS.
I'M...
...SICK OF IT ALL.
I WORK HERE ALL NIGHT...
...SHOW-ING OFF MY HYPNOSIS TO THESE CROWDS.
ONCE I'M DONE, I HEAD TO ANOTHER FESTIVAL FOR ANOTHER SHOW.

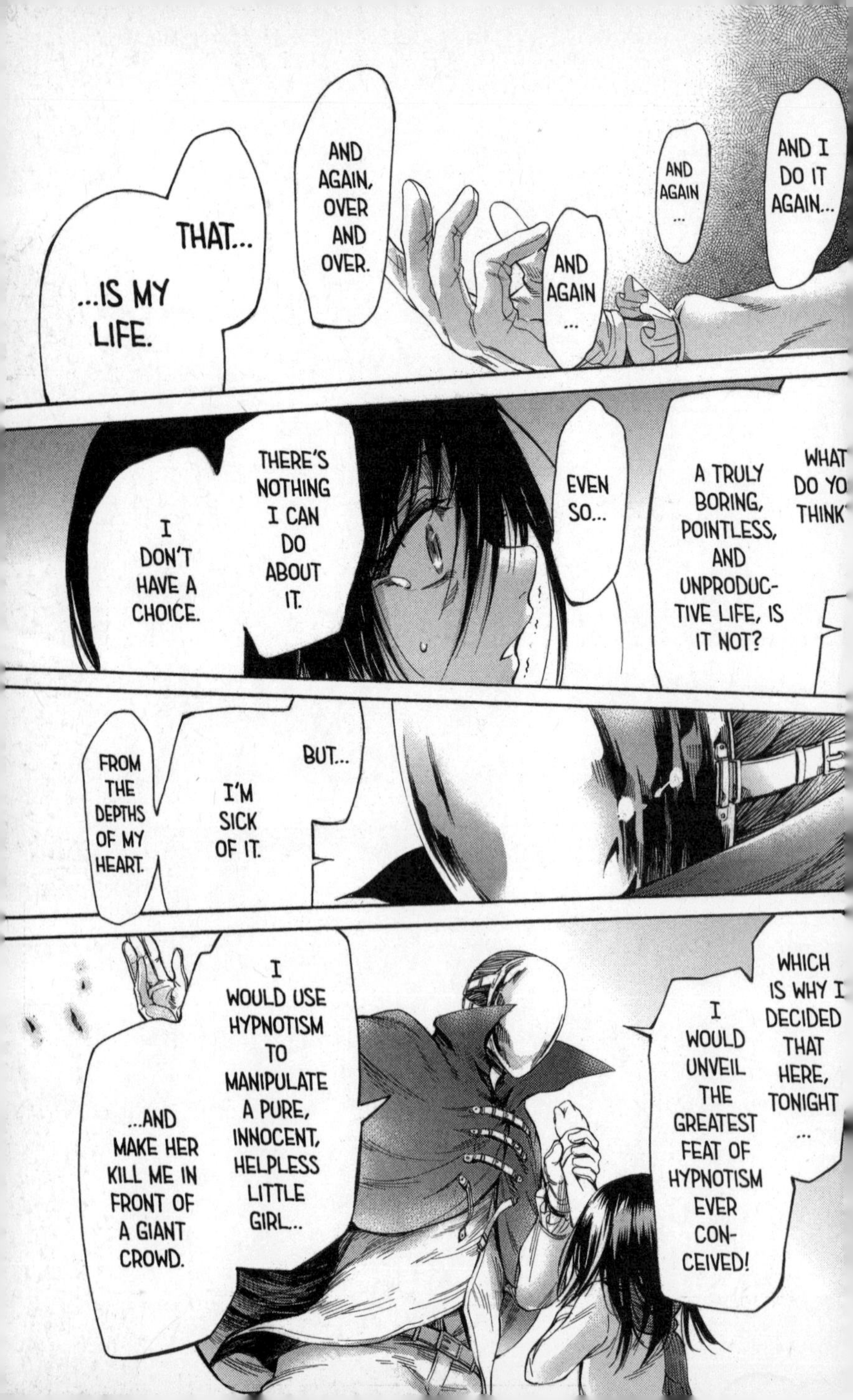
AND I DO IT AGAIN...
AND AGAIN...
AND AGAIN...
AND AGAIN, OVER AND OVER.
THAT...
...IS MY LIFE.
WHAT DO YO THINK
A TRULY BORING, POINTLESS, AND UNPRODUCTIVE LIFE, IS IT NOT?
EVEN SO...
THERE'S NOTHING I CAN DO ABOUT IT.
I DON'T HAVE A CHOICE.
BUT...
I'M SICK OF IT.
FROM THE DEPTHS OF MY HEART.
WHICH IS WHY I DECIDED THAT HERE, TONIGHT...
I WOULD UNVEIL THE GREATEST FEAT OF HYPNOTISM EVER CONCEIVED!
I WOULD USE HYPNOTISM TO MANIPULATE A PURE, INNOCENT, HELPLESS LITTLE GIRL...
...AND MAKE HER KILL ME IN FRONT OF A GIANT CROWD.

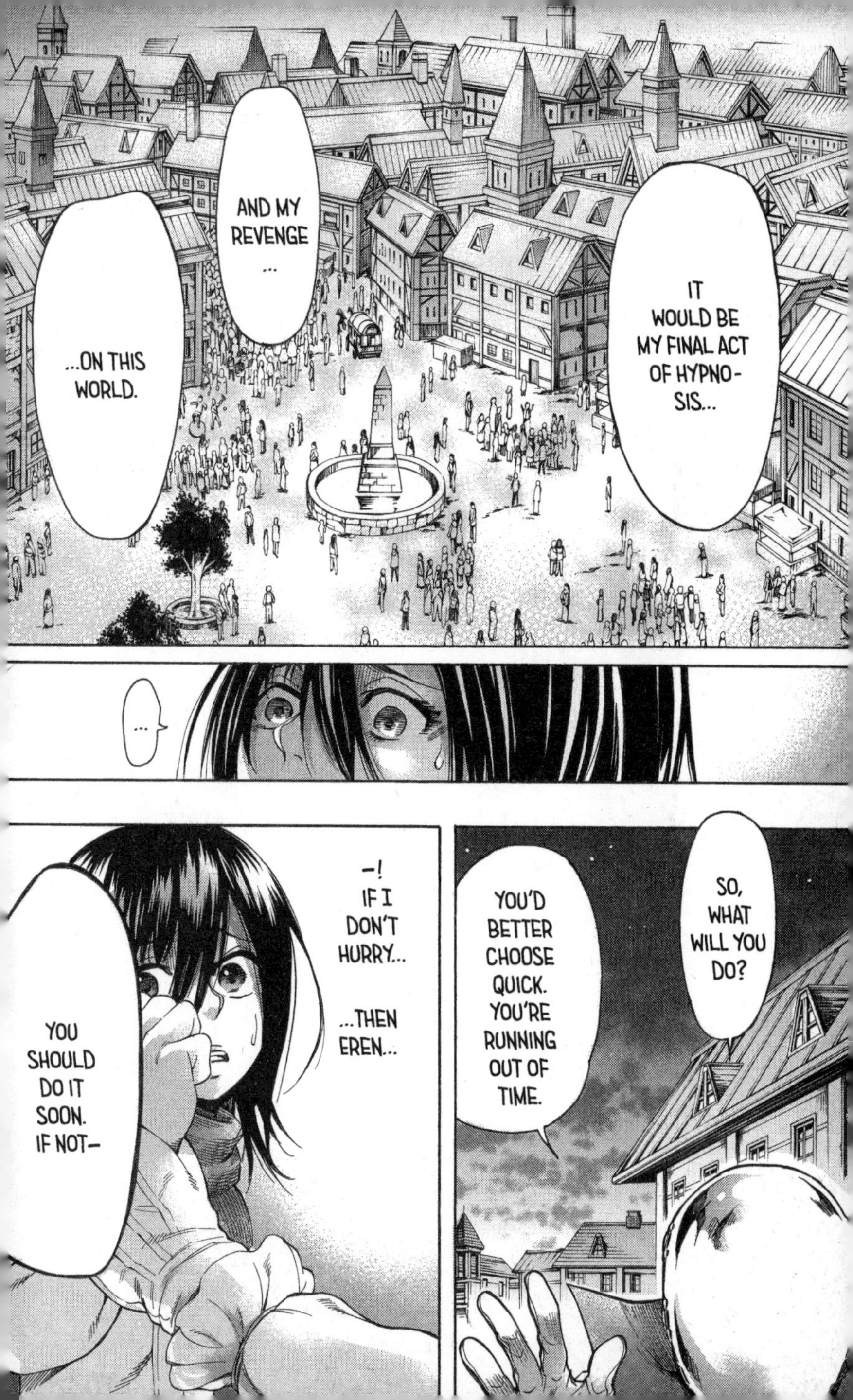
IT WOULD BE MY FINAL ACT OF HYPNO-SIS...
AND MY REVENGE ...
...ON THIS WORLD.
...
SO, WHAT WILL YOU DO?
YOU'D BETTER CHOOSE QUICK. YOU'RE RUNNING OUT OF TIME.
—! IF I DON'T HURRY...
...THEN EREN...
YOU SHOULD DO IT SOON. IF NOT—

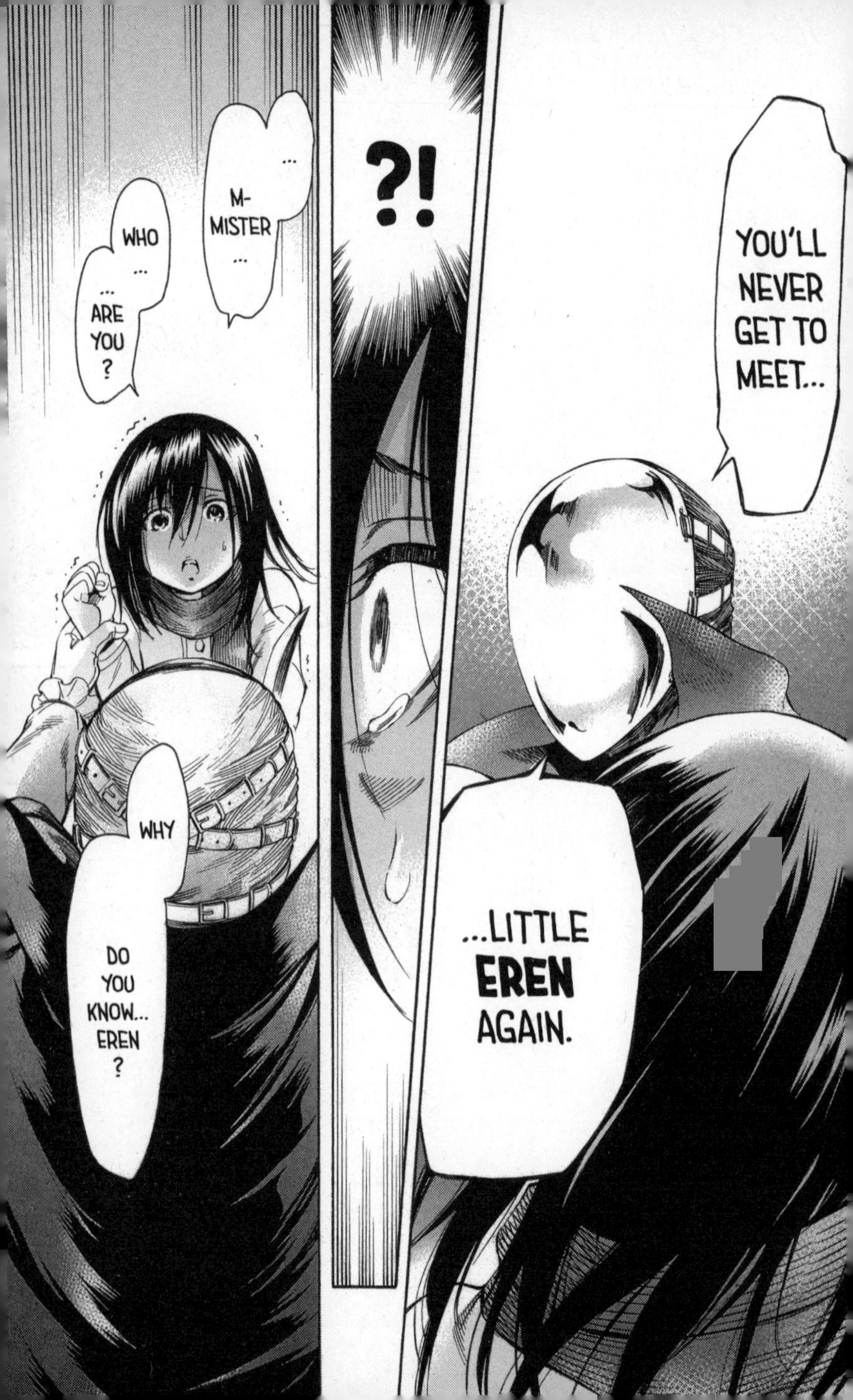
YOU'LL NEVER GET TO MEET...
...LITTLE EREN AGAIN.
?!
... M-MISTER ...
WHO ... ... ARE YOU ?
WHY DO YOU KNOW... EREN ?

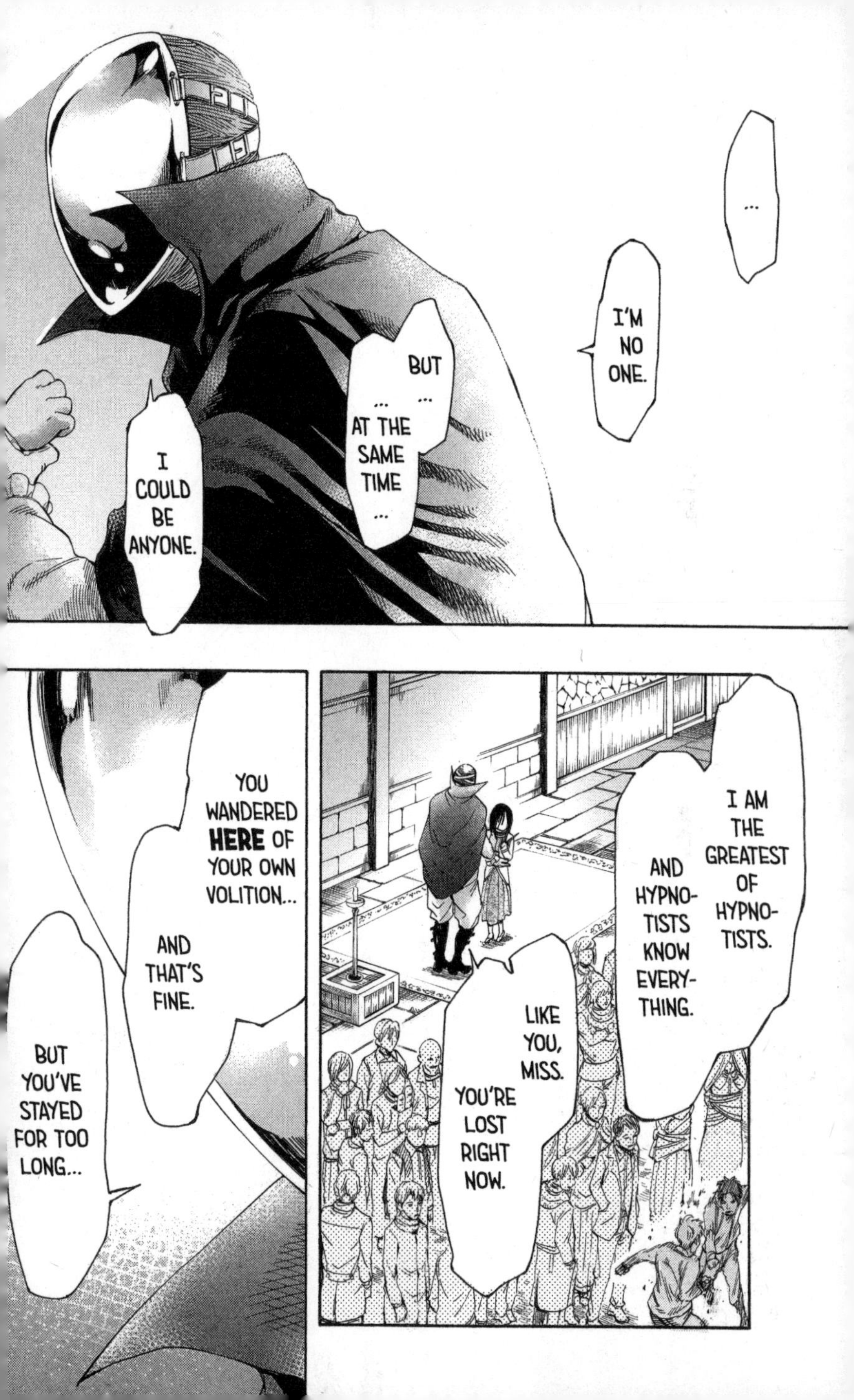
...
I'M NO ONE.
BUT ... AT THE SAME TIME ...
I COULD BE ANYONE.
I AM THE GREATEST OF HYPNOTISTS.
AND HYPNOTISTS KNOW EVERYTHING.
LIKE YOU, MISS.
YOU'RE LOST RIGHT NOW.
YOU WANDERED **HERE** OF YOUR OWN VOLITION...
AND THAT'S FINE.
BUT YOU'VE STAYED FOR TOO LONG...

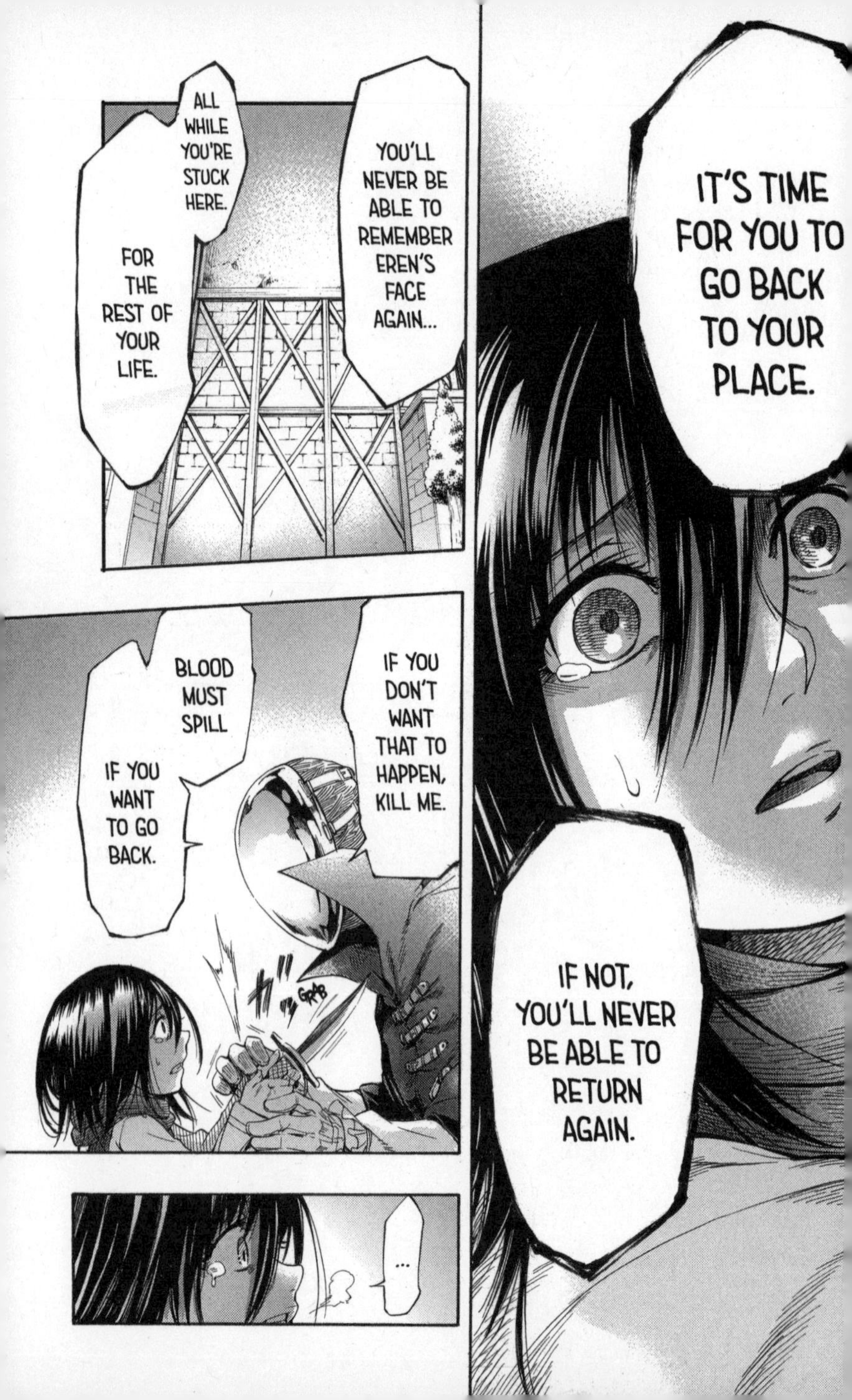
IT'S TIME FOR YOU TO GO BACK TO YOUR PLACE.
IF NOT, YOU'LL NEVER BE ABLE TO RETURN AGAIN.
YOU'LL NEVER BE ABLE TO REMEMBER EREN'S FACE AGAIN...
ALL WHILE YOU'RE STUCK HERE.
FOR THE REST OF YOUR LIFE.
IF YOU DON'T WANT THAT TO HAPPEN, KILL ME.
BLOOD MUST SPILL
IF YOU WANT TO GO BACK.
GRAB
...

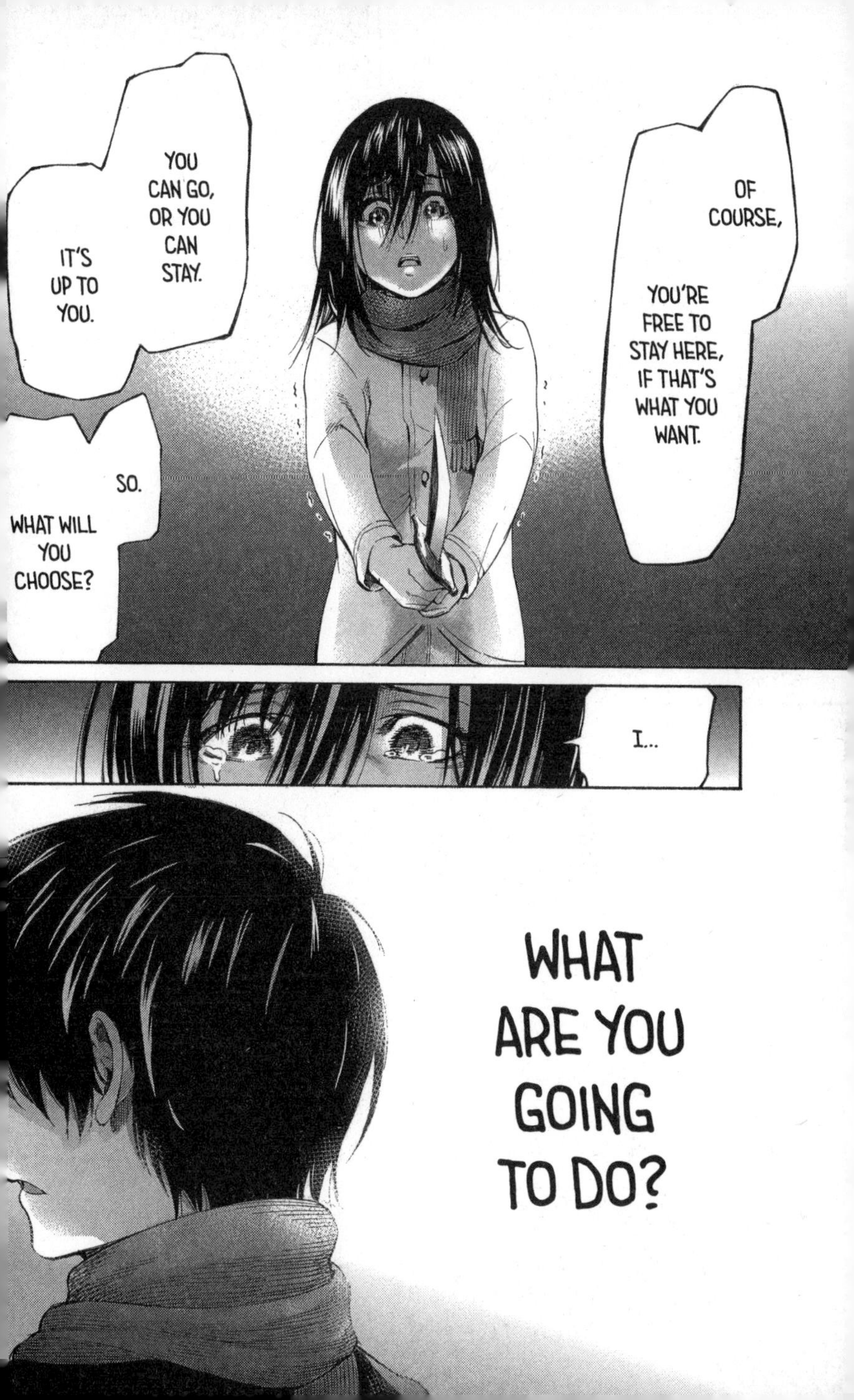
OF COURSE,
YOU'RE FREE TO STAY HERE, IF THAT'S WHAT YOU WANT.
YOU CAN GO, OR YOU CAN STAY.
IT'S UP TO YOU.
SO.
WHAT WILL YOU CHOOSE?
I...
WHAT ARE YOU GOING TO DO?

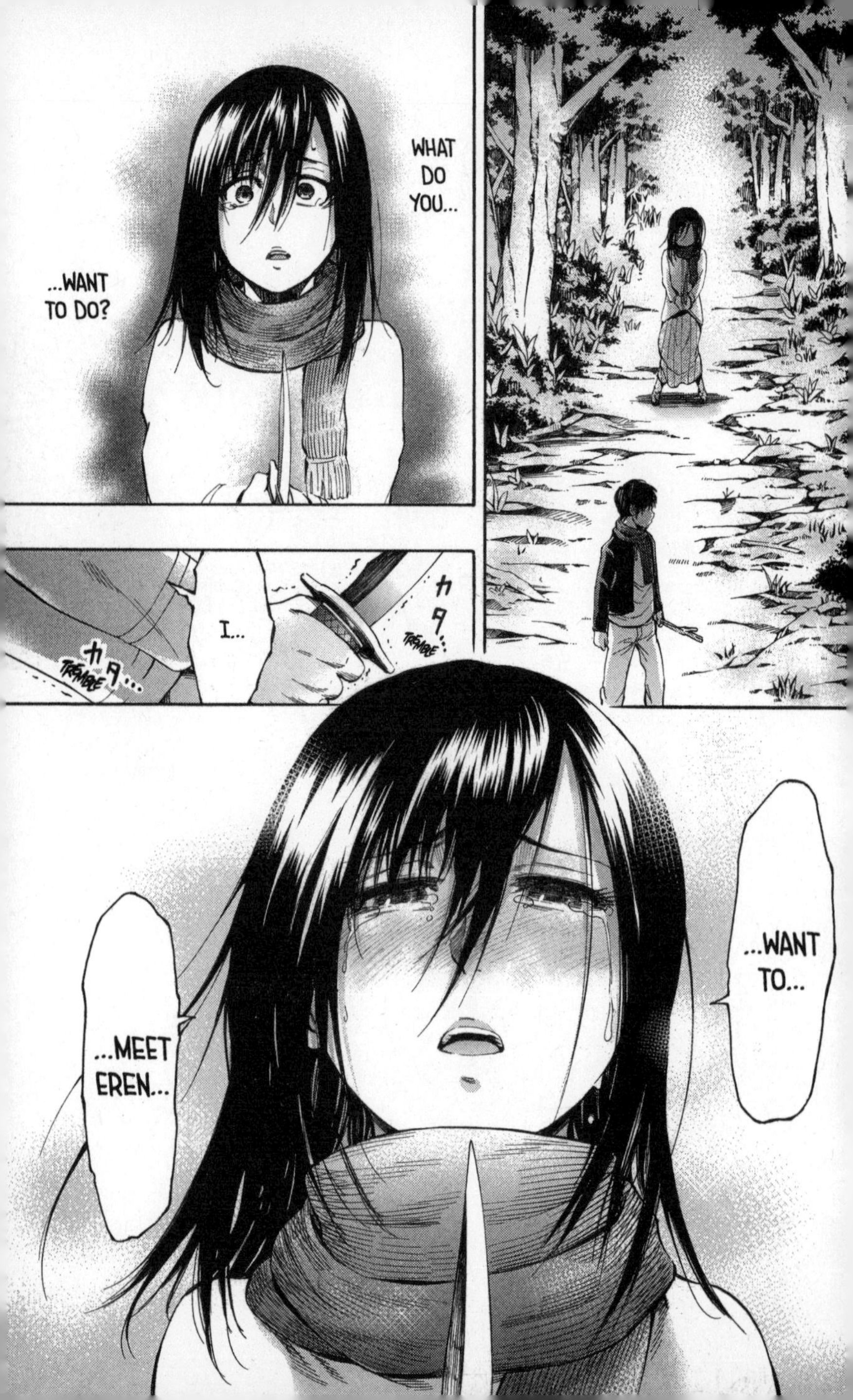
WHAT DO YOU...
...WANT TO DO?
カタ TREMBLE
I...
カタ TREMBLE...
...WANT TO...
...MEET EREN...

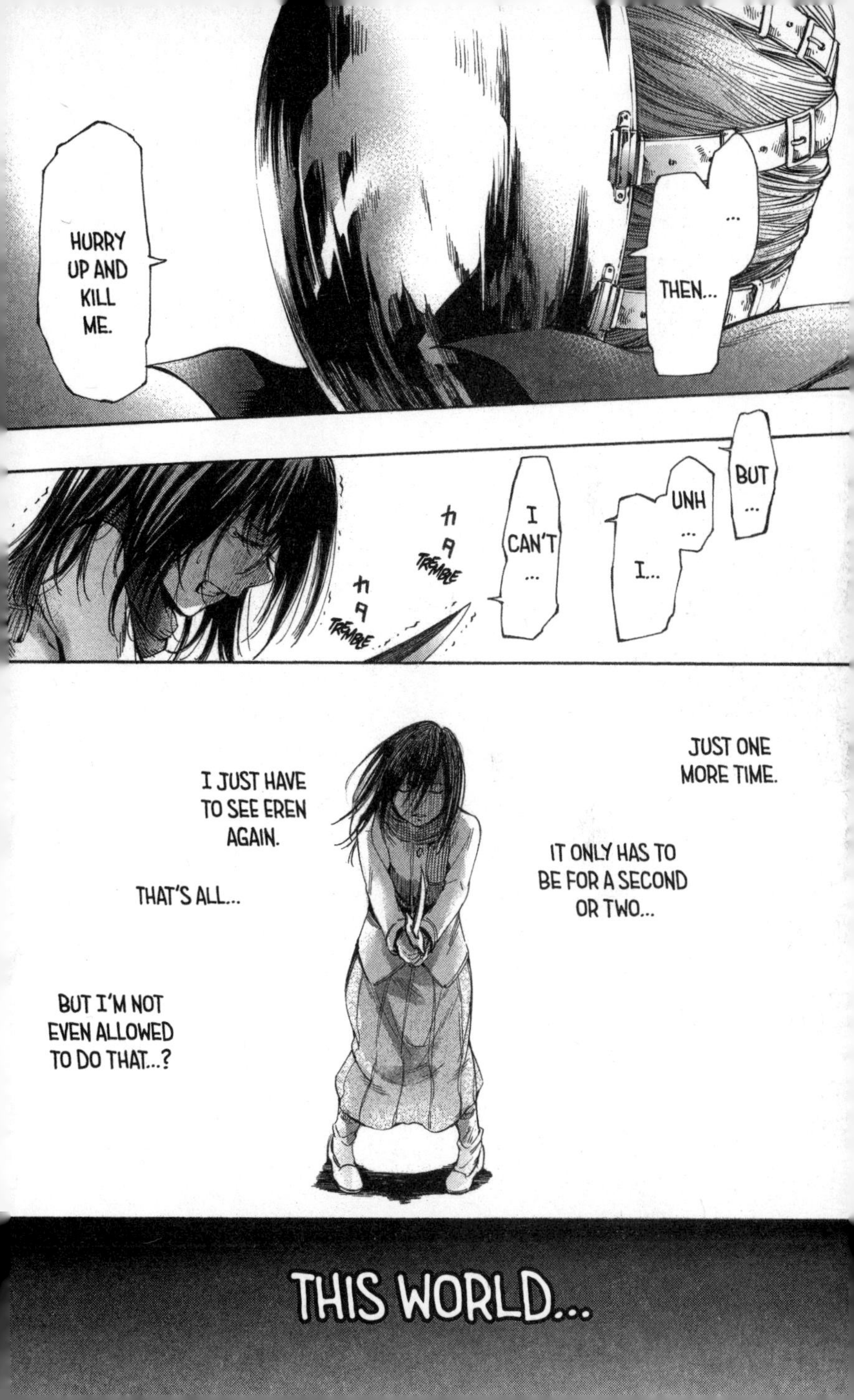
...
THEN...
HURRY UP AND KILL ME.
BUT...
UNH...
I...
I CAN'T...
カタ TREMBLE
カタ TREMBLE
JUST ONE MORE TIME.
IT ONLY HAS TO BE FOR A SECOND OR TWO...
I JUST HAVE TO SEE EREN AGAIN.
THAT'S ALL...
BUT I'M NOT EVEN ALLOWED TO DO THAT...?
THIS WORLD...

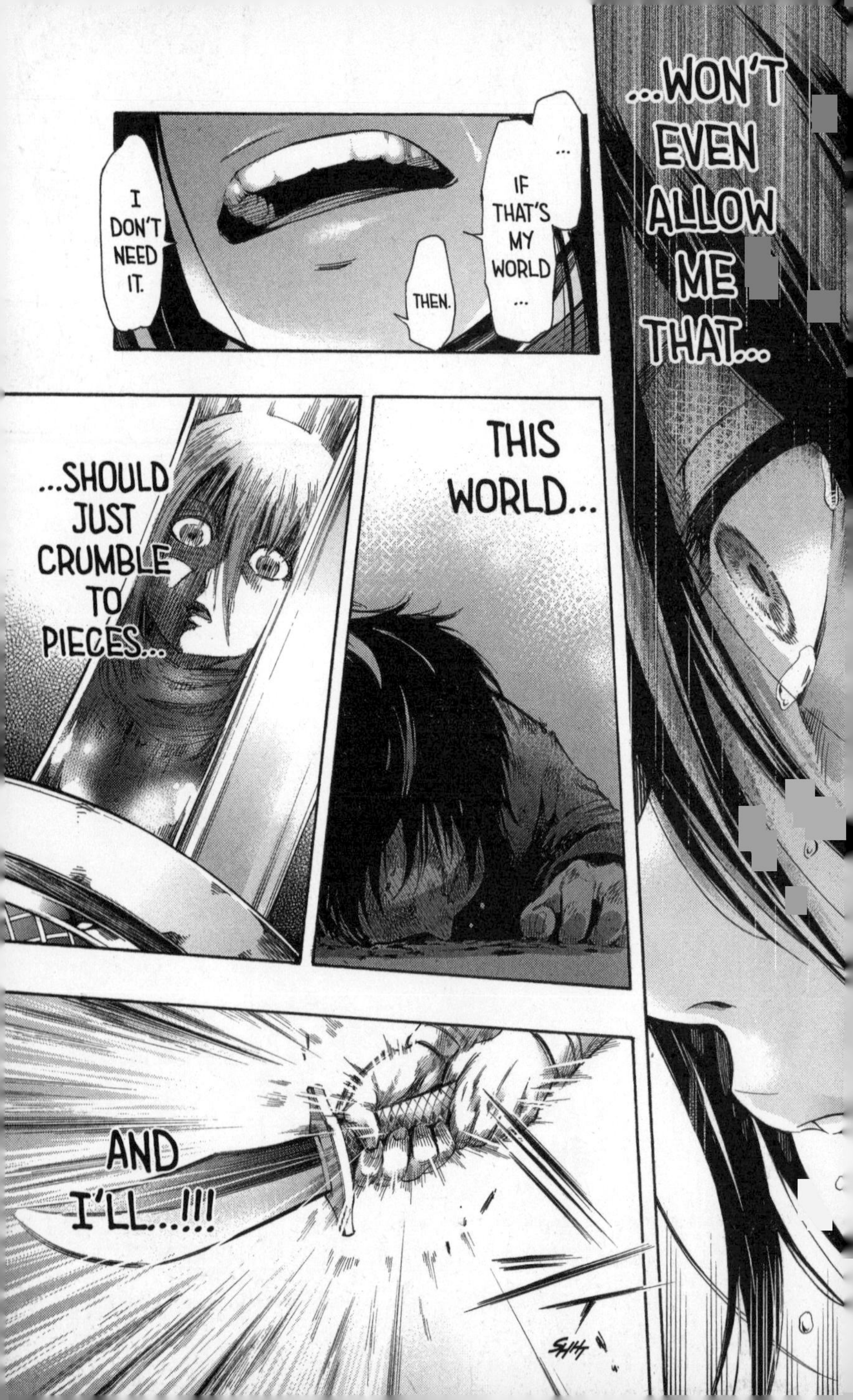

...WON'T EVEN ALLOW ME THAT...
... IF THAT'S MY WORLD ...
THEN.
I DON'T NEED IT.
THIS WORLD...
...SHOULD JUST CRUMBLE TO PIECES...
AND I'LL...!!!

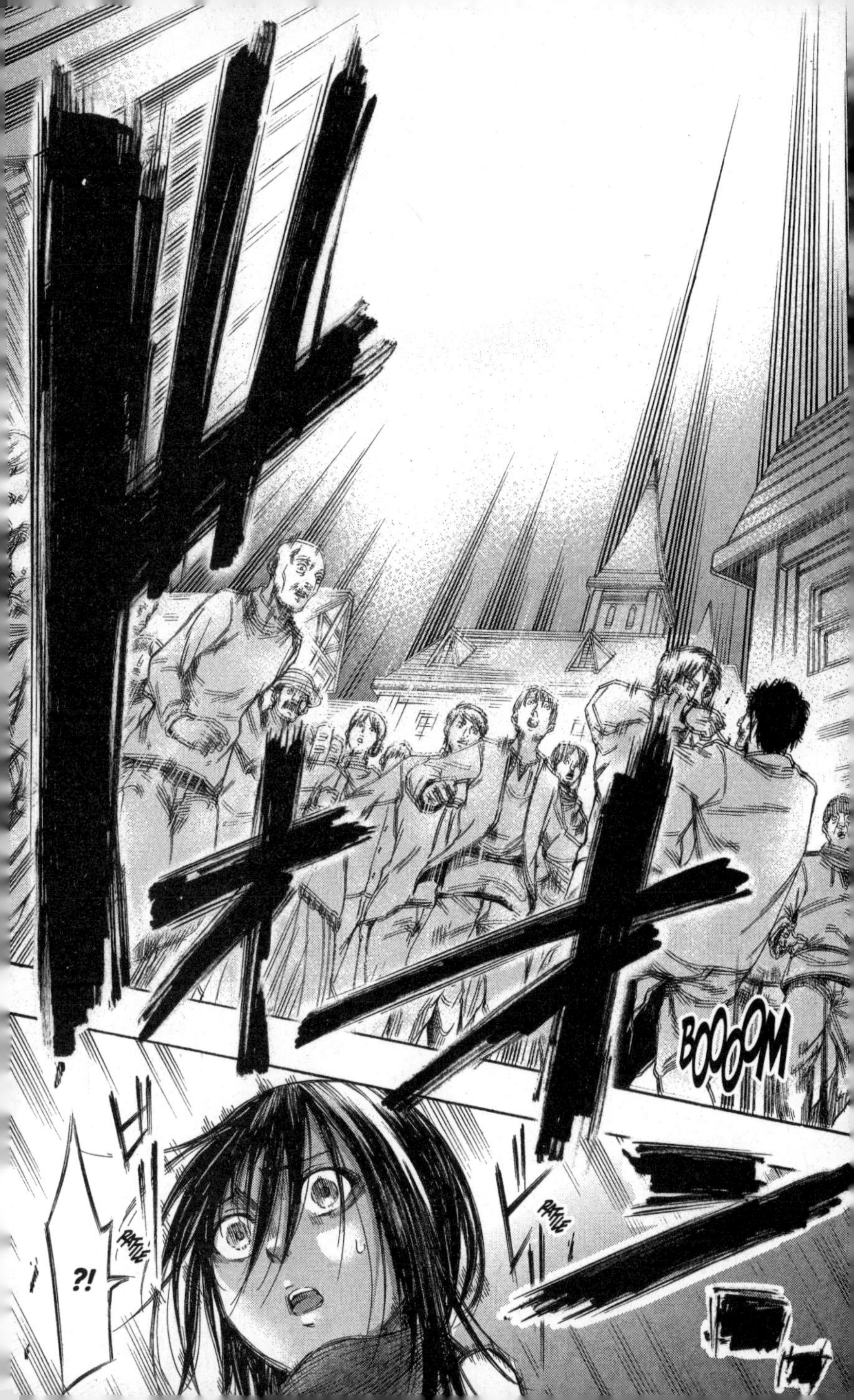
BOOOOM
RATTLE
RATTLE
?!

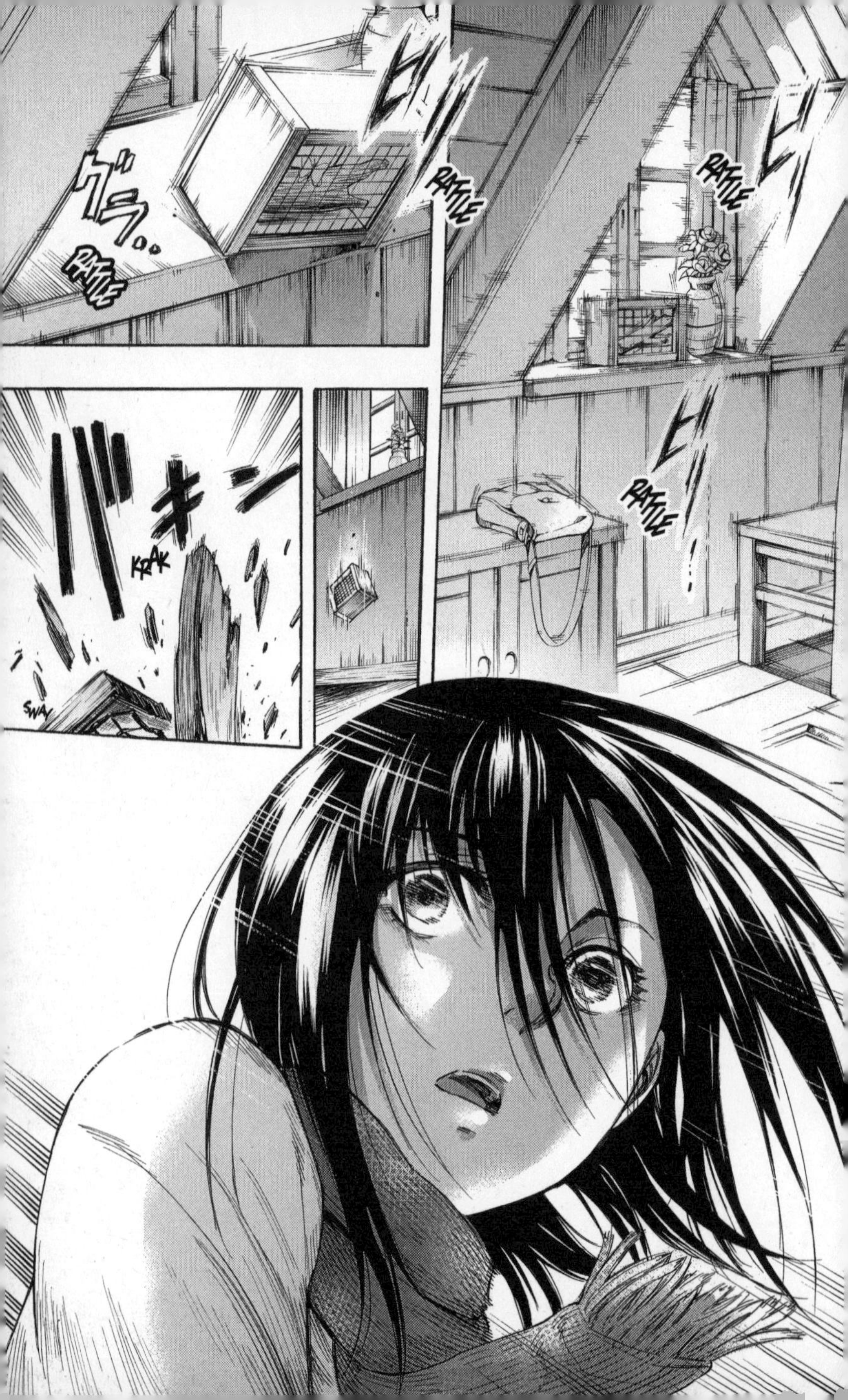
RATTLE
RATTLE
RATTLE
RATTLE
KRAK
SWAY

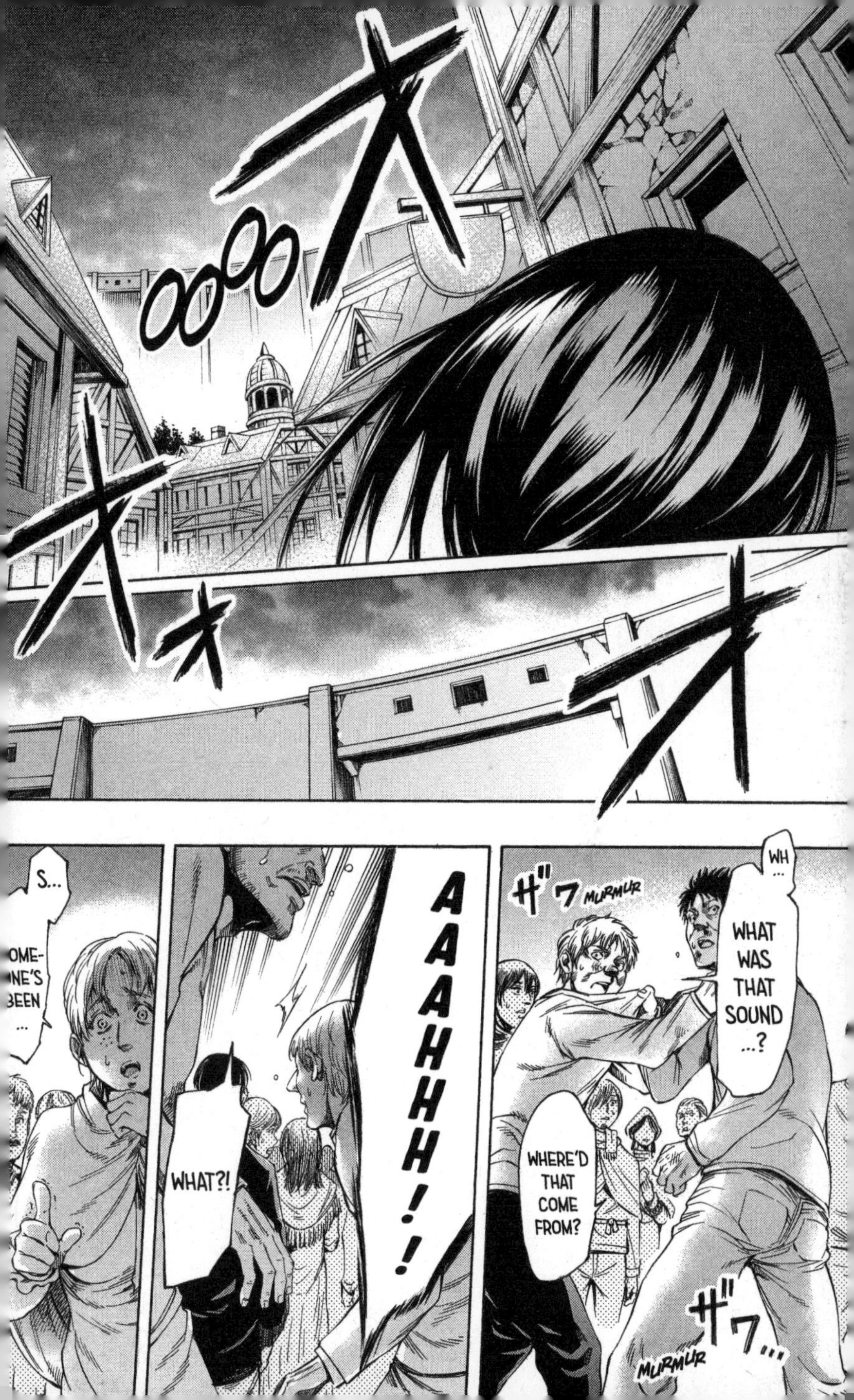

OOOO
WH ...
WHAT WAS THAT SOUND ...?
ザワ MURMUR
WHERE'D THAT COME FROM?
ザワ... MURMUR
AAAAHHHH!!!
WHAT?!
S...
OME- NE'S BEEN ...

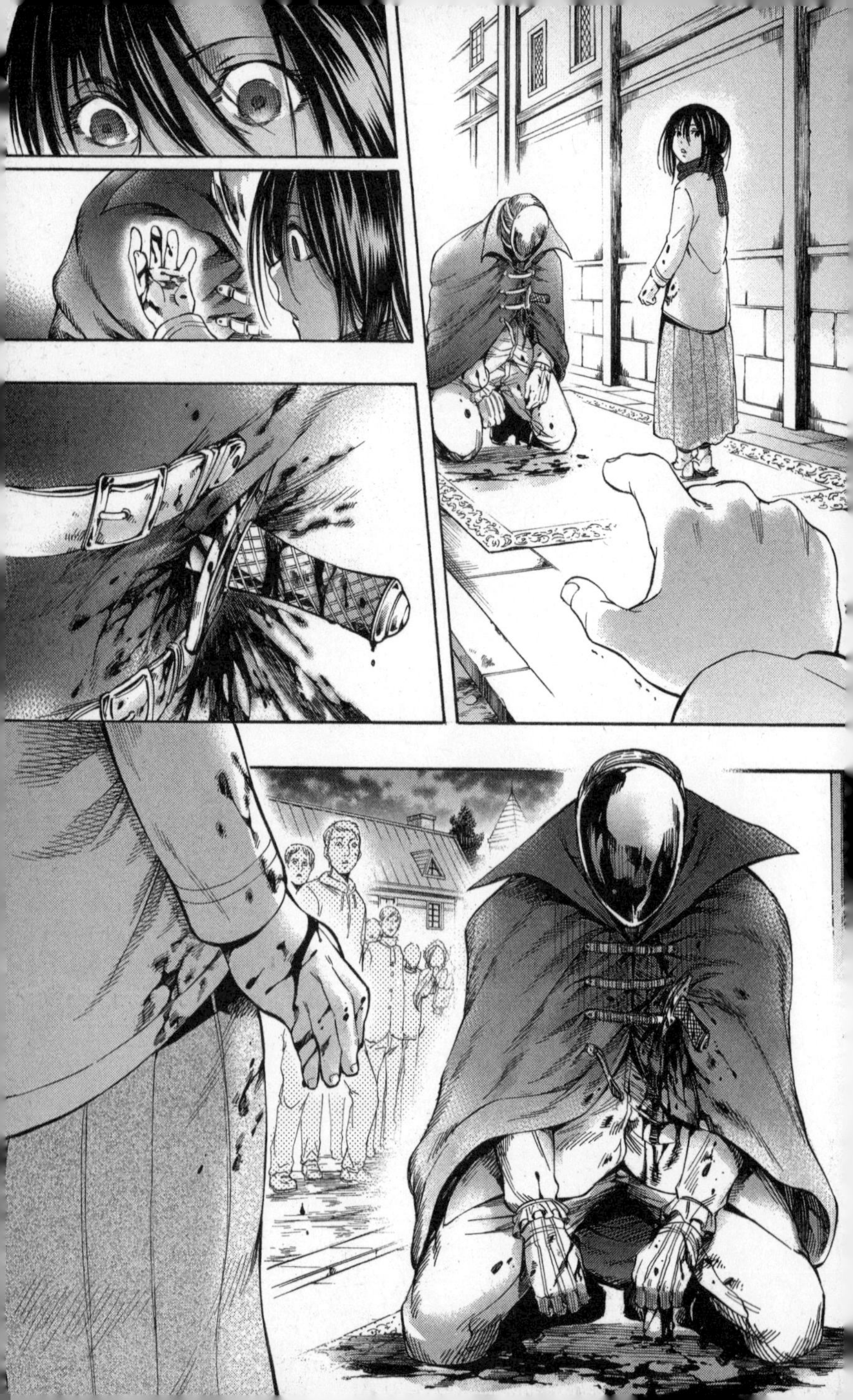

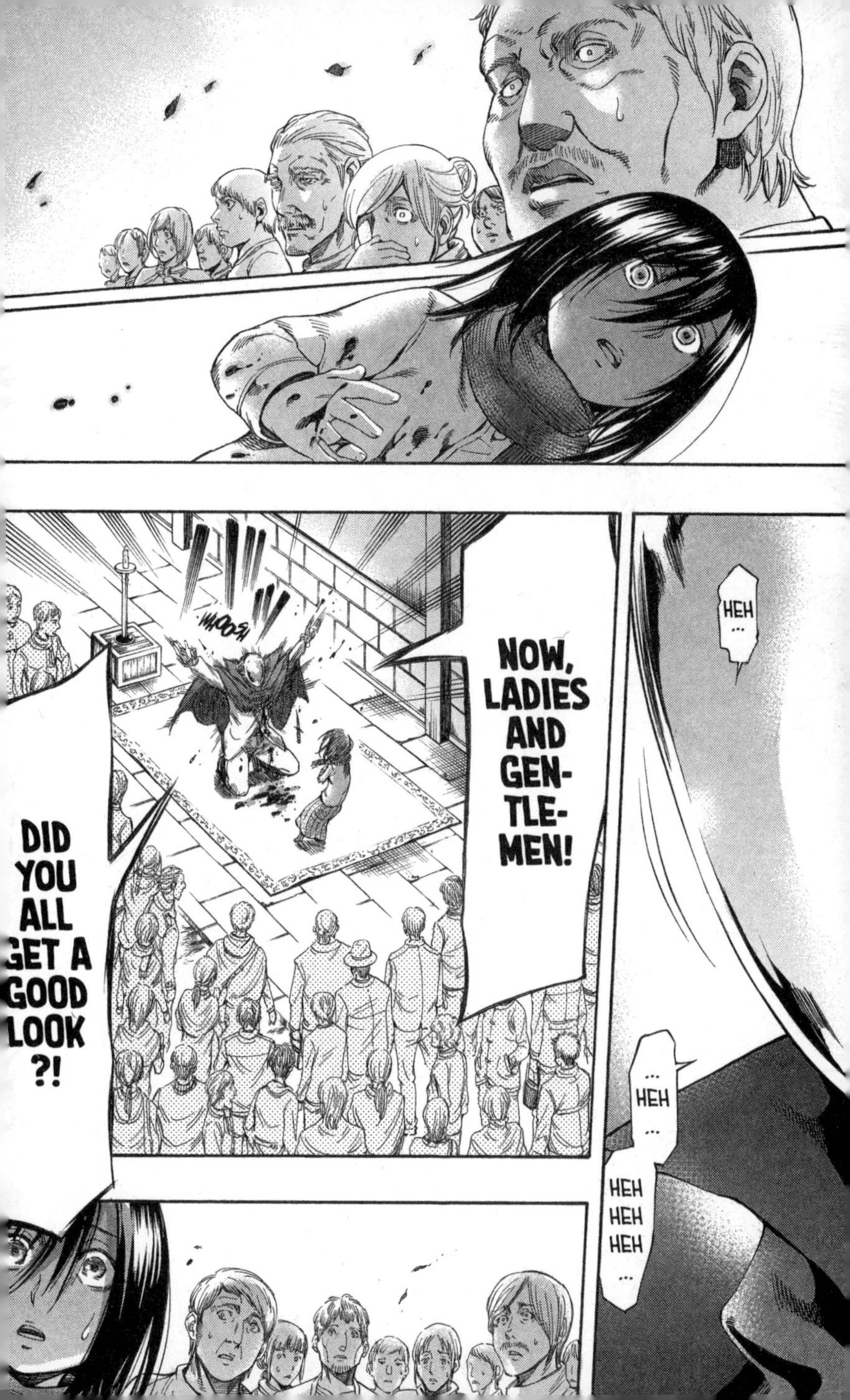
HEH ...
... HEH ...
HEH HEH HEH ...
WHOOSH
NOW, LADIES AND GEN-TLE-MEN!
DID YOU ALL GET A GOOD LOOK ?!

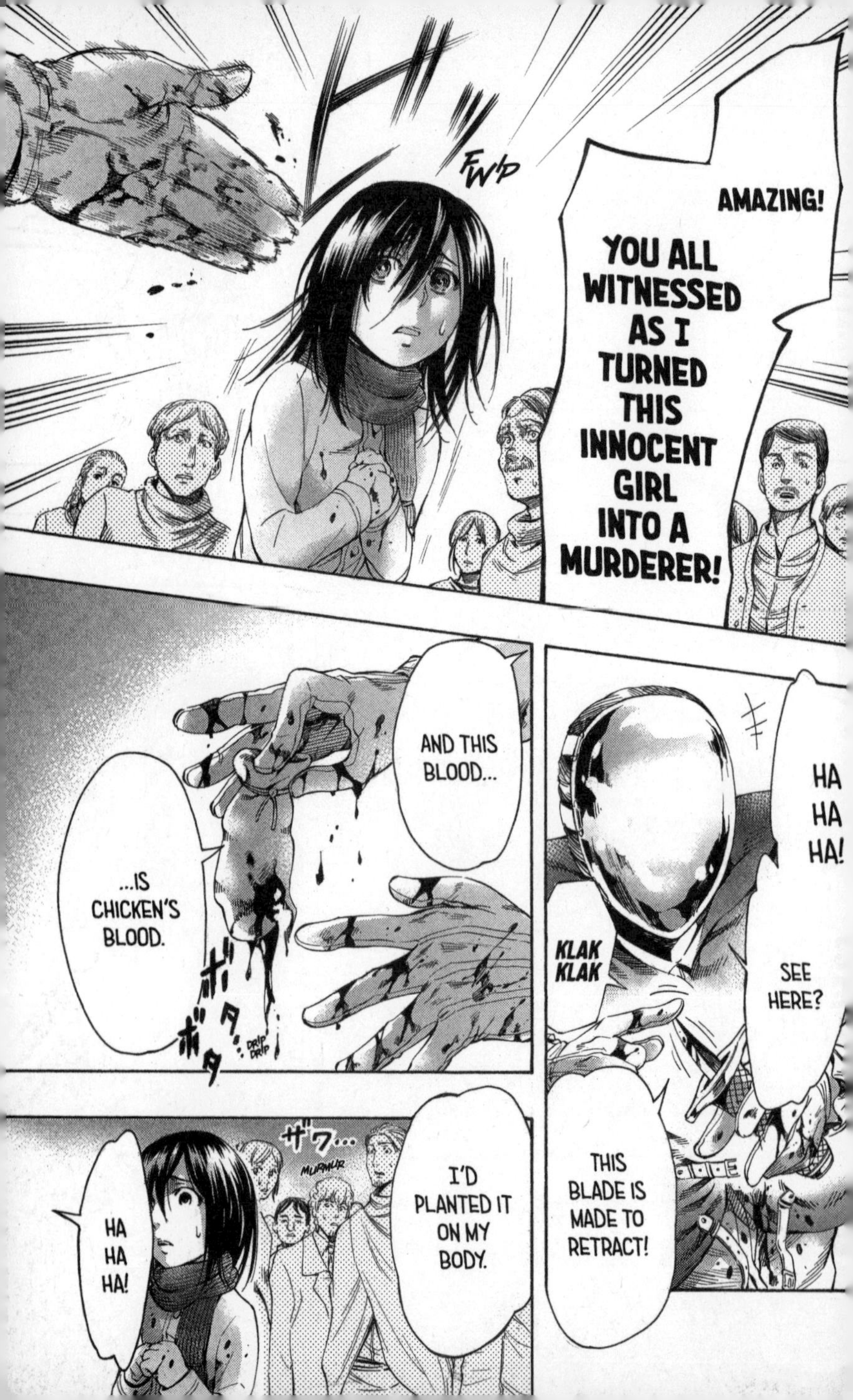
FWP
AMAZING!
YOU ALL WITNESSED AS I TURNED THIS INNOCENT GIRL INTO A MURDERER!
HA HA HA!
SEE HERE?
KLAK KLAK
THIS BLADE IS MADE TO RETRACT!
AND THIS BLOOD...
...IS CHICKEN'S BLOOD.
DRIP DRIP
I'D PLANTED IT ON MY BODY.
MURMUR
HA HA HA!

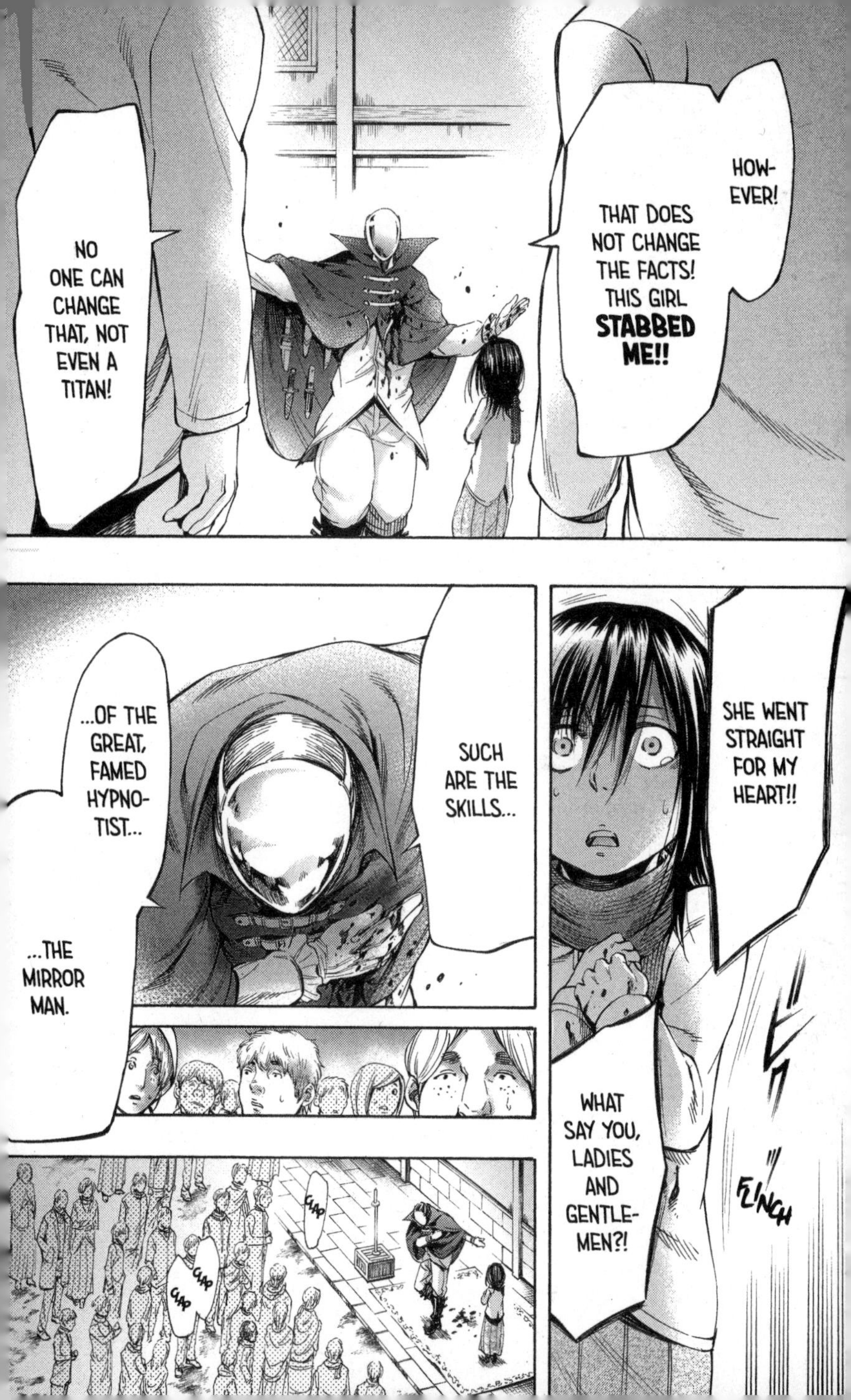
HOW-EVER!
THAT DOES NOT CHANGE THE FACTS! THIS GIRL **STABBED ME!!**
NO ONE CAN CHANGE THAT, NOT EVEN A TITAN!
SHE WENT STRAIGHT FOR MY HEART!!
FLINCH
WHAT SAY YOU, LADIES AND GENTLE-MEN?!
SUCH ARE THE SKILLS...
...OF THE GREAT, FAMED HYPNO-TIST...
...THE MIRROR MAN.
CLAP
CLAP
CLAP

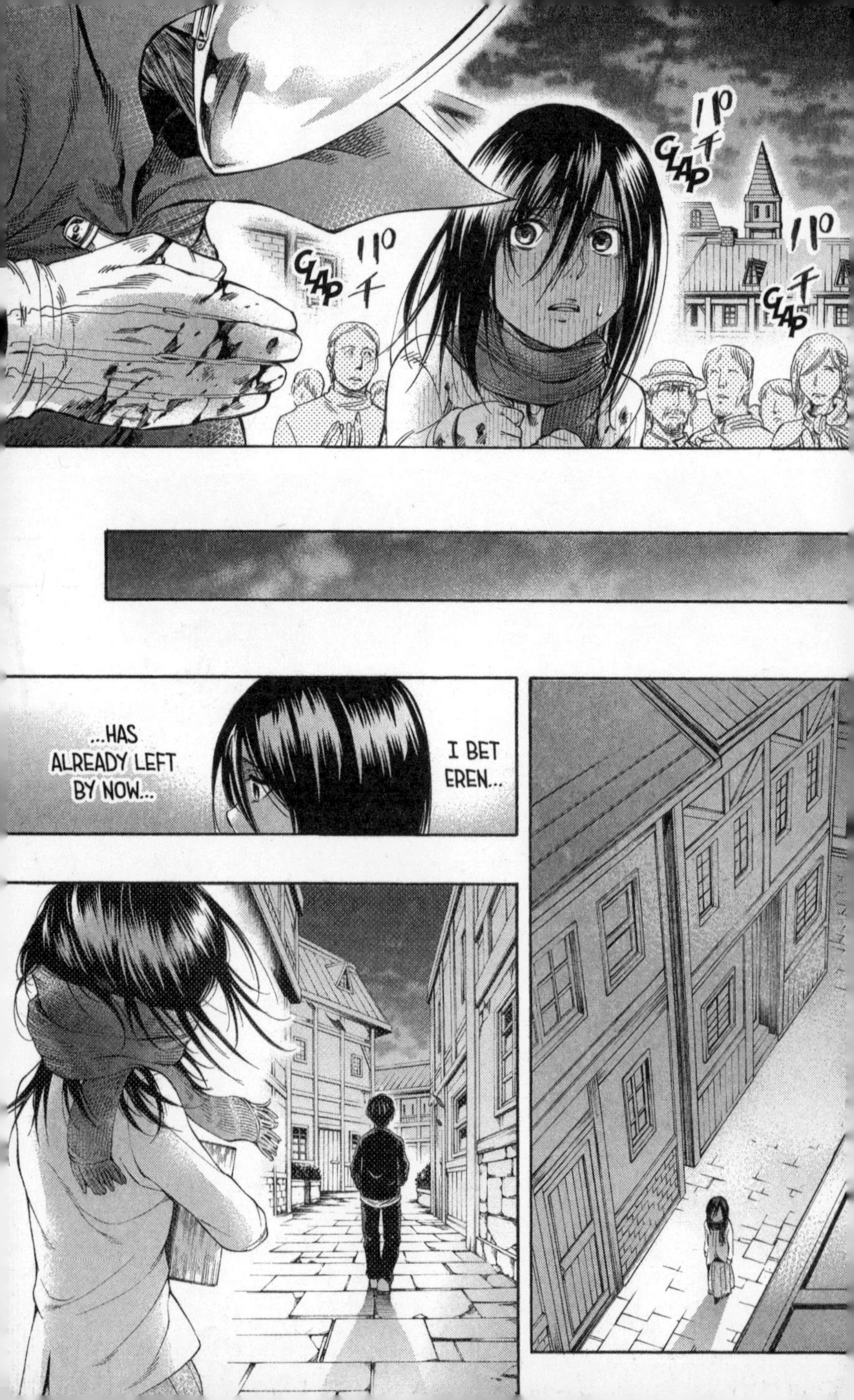
パチ
CLAP
パチ
CLAP
パチ
CLAP
I BET EREN...
...HAS ALREADY LEFT BY NOW...

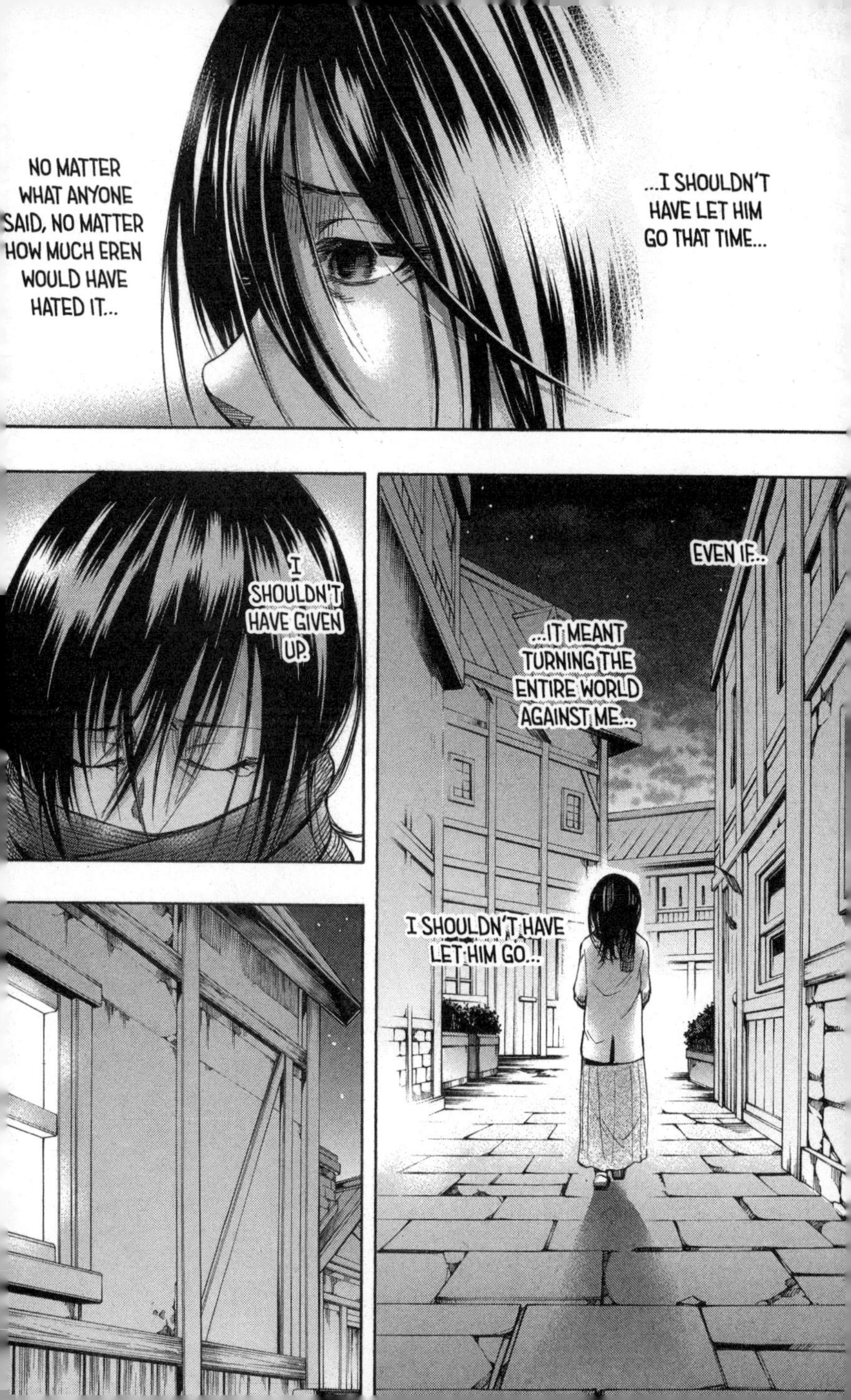
NO MATTER WHAT ANYONE SAID, NO MATTER HOW MUCH EREN WOULD HAVE HATED IT...
...I SHOULDN'T HAVE LET HIM GO THAT TIME...
EVEN IF...
...IT MEANT TURNING THE ENTIRE WORLD AGAINST ME...
I SHOULDN'T HAVE LET HIM GO...
I SHOULDN'T HAVE GIVEN UP.

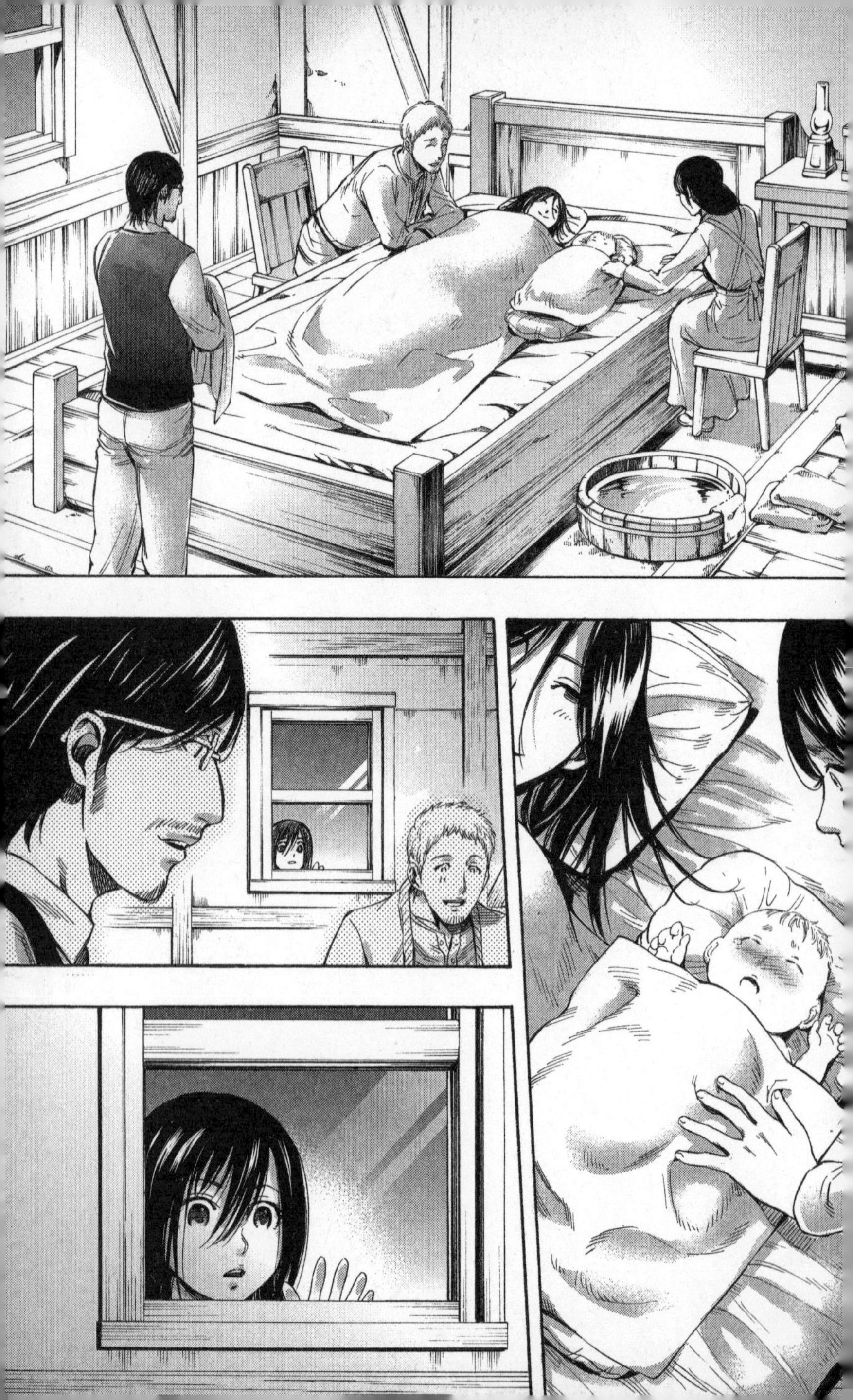

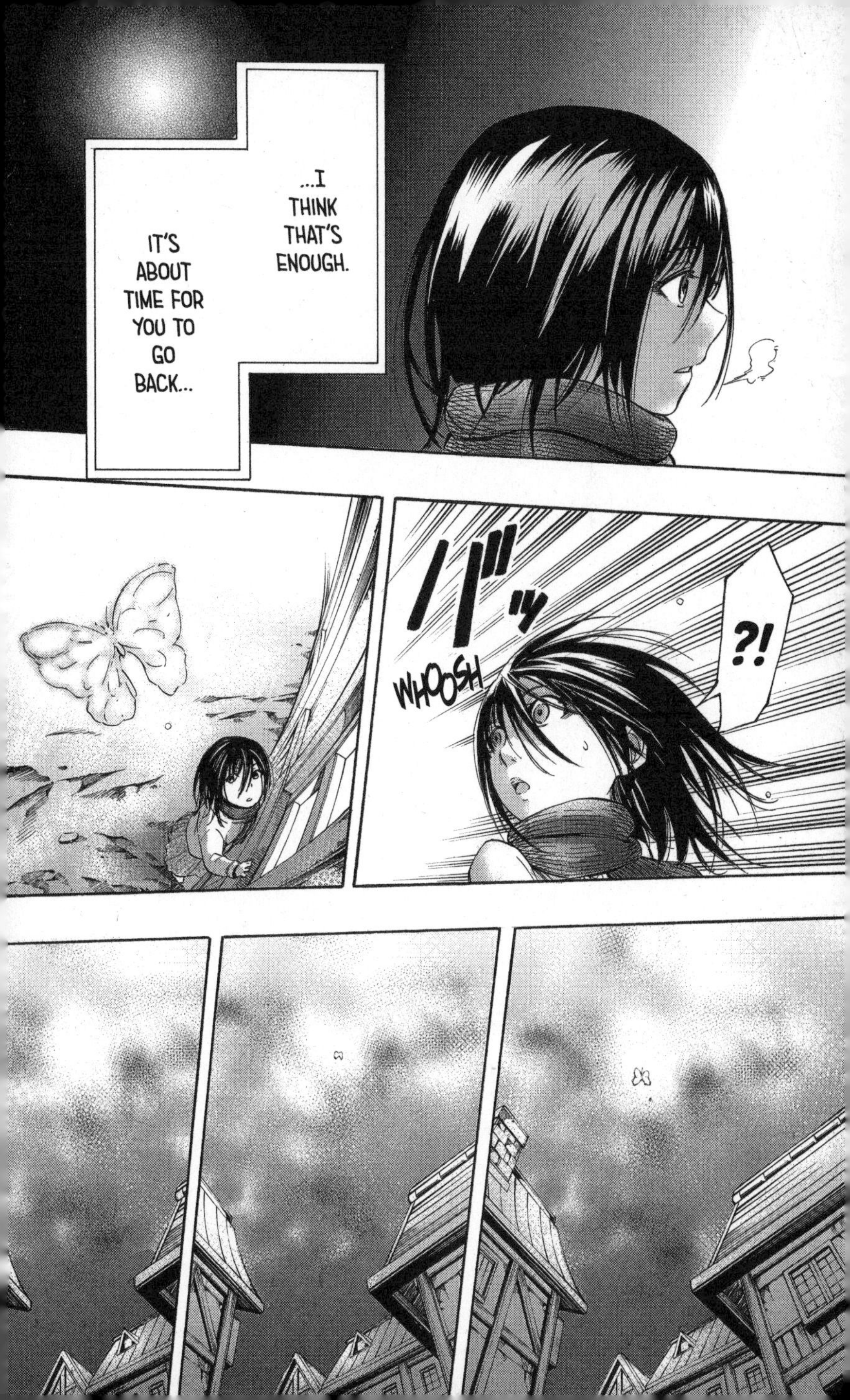
...I THINK THAT'S ENOUGH.
IT'S ABOUT TIME FOR YOU TO GO BACK...
バッ
WHOOSH
?!

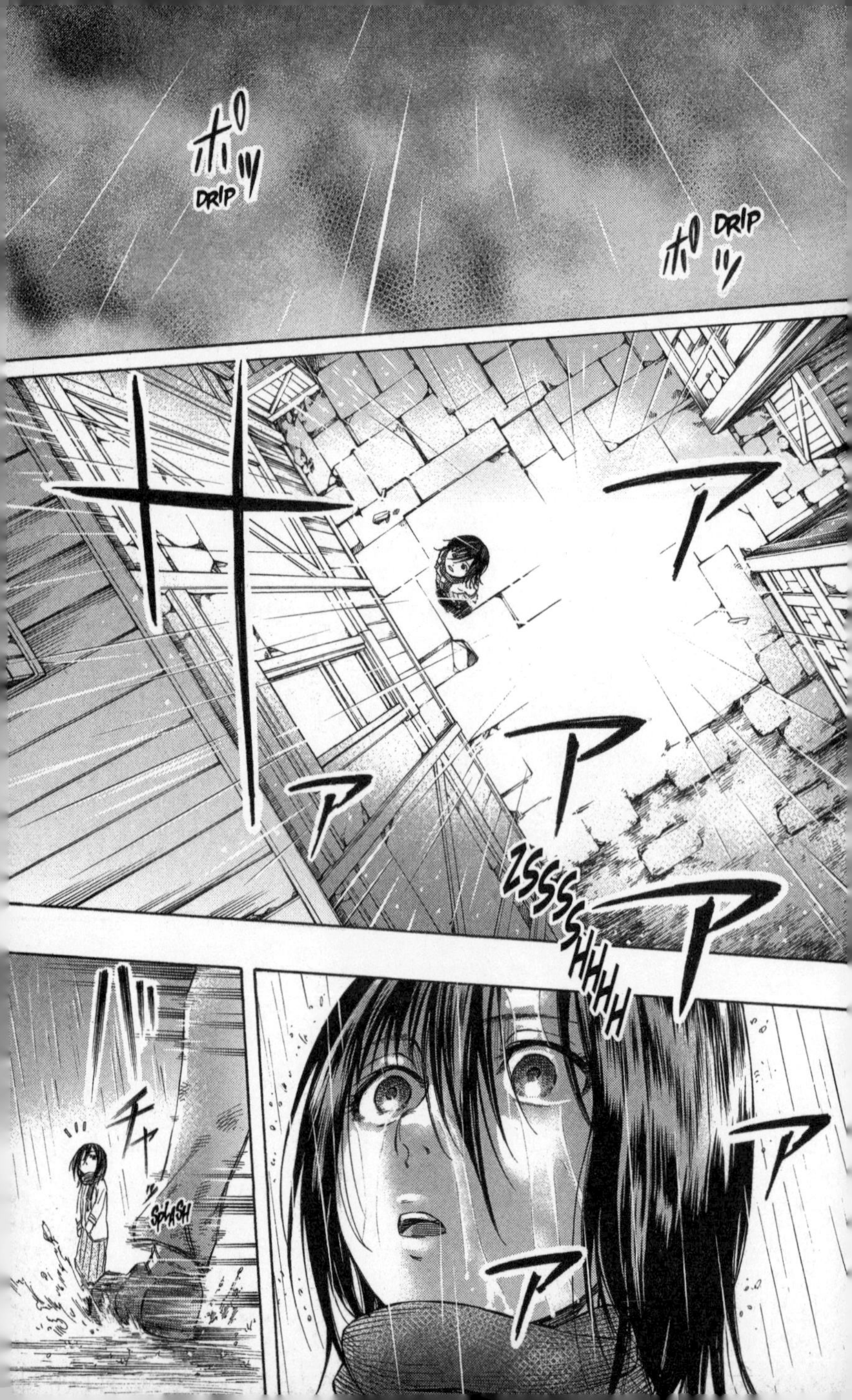
ポツ
DRIP
ポツ
DRIP
ザァァァァ
ZSSSSHHHH
ァァ
バチャッ
SPLASH

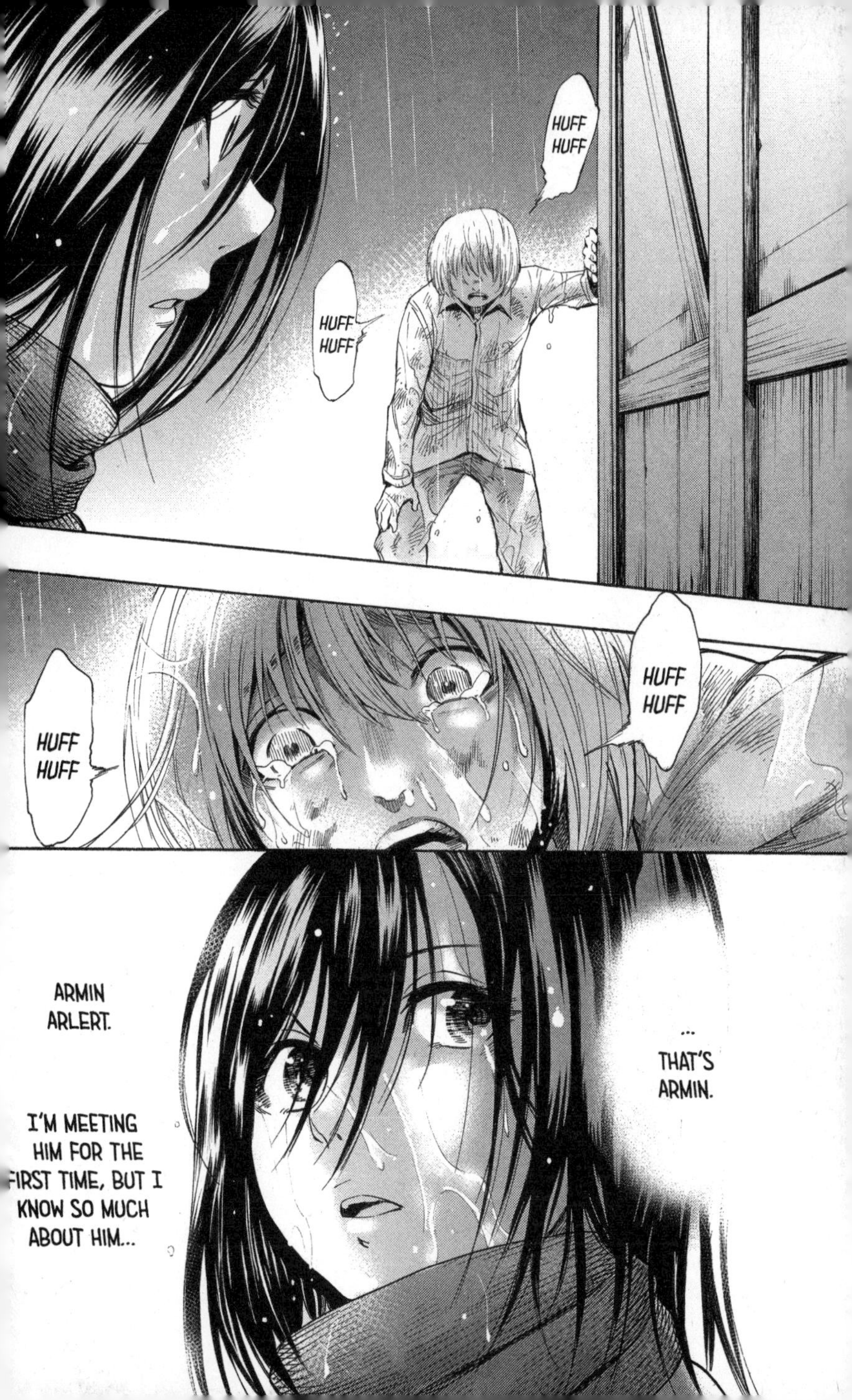
HUFF HUFF
HUFF HUFF
HUFF HUFF
HUFF HUFF
... THAT'S ARMIN.
ARMIN ARLERT.
I'M MEETING HIM FOR THE FIRST TIME, BUT I KNOW SO MUCH ABOUT HIM...

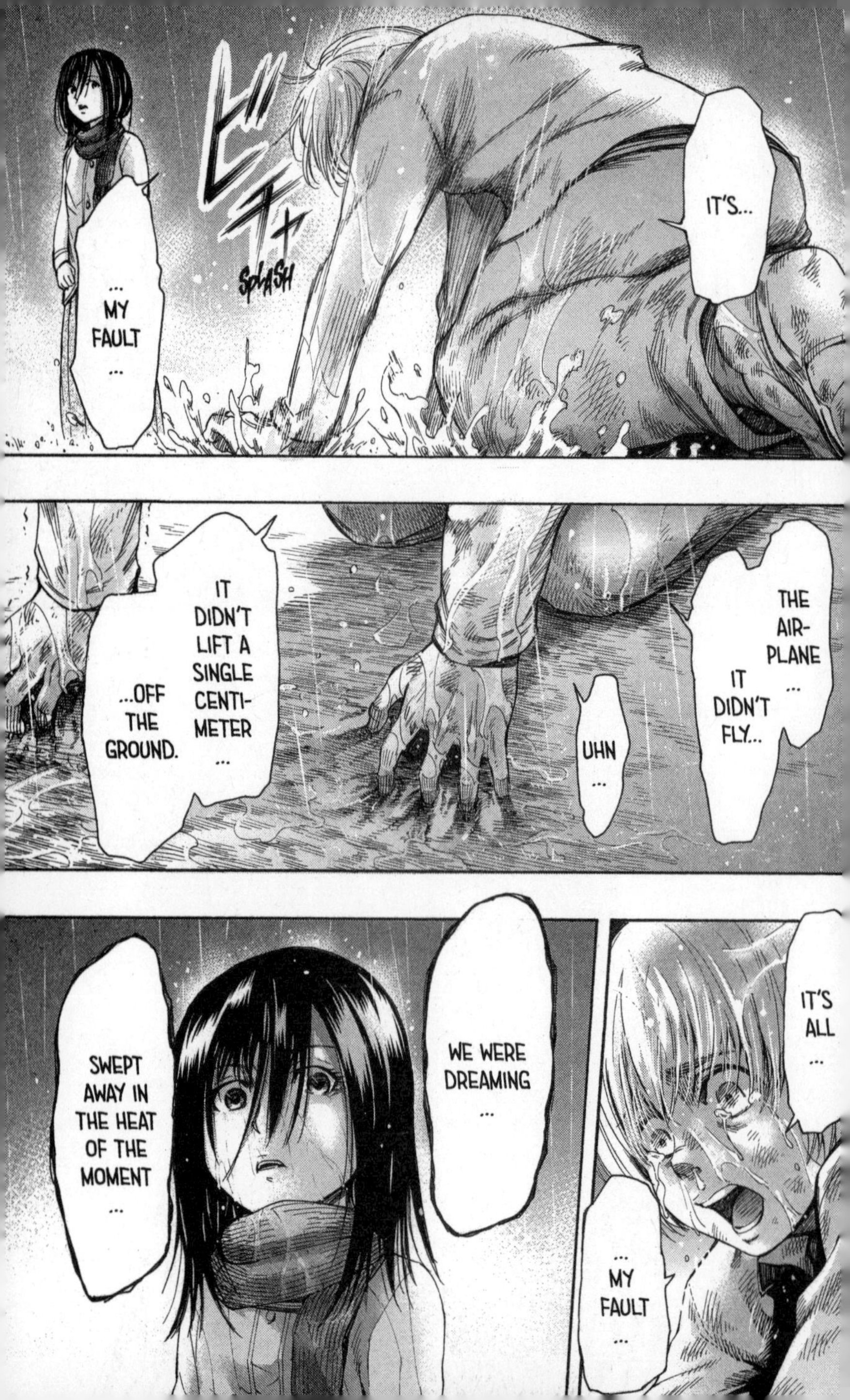
IT'S...
SPLASH
... MY FAULT ...
THE AIR-PLANE ...
IT DIDN'T FLY...
UHN ...
IT DIDN'T LIFT A SINGLE CENTI-METER ...
...OFF THE GROUND.
IT'S ALL ...
... MY FAULT ...
WE WERE DREAMING ...
SWEPT AWAY IN THE HEAT OF THE MOMENT ...

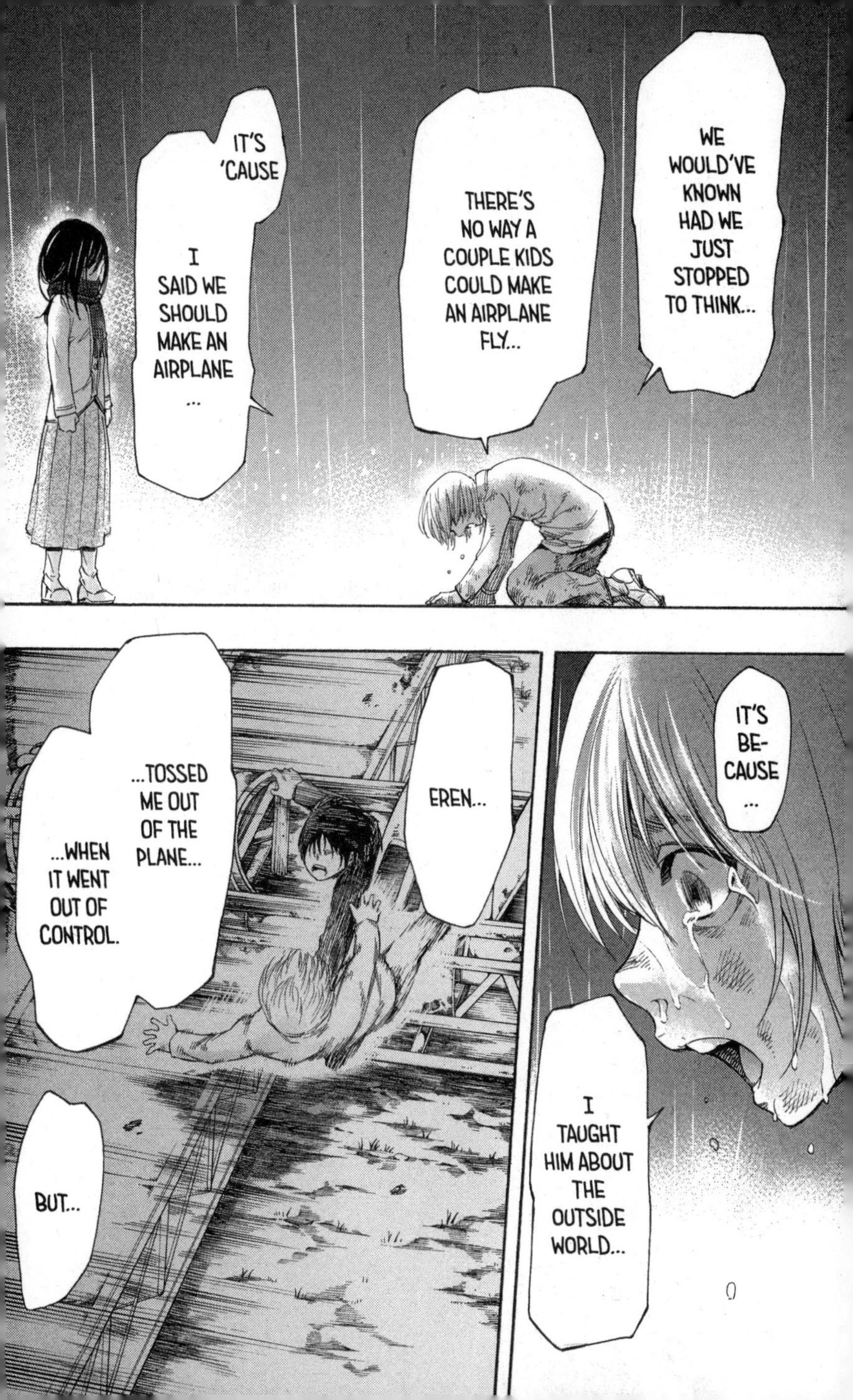
WE WOULD'VE KNOWN HAD WE JUST STOPPED TO THINK...
THERE'S NO WAY A COUPLE KIDS COULD MAKE AN AIRPLANE FLY...
IT'S 'CAUSE I SAID WE SHOULD MAKE AN AIRPLANE ...
IT'S BE-CAUSE ...
I TAUGHT HIM ABOUT THE OUTSIDE WORLD...
EREN...
...TOSSED ME OUT OF THE PLANE...
...WHEN IT WENT OUT OF CONTROL.
BUT...

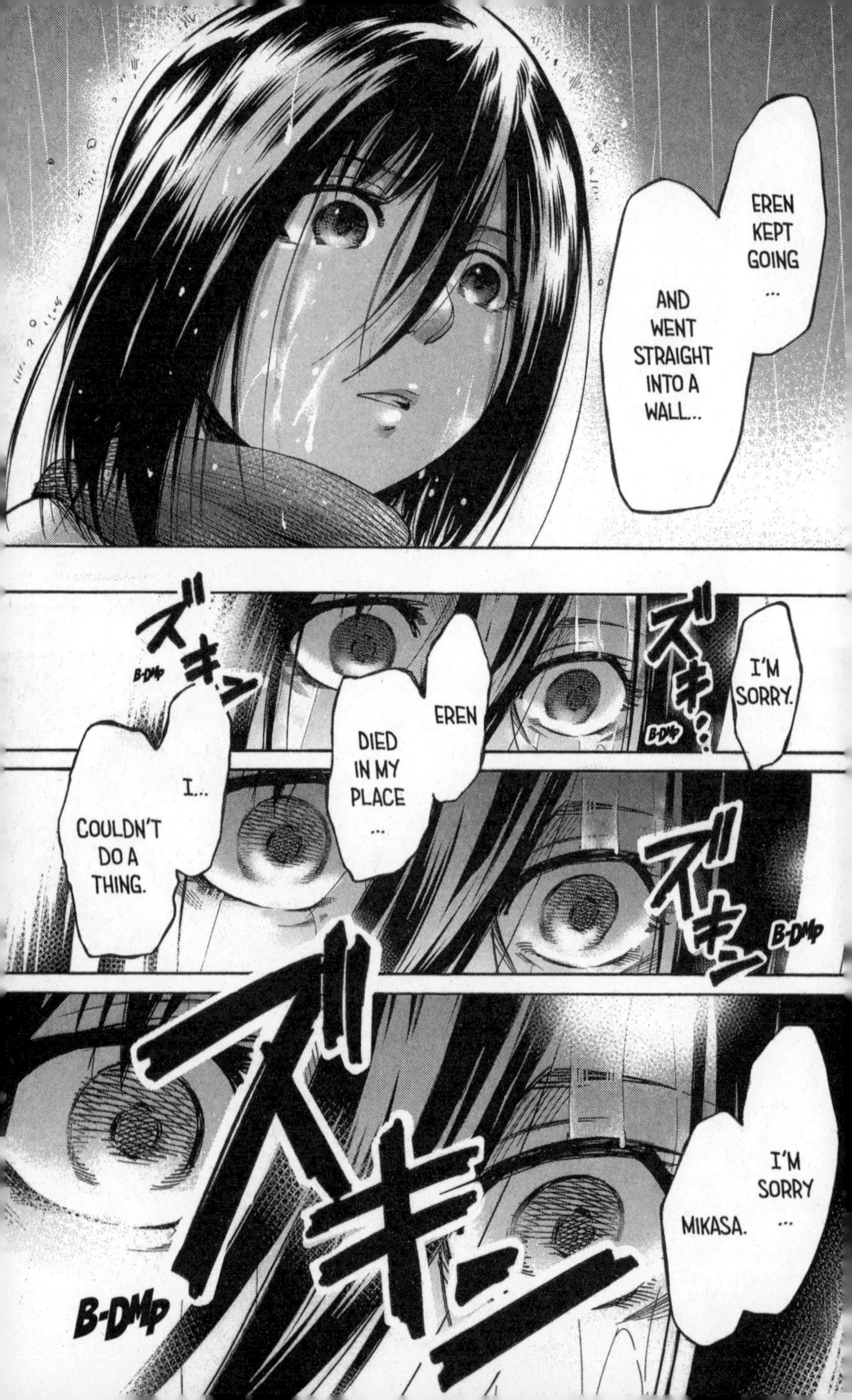
EREN KEPT GOING ...
AND WENT STRAIGHT INTO A WALL...
I'M SORRY.
ズキ…
B-DMP
EREN
DIED IN MY PLACE ...
ズキン
B-DMP
I...
COULDN'T DO A THING.
ズキン
B-DMP
I'M SORRY ...
MIKASA.
ズキン
B-DMP

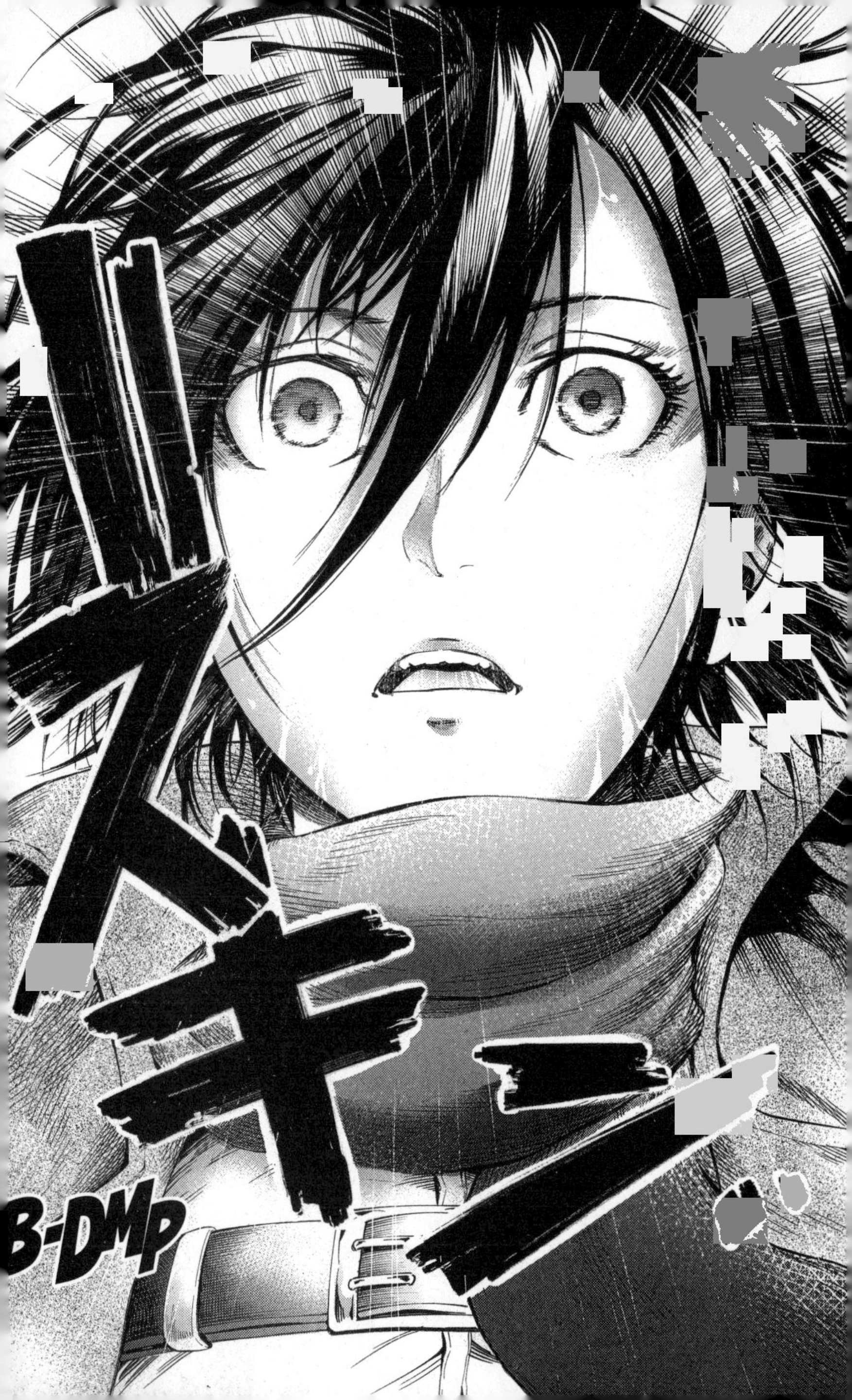
B-DMP

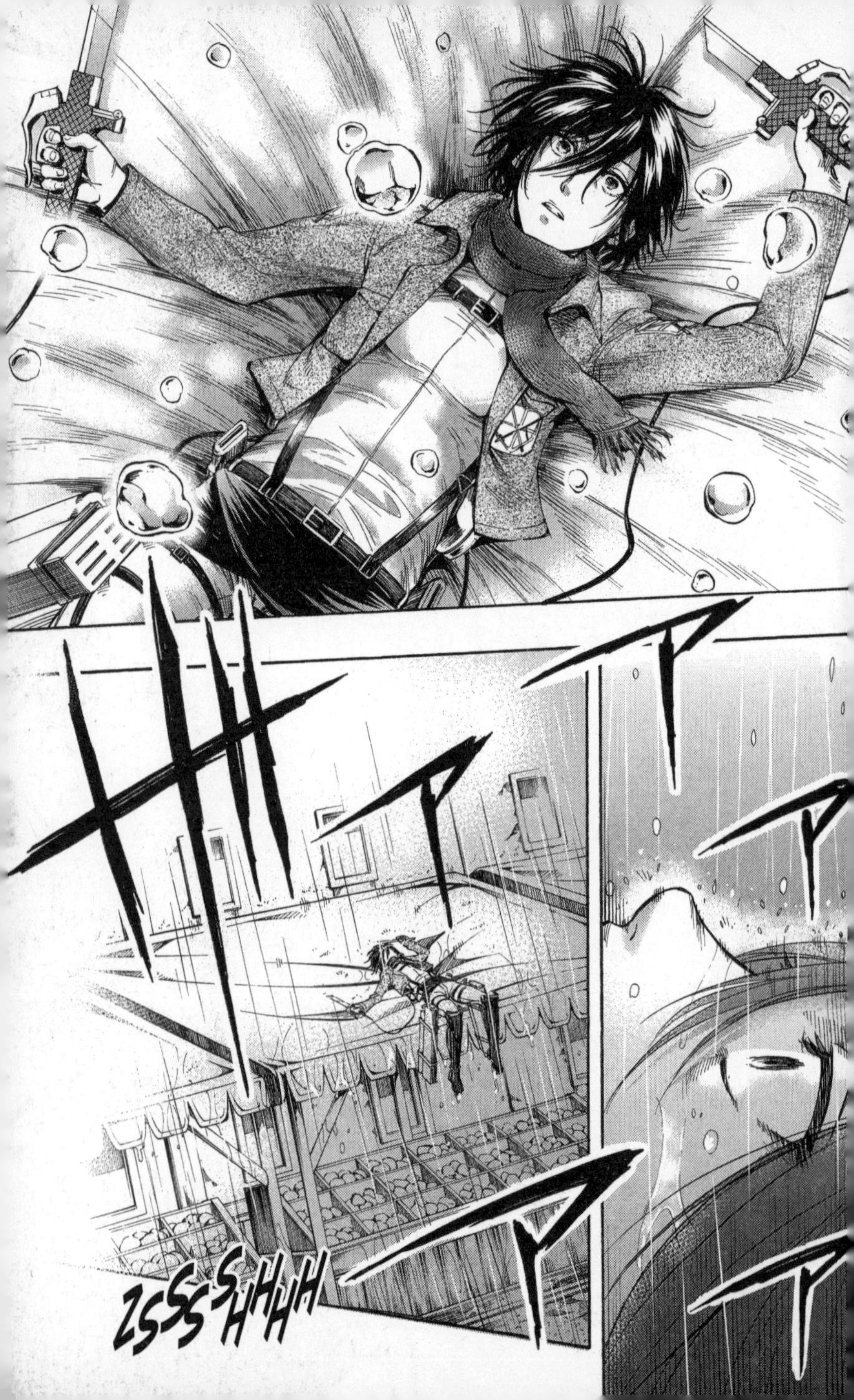

ZSSSSHHHH

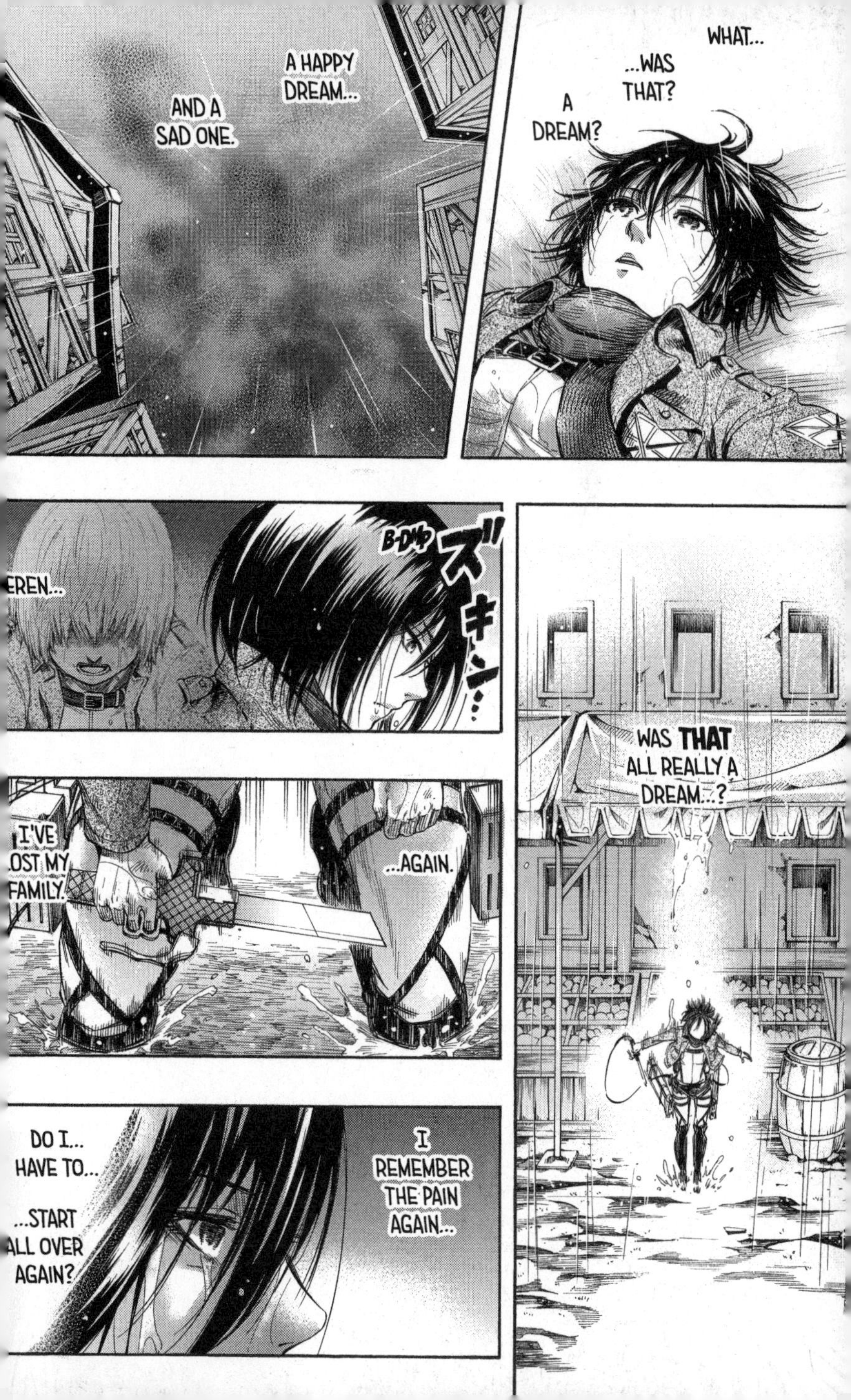
WHAT...
...WAS THAT?
A DREAM?
A HAPPY DREAM...
AND A SAD ONE.
WAS THAT ALL REALLY A DREAM...?
EREN...
B-DMP
ズキン
...AGAIN.
I'VE LOST MY FAMILY.
I REMEMBER THE PAIN AGAIN...
DO I... HAVE TO...
...START ALL OVER AGAIN?

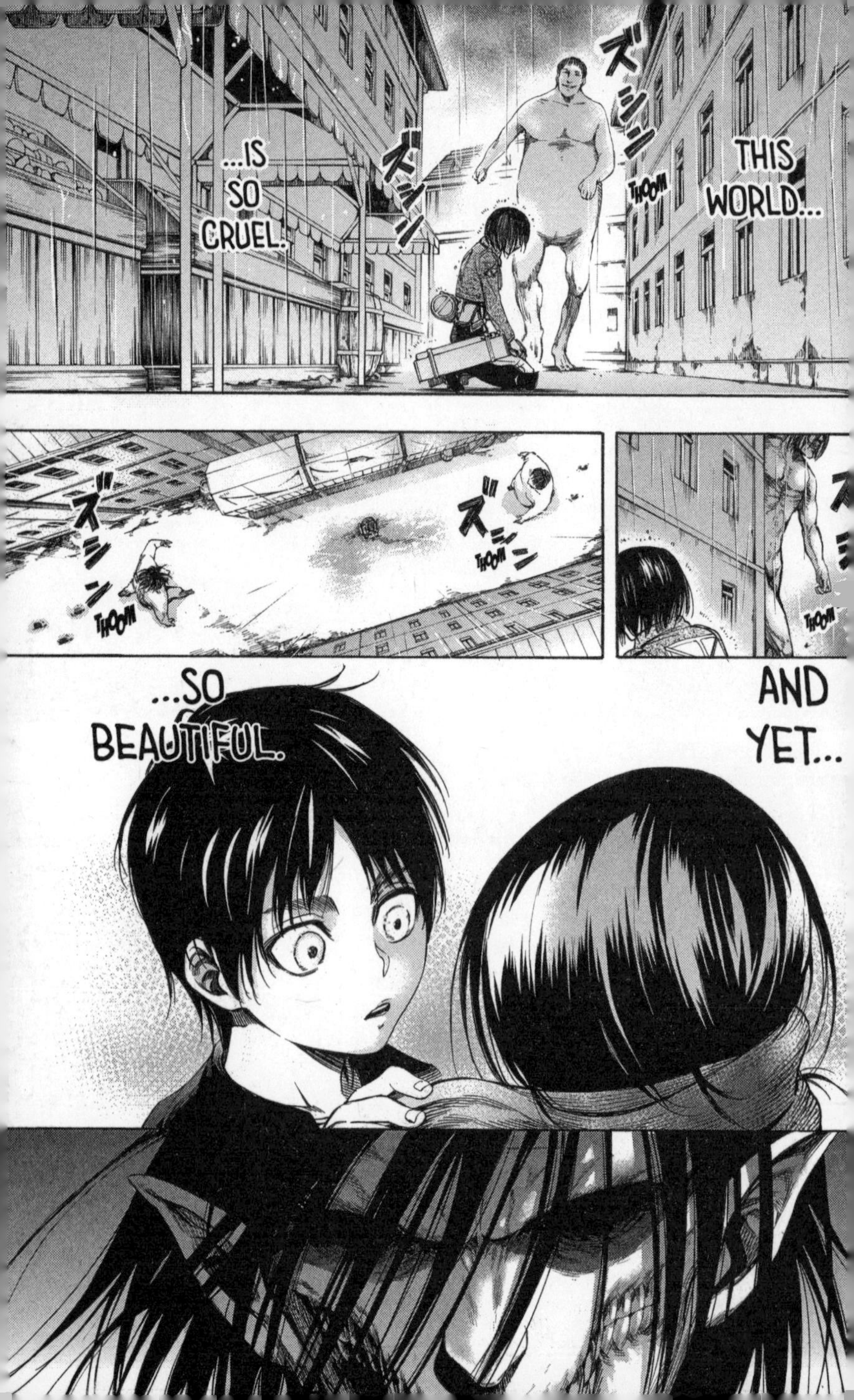
THIS WORLD...
ズシン
THOOM
ズシン
...IS SO CRUEL.
THOOM
ズシン
THOOM
ズシン
THOOM
AND YET...
...SO BEAUTIFUL.

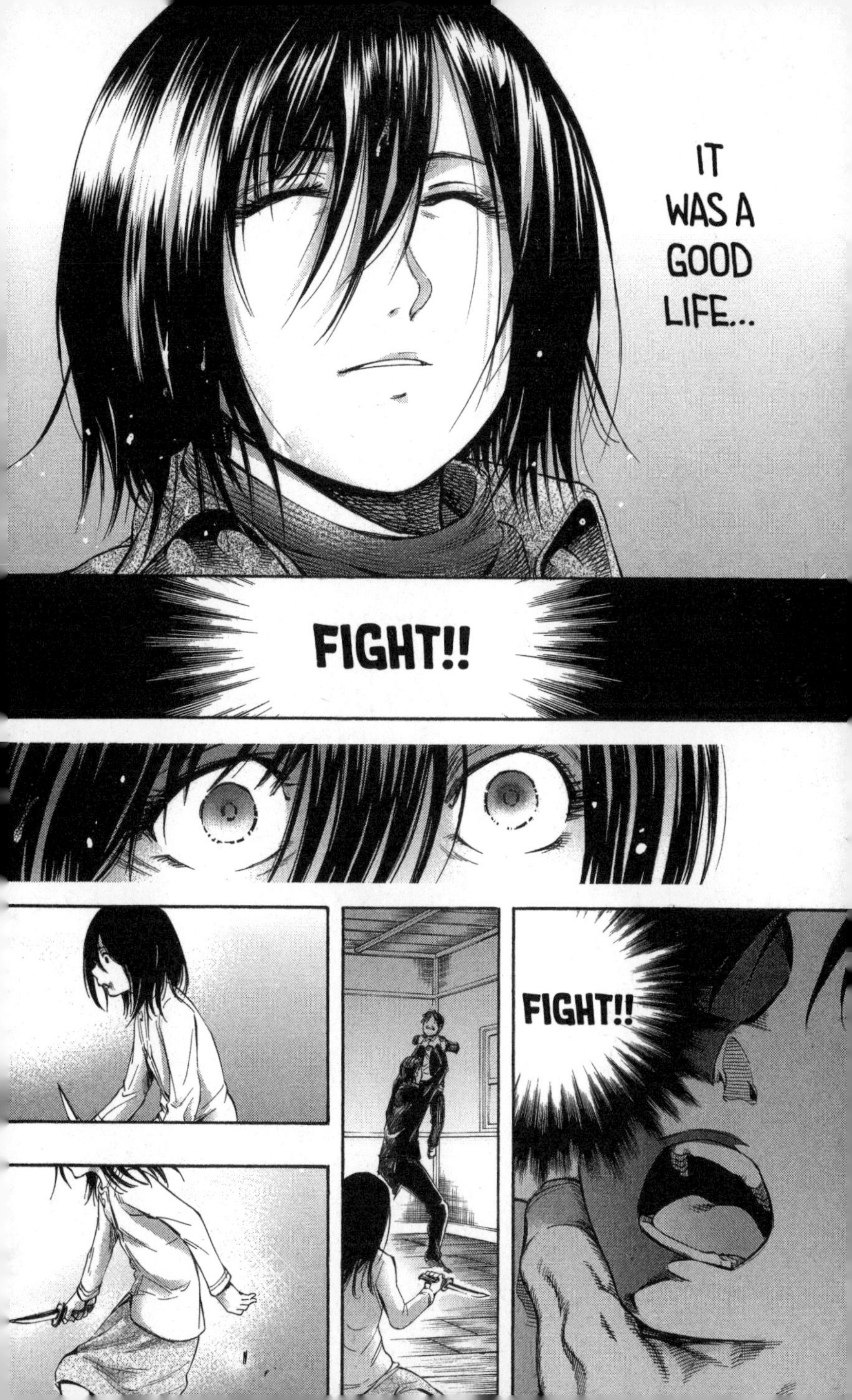
IT WAS A GOOD LIFE...
FIGHT!!
FIGHT!!

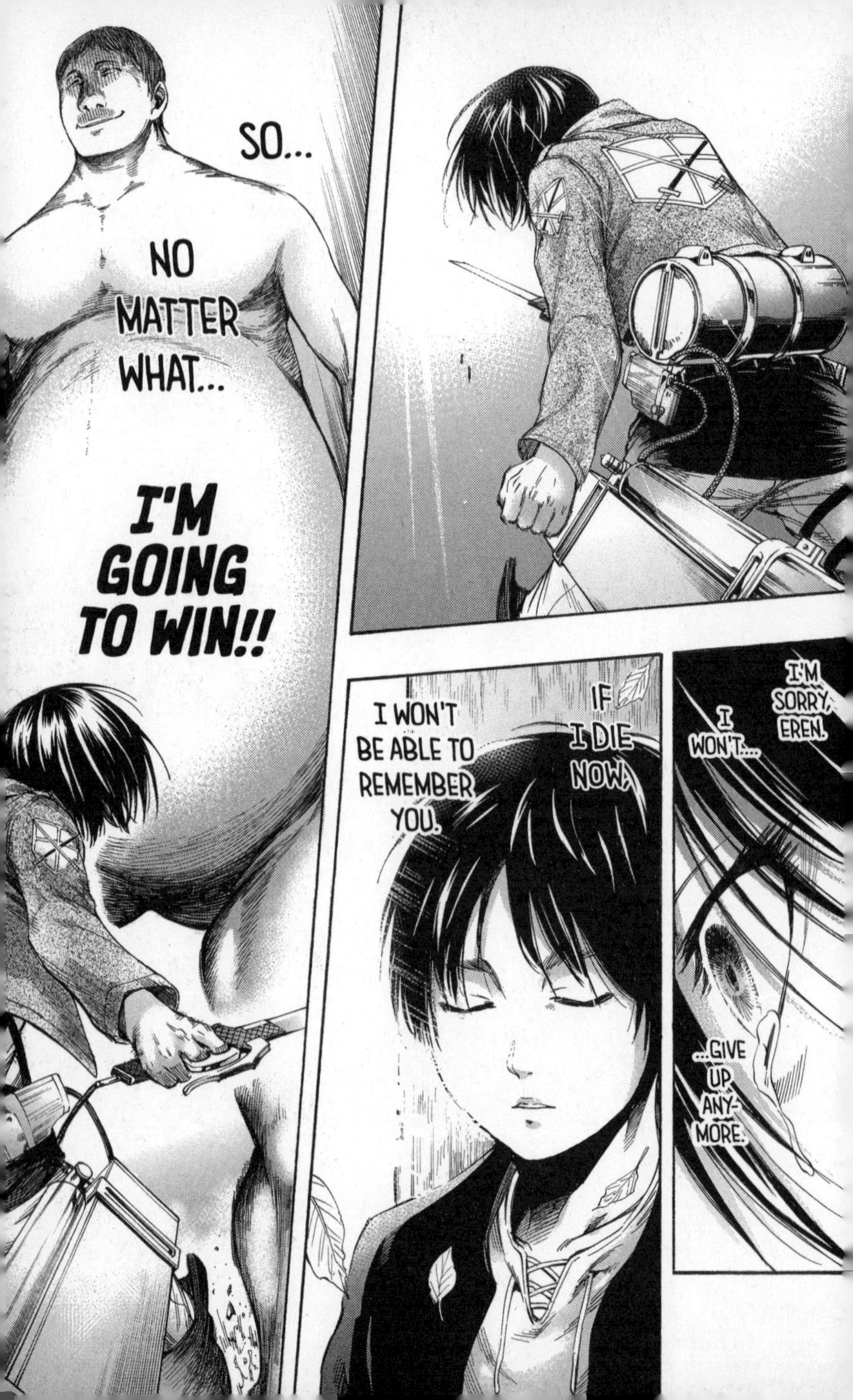
I'M SORRY, EREN.
I WON'T...
...GIVE UP ANY-MORE.
IF I DIE NOW,
I WON'T BE ABLE TO REMEMBER YOU.
SO...
NO MATTER WHAT...
I'M GOING TO WIN!!

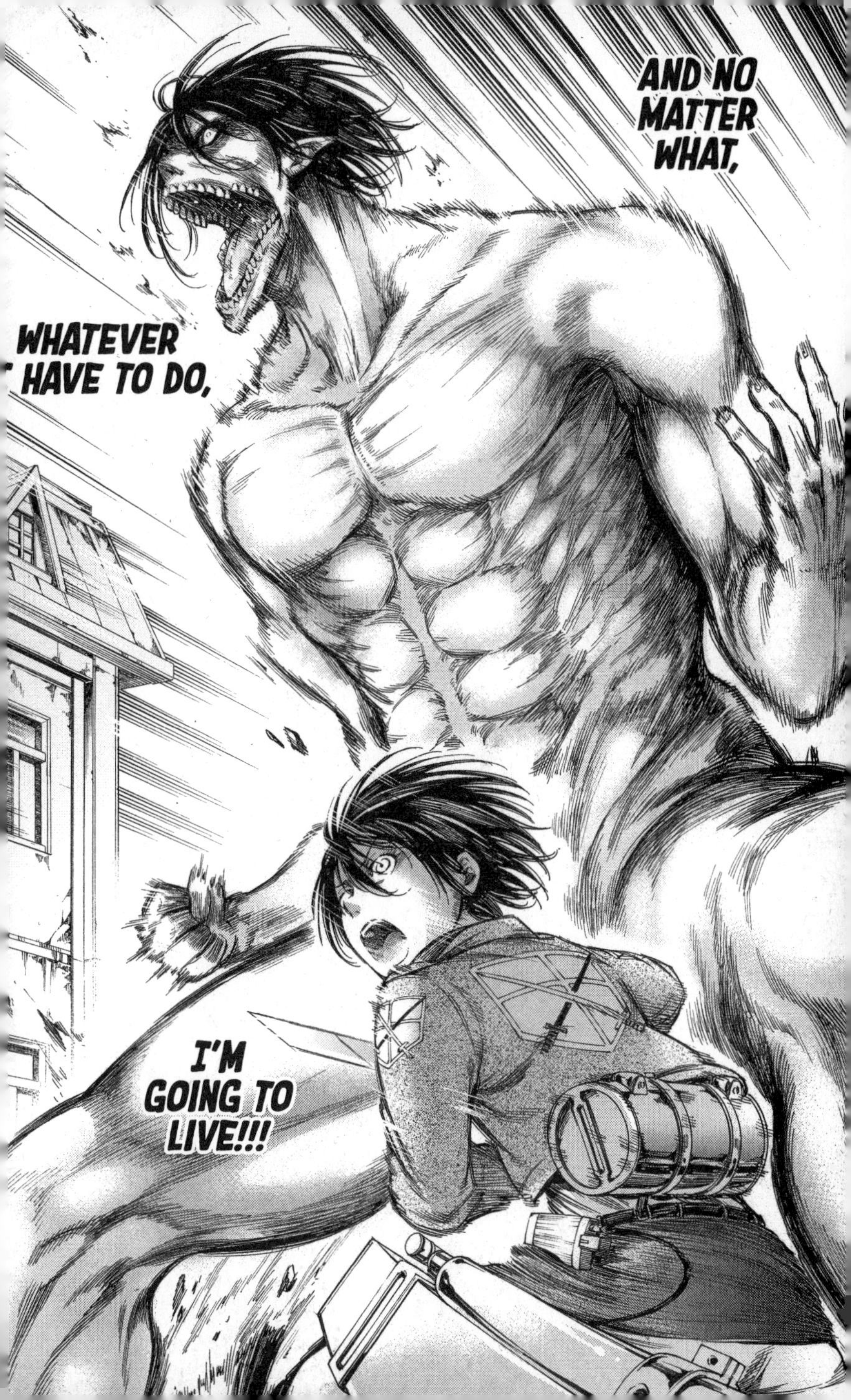
AND NO MATTER WHAT,
WHATEVER HAVE TO DO,
I'M GOING TO LIVE!!!

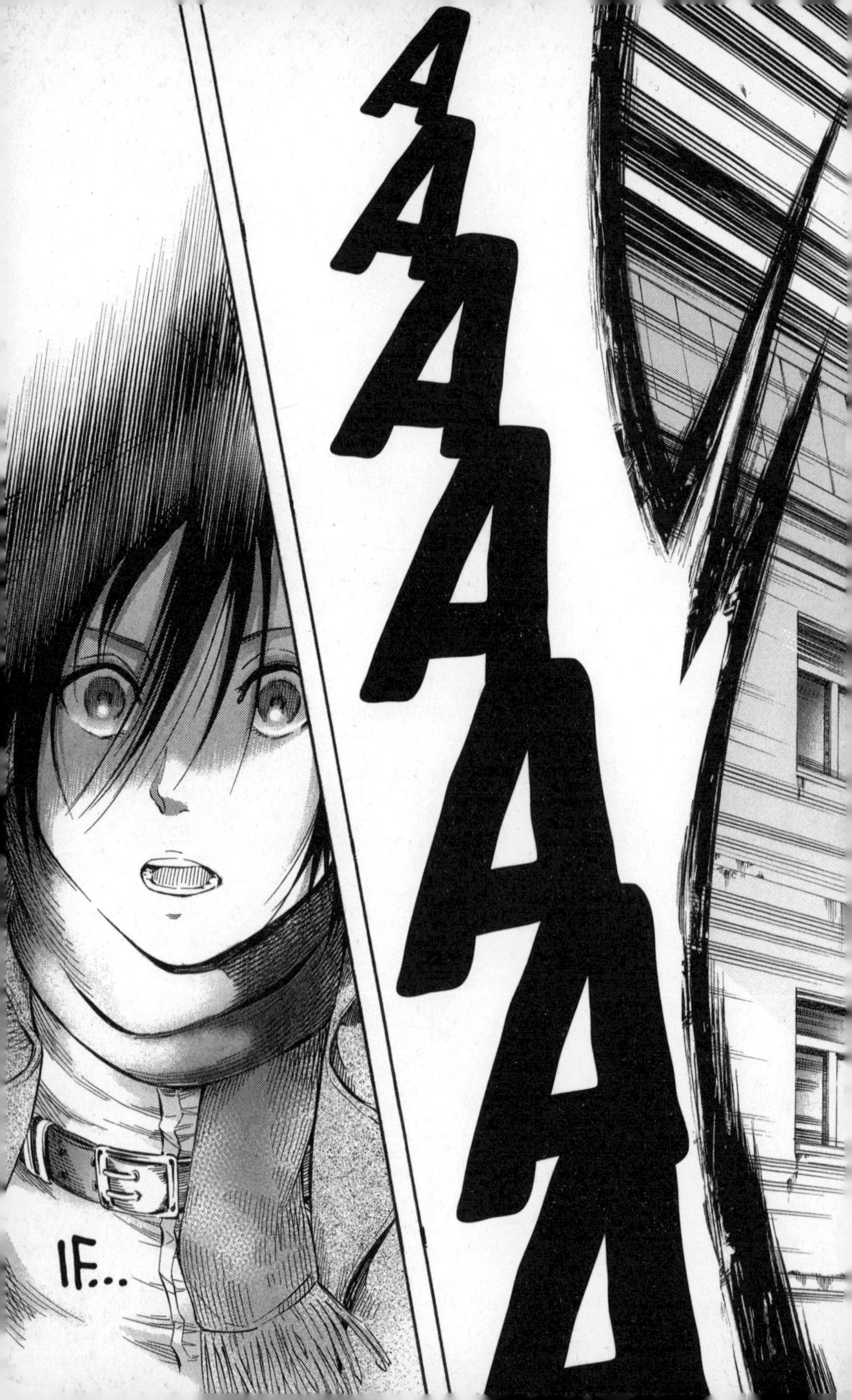
AAAAAAAAA
IF...

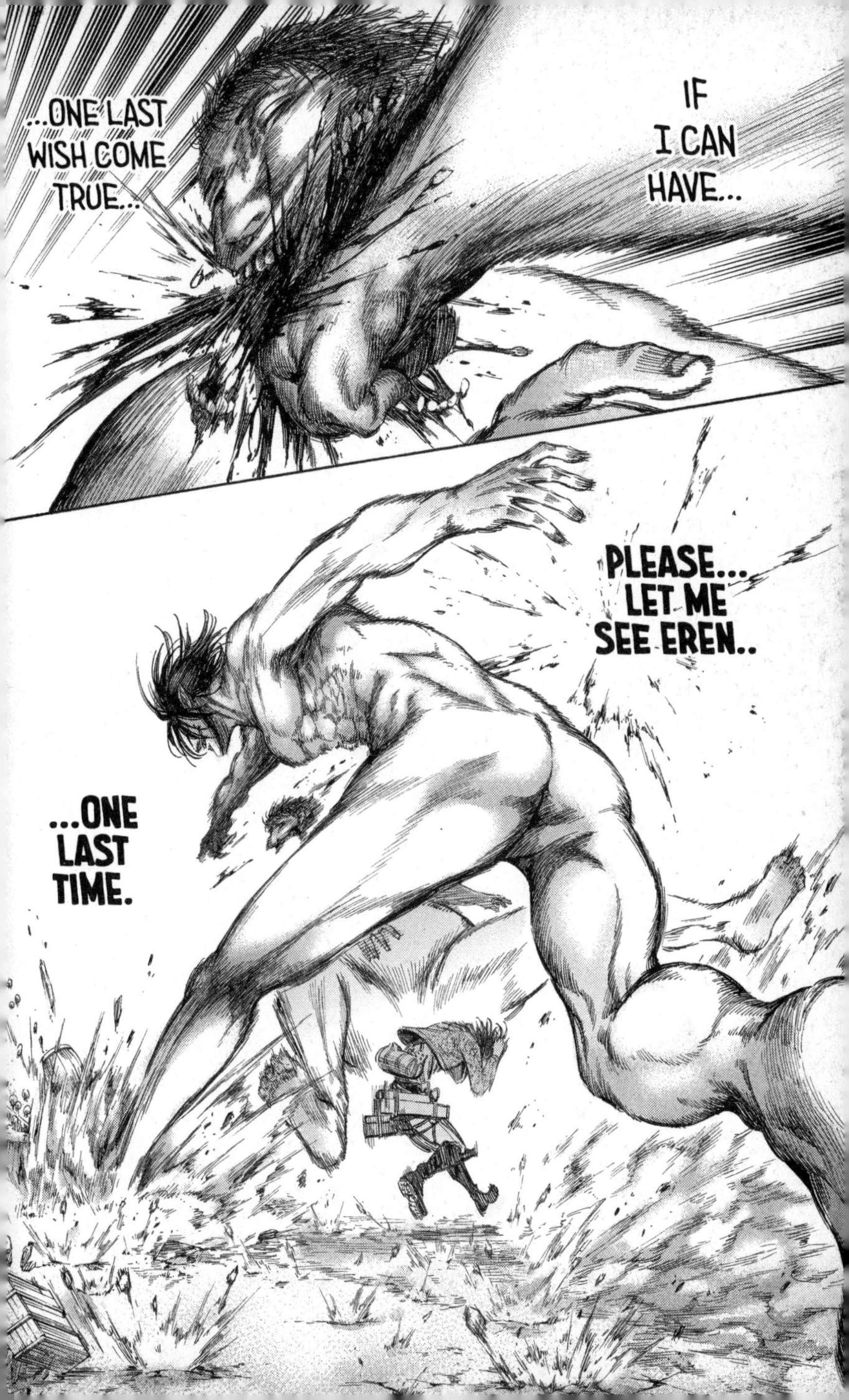
IF I CAN HAVE...
...ONE LAST WISH COME TRUE...
PLEASE... LET ME SEE EREN..
...ONE LAST TIME.

ATTACK ON TITAN

LOST GIRLS

850

—Wall Sheena

Trost District

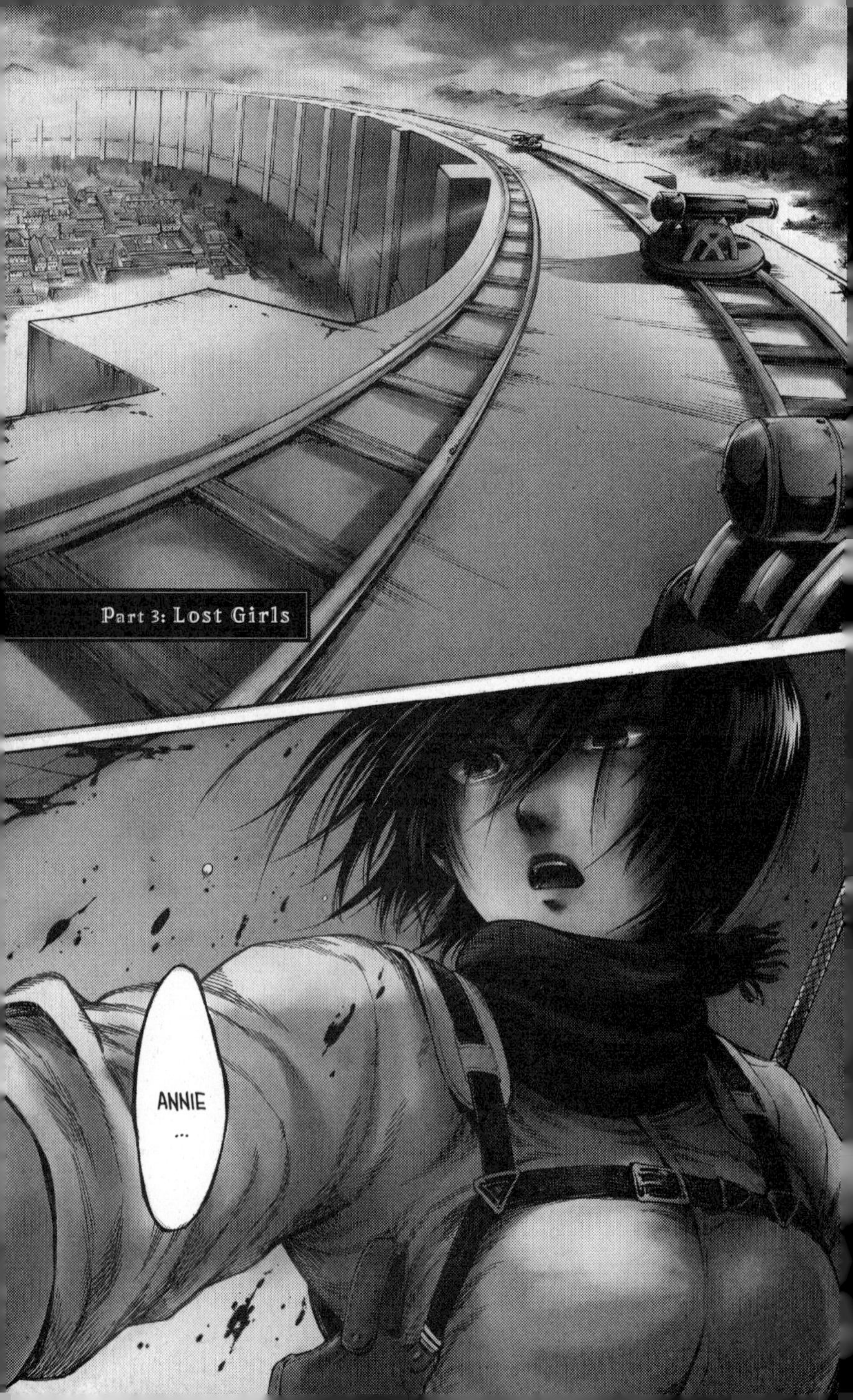
Part 3: Lost Girls
ANNIE
...

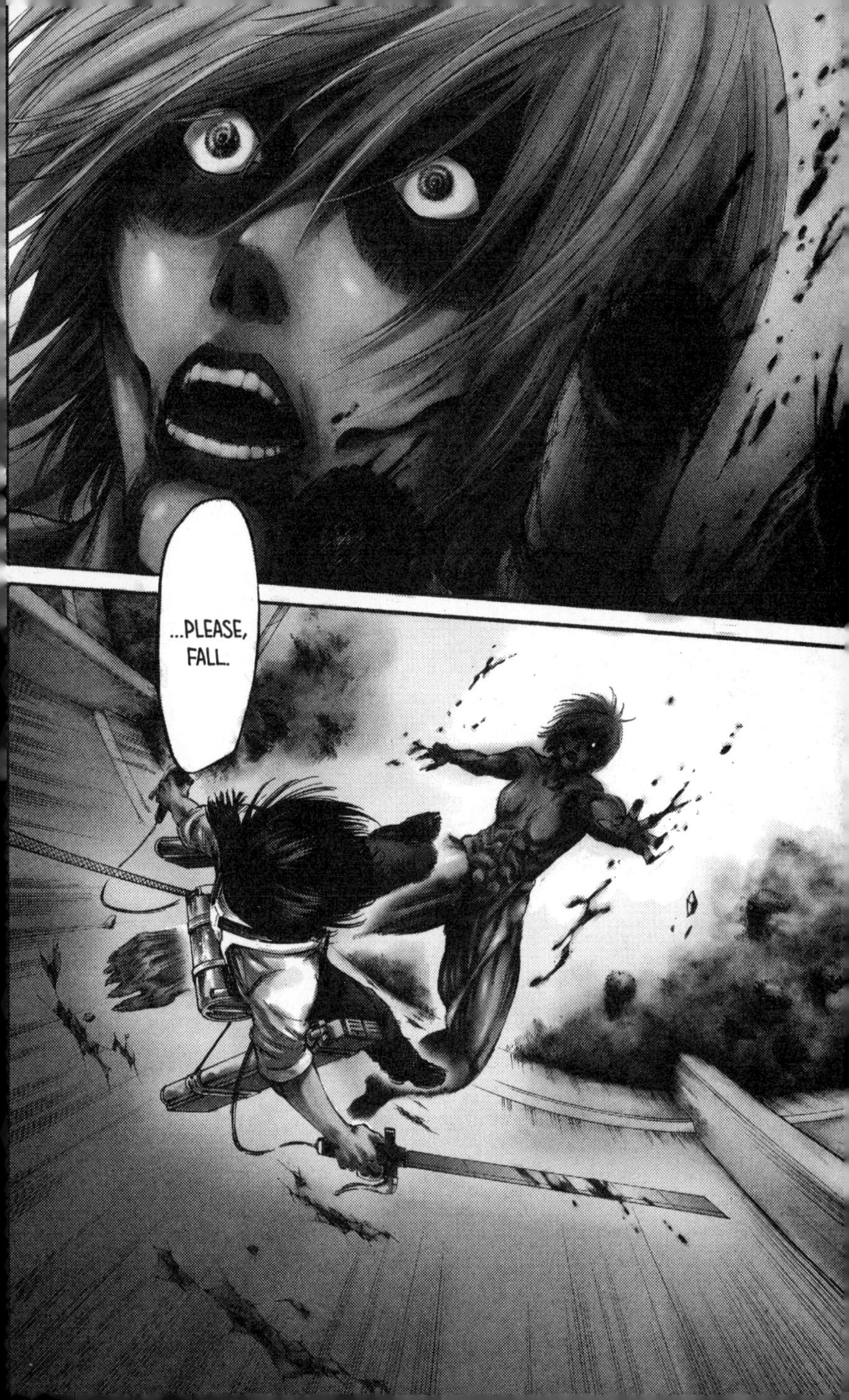
...PLEASE, FALL.

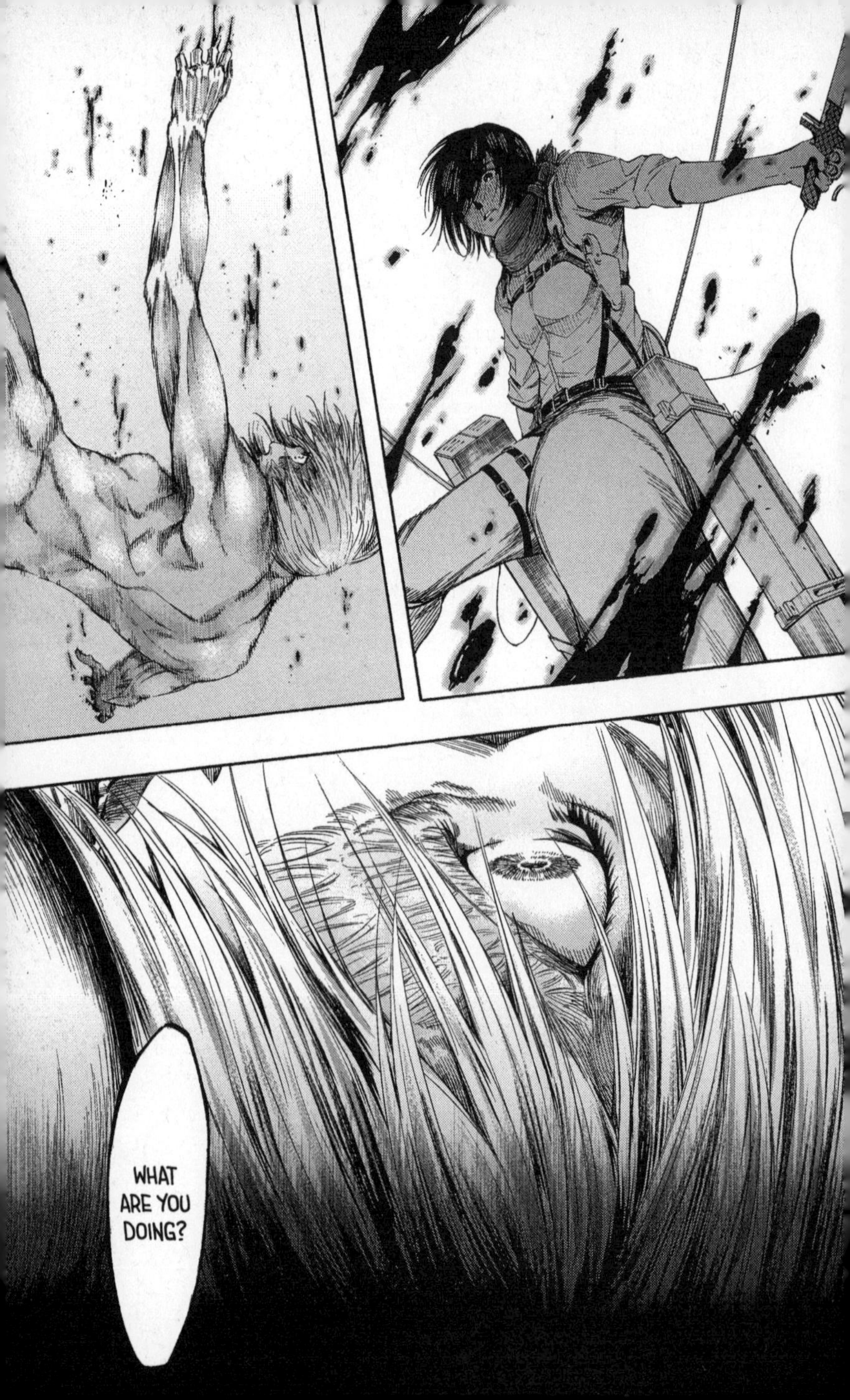
WHAT ARE YOU DOING?

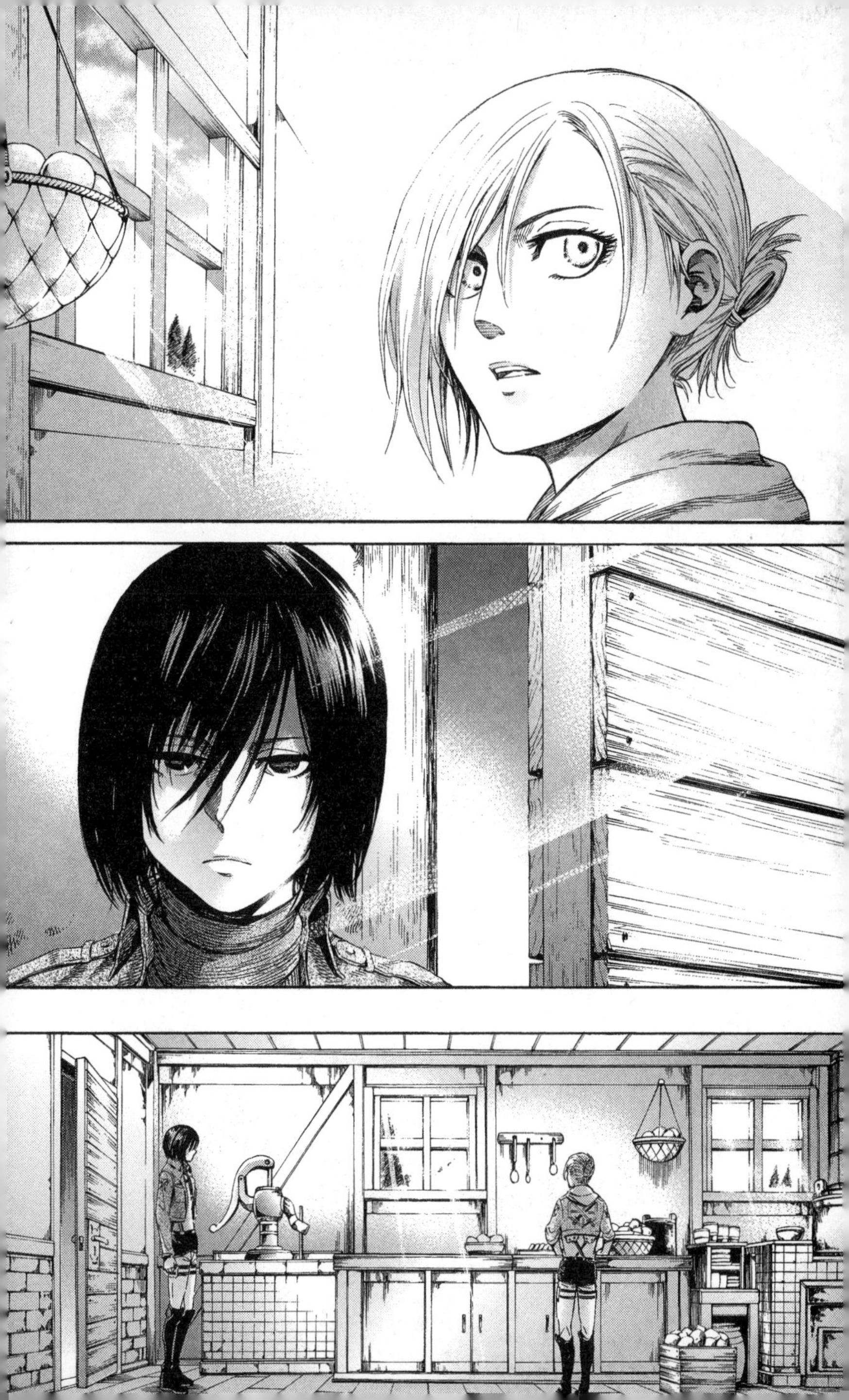

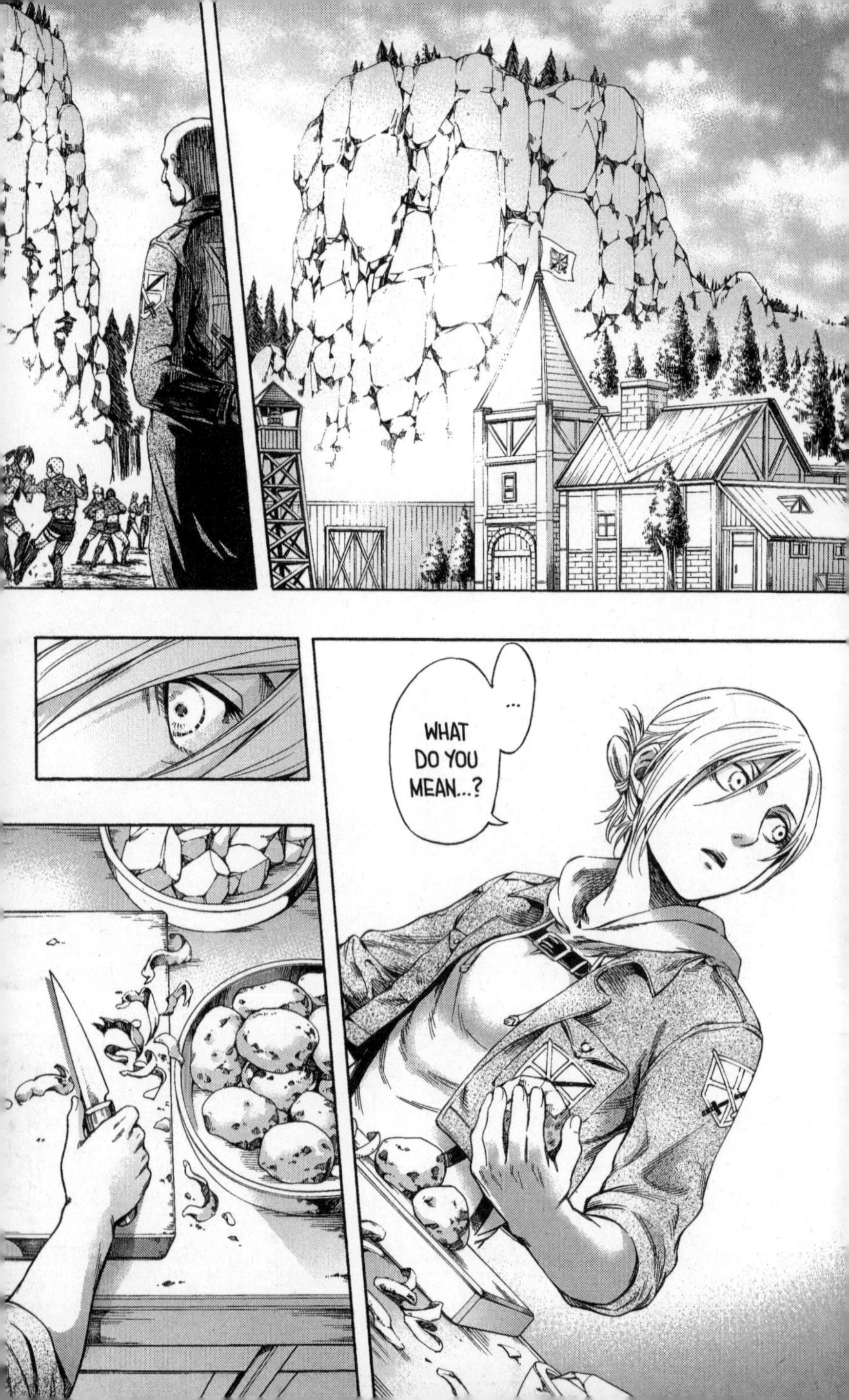
...
WHAT DO YOU MEAN...?

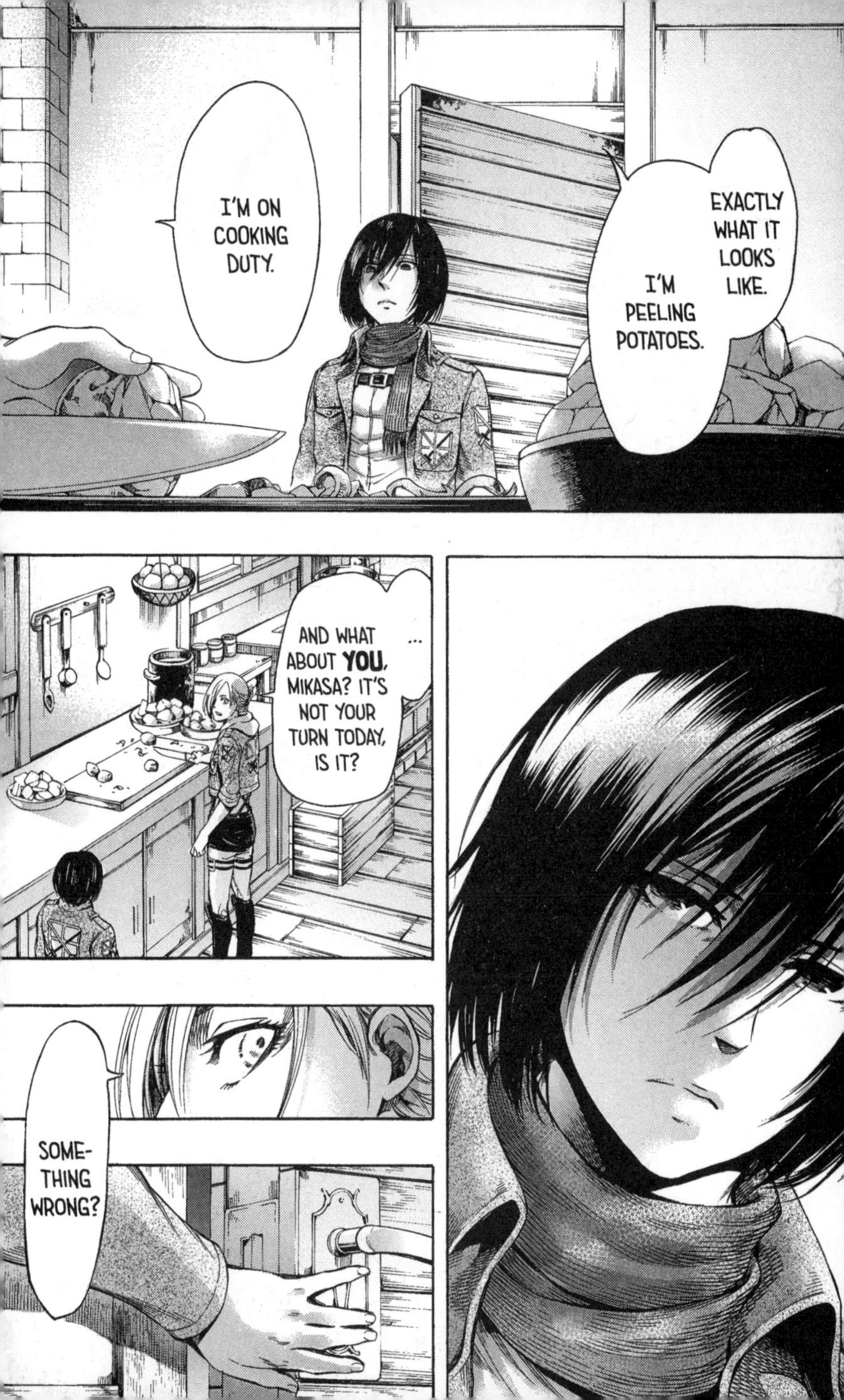
EXACTLY WHAT IT LOOKS LIKE.
I'M PEELING POTATOES.
I'M ON COOKING DUTY.
...
AND WHAT ABOUT **YOU**, MIKASA? IT'S NOT YOUR TURN TODAY, IS IT?
SOME-THING WRONG?

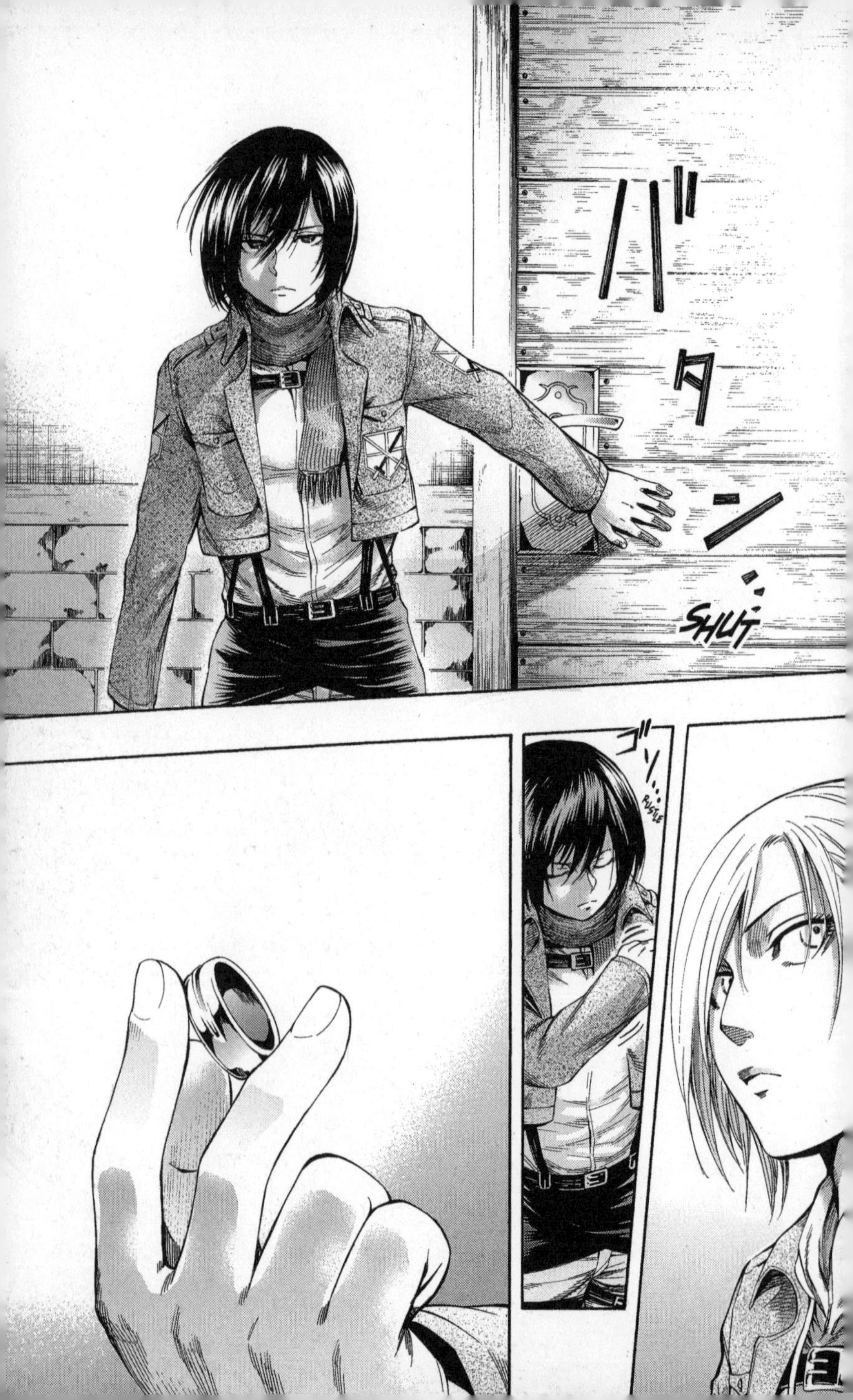
バタン
SHUT
ゴソ…
RUSTLE

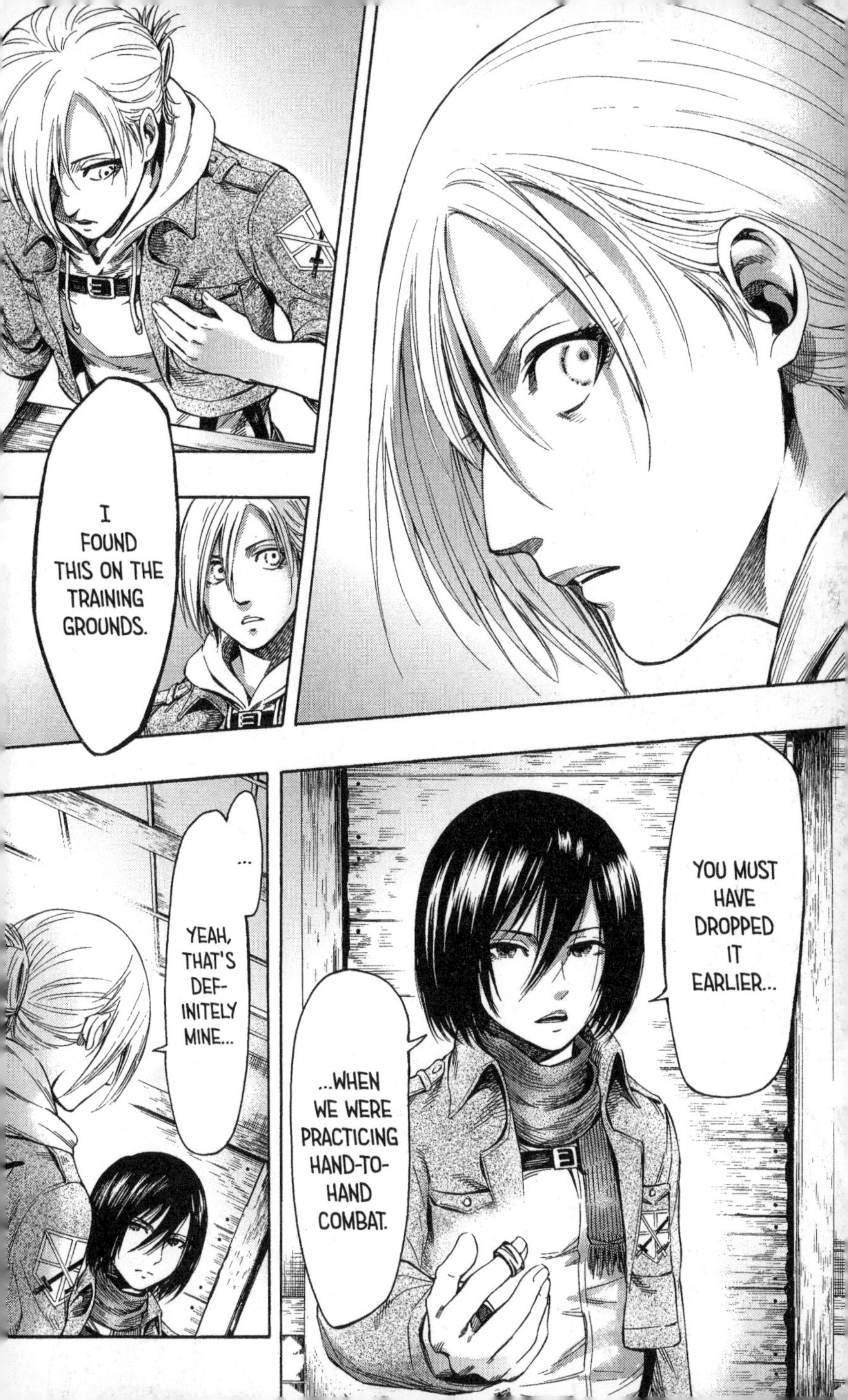
I FOUND THIS ON THE TRAINING GROUNDS.
YOU MUST HAVE DROPPED IT EARLIER...
...WHEN WE WERE PRACTICING HAND-TO-HAND COMBAT.
...
YEAH, THAT'S DEFINITELY MINE...

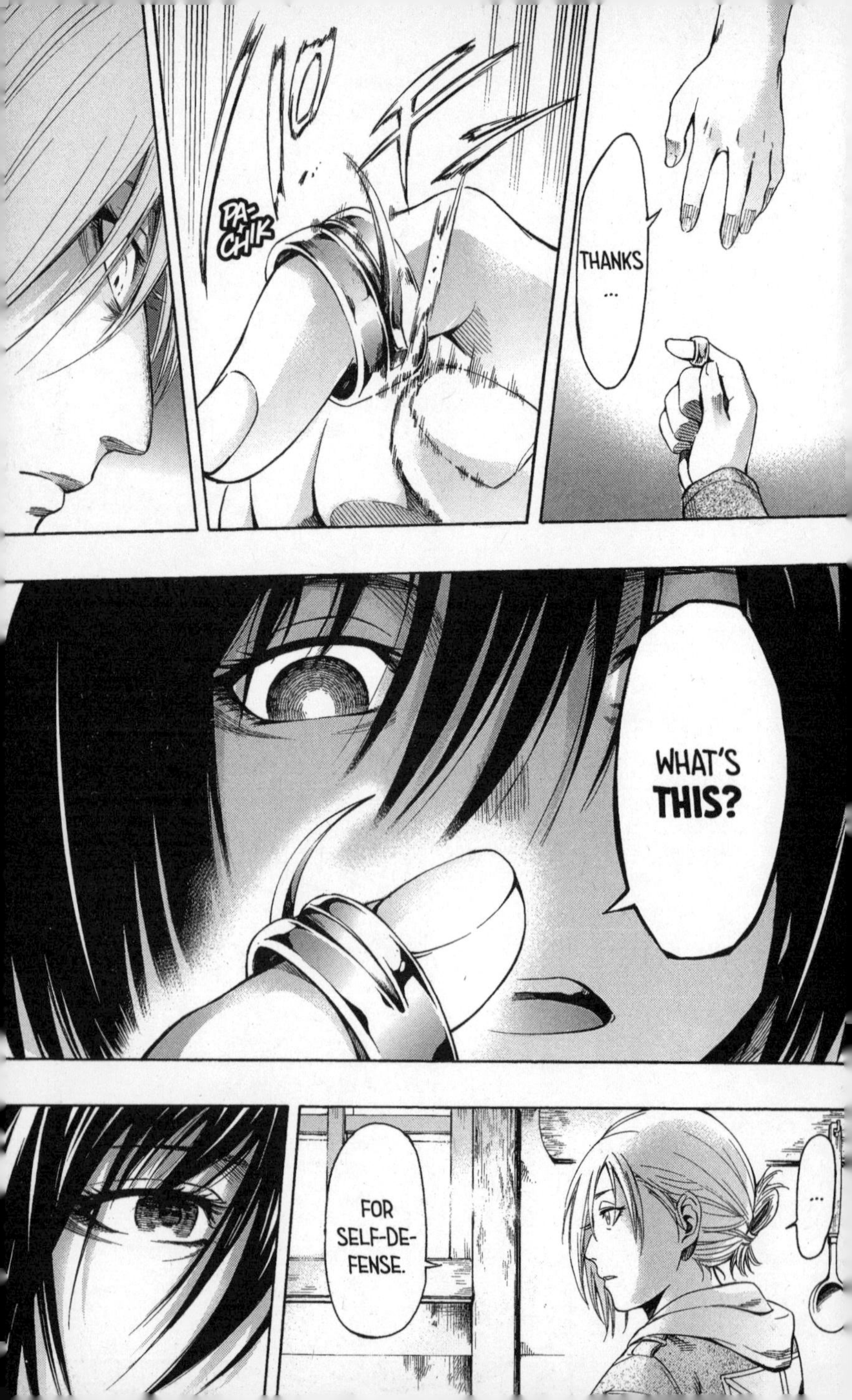
THANKS ...
PA-CHIK
WHAT'S **THIS?**
...
FOR SELF-DE-FENSE.

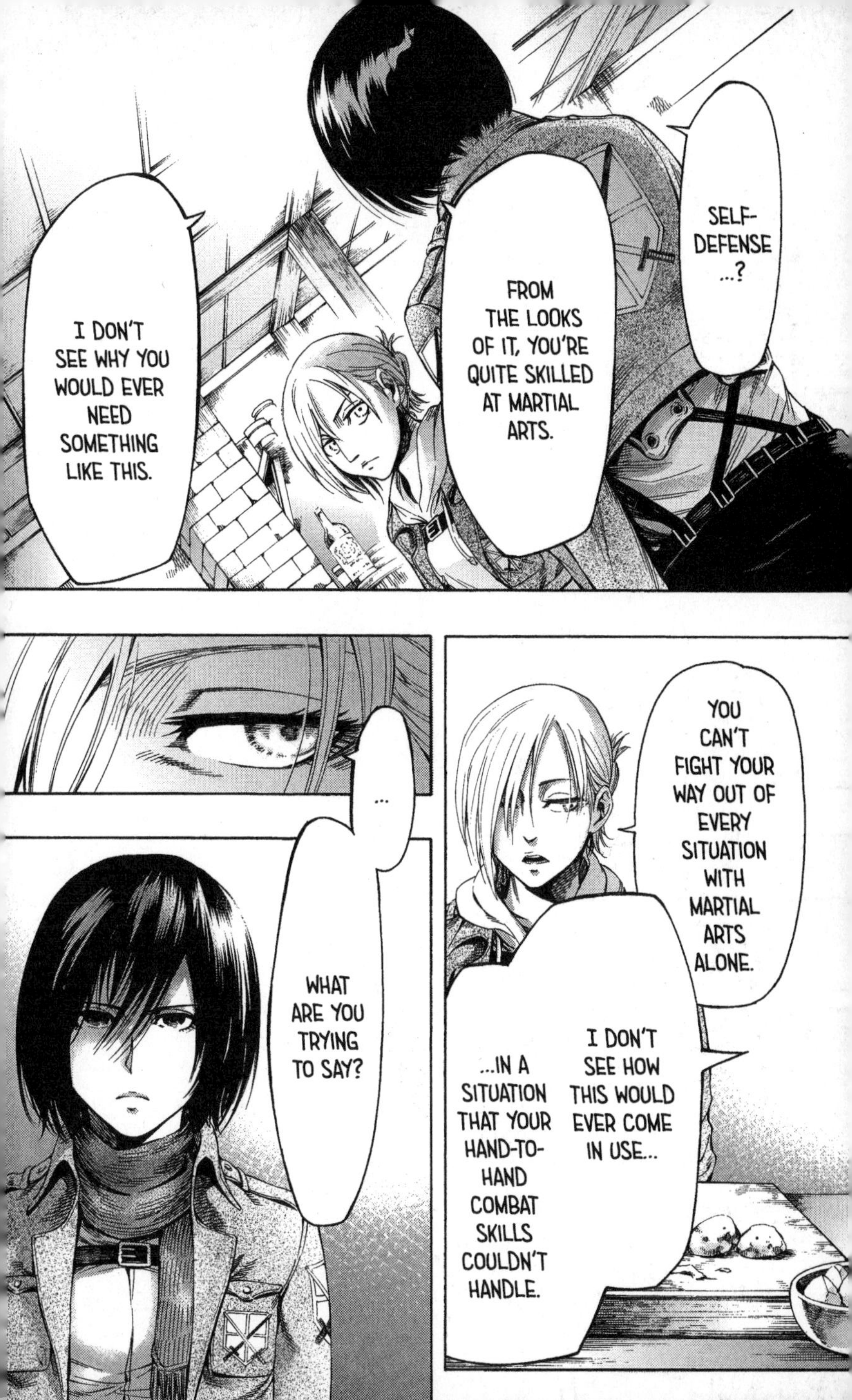
SELF-DEFENSE ...?
FROM THE LOOKS OF IT, YOU'RE QUITE SKILLED AT MARTIAL ARTS.
I DON'T SEE WHY YOU WOULD EVER NEED SOMETHING LIKE THIS.
YOU CAN'T FIGHT YOUR WAY OUT OF EVERY SITUATION WITH MARTIAL ARTS ALONE.
I DON'T SEE HOW THIS WOULD EVER COME IN USE...
...IN A SITUATION THAT YOUR HAND-TO-HAND COMBAT SKILLS COULDN'T HANDLE.
...
WHAT ARE YOU TRYING TO SAY?

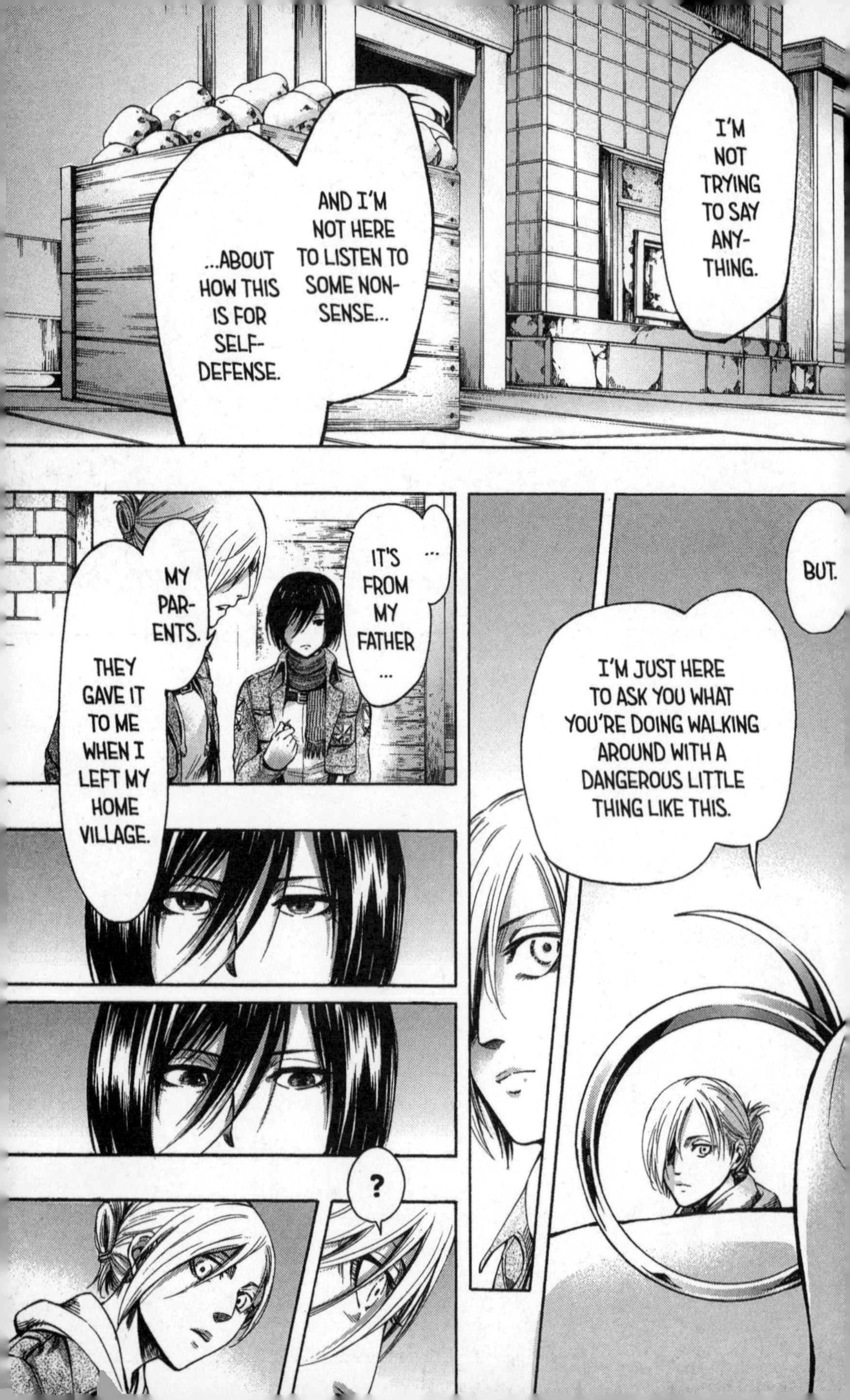
I'M NOT TRYING TO SAY ANYTHING.
AND I'M NOT HERE TO LISTEN TO SOME NONSENSE...
...ABOUT HOW THIS IS FOR SELF-DEFENSE.
BUT.
I'M JUST HERE TO ASK YOU WHAT YOU'RE DOING WALKING AROUND WITH A DANGEROUS LITTLE THING LIKE THIS.
...
IT'S FROM MY FATHER ...
MY PARENTS.
THEY GAVE IT TO ME WHEN I LEFT MY HOME VILLAGE.
?

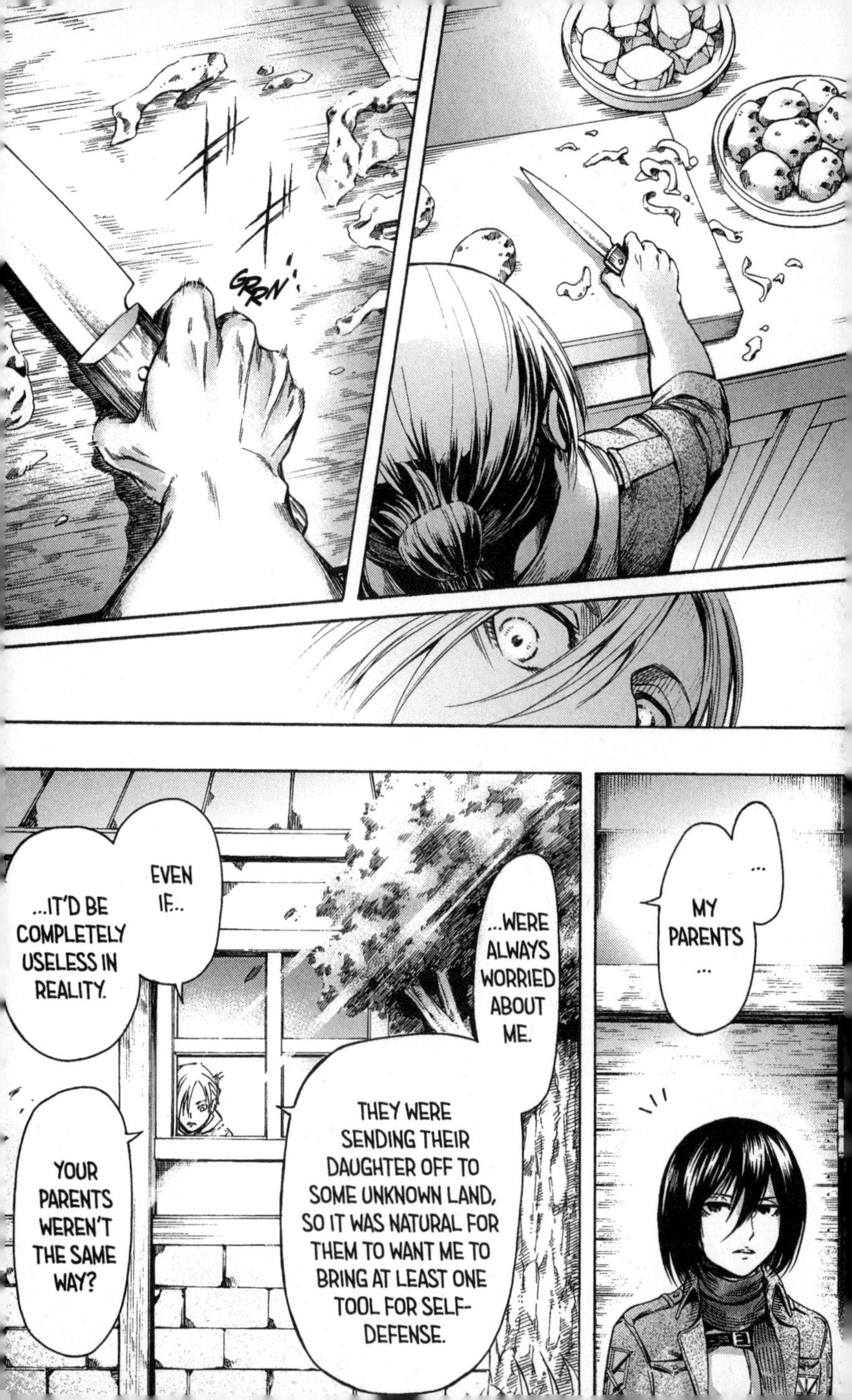
GRRN
...
MY PARENTS
...
...WERE ALWAYS WORRIED ABOUT ME.
THEY WERE SENDING THEIR DAUGHTER OFF TO SOME UNKNOWN LAND, SO IT WAS NATURAL FOR THEM TO WANT ME TO BRING AT LEAST ONE TOOL FOR SELF-DEFENSE.
EVEN IF...
...IT'D BE COMPLETELY USELESS IN REALITY.
YOUR PARENTS WEREN'T THE SAME WAY?

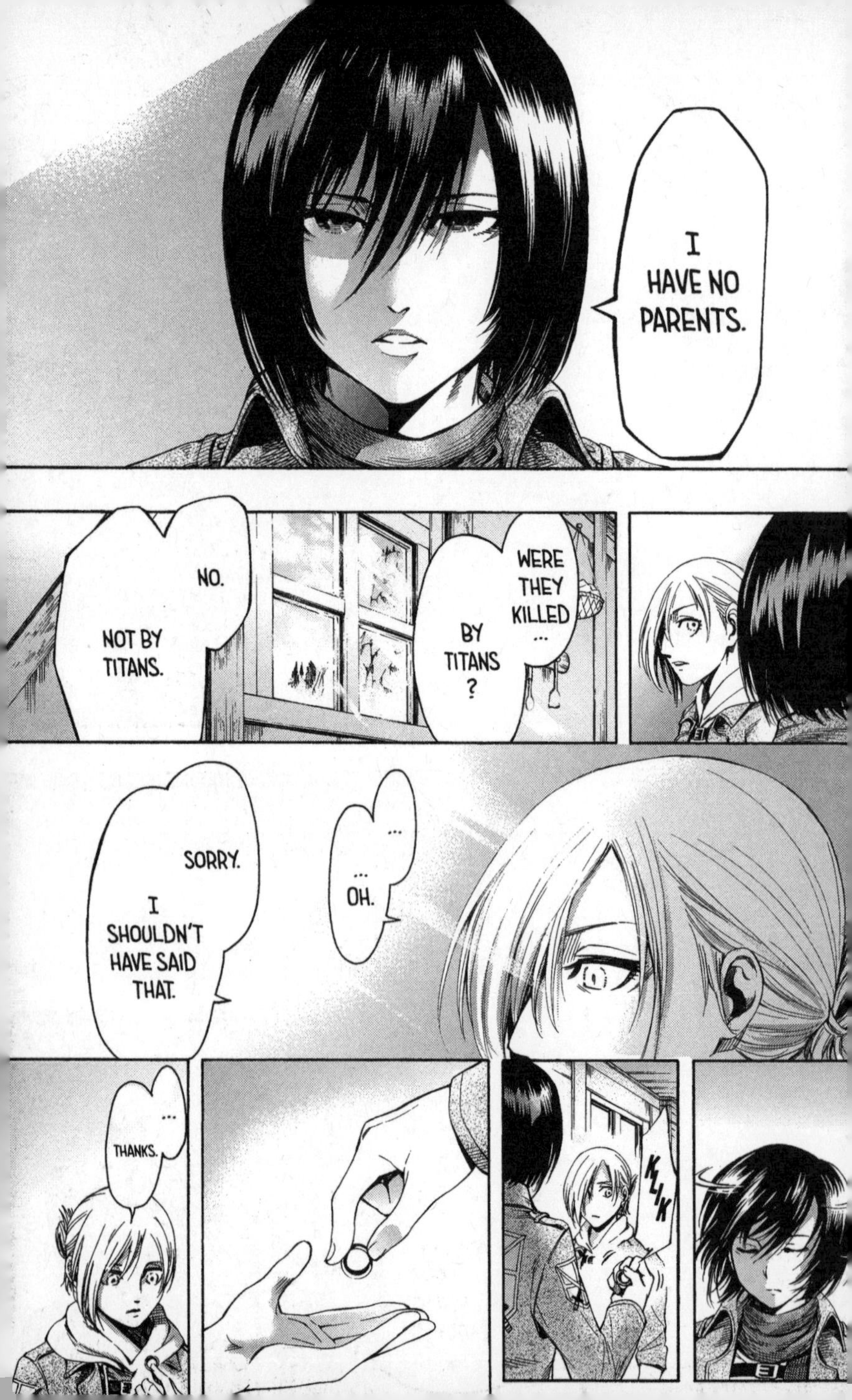
I HAVE NO PARENTS.
WERE THEY KILLED ... BY TITANS ?
NO. NOT BY TITANS.
... ... OH.
SORRY. I SHOULDN'T HAVE SAID THAT.
KLIK
... THANKS.

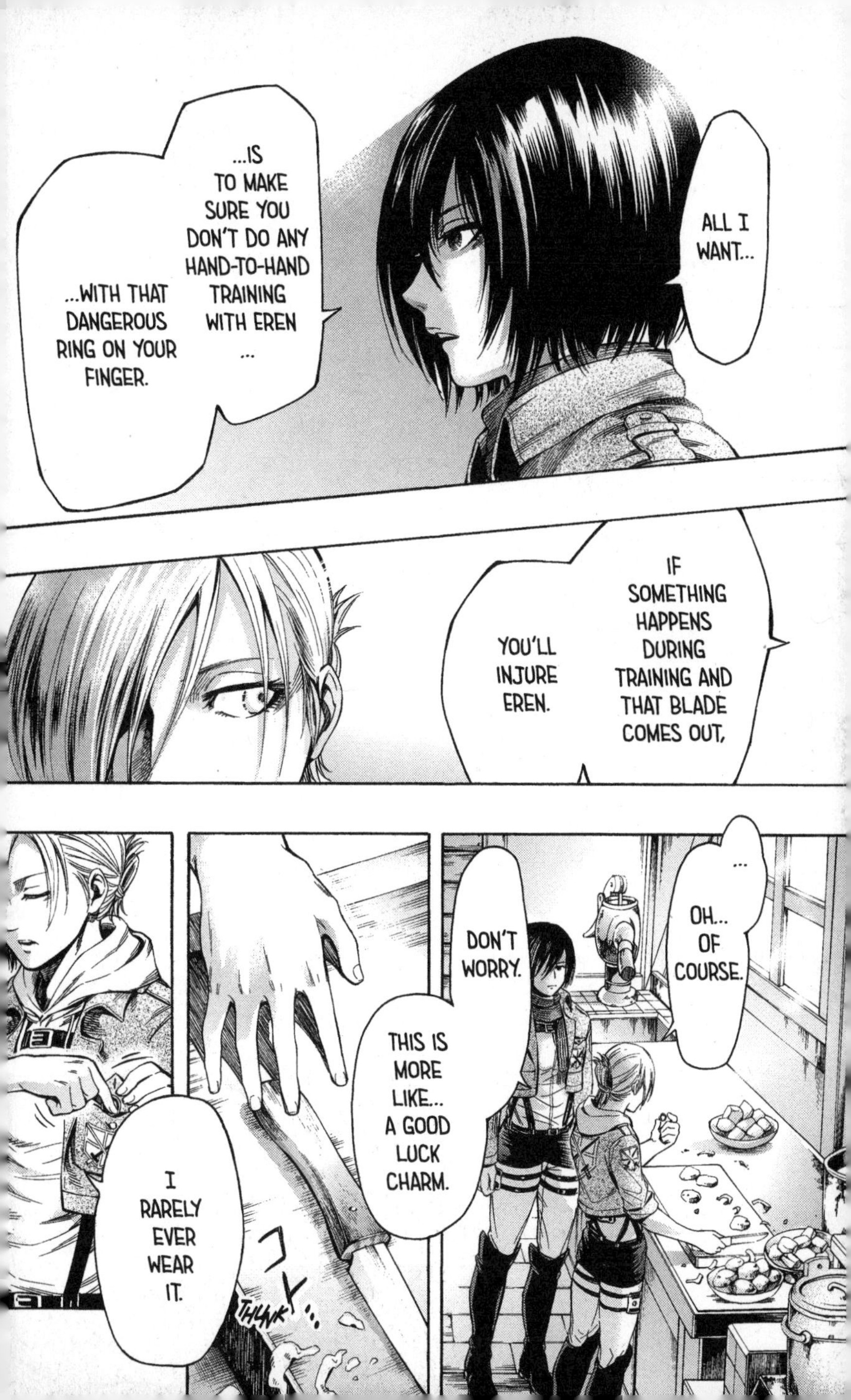
ALL I WANT...
...IS TO MAKE SURE YOU DON'T DO ANY HAND-TO-HAND TRAINING WITH EREN ...
...WITH THAT DANGEROUS RING ON YOUR FINGER.
IF SOMETHING HAPPENS DURING TRAINING AND THAT BLADE COMES OUT,
YOU'LL INJURE EREN.
...
OH... OF COURSE.
DON'T WORRY.
THIS IS MORE LIKE... A GOOD LUCK CHARM.
THUNK
I RARELY EVER WEAR IT.

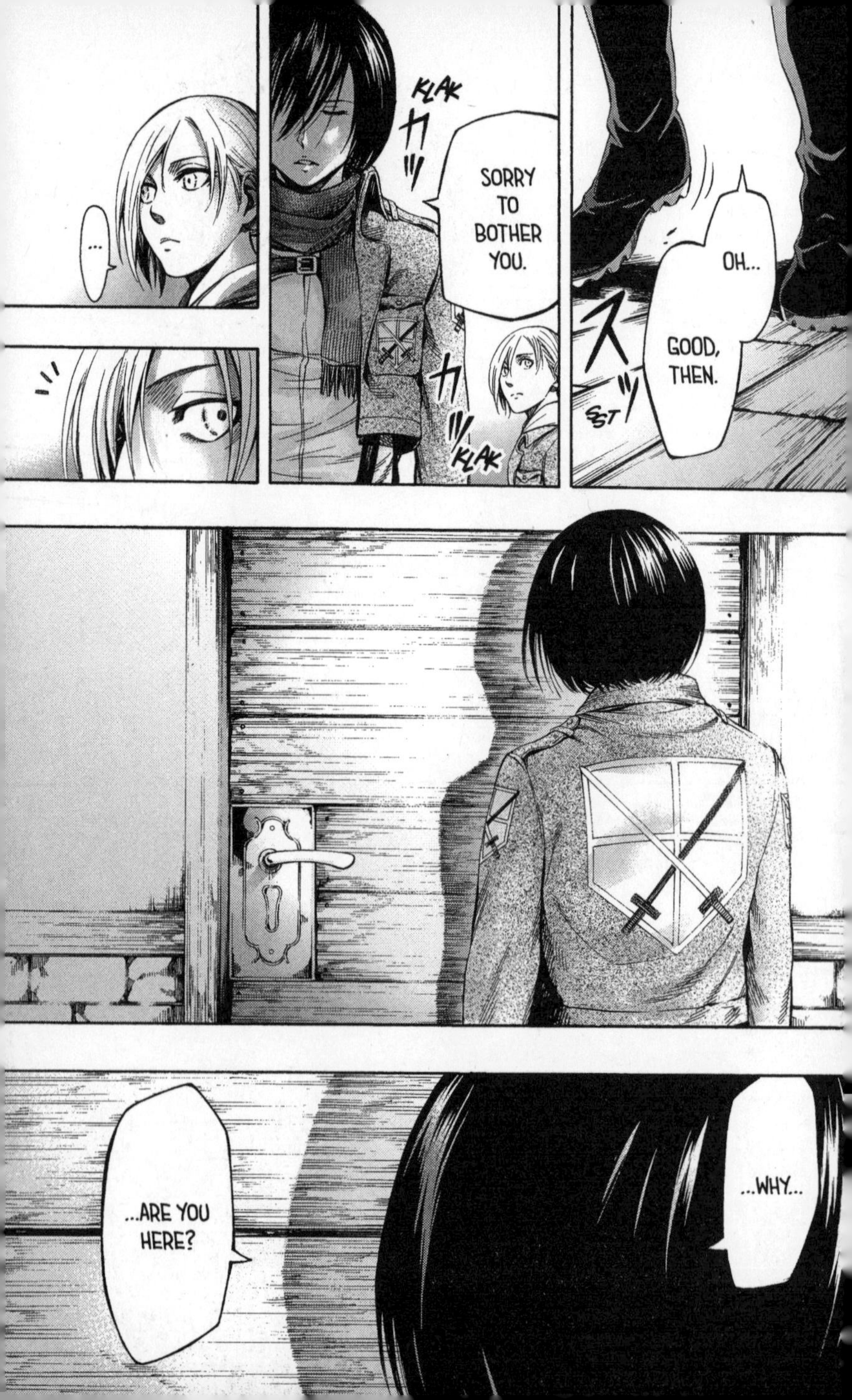
OH...
GOOD, THEN.
スッ
SST
KLAK
カッ
SORRY TO BOTHER YOU.
カッ
KLAK
...
...WHY...
...ARE YOU HERE?

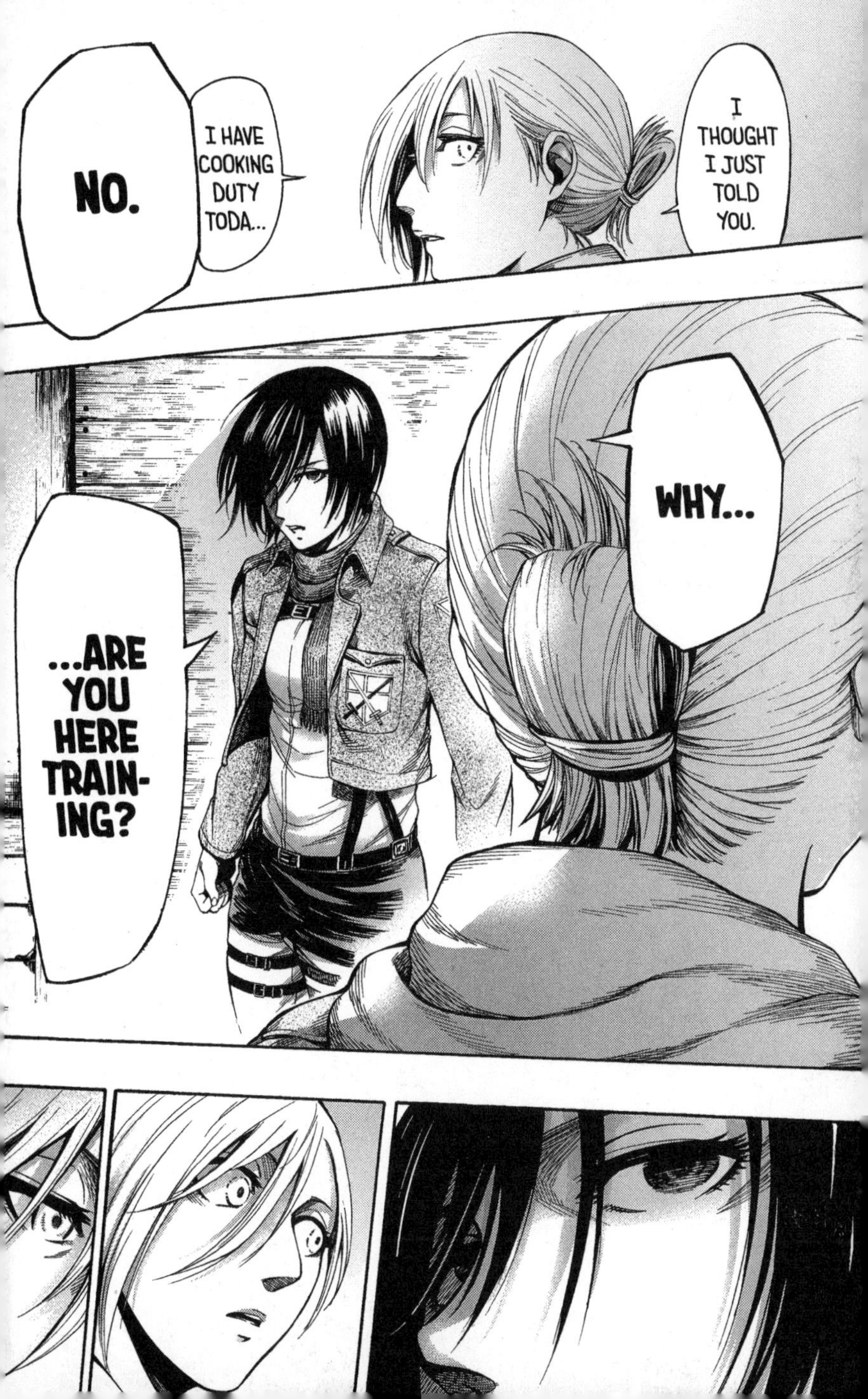
I THOUGHT I JUST TOLD YOU.
I HAVE COOKING DUTY TODA...
NO.
WHY...
...ARE YOU HERE TRAIN-ING?

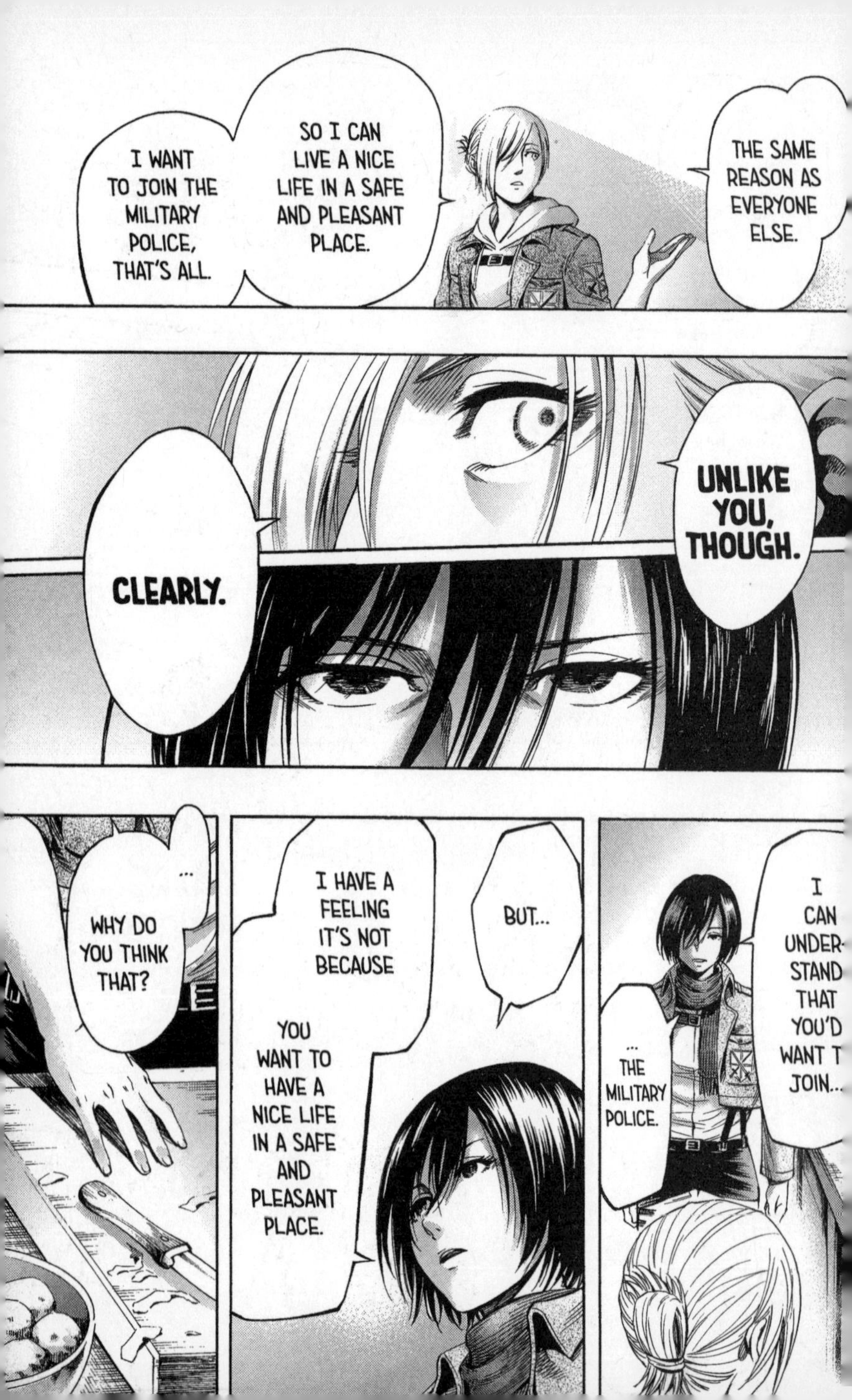
THE SAME REASON AS EVERYONE ELSE.
SO I CAN LIVE A NICE LIFE IN A SAFE AND PLEASANT PLACE.
I WANT TO JOIN THE MILITARY POLICE, THAT'S ALL.
UNLIKE YOU, THOUGH.
CLEARLY.
I CAN UNDERSTAND THAT YOU'D WANT T JOIN...
... THE MILITARY POLICE.
BUT...
I HAVE A FEELING IT'S NOT BECAUSE
YOU WANT TO HAVE A NICE LIFE IN A SAFE AND PLEASANT PLACE.
...
WHY DO YOU THINK THAT?

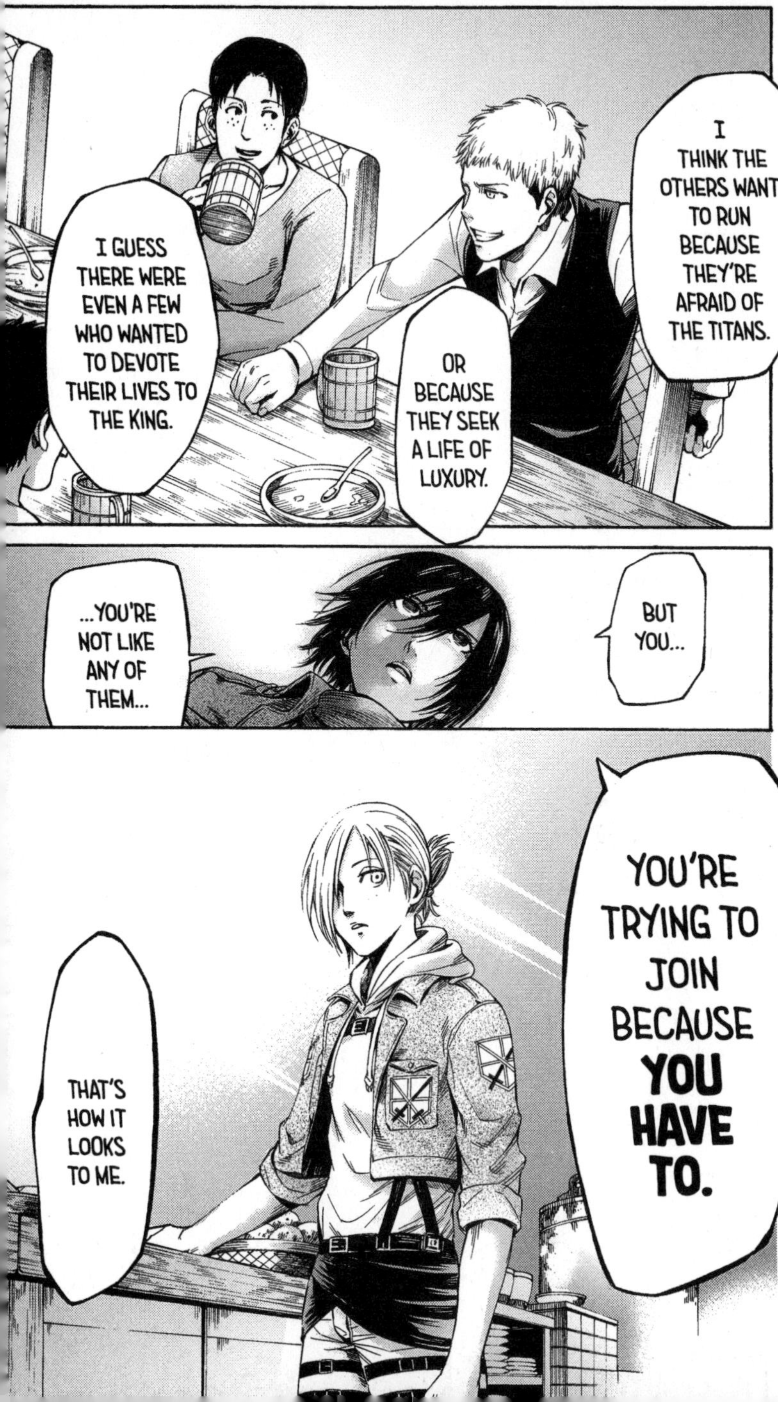
I THINK THE OTHERS WANT TO RUN BECAUSE THEY'RE AFRAID OF THE TITANS.
OR BECAUSE THEY SEEK A LIFE OF LUXURY.
I GUESS THERE WERE EVEN A FEW WHO WANTED TO DEVOTE THEIR LIVES TO THE KING.
BUT YOU...
...YOU'RE NOT LIKE ANY OF THEM...
YOU'RE TRYING TO JOIN BECAUSE **YOU HAVE TO.**
THAT'S HOW IT LOOKS TO ME.

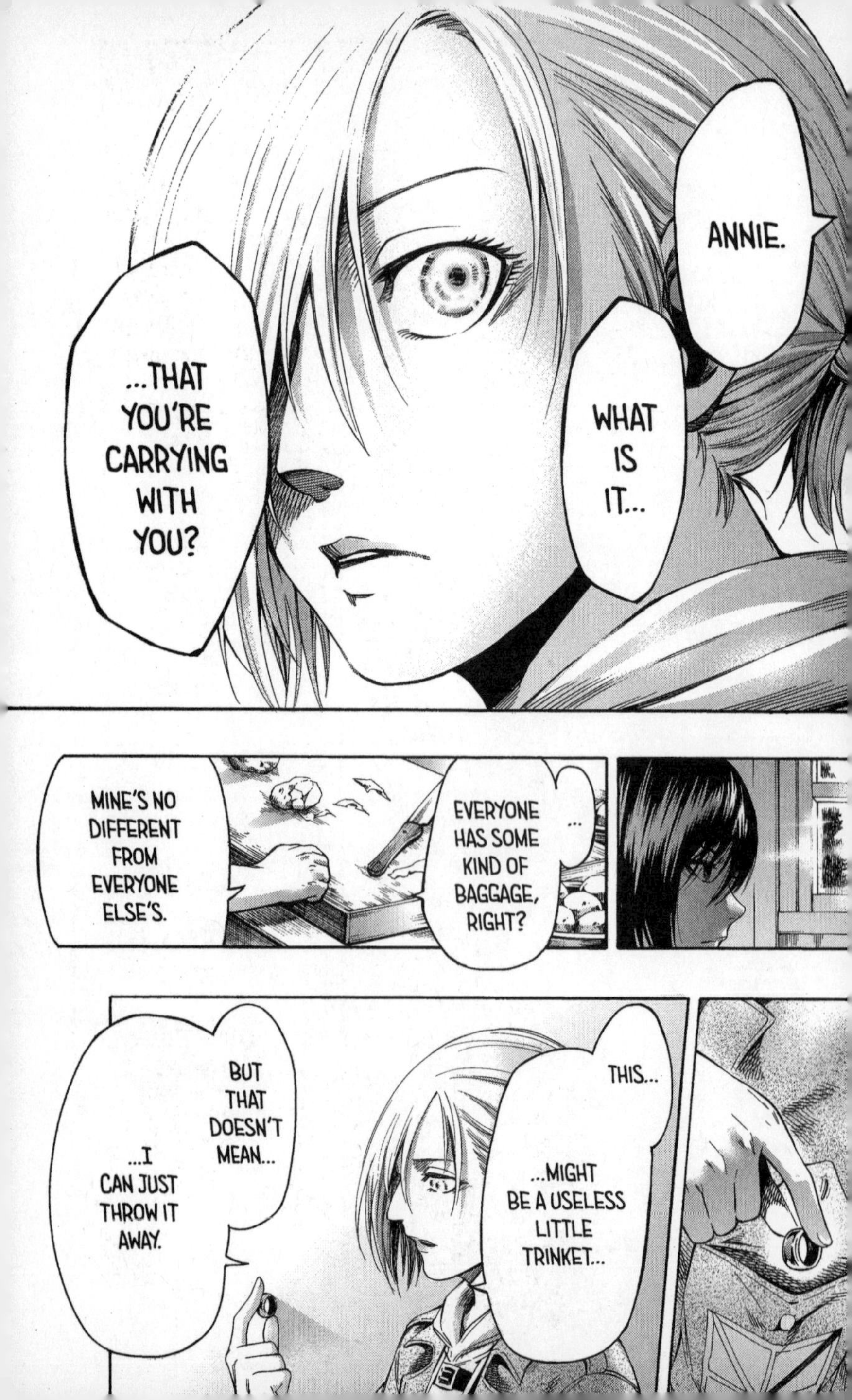
ANNIE.
WHAT IS IT...
...THAT YOU'RE CARRYING WITH YOU?
...
EVERYONE HAS SOME KIND OF BAGGAGE, RIGHT?
MINE'S NO DIFFERENT FROM EVERYONE ELSE'S.
THIS...
...MIGHT BE A USELESS LITTLE TRINKET...
BUT THAT DOESN'T MEAN...
...I CAN JUST THROW IT AWAY.

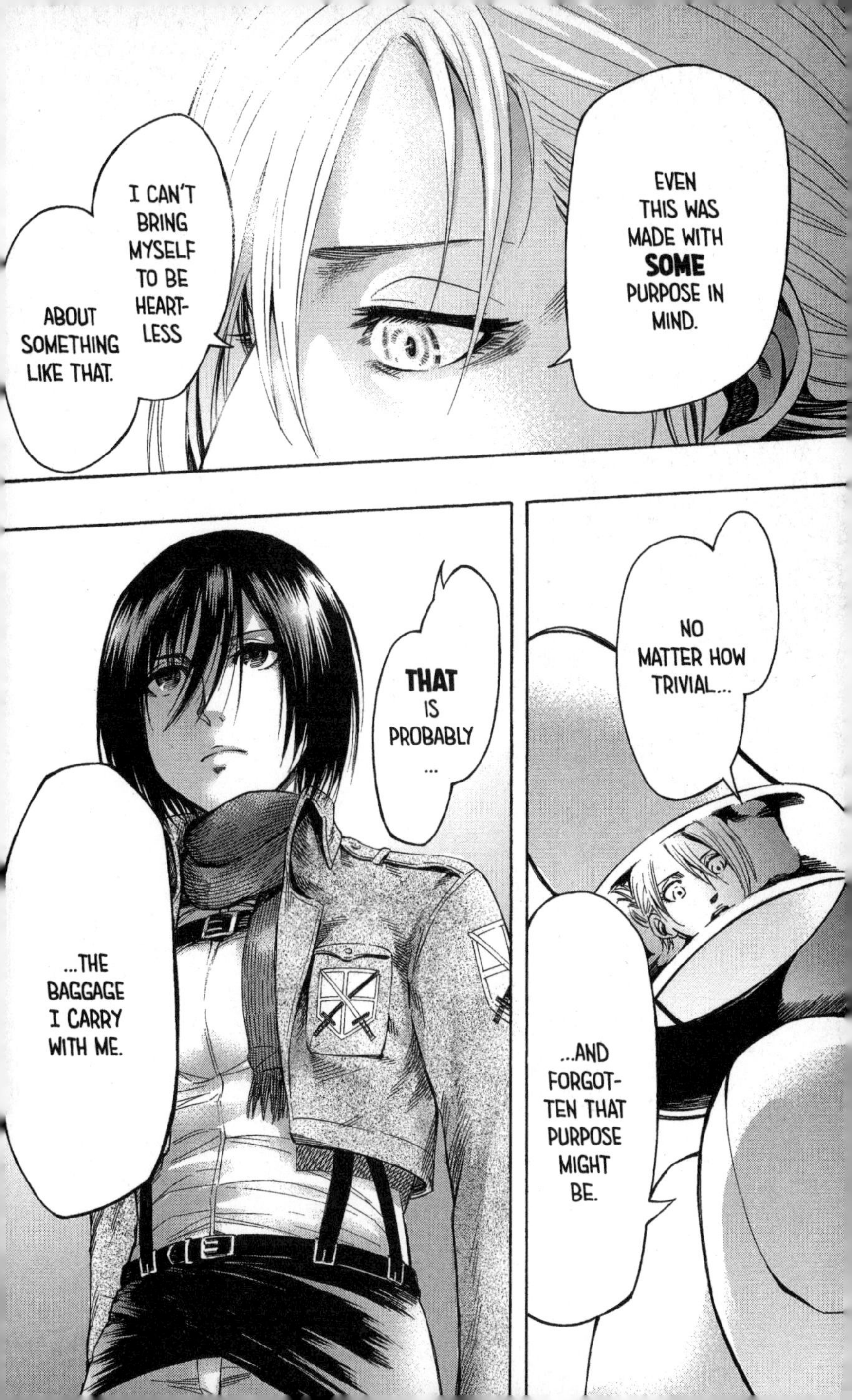
EVEN THIS WAS MADE WITH **SOME** PURPOSE IN MIND.
I CAN'T BRING MYSELF TO BE HEARTLESS
ABOUT SOMETHING LIKE THAT.
NO MATTER HOW TRIVIAL...
...AND FORGOTTEN THAT PURPOSE MIGHT BE.
THAT IS PROBABLY ...
...THE BAGGAGE I CARRY WITH ME.

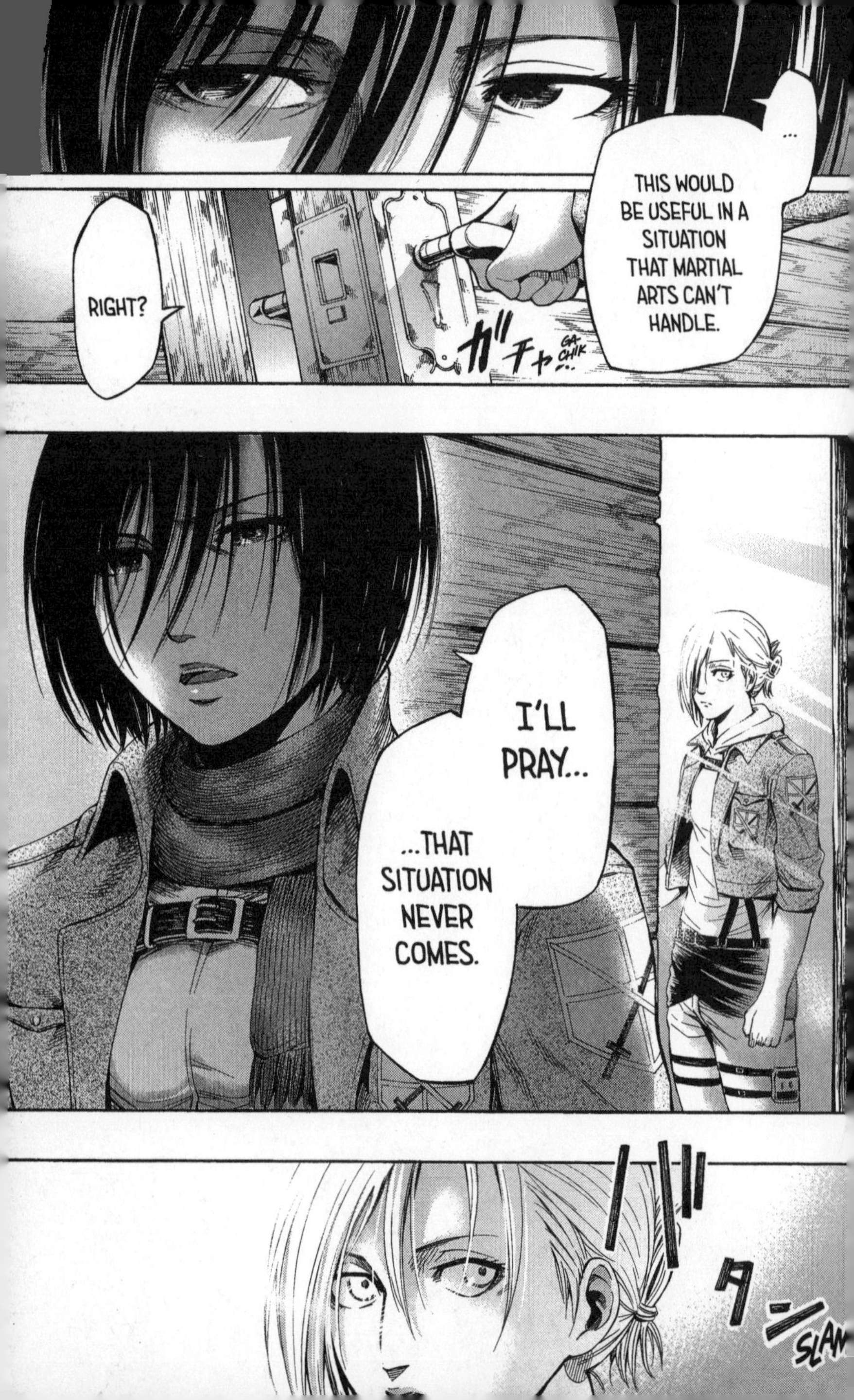
...
THIS WOULD BE USEFUL IN A SITUATION THAT MARTIAL ARTS CAN'T HANDLE.
ガチャ
GA CHIK
RIGHT?
I'LL PRAY...
...THAT SITUATION NEVER COMES.
バタン
SLAM

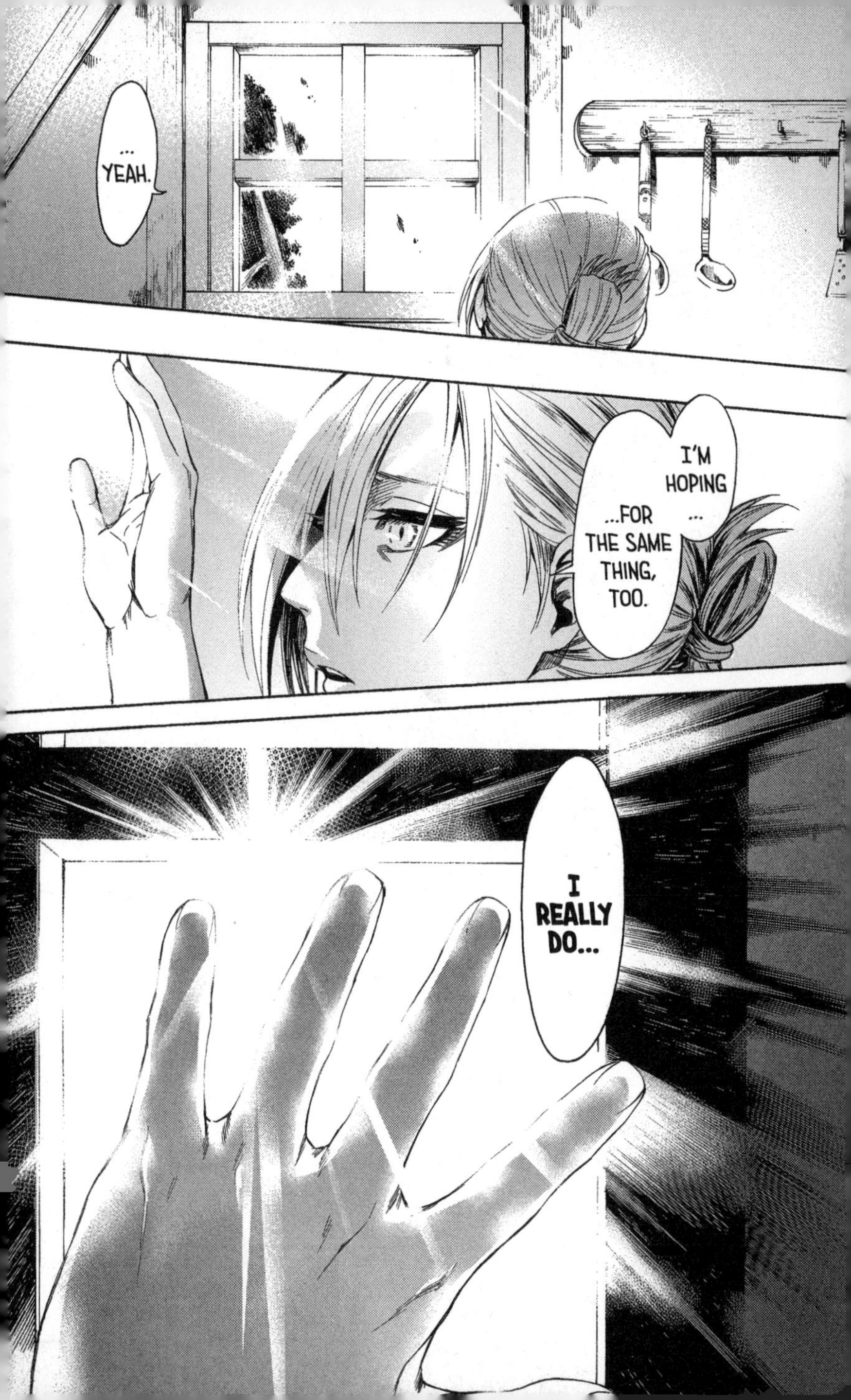
... YEAH.
I'M HOPING ...
...FOR THE SAME THING, TOO.
I REALLY DO...

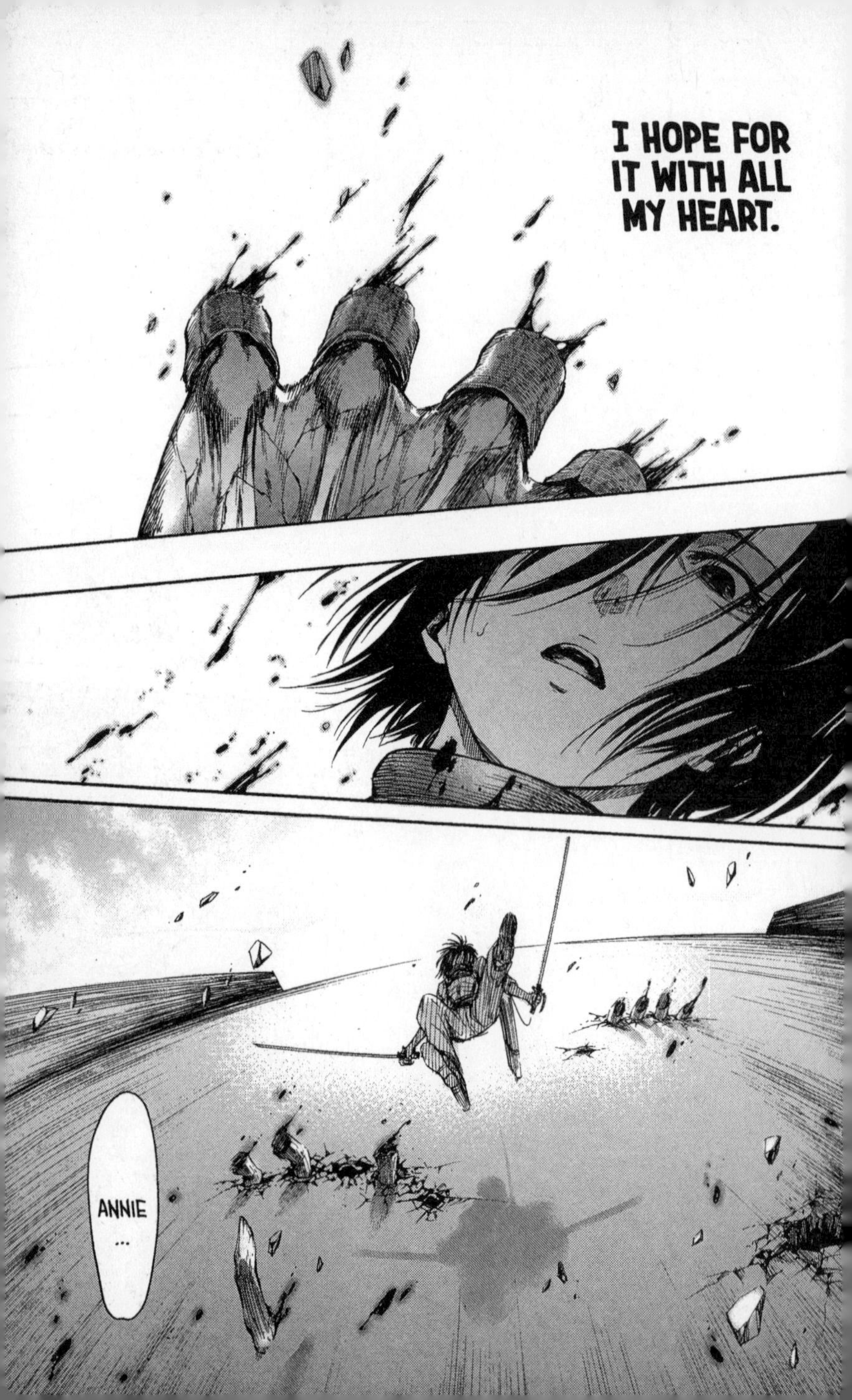
I HOPE FOR IT WITH ALL MY HEART.
ANNIE ...

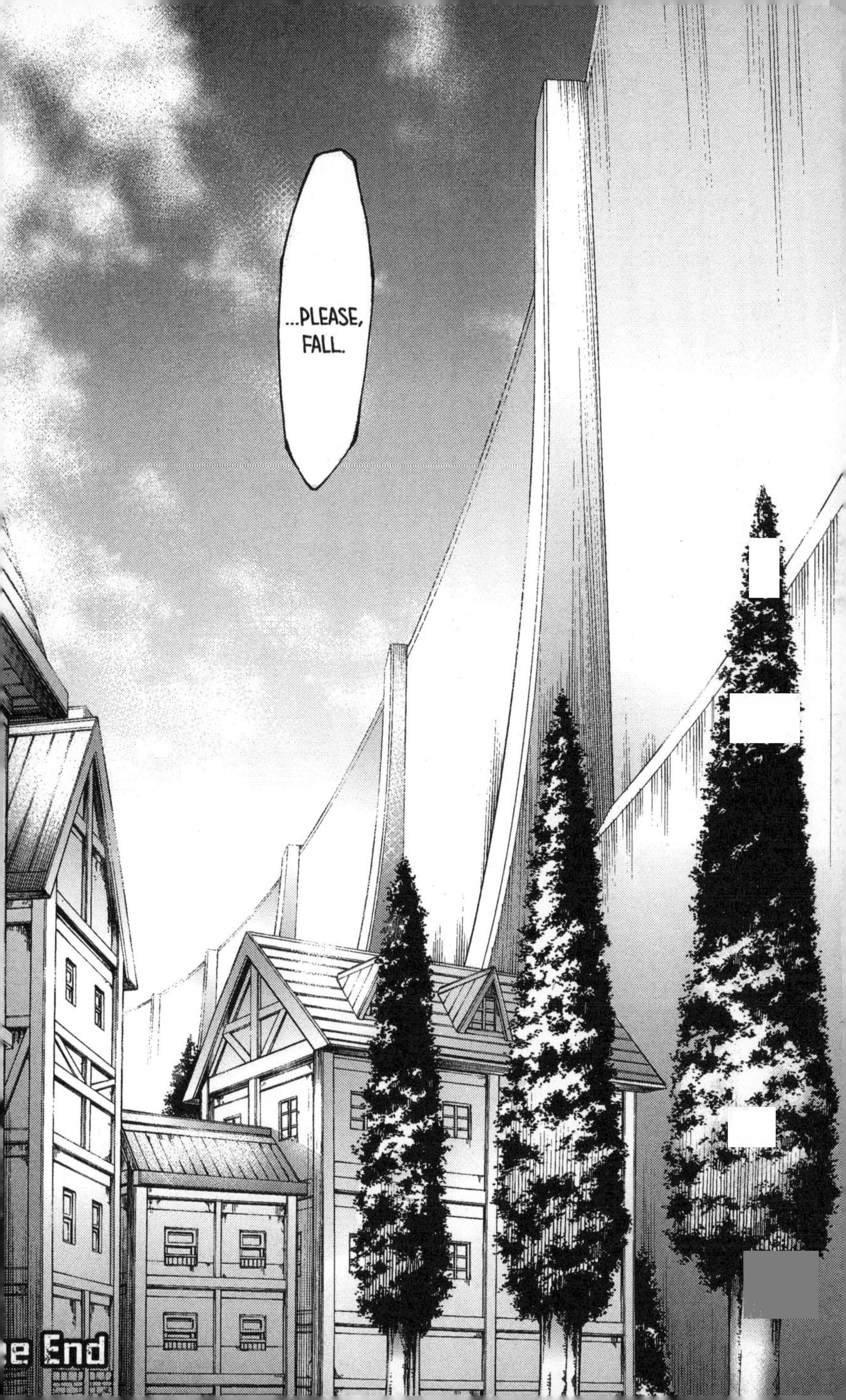
...PLEASE, FALL.
e End